BRITAIN AND THE ISLAMIC WORLD, 1558–1713

BRITAIN AND THE ISLAMIC WORLD, 1558–1713

GERALD MACLEAN
AND
NABIL MATAR

UNIVERSITY PRESS

OXFORD
UNIVERSITY PRESS

Great Clarendon Street, Oxford OX2 6DP

Oxford University Press is a department of the University of Oxford.
It furthers the University's objective of excellence in research, scholarship,
and education by publishing worldwide in

Oxford New York

Auckland Cape Town Dar es Salaam Hong Kong Karachi
Kuala Lumpur Madrid Melbourne Mexico City Nairobi
New Delhi Shanghai Taipei Toronto

With offices in

Argentina Austria Brazil Chile Czech Republic France Greece
Guatemala Hungary Italy Japan Poland Portugal Singapore
South Korea Switzerland Thailand Turkey Ukraine Vietnam

Oxford is a registered trade mark of Oxford University Press
in the UK and in certain other countries

Published in the United States
by Oxford University Press Inc., New York

© Gerald MacLean and Nabil Matar 2011

The moral rights of the authors have been asserted
Database right Oxford University Press (maker)

First published 2011

All rights reserved. No part of this publication may be reproduced,
stored in a retrieval system, or transmitted, in any form or by any means,
without the prior permission in writing of Oxford University Press,
or as expressly permitted by law, or under terms agreed with the appropriate
reprographics rights organization. Enquiries concerning reproduction
outside the scope of the above should be sent to the Rights Department,
Oxford University Press, at the address above

You must not circulate this book in any other binding or cover
and you must impose the same condition on any acquirer

British Library Cataloguing in Publication Data
Data available

Library of Congress Cataloging in Publication Data
Data available

Typeset by SPI Publisher Services, Pondicherry, India
Printed in Great Britain
on acid-free paper by
MPG Books Group, Bodmin and King's Lynn

ISBN 978–0–19–920318–5

1 3 5 7 9 10 8 6 4 2

Acknowledgements (MacLean)

First and foremost, my thanks to Nabil who has patiently persevered with this project during long periods when I have fallen behind or become preoccupied with other matters. We first discussed this project back in 2002, since when it has been almost impossible to keep track of the friends and colleagues who have helped along the way with stimulating suggestions, challenging questions, and useful recommendations (not to mention beds for the night in Algiers, Istanbul, and Damascus), and for invitations to share ideas with and learn from audiences in Abu Dhabi, Ankara, Berlin, Brighton, Bristol, Bucharest, Cambridge, Canterbury (Kent), Glasgow, London, Nashville (Tennessee), Neapoli (Greece), Nottingham, Reading, York, and Zaghouan (Tunisia). Special thanks to all who have allowed me the privilege of reading their work in early and draft form, and those who have raised and answered questions. A very short list must include Kate Arthur, Edmund Bosworth, Matthew Birchwood, Jerry Brotton, Matthew Dimmock, Ziad Elmarsafy, Caroline Finkel, Cornell Fleisher, Maria Fusaro, Robert Irwin, Donna Landry, Philip Mansel, James Mather, and Mahmut Mutman. My thanks too must go to all those who came to Exeter in April 2009 and delivered papers at the conference on 'Britain and the Muslim World: Historical Perspectives' for a stimulating three days during which I learned a great deal and was inspired to think about this project in new and exciting ways: without support from the British Academy and the Institute for Arab and Islamic Studies at the University of Exeter, this event could not have taken place. Special thanks are, as always, due to the staff of the Manuscripts and Rare Books Reading Rooms of the British Library for continuing to provide unparalleled patience and help. And, as ever, Donna Landry made it possible.

Acknowledgements (Matar)

Collaborating with Gerald on this book was both stimulating and enjoyable. Although we met only a few times during the past four years, we kept in close contact, and discussed together every part of the book. I had never been involved in collaborative work, but am thankful to Gerald for making the experience truly enriching.

As always, there are many friends I would like to thank: Alex Baramki (Washington, DC), Galina Yermolenko (De Sales University), Mazin Tadros (Union College), and Dina Matar (SOAS), all of whom discussed with me various sections of the book. For assistance with the theological and historical parameters of Islamic civilization, I turned to Mohammad Asfour and Muhammad Shaheen (University of Jordan), Anouar Majid (University of New England), and close to home, Wadad Qadi (University of Chicago, retired), and Giancarlo Casale (University of Minnesota). I also wish to thank Adnan al-Bakhit at the University of Jordan, who was kind enough to send me photocopies of material from the vast collection of microfilms at the University of Jordan.

The staffs of the following libraries have been gracious in their assistance: James Ford Bell Library (University of Minnesota), Wilson Library (University of Minnesota), Houghton Library (University of Harvard), Folger Library (Washington, DC), National Archives (Kew), British Library (London), National Library of Rabat (Rabat, Morocco), and Bibliothèque Nationale (Paris).

Gerald and I are grateful to Marguerite Ragnow, director of the Bell Library, University of Minnesota, for her advice regarding some of the illustrations and her help in locating them.

I wish to thank the editors of *The Journal of Islamic Studies* and the *Journal of Early Modern History* for permission to use material from the following articles: 'The Last Moors: Maghariba in Britain, 1700–1750,' *Journal of Islamic Studies* 14 (2003): 37–58; 'Ahmad al-Mansur and Queen Elizabeth I,' in *Journal of Early Modern History* 12 (2008): 55–76.

Not for a single moment during the past years of working on this book were Abraham and Hady ever out of my thoughts, as they forge ahead in their lives. May God continue to shine His face on them. And of course, Inaam is always there. And G.

And always remembered are Selim Kemal and Rudolph Stoeckel.

I wish to dedicate my portion in this book to Dominic Baker-Smith who served as my dissertation supervisor at Cambridge University many decades ago.

It is a dedication long overdue.

As years have passed, more and more have I come to realize how much the intellectual rigour that he instilled in me, along with the importance of religious and historical intersections, has guided my research. From the first time we met in his Fitzwilliam College rooms, to the many occasions when he hosted me and other graduate students at his home, and later in his retirement in Suffolk, Dominic has been the model of the scholar-humanist whose work inspires not only his own life, but the lives of those around him. His breadth of knowledge and sharpness of criticism helped me finish my dissertation in record time, and leave Emmanuel completely transformed. As I look back, I cherish the civility and elegance of the academic in him, his courtesy in the exchange of ideas, and the firm gentility in disagreement. We came from different cultures and worlds, he an Englishman and I a Palestinian, but Dominic built a bridge that opened new paths for me, leading to my first appointment at the University of Jordan and to the unforgettable experience of Quarr Abbey on the Isle of Wight.

As he works on his translation of *Utopia*, he continues to embody for me the dignity of scholarship and the sincerity of research—qualities that now, more than ever, I try to emulate.

To him, I will always be deeply grateful.

Contents

List of Illustrations   x
List of Abbreviations   xii
Map: Britain and the Islamic World   xiii

Introduction   1
1. Islam and Muslims in English Thought   13
2. First Diplomatic Exchanges   42
3. British Factors, Governors, and Diplomats   79
4. Captives   124
5. The Peoples of the Islamic Empires   156
6. Material Culture   198
7. Conclusion   230

Notes   239
Works Cited   292
Index   321

List of Illustrations

Map: Britain and the Islamic World. Prepared by Alphonce Nicholaus, University of Minnesota — xiii

1. *The Alcoran of Mahomet* (1649), title page to the first English translation of the Qur'an. MacLean copy — 35
2. Queen Elizabeth I (r. 1558–1603), from Edward Grimseston, *A Generall Historie of the Netherlands* (1609). From the James Ford Bell Library, University of Minnesota, Minneapolis, Minnesota — 44
3. Sultan Murad III (r. 1574–95), from Richard Knolles, *The Generall Historie of the Turkes* (1603). From the James Ford Bell Library, University of Minnesota, Minneapolis, Minnesota — 46
4. Shah 'Abbas, from Thomas Herbert, *A Relation of some Yeares Travaile* (1634). From the James Ford Bell Library, University of Minnesota, Minneapolis, Minnesota — 65
5. Muhammad Sadiqi Bichitr, *Jahangir Preferring a Sufi Shaikh to Kings*, from the St Petersburg album. Mughal dynasty, reign of Emperor Jahangir (1615–18). Opaque watercolour, gold and ink on paper: H x W (image): 25.3 x 18 cm (9 15/16 x 7 1/16 in). Freer Gallery of Art, Smithsonian Institution, Washington, DC: Purchase, F1942.15a — 73
6. A panoramic view of the port of Libyan Tripoli, from John Ogilby, *Africa* (1670). From the James Ford Bell Library, University of Minnesota, Minneapolis, Minnesota — 80
7. 'The Triumph of a Christian that has renounced the Faith', from Jean Dumont, *Nouveau voyage du Levant* (A la Haye, 1694). From the James Ford Bell Library, University of Minnesota, Minneapolis, Minnesota — 125
8. 'A Merchant Jewe', from Nicolas de Nicolay, *The Navigations into Turkie* (1585). MacLean copy — 173
9. 'A Merchant of Armenia', from Nicolas de Nicolay, *The Navigations into Turkie* (1585). MacLean copy — 179

10. Types of Persians—an 'Abdall or Preist,' and a 'Coozel-bash' (Kızılbaş or 'red head') warrior; William Marshall's engraved title page to Thomas Herbert, *A Relation of some Yeares Travaile* (1634). From the James Ford Bell Library, University of Minnesota, Minneapolis, Minnesota   190

11. A Moor smoking; title page to Richard Brathwaite's *The Smoaking Age* (1617). By permission of the British Library; shelfmark C.40.b.20. Copyright belongs to the British Library and further reproduction is prohibited   205

List of Abbreviations

CSP   *Calendar of State Papers,* followed by series
CSPD   *Calendar of State Papers Domestic*
CSPV   *Calendar of State Papers Venetian*
ODNB   *Oxford Dictionary of National Biography,* online version

Short-Title Catalogue: A. W. Pollard and G. R. Redgrave, *A Short-Title Catalogue of Books Printed in England, Scotland, and Ireland, and of English Books Printed Abroad, 1475–1640.* 1926; 2nd ed., 3 vols. London, 1986.

Wing, *STC:* Donald Wing, et al, eds., *Short-Title Catalogue of Books Printed in England, Scotland, Ireland, Wales, and British America, and of English Books printed in other countries, 1641–1700.* 1945; 2nd ed., 4 vols. New York, 1994–98.

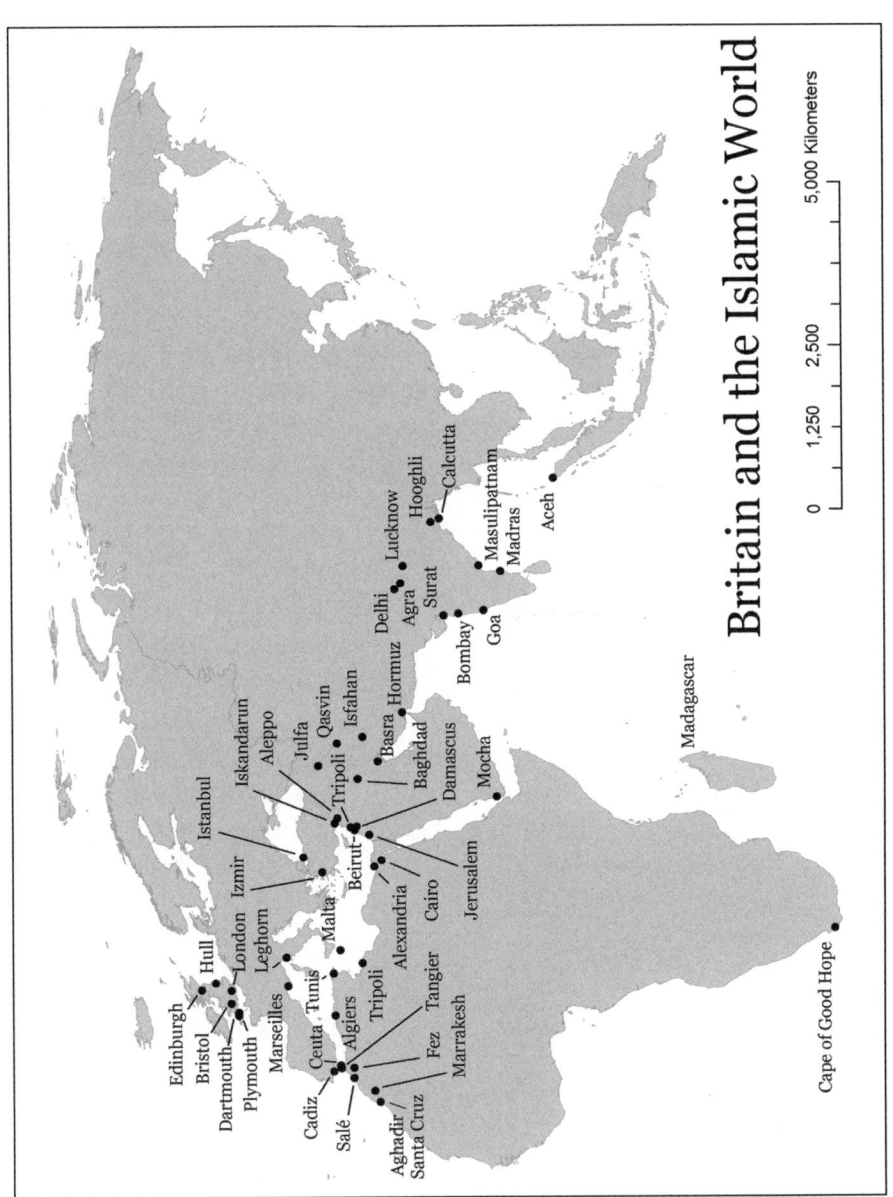

Map: Britain and the Islamic world
Prepared by Alphonce Nicholaus, University of Minnesota

Introduction

> Perhaps the last place in the world where we should expect to find Mahommedanism is England, and yet it is a fact that this religion has been established in our land of late years, and, strange to say, by an Englishman.
>
> John J. Pool, *Studies in Mohammedanism* (1892)

The above words were written in 1892 by a civil servant, 'late of Calcutta', one John J. Pool. The author continued by describing the 'Church of Islam', which he visited at the Liverpool Moslem Institute. The first mosque in Britain, it had opened the year before. Although he was sharp enough to note the mistake in a sign that announced 'There is no God but God, and Mohammed was His Prophet', which he urged should be 'is' not 'was', Pool was clearly unaware of how long had been his country's engagement with Muslims and the Islamic world.[1] Three hundred years earlier, Queen Elizabeth I had received a petition from a Muslim in London who wanted to join her navy and fight against the Spaniards.[2] Elizabeth was building strong commercial and diplomatic ties with the Ottoman and Moroccan Empires—so strong that she was the first monarch to welcome Muslim ambassadors to England and to receive them with all due pomp and ceremony in her royal palaces.

What did English-speaking men and women in the early modern period know about Muslim peoples and societies, about Islam as a theology, and about Islamic lands? How were their lives influenced by increasing knowledge of, and contact with, the diverse peoples and disparate cultures of the Islamic world? In this book, we explore encounters between Britain and the Islamic world from 1558 to 1713, showing how scholars, diplomats, chartered company officials, factors, captives, travellers, clerics, and chroniclers were involved in developing and describing those interactions. We indicate some of the ways that religious and national identities, as much as cultural and domestic life in Britain, were being shaped by ideas, goods, styles, and techniques imported from Islamic lands. All periodizations are problematic, but we begin with Queen Elizabeth I since it was under her reign that diplomatic and commercial relations with the Islamic world, from Morocco to Persia to India, first began. All but one of the four trading companies that received her royal charter took Britons to Islamic regions (Turkey Company, 1581 renamed Levant Company, 1592; Barbary Company, 1585; East India Company, 1600), while the fourth brought English traders in limited contact with Muslims (Guinea Company, 1588). We end with the Peace of Utrecht in 1713 between Britain and France that concluded the War of the Spanish Succession. With the relative decline of Spain as a naval and imperial power after the 1640s, with the partial withdrawal of the States General from international rivalry after the three Anglo-Dutch wars in the second half of the seventeenth century, with the establishment of fortified settlements on the coasts of India by the East India Company in the later decades of the seventeenth century, and with the fragmentation of the Mughal Empire after the death of Aureng-zebe in 1707: following these changes, by 1713, London had become the 'centre of world trade', and England, in the envious words of Montesquieu, 'mistress of the seas (a thing without precedent), and combining trade with empire'.[3]

During this century and a half, Britons met Muslims for the first time since the Crusades and began re-examining their understanding of Islam in which there had been 'little innovation' since the thirteenth century.[4] Decisive changes were taking place in the ways Britons thought about themselves and the ways they acted in, and upon, the international scene. These changes were brought about by trade, cultural, and commercial rivalry, and fascination with foreign and exotic goods and ways of life that, in turn, generated needs for export markets and for the importation of natural resources from countries as near as Morocco—gold and salt-petre—and as far as Bengal. From Safi to Mocha, and from Izmir to Surat and Madras, Britons imported horses and coffee, gold and sugar, silk and spices, carpets and manuscripts, ivory, calico, and indigo, all of which changed the course of their cultural history. If, as Donald F. Lach has argued, Asia had a role in the making of Europe,[5] so we will argue, the Islamic world had a specific and important role in the making of Britain. What we will show is the wide range of exposures and conflicts, sources and

INTRODUCTION 3

texts, people and objects, that were instrumental in that process. To do so, we will approach the discussion through these perspectives:

1. Muslims and Islam in English Thought
2. First Diplomatic Exchanges
3. British Factors, Governors, and Diplomats
4. Captives
5. The Peoples of the Islamic Empires
6. Material Culture

Different social groups and classes in Britain developed different ideas and opinions about the Islamic world, its geography, history, and peoples. Not only did Britons encounter a variety of non-Muslim religious communities during their sojourns into Islamic lands, they also found new ideas and resources, which they proudly took back to their homes. In the 1580s, English physicians turned to the Egyptians to learn about antidotes to poison;[6] by the 1590s, Queen Elizabeth sweetened her food with Moroccan sugar.[7] As much as the English were eager to learn about novelties from their European neighbours,[8] so were they also eager to learn from Muslims. In Persia with the Shirley brothers, George Manwaring wondered at spectacular firework displays, agricultural techniques, and the production of muskets and firearms;[9] on 15 July 1620, Samuell Sharpe and Richard Wilton, 'cittizens of London', acquired a patent for 'makeing of grogram . . . and sundrie other sortes of silke and other stuffes after the Turkie manner of chamletting'.[10] In that same decade, Englishmen of the Surat factory in India gave up on medicines sent from England and took the 'advice of local Mughal doctors', and were thereby considered to be tempted to 'swap religions and cultures' with Muslims.[11]

Meanwhile, accurate first-hand reports about Islam and its various peoples appeared by writers as different from each other as George Sandys and Henry Blount (travellers), Edward Pococke and Sir Thomas Hyde (orientalists at Oxford), Sir Thomas Roe (envoy to the Levant and India), Sir Paul Rycaut (diplomat and historian), and Thomas Smith (chaplain). There were also numerous translations from French travellers, captives, and theologians: Nicholas de Nicolay and Guillaume Joseph Grelot (both of whose accounts included illustrations), Sir John Chardin, Tavernier Bernier, Jean de Thévenot, and others. By the middle of the century, corantos and newsbooks began to include sections on the Islamic World, chiefly from the Ottoman Empire, reporting on festive occasions, battles, changes of government, and unusual events.[12] But nothing compares in the magnitude, detail, and breadth of the information available about the different parts of the Islamic world with the writings of factors, merchants, consuls, agents, and ships' captains that were exchanged among themselves as well as those that were sent to London. The letters and reports from the East India Company, covering India and Persia, from the Levant Company, covering the eastern Mediterranean, and from representatives and consuls in North Africa, extend to tens of thousands of pages, all about trade, commodities, markets, exports and imports, European rivals, ports, governors and kings, and multi-religious societies. Although the trading companies tried to control the information about the regions to which their ships sailed, and did not sponsor its publication, an encyclopaedic range of information about the British experience in Islamic lands piled up in the offices of the chartered companies, as well as of the Secretary of State to whom letters from North Africa were addressed. At the same time, armchair scholars at Oxford and Cambridge studied medieval Islamic science, history, and Qur'anic exegesis, learning of and describing a different kind of Islam from the one encountered by sailors wandering the streets of Izmir, or captives labouring in the fleets of Algiers. Theatrical representations of Muslims by dramatists such as Christopher Marlowe, Thomas Greene, Thomas Heywood, John Massinger, Elkanah Settle, John Dryden, and Aphra Behn may have differed vastly from what a radical theologian like Thomas Brightman, or Warwickshire physician such as Henry Stubbe, or an administrator such as Samuel Pepys, or a Quaker such as George Fox, purported to know. And all of these differed in their purview of Islam from writers like Alexander Ross and Humphrey Prideaux, and in their conception of the Islamic world from geographers and cartographers with access to the most up-to-date atlases and Portolan maps.

Many Britons, from the groundling gaping at Thomas Heywood's Mullisheq, to the parishioner staring at a kinsman returning from captivity, to the London agent calculating company profit, wondered about Islam, the Muslims, and their lands. And similarly, Muslim rulers were eager to engage Britons in trade and to learn about their society. The Ottoman Sultan, the Safavid Shah, the Great Mughal, the Deys and Beys of the North African regencies, and the Moroccan Mulay wanted to negotiate commercial, and sometimes diplomatic, agreements with Britons, and tried to find out as much as possible about their lands and rulers. They faced pressing concerns at home and on their borders that encouraged them to view these infidel visitors and merchants in a strong military light. The Moroccans had the Ottomans in Algeria and eastward along the North African coast to worry about, given the Ottoman desire to conquer the whole of the Maghrib. The Ottomans, for their part, had the Savafids challenging their eastern borders, while the latter were constantly threatened by Ottoman military encroachment, culminating in the re-conquest of Baghdad in 1638. Both of these Islamic empires sought British support, as the numerous initiatives by William Harborne, the Shirley brothers, and other emissaries indicate.[13] The close association with the Safavids led to numerous exchanges of emissaries, while the Persian ambassador who reached Chinapatan in the late 1680s found much to admire in British administration, writing about the city and the fort that the 'English have built themselves'.[14] Further east, the Mughal emperors had the vast Indian Ocean for their commercial exploitation, but also had internal rivalries with contenders and local princes that often led to military conflicts—in which the British, from the second half of the seventeenth century, began to participate. Mughal governors reported on the number of British settlements, both in the shape of forts and towns, and on their belligerent growth. By the end of the seventeenth century, internal changes within the three great Muslim empires of the Ottomans, Safavids, and Mughals may have been largely similar,[15] but it was only in India that British policy began to entertain military force as a means for promoting settlement and to ensure commercial monopoly. Britons had tried, and failed, in Tangier, but they successfully maintained over a dozen fortifications on the west coast of Africa, expanded Bombay, and fortified Madras after receiving a grant in perpetuity from the Indian ruler in 1678.[16] Although English trading settlements were typically defended by garrisons, Sir Joshua Child's benighted war against the Mughal Empire in 1688–89 marked the first signs of a hardening of attitude and willingness to engage in military aggression that would return in the mid eighteenth century.[17]

British knowledge of the Muslims and the Islamic world varied in accordance with regions and times. In this book, we examine comparatively and thematically three geo-political regions. This division follows the very different organizational, financial, and naval dynamics that governed British expansion, and the different balance, or imbalance, of power that prevailed in various parts of the world. To approach Muslims as a single, homogeneous category would be to ignore historical and national distinctions that changed during the course of the period. It would also be to ignore geographical, commercial, and ideological distinctions among the different trading companies. Writers of most travel accounts and chronicles specifically mention regions and countries, but do not conceive of a generalized Muslim world stretching from Marrakesh to Agra: university chairs established at the time were in 'Arabic' or 'Oriental' Studies not 'Islamic' Studies, as has become common today. While most of the people that Britons met in the three regions were Muslim, the factors, travellers, and consuls were not always sure about that—as we shall show in the course of this book. The Islamic empires were noteworthy too because within their domains resided a number of people who were not Muslims. The unexceptional mingling of Muslims, Christians, and Jews, to say nothing of other faiths, and the very existence of seemingly harmonious multi-ethnic, multicultural communities surprised and impressed many European visitors.

The three trading companies represent the three regions in which Britons first encountered the Islamic world. First comes Anatolia and the eastern Mediterranean of the Ottomans, where the Levant Company operated. Extending from Alexandria, Jerusalem, Lebanese Tripoli, Izmir, Istanbul, and Aleppo, this region was quite familiar to educated English Britons from Graeco-Roman geographical writings and biblical texts. In the light of the military and cultural confrontations between western Europe and the Ottoman Empire during the sixteenth and seventeenth centuries, a vast body of writing appeared in Latin, French, German, and Italian, to which Britons turned for information about those they called the 'Turks'. These writings described battles and dynasties, often prefaced by accounts of the rise of 'Mahomet' and the beginnings of Islam. Produced against the backdrop of the Ottoman armies and navies as they pushed toward Vienna in 1529 and Malta in 1566, they could not but express deep fear and hostility. As the Ottoman sultans and their subjects, however, lost their military edge in the final decades of the seventeenth century, and no longer posed a threat to British interests in the eastern Mediterranean, English writings changed, no longer expressing the vituperation that had marked influential tomes such as Richard Knolles's *Generall Historie of the Turkes* (1603). The letters of Lady Mary Wortley Montagu written during the early 1700s from Istanbul and Edirne reflect British curiosity and ease rather than fear at what Richard Knolles had earlier described as the 'present terrour of the worlde'.

The second region is that of the Ottoman regencies of Libya, Tunisia, Algeria, and the kingdom of Morocco, a region that was encountered every time Britons sailed to the Levant, since their ships needed to avoid waters dominated by unfriendly Catholic powers to the north. During Elizabeth's reign, this zone attracted much commercial and political attention. A century later, however, while its naval usefulness continued, the region became less important—even Moroccan saltpetre, which had been much needed, was replaced by Indian imports. This region was not overseen by a centralizing company similar in power and longevity to the Levant or East India Companies: factors and consuls reported directly to the Secretary of State without a board of investors to coordinate their activities, and enjoyed only limited royal intervention; after Queen Elizabeth, letters by the monarchs to the rulers of the regencies are few. Further, and although the Iberians possessed numerous outposts in North Africa, the English went to the Mediterranean to trade and pillage, not to seize and settle: even Tangier in 1661 was a dowry gift not a conquest. This region was nevertheless decisive in imprinting an indelible, and antagonistic, image of Muslims, because it was here that large numbers of Britons were taken captive by 'Barbary' pirates. Captives who returned home, while denouncing Muslims and Islam, told and wrote about the brutal conditions they had endured. One of the most enduring images that continued to demonize Muslims originated in the sixteenth and seventeenth centuries: that of the Muslim, North African captor, holding to ransom or forcing to convert the innocent English captive, who was usually male, but sometimes, female. The consular archives recording English activity in this region, with their extensive documents about captivity, ransom, apostasy to Islam, and naval battles, have received relatively little scholarly attention in contrast with those concerning relations between early-modern England and the Ottoman, Safavid, and Mughal Empires. Among our objectives in this book is to redress the imbalance by focusing on Britain's early encounters with North Africa in some detail.

The third region reaches from Persia across India to the edge of South East Asia, including what R. J. Barendse has called *The Arabian Seas* (2002). By the end of the seventeenth century, this zone had become the most important trading partner with Britain of all the Islamic regions: it was here that trade joined the 'Indian Ocean World' to the American colonies. This zone begins in Aleppo since it was from here that information and letters about inter-European affairs that had been collected in Istanbul or Izmir travelled to Isfahan, Basra, Lahore, and Surat, all the way to Madras, Bantam, and Aceh. This zone was administered by the East India Company and employed the highest number of men—who sometimes took their families with them. Throughout this region, factors and other company agents shared information, writing to each other while copying their letters to London. The records of the East India Company reveal a vast network of Britons, in forts and on ships, in the hinterland and in harbours, sometimes in rivalry, but more often writing to each other for commercial instructions and naval support, as well as for casks of English beer, ink, paper, and Shiraz wine. This zone was rich and offered the largest potential for trade and profit, not only in terms of the goods that Britons carried back to Europe or from one region to another, but also in terms of financial cooperation with wealthy local governors who extended capital to the English entrepreneurs.[18] Because of the magnitude of investments, the London offices of the East India Company maintained a firm system of control, ensuring that factors, consuls, and eventually soldiers, abided by commercial priorities and courses of action.

Strikingly, in this vast archive of East India Company writings from Persia and India, there is none of the intense religious polarization that appears in writings about North Africa or the Levant. Although there were a few captivities—or as the records term them, 'imprisonments'—of Britons in India and Ceylon, no accounts were published that depicted the horror of captivity in divisive religious terms. Nor are there repeated references to Islam or Muslims: when early travellers and later factors described the 'superstitions' they observed—of fasting, 'Lent', feasts, 'priests', and 'Mesquits'—they did not use their observations to incite fear or opposition, and more often used the ethnic terms, 'Moor' and 'Arab', rather than the religious term 'Mahometan'. In India and South-East Asia, Britons encountered new societies, cultures, and peoples, but they did not react adversely to Islam because they did not find the Muslims as threatening as those in the Mediterranean, and because they often found the 'Moors' mixed with Hindus, 'Gentiles', and 'Hindustanis', which meant the encounter was much less defined in terms of religion. Writings about North Africa were heavily polemical and focused on Muslims since they were the dominant religious community in that region, although English reports regularly maligned the small Jewish community too. But in India and further east, the discourse concerned trade, difficulties with local rulers, anger at interlopers, not to forget rivalry with the Dutch and the Portuguese, and to a lesser extent with the Venetians and Danes. The Indian Ocean failed to evoke the religious anxiety and defensiveness of the Islamic Mediterranean, since here the danger of religious conversion came from the Portuguese

Catholics not the Muslims. Perhaps, had Aureng-zebe imposed the *jizya* tax on the English as he did on his subjects in 1679, they might have been alerted to the distinctness of Islamic law. But he did not.[19]

In this context of differentiating attitudes to the three regions in English writings, there are three factors to consider. First, descriptions, reactions, and responses to the Islamic empires were not separable from the balance, or imbalance, of power, nor from British advances in navigation and warfare. In the Ottoman Mediterranean, the Levant Company did not rely on naval or military force to pursue its goals. No British fleet ever bombarded Izmir or Iskenderun in intimidation or reprisal. In the North African zone, however, following Sir Robert Mansel's failed attack on Algiers of 1621, the British fleet intervened in 1637 in Salé and continued to do so, with devastating attacks on Algiers in 1669 and Libyan Tripoli in 1675, until the end of the century—by which time it, along with France, had disabled the naval capability of Morocco and all the regencies. Similarly, as early as the 1650s, East India Company officials in London began instructing their agents in India to use force when negotiating 'terms' to their 'reasonable satisfaction', and to send out vessels, for both 'offensive and devensive' actions—at the same time that they oversaw the establishment there of 'garrison towns controlled by military governors'.[20] Views of Islam and Muslims were determined by the amount of military or diplomatic clout that Britons had, or did not have.

Second, by the middle of the sixteenth century, there was a large body of English publications about the Ottoman Empire and the religion of its people, from travellers' reports to theological treatises, biblical commentaries, and even plays. There were also the popular captivity accounts. About Persian and Indian Islam, and about the Muslims in those regions, there were fewer publications, and writings that did appear lacked the same intensity of polemical focus on religion. Consequently, Mughal and Safavid rulers were never denounced in sermons or on stage, unlike the 'Grand Turk', who served as a commonplace figure of despotic tyranny and violence. 'Turk Gregory never did such deeds in arms as I have done this day,' boasts Falstaff in *I Henry IV* (5. 3. 45), reminding us that the Ottoman sultan was an arch-enemy who was often connected with that other arch-enemy of Protestant England, the Pope. And no captives wrote of ill-treatment among the Persians or the Indians with the anger of returnees from North Africa. Many seventeenth-century English printed texts about North Africa and the Ottoman Levant were written by English captives, or translated into English from French captivity records: no consuls or factors from Surat, Isfahan, or Aceh in Sumatra published accounts about their experiences—experiences that were largely non-confrontational, and would have offered a different image of Muslims. Although writing was a powerful tool in the process of expansion and domination,[21] none of the East India Company archive, which could have given an alternative impression of the religion and the peoples of Islam, was published at the time. Unlike France, where there was an impressive pre-imperial body of oriental studies,[22] England produced very little in comparison, except a few studies by Oxford scholars such as Edward Pococke, father and son; Richard Greaves; and Thomas Hyde, and these were clearly aimed at academic readers. Then as today, it would seem, accounts of conflict, captivity, and religious polarization were deemed more marketable.

Third, when Britons sailed into the Mediterranean, they carried with them vague and prejudiced memories of the Crusades, a hostile attitude fortified by images of the 'Turk's Head' decorating public houses and archery butts, and the numerous plays, ballads, and epics that recalled the glorious deeds of heroic Britons battling Saracen and Turk. Elizabethan sailors arriving in the Mediterranean and encountering Muslims for the first time were most likely burdened by centuries-old images of confrontation and eschatological holy war. In the western Mediterranean, Britons found themselves in a region seething with hostility from the North African Moriscos. Expelled from, and robbed of, their homes and history, the Moriscos attacked Christian shipping, seldom distinguishing between Spanish Catholics and British Protestants. At the same time, governors in the Ottoman regencies recalled attacks on Algiers (1541) and Tunis (1573), while Moroccan rulers resented the settlements and forts that had been planted on their shores by European Christians from the late fifteenth century. North Africa, from Libyan Tripoli to Agadir, was a region of European colonialism and consequent Muslim anger and volatile memories—and it was here that English seamen and merchants first ventured in search of markets, resources, and employment.

The Islam that appears in the early modern archive and imagination of England belongs, therefore, chiefly to the first two regions, and only tangentially to the lands and peoples of the Mughal and Safavid Empires. Britons did, on occasion, write about being insulted by Safavid and Mughal rulers for being Christian—such as Anthony Jenkinson by Shah Tahmasp in 1562, and Thomas Kerridge in Surat in 1616.[23] And some travellers—but not, suggestively, company factors—who wrote about their journeys this far east also denounced Islam and Muslims.[24] But these were exceptional instances. The importance of the Persian-Indian region lay in British commercial, and later colonial, interests, with the result that the East India Company correspondence rarely concerned itself with religious differences or the problems of conversion. The first accounts of India from the 1580s, some of which were published by Richard Hakluyt, described in great detail, and awe, the wonders of Indian civilizations, peoples, customs, and trading possibilities, but showed very little interest in religious beliefs. Later resident factors and agents did not confront religious difficulties so much as commercial and military challenges from other Europeans, and occasional problems negotiating with local rulers. Had some of this correspondence been published in the seventeenth century, a different view of Muslims might well have supplanted religious hostility.[25]

During the sixteenth century, the English were never more than relatively minor players on the global scene, and little was known about them beyond their shores. Even in 1642, King Charles I still had to write to the Ottoman sultan expressing his desire for 'Amitie' and imploring him to maintain 'the entercourse of Trade between Our Subjects and Yours'.[26] But as the balance of power shifted, so did relations with Muslims, as well as attitudes towards them and their religion. Consuls writing from Algiers in 1600 lacked the assurance of factors writing from Madras in 1700. Had an Othello really slain a 'circumcis'd Turk' in Aleppo, he would not have lived to tell of his deed, but eighty years later, in 1684, when English sailors in Karwar killed two Muslim boys, the British factory had enough power, and money, to buy their safety.[27] Back in 1608, when William Hawkins began trading in Agra, he would have felt none of the religious and cultural superiority that military might bestowed on his compatriots after conquering Bombay from the Portuguese in 1662, or bombarding Libyan Tripoli in 1675, or defeating the French in the Mediterranean in 1713. By the terminal year of our study, a substantial shift had taken place in British attitudes to Islamic societies from that which had prevailed in the Elizabethan era. Popular historians of Anglo-Islamic relations often sacrifice historical and geographical context for racy narrative, jumbling examples from across centuries and regions without recognizing the crucial differentiations in naval, diplomatic, and commercial power that determined specific reactions at specific times, and that brought about the change in British presence from confused factors to imperious consuls and military commanders.

This book tells the story of this change from the point of view of how the different Muslims and Islamic cultures of the North African, the Ottoman, and the Persian-Indian regions became increasingly known and influential in the thought and life of early modern Britain.

I
Islam and Muslims in English Thought

Muslims

From the Elizabethan period on, traders from Britain could no longer exclude Muslims from their commercial outreach any more than English, Welsh, and Cornish pirates and privateers could resist attacking ships in the Mediterranean basin. The English, after all, had been profiting from—and enslaving—North Africans for generations.[1] British and European economies were changing as a result of the arrival of gold and silver from the Americas. Every commercial nation, Christian and Muslim, wanted to gain from that wealth by expanding trade and attracting investors and even immigrants. The conflict between Elizabethan England and Catholic Spain, followed by the devastations of the Thirty Years War on the continent, compelled British merchants to seek alternative markets and seaports in the Mediterranean as well as the Indian Ocean. New sea routes were explored, factories established, and a few expatriated Britons married and acculturated to new lives in countries as different as Algeria, Japan, Persia, and India.[2] A new world order of commercial rivalry, diplomatic intrigue, military alliances, counter-alliances, and religious reconfigurations was emerging, bringing British ships and travellers into Tangier, Alexandria, Mocha, and Hormuz. At the same time, North African, Ottoman, and Persian emissaries came to London, where they wandered about, visited cathedrals and centres of learning, observed social and industrial changes, and variously charmed and mystified the locals.

This was an era when Britons and Muslims first met each other and learned about each other's religion, customs, laws, and society, about differences in the roles of women, and the status of rulers, as well as about similarities in desire, greed, and curiosity. From the Mediterranean that encompassed Morocco and the Ottoman Empire, the initial British experience of Islam rapidly moved eastward, toward Safavid Persia and Mughal India—the two most powerful centres of Islamic civilization and religion after the Ottoman Empire. In contemporary literature, Persia regularly featured as a biblical as well as a romantic past rather than as an existing present. From the book of Isaiah with its celebration of the Persian king Cyrus, to Herodotus and later Greek historians, the ancient imperial civilization of Darius was most likely to have been more familiar to English readers than the contemporary world of the Safavids. Unlike the upstart Ottomans, the Persians had established a great and glorious empire rivalling those of Greece and Rome, as described in works such as Joannes Philippson's *Briefe Chronicle of the foure principall Empyres. To wit of Babilon, Persia, Grecia and Rome* (1568, rpt. 1627).[3] But beyond the ranks of the imaginatively or biblically minded, Persia was also known for being the source of one of the nation's greatest and most profitable commodities: raw silk. Further afield lay India, fabled land of aromatic spices, pearls, and precious stones, and source of what was rapidly becoming the most important import, calico. Realizing the potential in the markets of these empires, both for export and import, Britons set out to get rich by exploring trade routes and negotiating agreements. Their activities irked the French, Venetians, Spanish, and Portuguese who had preceded them in commercial entrepreneurship in the Islamic dominions. But supported by the Crown, they established chartered companies to coordinate and eventually monopolize what would become a vast exchange in cloth and currencies, slaves and ideas, foods and luxury items, exotic animals, and even portraits. Given the large amount of imports, the impact of Islamic material culture on British society was extensive. Chapter 6, on material culture, examines a few of those imports.

Although people living in the British archipelago were never really threatened by the armies of the Ottomans, Elizabeth became queen while Sultan Süleyman 'the Magnificent' (r. 1520–66) commanded the most formidable army in Europe. Elizabeth fully understood the value of being able to consolidate national unity by invoking a distant enemy. In July 1565, the Spanish ambassador reported that Elizabeth had 'ordered a general prayer for victory' against the Ottoman forces that had been attacking Malta since May.[4] Forms of public prayers to be read twice a week 'for the delivery of those Christians that are now invaded by the Turke' were duly printed, but swiftly replaced with prayers 'of thanksgeving' when the Ottoman armada finally retreated in September.[5] The Ottoman invasion of Hungary the following May occasioned yet another set of prayers 'for the preservation of those christians and their countreys, that are nowe invaded by the Turke', though Süleyman's death in September while on campaign seems to have gone unnoticed.[6] At home, the Ottoman threat, however remote, could be used to browbeat the pious into contemplating their own sinful lives. Later, the militarism and pomp of the Ottoman armies fascinated and awed British visitors, even as various authors wistfully began predicting the imminent collapse of the great Islamic empires. The retreat of the Ottoman forces from the gates of Vienna in 1683, and the subsequent Peace of Karlowitz in 1699, encouraged widespread optimism that the military threat of 'the terrible Turk' was under control. 'But,' as Suraiya Faroqhi notes, 'when it came to the judgement of practical politicians, before the defeat of the sultan's armies in the Russo-Ottoman war of 1768–74, the power of that potentate was taken seriously indeed.'[7]

Meanwhile, Muslim local officers, administrators, and rulers from Marrakesh to Libyan Tripoli, and from Izmir to Jerusalem and Agra, were also learning about the Euro-Christians who sailed into their harbours or travelled to their cities, bringing with them commodities and stories about their lands, their monarchs, their cultures, and differences in their Protestant and Catholic versions of Christianity. Britons were driven by commercial need and by the desire to trade—not by some curiosity peculiar to 'western' Europeans, or a heroic spirit of 'adventure', as often claimed. Like immigrants today into the West, early modern Britons sailed and trekked to the lands of Islam in search of employment, opportunity, and remuneration. And they were able to do so because Islamic society, following Qur'anic injunction, is multi-religious and allows separate spaces for Christians and Jews. Consequently, Protestant Britons were free to travel into the Ottoman and Safavid Empires at a time when they would not have been as safe travelling into Spain or other Catholic countries with anti-Protestant ideologies. While living in Istanbul, Sanderson regularly went about sightseeing. He records spotting elephants, tame lions, and even a giraffe, at a time when no Moroccan, or Indian, or Persian would have felt comfortable about being a tourist in England—assuming he would have wanted to be one.[8] In the Islamic world, British travellers regularly bumped into each other: William Lithgow dined with the pirate John Ward in Tunis, Robert Shirley and his wife met Thomas Coryate in India, and the chaplain Henry Teonge met an old college friend from Christchurch while in Aleppo. They met plenty of foreigners too: in Jerusalem George Sandys records meetings with Italians, French, Portuguese, and Germans; some were traders, some sailors, and others consuls.[9]

This inherent, and historical, openness of Islam to the Peoples of the Book encouraged Britons in search of trade, markets, and profit to travel to Egypt, Anatolia, Persia, and India—hence the repeated issuances of *firmans* by Ottoman and Mughal rulers. Although they ventured into regions where no previous Britons had gone, they were not really discovering new routes, but were following commercial trails that the Ottomans, Safavids, Mughals, and other Muslims had been using for centuries, even millennia.[10] They adapted to local customs such as clothing and diet, and joined local caravans that were, for a fee, willing to protect them.

When they arrived at their destinations, from Isfahan to Agra, they were received by the ruling monarchs as any other foreign merchant: they were invited to the courts in order to be seen and questioned. Numerous accounts by English travellers and merchants tell of Muslim potentates quizzing them for hours, even days, about their native countries. Thus was the case of Sir William Hawkins, as well as Sir Thomas Roe, of whom there is a colourful portrait in the Mughal court showing him sitting at the feet of Shah Jahangir (r. 1605–27). On some occasions, reports of these meetings were written down and kept in the court depositories for future use. Earlier, in 1599, Jasper Tomson, the English agent in Marrakesh, was asked to report on the Ottoman invasion of Hungary in 1596 in which he had participated. His account was 'sett downe Larbie tonge [in Arabic]... [by] the Kinges cheiffe interpretour for the Latine and Spanish tongues. Where we spent 6 howres together till the night approched.'[11] Such information was rarely transformed, however, into publically available documents, histories, or chronicles similar to the world histories and geographies that were beginning to appear from the presses of England and the rest of Western Christendom. Printing in Arabic script was, after all, forbidden throughout the early-modern Islamic world. Although Sephardic exiles had, from the late fifteenth century, established printing presses using Hebrew script in a number of Ottoman cities, and Paul Rycaut was able to have an English text of the trading licence of 1663 printed in English in Istanbul, it would not be until 1706 that, in Aleppo, the first Arabic-script press—brought by Orthodox Christians—appeared anywhere in the Ottoman Empire.[12]

Trade between England and the Ottoman Levant started as early as 1511, according to Richard Hakluyt, but by the middle of the century, it had ground to a halt.[13] In 1553, however, Anthony Jenkinson was granted a personal licence to trade throughout the Ottoman Empire by Sultan Süleyman I,[14] and in 1580 Sultan Murad III (r. 1574–95) issued a formal trading licence, or *ahidname*, to the English nation as a whole. This agreement was similar in kind to trading privileges that had earlier been granted to the Genoese, Venetians, and the French.[15] Meanwhile, in 1566 and 1568, commercial privileges had been granted to the English by Shah Tahmasp (r. 1524–76) in an attempt to lure them away from Ottoman markets.[16] These privileges were confirmed in the next century, culminating in the Grant of Capitulations of July–August 1629 by Shah Safi (r. 1629–42), which remained in effect until 1722 and the end of the Safavid dynasty.[17] Throughout this period, Britons were signing ad hoc commercial treaties and diplomatic agreements with local rulers in the North African Mediterranean at regular intervals, renewing their terms as facts on the ground changed in favour of Britain's growing power.

How much information about the Ottomans, the North Africans, the Persians, or Mughals was passed back to people at home by the traders and merchants remains unclear. Although there was a vast legacy of classical and biblical geographical lore that English readers could consult, information about the Islamic world was first treated with the same jingoistic rhetoric as information about the Americas—as a product of European discovery. The Mughals, wrote Robert Morden in 1680, 'lived in peace under their several Kings until the year 1587, when discovered by the Portugals, after by the English, Dutch, &c.'[18] The reports printed in Hakluyt's *Principal Navigations* (1589) and Samuel Purchas' *Hakluytus Posthumus* (1625) furnished the first body of reasonably reliable information, but uncertainty and confusion persisted. Many accounts were translations from Italian, French, and Latin, while original works by English travellers generalized about 'Mahometanism' and 'Mahometans' from their experience of specific Muslim communities, and from observing the customs and rituals of specific regions, they applied them to the religion of Islam as a whole. In 1558, Jenkinson—the first writer to describe the Muslims of Central Asia—could not have realized that the 'Mahometists' whose customs he recorded differed dramatically from the 'Arabians' of 'Jerusalem and Tripolis' that Laurence Aldersey later encountered in 1581, or from the 'Moors' of North Africa described by Leo Africanus in his *Geographical Historie of Africa* (1550), which was translated into English in 1600.[19] The earliest English writers were entirely unaware of the vast variety of customs, rituals, and beliefs that separated the Ottomans from the Persians, and both in turn from the Mughals.

Contacts

One manner in which Britons learned about Muslims and members of other eastern religions and nations was by the personal contacts they established with those whom they variously termed Turks, Moors, Arabs, eastern Christians, Indians, Persians, Jews, and Armenians. English writers regularly mention formal associations, and even personal friendships developing between Muslims and other minorities under Islamic rule—suggesting that some knowledge of Islamic culture and history, however partial, was inevitably conveyed back to home. In recounting his journey to Jerusalem in 1601, Henry Timberlake describes becoming close friends with an un-named Moor without whom he would not have survived.[20] Although Timberlake doubtless learned something about his friend's North African homeland, he wrote nothing. The writings of John Harrison, who served as agent for the Barbary Company in Morocco during the first decades of the seventeenth century, constitute the first archive in English about that region.[21] While visiting Morocco in December 1637, Edmund Bradshaw introduced a powder that 'benefited' the Moroccan queen. When he was later accused of witchcraft by Robert Blake, a resident trader, 'some of the most learned' men in the country joined Bradshaw in discussions about, and experiments in, 'chemical arts'—forming what must have been the first Euro-Maghariba scientific community.[22] Edward Pococke studied Arabic at the hands of an Ottoman Christian in Aleppo, and the annotations to his *Specimen Historiae Arabum* (1650) show detailed knowledge of Arab-Islamic history. Paul Rycaut and John Finch became familiar with Ottoman society and culture, travelling widely in Anatolia. At the same time, Levant Company and East India Company consuls and factors, from Lebanese Tripoli to Surat, established close working relations with the local rulers and members of the court. They wrote about visits to homes, courts, and even mosques. Many 'Franks', Britons included, visited the Aghia Sophia mosque in Istanbul—starting with Fynes Moryson in 1597—while Thomas Smith was in a mosque 'at Evening-prayer in the time of Ramazan'—amidst an

'Assembly of no less than two or three thousand'.[23] In 1658, Captain John Durson offered his services to the prince of Bengal, while his friend, William Pitts, married 'a Moorish woman'.[24] Toward the end of the seventeenth century, Francis Brooks befriended a Moor who helped him escape after many years in Moroccan captivity. Having become proficient in Arabic, Brooks was able to impersonate the language and culture of his companion.[25] And there were the few Muslims who converted to Christianity and came to England: the two 'Turks' who were, allegedly, in the inner circle of King George I's retinue are a case in point.[26]

The visits of Muslim ambassadors and emissaries to London, along with Jewish and Christian subjects sent by Muslim potentates, produced magnificent processions and exhibits of horses, slaves, turbans, scimitars, priests, jurists, and cuisines. The majority of visitors came from North Africa, with Ottoman, Safavid, and Indian emissaries trailing behind. The most elaborate procession was described in *The Arrivall and Intertainements of the Embassador, Alkaid Jaurar Ben Abdella* (1637),[27] an emissary from Morocco, whom king Charles preferred to meet rather than the Polish ambassador whom he kept languishing for months.[28] Jaurar and other visitors sometimes stayed longer than their hosts wanted—they wandered in the city, mingling with the populace, eating, drinking, and observing. In 1682, a Christian convert to Islam by the name of Lucas (also James) Hamet accompanied the Moroccan ambassador, Mohammad ibn Haddu, to London. During his stay, he married an English servant, an episode which Thomas Rymer, a decade later, recalled: 'With us [in England] a Moor might marry some little drab, or Small-coal Wench.'[29] Such visitors, with their exotic clothes and dignified demeanour, became familiar to many Londoners: the anxious neighbours, the greedy landlord who wanted extra payments from them, the gawking street urchin, and the amused aristocrat—they either admired these Muslim visitors or berated them, reflected on their civility, or suspected them of being spies. At the same time, upon their return, the visitors described the wonders they saw in the changing society of Christians. On 25 Shawwal 1135 (28 July 1723), Mulay Isma'il of Morocco wrote to King George I praising the '*ingliz*'—the English—as '*afdal ajnas al-nasara*'—'the best of Christians'.[30]

This wide interest in Muslims among the English sometimes attracted imposters who donned Turkish clothes and arrived in London, claiming to represent the Ottoman court. And the English fell for them—as in the case of 'jolly Mustafa' who arrived in London in 1607, 'saing that he came from the King of the Wourld', or 'Mahomed Bei' who 'Frequented the Court in his Ottoman Garb and the Eastern-mode'.[31] Londoners both feared and enjoyed the visits of these 'Mahometans'—depending on the time. When 'Abd al-Wahid al-'Annouri met Queen Elizabeth in 1600, the populace was so terrified at his august might and 'Moorish' religion that captains refused to allow him and his entourage of infidels on board their ships until the queen intervened.[32] But other Muslims reached England and some of them stayed. In 1611, Thomas Coryate wrote about the numerous Muslims in London who could be identified by the 'rowle of fine linen wrapped together upon their heads'—their turbans.[33] By the second half of the century, when the image, and power, of 'the terrible Turk' was changing, it became possible for William Davenant to represent the Grand Signor in his operatic *Siege of Rhodes* (1656), singing (and perhaps even dancing?) on an Interregnum stage, together with his consort, the fearsome Roxolana, ever in maudlin tears. At the same time, the first coffee shop selling the 'Turkish berry' opened in Oxford; a few years later, King Charles II started wearing clothes designed in the 'Persian' fashion.[34] In 1681–2, the Moroccan ambassador was widely feted and taken to see the Royal Society— where he signed his name on the visitors' chart—and the University of Oxford.[35]

At home, Britons came to know not only royal Muslim delegates, but also Muslims—very few admittedly—who were seeking conversion to Christianity. Although the goal of converting Muslims was ever paramount in English evangelical thought, there was little success, and only a few Muslims from the Ottoman Empire ever converted and settled in England. But, as Imtiaz Habib has so carefully shown, numerous men and women, described in church records as 'Moors', 'Blackamoors', and 'Negros', were baptized, married, or buried all around England, although the vast majority appeared in London. From between 1500 and 1677, there are records attesting to no fewer than 448 'Black lives' in the country; most if not all of them presumably Muslim.[36] Only a few accounts about the conversion of Muslims to Christianity in England, however, have survived, and judging from those accounts, the men—there were no accounts of women converting— presented to parishes the opportunity of seeing and touching a 'Turk' or a 'Moor' for the first time. Whenever such a conversion occurred, a sermon was delivered, and sometimes published, to explain from where the 'Mahometan' had come and why he had chosen to convert to Protestantism—not Catholicism—and become 'English', since after his conversion, he adopted an English name, took on English clothes, and partook of the English church communion. The congregation marvelled at the 'Turk' standing before them, un-turbanned and de-Islamicized. Similar marvelling took place whenever a Christian convert to Islam, a 'renegade', returned to his parish and sought repentance and readmission. Preachers denounced such renegades, attacking them vehemently for abandoning the true faith. Especially after the Laudian rite of 1637 for reintegrating renegades back into English Christianity, the 'English Mahometan'—a phrase that was frequently used—stood in the church where children and women went up to taunt him, while the preacher urged the returnee's relatives to spy on him when he went to the 'privy' to ascertain whether he had received the mark of the beast—circumcision. Whenever such men-turned-Muslim returned from North African captivity, God, king, and St George were all praised that the 'Turk' had been defeated—both in the military as well as the religious conflict.[37]

By the early eighteenth century, as Britain was growing in wealth and power, many impoverished merchants from North Africa arrived in London seeking compensation for losses incurred during attacks on British ships carrying them and their cargoes. They wandered the streets of the metropolis, sometimes completely disoriented and confused, and wrote petitions with the help of locals who, as translators, made the petitions more palatable to English reading taste.[38] They used phrases and expressions of supplication that the English translator deleted, but that have remained in use until today, such as '*Allah yirham walidayk*', or 'May God have mercy (on the souls) of your parents'. From such petitioners, Britons sometimes learned idiomatic Arabic, like Simon Ockley, who went down to the London docks and talked to Muslim merchants, while at the same time captives and consuls returned often claiming to know Turkish, North African languages, Arabic, and *aljamiado*—non-standard Spanish written in Arabic script used by Iberian Muslims.[39] They also read their petitions and learned about Muslim experiences at sea—how some had been sailing on British ships when they were attacked and robbed by European pirates and how they had journeyed to England seeking restitution, despite the cold and hunger encountered in *Londra*.

Meanwhile, numerous British merchants, would-be converts, and mercenaries migrated to North Africa and the Levant in search of work, income, booty, and advancement. In 1600, the Bey of Algiers was pleased to welcome an English pirate named Griffon who 'brought to this place a prize consisting of stuffs & other merchandise, which belonged to our natural common enemies the Spaniards... [he] has received from us every courtesy'. A few days later, two other 'English' captains showed up, claiming to be from London, and bringing 'wool & brasil wood' for which they received from the Algerians 'the usual favours & caresses'.[40] The number and influence of these pirates grew during the early seventeenth century, such that British consuls as well as North African rulers complained about the damage they were doing. Seeking to redress the situation, James Frizell, the consul in Algiers, wrote in August 1631 that it was not the 'English' who were doing 'wrongs' to the 'Cursaires' of Algeria. As the Dey of Algiers complained in 1660, it was rather those, who by 'ffraud & decipt haue owned the ships of Enimies (wearinge English Colours) pretendinge them to be English'.[41] But there are many references to English pirates joining forces with Muslims and other Euro-Christians in ports extending from Agadir to Tunis. The notorious John Ward was one among many, and was celebrated in English as well as in Arabic writings, while an Algerian pirate known as 'Cannary' operated quite safely out of the Isle of Wight, attacking Dutch (before 1688) and later French shipping.[42]

Britons migrated and emigrated to Islamic North Africa decades before they started their Great Migration to North America after 1629. For would-be emigrants, the appeal of Islamic cities and ports was great, all the more so after the first thirty years of the Roanoke plantation in Virginia had made it widely known just how grim prospects in the New World really were. By 1610, the Virginia Company needed to publish a rebuttal to the 'scandalous reports' about the colony that were seriously discouraging immigrants.[43] Moreover, the journey across the Atlantic Ocean was extremely hazardous, while much closer to home were the sunny and welcoming regions of the Mediterranean and Levant which offered the dazzling wealth and alluring ease of Islamic culture. There was Marrakesh with the gold-rich legacy of its Sa'adian dynasty: it is not surprising that Thomas Heywood's *The Fair Maid of the West Part I* (*c.*1600) ended with the English couple receiving a fabulous dowry from the generous Moroccan king. There was Algiers with its quaint white buildings, clean streets, thriving commerce, and delicious fruit. And there was Istanbul with its fabulous wealth, dazzling bazaars, and magnificent buildings. And then there was Isfahan, and the emporia of riches in India the like of which had never been seen before by British eyes. By the second half of the seventeenth century, the fort-settlement in Tangier looked financially promising to King Charles II, and threatening to the

Moroccans, while the fortified garrison settlements in India had become permanent, and were producing huge profits.

The origins of the British Empire are often described in abstract ideological terms: Protestantism, anti-Catholicism, freedom, trade, adventure, cosmopolitanism, enthusiasm, curiosity.[44] These and other religious and national motivations have been proposed to explain the imperial project. So it is easy to forget that the lands of the early-modern Islamic empires, some of which would eventually fall under British and other European hegemonies, were abundant with natural and mineral resources that brought wealth to European settlers and entrepreneurs. It was not men with high moral ideals, Christian visions, and cosmopolitan imaginations who ventured to Virginia or Guiana, Tangier or Izmir, Hormuz or Surat, but men—persevering and determined—who were on the make: from Anthony Jenkinson who, in the middle of the sixteenth century, declared to Shah Tahmasp that he was there to 'treate of friendship, and free passage of our Merchants and people, to repaire and traffique within his dominions', to William Hawkins who openly admitted to trying to 'feather my Neast' at the Mughal court in 1609, to the 'needy and the greedy' who ventured to the British bastion of Tangier in the second half of that century, along with 'the Smiths, Caprenters, Sawyers, Coopers, Whelwrights, Carters, Masons, Miners, Drill-men, Quarry-men, and Stone-cutters, making a pretty confused Musick'.[45] Whenever such men wrote about regions previously unknown to their countrymen, they described the plenty they saw: the gold, horses, and saltpetre of Barbary, the currants of Zante, the silk of Persia, the indigo, jewels, spices, and ambergris of India—and the multitude of fruits, vegetables, and legumes, as well as myrrh, aloes, cinnamon, and nutmeg. Afterwards, fleets sailed out in search of these commodities, manned by seekers of profit, and sponsored by London officials of companies chartered by monarchs demanding maximum returns on their investments. Tenacious and heavily armed, these men transformed the seas of the early modern world into roads for the internationalization of commodities and trade, setting in motion the beginning of British commercial and colonial settlements throughout the Islamic world, from Tangier in western Morocco to Surat in western India.

Consuls and members of the expatriate trading communities became the foremost Britons to understand the physical and mental world of their Muslim hosts. They sometimes engaged members of the local communities in proscribed drinking bouts, listened to their strategies, counted the number of naval vessels in their harbours, negotiated for captives, argued for compensation of stolen or sunken goods, and, when they felt comfortable enough, discussed differences in politics, religion, and custom. Thomas Roe left an extensive correspondence from his ambassadorial years at the Mughal and Ottoman courts, making him the first Englishman to be able to write perceptively about differences between Islamic civilizations. Half a century later, Paul Rycaut, who lived in Izmir for about ten years, wrote the most comprehensive study of the Ottoman Empire in English (1667), which he kept on expanding for years to follow. The chaplain Thomas Smith wrote a fascinating account of the Ottoman Islamic world (1678). Meanwhile, scores of other factors, consuls, and ambassadors in North Africa, most of whose massive writings have not been examined in English scholarship, provided the intelligence that British policymakers needed in designing strategies for import and export, war and peace.[46] This vast body of diplomatic correspondence demonstrates the extent of knowledge that circulated: chapter 3 only scratches the surface of a vast and fascinating archive, some of which remains uncalendared in boxes at the National Archives in London.

Britons also encountered Muslims as slaves and captives, chained in the gaols of London and Plymouth, crammed in Spanish galleys, and for sale in the markets of Algiers, Cadiz, Genoa, and Valetta. Paradoxically it was piracy, the seizure of captives, and the subsequent ransom negotiations, that led to closer familiarity between Britons and North Africans—and therefore a fuller understanding of Islamic ritual, custom, and doctrine. Meanwhile, Maghariba travelled to London and other European cities, to ransom their compatriots, familiarizing themselves thereby with the cultural environment and diplomatic codes of engagement. They needed to learn to negotiate with Christians—in order to report back to their *diwans* and courts. Given the high volume of Muslims seized by European pirates and privateers, there were frequent Muslim, Jewish, and even Christian delegations of ambassadors and emissaries crossing the Mediterranean to negotiate with their French, British, Maltese, or Spanish counterparts. In 1621, two envoys from Tetuan met with the English fleet admiral to 'treat with him concerning the Redemption of such of their People as had been taken by our Ships'.[47] Three years later, an ambassador from Istanbul arrived in London with a list of the names of the Ottoman and Moorish captives in England, '& some fewe, that are soulde into spaine, & Italie'.[48] Many Mediterranean Muslims learned about the English after falling prey to piracy in the same manner that many Britons learned about Muslims after being seized into captivity.

From these encounters grew the English and European literature of captivity, with its hostile image of Muslim captors lording it over, but then being outwitted by, English captives. Europeans had been taken captive in the New World as early as the first half of the sixteenth century, but the English, with their limited exposure, had yet to encounter and write about the Native Americans as captors—though they wrote about Spanish captors in Mexico. In the Mediterranean, however, the situation differed greatly. Large numbers—though the exact number continues to be a matter of dispute and exaggeration—of Britons were taken captive. Although Britons were less exposed to the threat of captivity than the French, Spanish, or Italians, having been late arrivals in the Mediterranean, it is striking that they produced some of the earliest texts in a genre that would dominate European and Western imaginations for centuries.[49] The dozens of accounts that appeared and reappeared in print, written in English or translated from French and Spanish, along with lists naming captives and their ransoms, shaped early-modern English attitudes to Muslims and Islam. Only in the Mediterranean did Islam and Muslims become inextricably associated with the violence of captivity. No such accounts with anti-Muslim animus appeared from, or about, the Indian-Persian region, since captivity never loomed as large there as it did in the western Mediterranean. It was the Islam of the Mediterranean that was to generate and give shape to British fears of Islam.

While travelling among the Muslims, or living in Islamic lands, Britons encountered large communities of Jews and eastern Christians for the first time. Since the expulsion of the Jewish community from England in 1290, the earliest meetings of Britons with large societies of Jews—larger than in Venice or Amsterdam—took place in Islamic cities: Istanbul, Aleppo, Izmir, Meknes, Algiers. In these Islamic cities, Britons were obliged to rely on local Jewish populations for help finding places to live, and for help arranging commercial and financial transactions. Both armchair chroniclers as well as on-the-scene traders described Jewish communities in detail, mixing biblical images with contemporary facts, while some British theologians and 'mechanick preachers', with ambivalent bigotry, advocated the heresy of Restorationism in an attempt to keep Jews out of England.[50] At the same time, numerous Anglican divines encouraged dialogue with the Orthodox Churches in the hope of converting the eastern Christians to the true faith of the Protestants—thereby establishing a common front against Catholic France and its busy Jesuit missionaries. Britons also met for the first time some of the oldest communities of Christians: Maronite, Coptic, Nestorian, Syriac, Armenian, and Eastern Orthodox, both Greek and Arabic speaking, and other 'Nations and distinct Denominations of Christians'.[51] Encounters with these communities helped to shape English views of Islam, since these diverse communities all belonged to the world of the Bible, and that world was currently being ruled by Muslims.

Images

Despite numerous interactions with 'Turks', Moors, Persians, and Indians, most Britons formed their image of Muslims in the theatres and churches, while travellers to Europe might well have seen representations of Muslims in the continental cathedrals with their rich iconography. Although it became increasingly complicated and nuanced during the course of the seventeenth century, the sense of Muslim danger persisted, especially at times of military conflict. From the reign of Queen Elizabeth to that of Queen Anne, Islam and Muslims were viewed through the prism of the powerful—and expansionist—empire of the Ottomans, and of the North African pirates and privateers who threatened British shores and navigation. As a result, Islam became inextricably associated with war and its threat, and Britons constructed an imaginary sense that Muslims—and 'imaginary' it was—were a tribe of warring anti-Christians intent on establishing the universal monarchy of their long-dead leader known as 'Mahomet'. Sir Thomas More wrote extensively about those he called 'Turks', and how they posed a theological and expansionist danger.[52] At the same time, the two formative figures of the Protestant Reformation, Martin Luther and John Calvin, urged war against the Ottomans in their theological writings and correspondence. Despite initial wavering, Luther committed himself to bellicose rhetoric damning Islam.[53] Contributing to this hostile representation was the most popular sixteenth-century tome, after the Bible: John Foxe's *Acts and Monuments* (1563). Foxe's lurid descriptions of Christian, chiefly Protestant, martyrs nurtured the anti-Catholicism that became a hallmark of Puritan and Non-conformist theology. With the addition of a section entitled 'The History of the Turks' in 1570,[54] Foxe joined the chorus of anti-Muslim detractors. With every re-publication of the book, the anti-Christian violence and danger of the Muslims was further consolidated in the minds and hearts of Anglican congregations, especially as they intoned the 'Prayer against the Turks' with which he concluded this section:

> O lord God of hosts, grant to thy church strength and victory against the malicious fury of these Turks, Saracens, Tartarians, against Gog and Magog, and all the malignant rabble of Antichrist, enemies to thy Son Jesus, our Lord and Saviour. Prevent their devices, overthrow their power, and dissolve their kingdom.[55]

Alongside Foxe, there were numerous translations from European texts that reported on the history and military activities of the Ottomans. In most cases, as with Foxe's *Acts*, the texts opened with a brief slander about the origins of Islam, and then, ignoring half a millennium of Arab-Islamic civilization, jumped to the rise of the Ottoman dynasty and its military empire.

Many Britons learned about Muslims exclusively through Foxe and from sermons and tomes of exegesis. Theologians introduced those they termed 'Mahometans' into their eschatological and millenarian schemes denouncing them as agents of Antichrist. These writings were among the most pervasive sources of information about Muslims—but these were Muslims imagined and determined by wild theological interpretations. This tradition of exegesis started with the seminal, and formidable, writings of Thomas Brightman and Hugh Broughton, who associated both Muslims and Catholics with the anti-Christ, all to be destroyed at the Second Coming of, or in preparation for, the Messiah.[56] Such thinking found its way into sermons, political polemics, histories, chronicles, devotional pamphlets, and tracts on military strategy, especially during the unsettled years of the Civil Wars and the Interregnum. Their arguments were adopted and modified by Joseph Meade, Thomas Goodwin, Peter Sterry, and non-'Puritans' such as Henry More—all of whom played a decisive role in the theological and political confrontations during Britain's 'century of revolution', to borrow Christopher Hill's phrase. In the writings of these millenarians, English parishioners and readers, students and scholars, encountered Muslims in the most terrifying shapes and manners—and all within the piety of their daily readings of the Scriptures. Meanwhile, for John Milton, Islam seems to have been regarded as a political ideology not a religion.[57]

In the privacy of their worship, British congregations confronted images of villainous and monstrous Muslims—not only in the present, but also in the historical past when the 'Turks' had paraded their crescents near the cross on Golgotha. This a-historical history of the Muslims, presenting them as eternal enemies of Christianity, had featured in the Mystery and Miracle plays which systematically vilified Muhammad. Although these plays declined during the Elizabethan period, audiences doubtless remembered how 'Mahound' had been the false god who sent Pharaoh chasing Moses across the Red Sea in the York cycle. In the Coventry cycle, it was he who had been instrumental in the Massacre of the Innocents by Herod, a Mahometan who dressed in Saracen clothes, and who was the inspiration for crucifying Christ. In the public theatres that replaced the Mystery plays, urban audiences witnessed complex, fearsome, and alienating portraits of Turks-as-Muslims who raged and killed their own children, and enslaved and brutalized Christians. Theatre audiences learned about turbaned Turks who were as cruel as their scimitars, and about black-skinned Moors who were evil descendants of Ham.[58]

Although English dramatists never attempted to offer any serious explanation of the differences between Sunni and Shi'ite Muslims, plays presented images of Muslims in remote regions of the world where Christians—never English though—were held in captivity or enslaved into harems simply to serve the lusts and arbitrary powers of those who worshipped their false prophet.[59] Such theatre was entertaining and brilliant, but it also disseminated disinformation in the form of standardized themes, costumes, religious phrases—'By Mahomet' and 'O Haly'—and dramatic gestures that became indelible markers of Muslims. Many Londoners must have left performances of Robert Greene's *Selimus: Emperor of the Turks* (1594) with their blood curdling at the mention of a Turk; others cringed at the cruelty of Muslims after learning how Sultan 'Mahomet' (i.e. Mehmed II, r. 1451–81) executed 'cursed cruelty upon a Greek maiden, whom he took prisoner, at the winning of Constantinople' in William Painter's *Palace of Pleasure* (1566).[60] Published in 1567, the second edition of Painter's *Palace* tells how Sultan Süleyman gave in to his devious wife Roxolana, and condoned the murder of his son Mustapha: this tale created one of the most damaging portraits of the 'Turk' to enter the English imagination. It was a story that was frequently dramatized on stages, not only in England, but throughout Europe. Roxolana became proof positive of what Muslims could do to Christians: having been abducted from her own Christian community, she had been transformed by life in the harem into a bloodthirsty virago.[61] Even the legendary Sir Gawain was recruited to fight 'a Sarasin, which after was taken and became Christian'.[62]

Cheap books and broadsheets introduced engravings, woodcuts, and lithographs of Muslims to increasingly large audiences. By such means, even those who could not read might gape at pictures of the grim Turk or the lascivious Moor just as, during the Reformation, their ancestors had looked at demonized portraits of the Pope or of Luther. Those living in provincial towns and rural areas might buy from any wandering print-seller a picture of the 'Mahometan', or a scene of Muslim atrocity.[63] Such images soon appeared on glazed earthenware, large plates, medals, and the tapestries that adorned wealthy and royal households. In Europe, the greatest example of such tapestries was the sixteenth–century 'Conquest of Tunis', depicting the Spanish-led attack on Tunis by Charles V in 1535, that decorated the marriage hall of Philip II of Spain and Mary Tudor and now decorates the walls of Reales Alcázares de Sevilla.[64] Such tapestries served as a form of travelling propaganda on behalf of the Habsburgs since they accompanied the kings and queens in their progresses around the country, and 'made political points'.[65] More modest tapestries served for wall hangings in private mansions, such as the seventeenth-century Italian silk on canvas piece depicting scenes from Torquato Tasso's crusader epic, *Jerusalem Liberated* (1580), which Edward Fairfax translated into English in 1600.[66] Bess of Hardwick's collection of textiles included an embroidered appliqué tapestry of 'The Virtues and their Opposites' from 1575 that portrays the Prophet Muhammad as the 'opposite' of 'Faith'.[67] Images of Muslims were being produced and transported all around European palaces and households. The figure of the Turk was growing more familiar as art and propaganda depicted him in the stock forms of powerful ruler and heinous executioner.[68]

At home, Protestant iconoclasm discouraged visual representations in churches, but illustrations in prayer books and liturgical collections, as Matthew Dimmock has shown, presented images of 'Mahomet' defeated by Christianity.[69] Wealthy Englishmen on the Grand Tour would have seen European ecclesiastical art—paintings, sculptures, frescos, mosaics— which exhibited the fearsome image of Muslims, again de-historicized. 'The Crucifixion' from the workshop of the German Hans Mielich (1516–73), depicts a turbaned soldier at the foot of the Cross.[70] The magnificent altarpiece by an unknown Flemish artist, c. 1535, that is now in the Philadelphia Museum of Art, shows 'Turks' and other turbaned horsemen at the foot of the Cross, carrying spears and sponges. In such and many other paintings, to witness Christ being crucified is to observe Muslims crucifying him. The message is simple: just as Muslims persecuted and helped crucify Christ, so they continue to persecute his followers in Eastern Europe, the Mediterranean, and even the New World. Because the victory of Lepanto took place on St Justina's day on 7 October 1571, from 1572 on, processions were held in Venice to celebrate the saint while decrying the Ottomans whom she had defeated—annual repetitions of this celebration enforced the association between worship and hostility to Islam.[71]

It has been argued that the encounter with the Ottoman Turks, whether in image or in reality, brought to the fore the idea of a 'common corps of Christendom', and helped forge religio-national identity in a period that was witnessing the confessionalization of Europeans.[72] English writers, travellers, and politicians tried to keep abreast of the continental confrontations with Muslims, and reported on battles, victories, and defeats in weekly news books. Whether the Ottomans were defeated in Malta, or in Croatia, by Papal vessels or Habsburg armies, these accounts confirmed the image of the anti-Christian enemy, and consolidated an Englishness that might one day have to confront Islam in the same manner that, in 1588, it had confronted Catholicism. After the Ottoman retreat from Vienna in 1683, English combatants in the battle wrote home, and published accounts, about their proud 'preservation of a great part of Christendom'.[73] From then on, the image of Muslims declined in stature in all respects, as dangerous Ottomans and powerful Moors became mere consumers of British products and exporters of raw material. Eventually, from Rabat to Aleppo to Isfahan, they came to be viewed as pegs in the cycle of trade:

> The Turkey trade is very useful, the goods we send being fully manufactured, and carried to them in our own shipping; and the commodities we take from them in returns, are also in our own navigation. The commodities we take from them are chiefly raw, and very proper to carry on our home manufactures, and employ our poor, as well as for re-exportation.[74]

By the middle of the eighteenth century, the peoples of the Islamic empires were being viewed as a means to a British imperial end.

Islam

Britons learned about the theology, jurisprudence, and legal system of Islam from writers who presented summaries of the beliefs and practices of Muslims, often in order to refute them and thereby celebrate England and Englishness. Contemporaries of John Foxe presented inaccurate accounts of the life of Muhammad, but their ignorance of the historical facts did not thwart their efforts to show the lewdness and blasphemy of the 'imposter'. As early as 1542, Richard Grafton translated a French text about the Ottomans and 'the summe of Mahoumetes doctrine' in which the Prophet and his teachings were compared to the outpourings of Antichrist, a serpent, an adder, and a wolf.[75] In 1543, selections from the first Latin translation of the Qur'an by the English monk, Robert of Ketton, were printed, including information on 'Leges de Homicidis', 'De Matrimoniis', 'Resurrectionis Modus', and other spurious aspects of Muslim belief and practice.[76] Chroniclers of world histories also included accounts about the rise of Islam, often lamenting how Islam had replaced Christianity in the lands of Christ, and how it was undermining the continuance of any knowledge of Christianity among the Greek, Armenian, and Arab Christians living under Ottoman rule.[77]

Unable, in most cases, to read the texts of Islam in the original languages, deprived of opportunities to discuss theology with Muslims, and assured of the absolute truth of their own Christian beliefs, British travellers and merchants, however well-intended, regularly recycled mistaken ideas about the fundamental pillars of Islam. With little or no understanding of Islamic history or ethnography, or of Arabic, Turkish, Persian, Armenian, 'Hindustani', or any of the numerous dialects of the Indian subcontinent, English writers explained everything that one society did in terms of religion—so much so that the tyranny, harems, slavery, and cruelty that were witnessed in some regions, and practised by different societies, became intrinsic to a generalized concept of Islam. Furthermore, in an age when writers did not verify their sources, numerous chroniclers reproduced extant material without checking its accuracy. A misconception about Muslims, or a deliberate slander of Islam, would thus be repeated without verification—even if it was most egregious or outrageous.[78] Muslims never drank wine, explained Sir John Mandeville, whose popular account was even included in Latin in Hakluyt's *Principal Navigations* of 1589, because the Prophet had been 'drunken of good wine'. And Muslims never ate pork, because 'Mahud' had stumbled into 'a dung heap, where he fell down, and rolled about, gnashing with his teeth and foaming: on seeing which, a number of swine, which were there, ran and tore him in pieces, and so put an end to him'.[79] Ignorance legitimated prejudice, and prejudice turned into exclusion, derision, and hostility.

Many writers, theatre-goers, and sailors conflated Muslims with 'Turks', and the repeated confusion of terms led to a superimposition of the Ottomans' imperial danger onto religion so that Islam became synonymous with Ottoman military expansion. From one of the earliest English texts on Islam—Wynkyn de Worde's *Treatyse of the Turkes Lawe called Alcoran* (c.1519) that was based on Mandeville—to the first English translation of the Qur'an in 1649, Muhammad was presented as prophet of the 'Turks', a term used throughout Christian Europe to refer to all Muslims regardless of origin. Such confusion had a lasting effect on British perceptions of Islam, since this association of a religious creed with an empire cemented the identification of faith with military conquest. As late as 1709, Islam was still termed the 'Turkish *Religion*'—and that was by Aaron Hill, a man who had lived and travelled in the Ottoman Empire for 'many Years'.[80] Islam also became associated with North African pirates at the same time that it became a byword for the evils of coffee and of 'Mahometan' sodomy. In short, the concept of the 'Turk' and these notions of Islam were largely the product of the English imagination—as is amply illustrated in a fanciful illustration of 'Mahomet Communicating his Doctrin to the People, with their Pilgrimage to Mecca' that appeared in a popular book on the 'Prodigious Religions' of 'Sundry Nations' in 1683.[81]

Be that as it may, the earliest printed source for reasonably accurate information about Islamic theology and doctrine in Europe was *Machumetis Saracenorum principis, eiusque successorum vitae, ac doctrina* ('The Life and Teachings of Machumet, Prince of the Saracens') produced in 1543 by Theodor Bibliander, which included a Latin version of sections from the Qur'an. The 'Bibliander' Qur'an was based on Robert of Ketton's inaccurate translation. An Italian version of Bibliander's edition became available in 1547, and a German one followed in 1604, but these were hard to come by and would only have been legible to scholars.[82] More commonly available were various forms of refutation that sought to defend Christianity by discrediting Muhammad and thereby exposing the flaws in Islamic theology. Reprinted no fewer than seventeen times between 1593 and 1676, Henry Smith's sermon, *Gods Arrow Against Atheists*, was typical in its claim that the reason for discussing Islam was to bring the reader to a clearer understanding of the evident truths of the Christian revelation. 'If I shall speake something of the Mahometish Religion,' Smith declared:

> I thinke the truth of the Christian Religion will appeare so much the more: for when blacke and white are laid together, the white carrieth the greater estimation and glorie with it. And beside, Mahomet himselfe testifieth of Christ to be a great Prophet of God, and a great worker of miracle.[83]

Smith argued that Islam is a 'patched religion' made up of elements from various sects, while Muhammad was no more than 'a deceiver, a false Prophet, and a king over those whom he had already infected throughout Arabia'.[84] William Percy's *Mahomet and his Heaven* (c.1600), is the only play that has survived which actually dramatized Muhammad—though in caricature—and some Islamic beliefs, including allusions to 'Ali and Shi'ism. But it was a closet drama which did not reach a wide audience.[85]

While Smith and others were content merely to reiterate various false claims against Islam that had been commonplace since the later Middle Ages, by the seventeenth century scholars trained in Arabic initiated attempts to provide more accurate accounts of the Prophet and his religion, though the purpose of such works continued to be refutation of Islam and defence of Christianity. One of the earliest English translations from an Arabic source aimed at discrediting Islam is William Bedwell's *Mohammedis Imposturae: that is, A Discovery of the Manifold Forgeries, Falshoods, and horrible impieties of the blasphemous Seducer Mohammed* (1615). In presenting his translation to his readers, Bedwell observes that the work provides an account of the absurdities of Islam in the form of a dialogue between two learned Muslims that was written in Arabic 'about 600 years since', and that he believes 'it to be written by some Saracen or Mohametane, who did in truth make these doubts and demands, as being desirous of better satisfaction.'[86] Bedwell's source, the '*Musahaba ruhaniya baina-l'alimain* ('A Spiritual Conference between Two Doctors') originally printed in Rome in the 1570s, was 'in reality, the work of a Catholic propagandist' and not a sceptical Muslim.[87] Nevertheless, claiming to be exposing the 'Forgeries, Falsehoods, and horrible impieties' of the Prophet in the words of a Muslim was no insignificant rhetorical achievement.

Other notable attempts to provide accurate information about Islam from Arabic sources include John Gregory's *Gregorii Opuscula* (1650) and Edward Pococke's compendious *Specimen Historiae Arabum* (1650), which, in hundreds of notes to an Arabic text of only thirty pages, set out to correct some of the more egregious errors by providing account of Arabs, Muhammad, and Islam based on the work of a thirteenth-century Arabic-speaking Jacobite, Abul-Faraj, and other Arabic manuscripts. The expansion of the Laudian collection of Arabic manuscripts at the Bodleian was instrumental in making available to scholars the first Arabic theological, historical, and literary materials to reach England. Translations and editions by Dutch orientalists of Arabic material were closely read in England, and in 1671, Edward Pococke the younger translated into Latin the Arabic tale of Hayy ibn Yaqzan, which was subsequently translated into English, and met with wide appeal. By the beginning of the eighteenth century, the centre of gravity for oriental studies had moved from Italy to France and England: Simon Ockley's two-volume *History of the Saracens* (1708, 1718) was similarly based on Arabic sources,[88] while the two volumes of *Mahometanism Explained* by Joseph Morgan (1723 and 1725) included the first material about the rise of Islam translated from *aljamiado* into English. The aim of these scholarly efforts was to enable defenders of Christianity to correct false ideas and thereby to refute Islam on better, sounder, and more accurate grounds. However, *The True Nature of Imposture Fully Display'd in the Life of Mahomet* by the Dean of Norwich, Humphrey Prideaux (printed twice in 1697 and twice again in 1698), was one of the most bigoted, and popular, attacks on Islam to appear in English.

It was in the signal year of 1649 that the first English translation of the Qur'an became available, but only after considerable legal problems and a certain degree of confusion over responsibility for its production. On 19 March of that year, the Sergeant at Arms was ordered 'to search for the press where the Turkish Alcoran is being printed, and to seize the same, and the papers; also to apprehend the printer and take him before the Council of State.' Two days later, the Sergeant at Arms reported that he had 'apprehended the printer of the Turkish Alcoran', who had been 'licensed by Dr. Downham', and was ordered to discharge the prisoner or proceed against him. On 29 March, a committee was assembled to enquire into 'the business as to printing the Turkish Alcoran', and one 'Stevenson, the stationer, and Downam, the licenser' were ordered to attend Council that day. Two days after this, on 31 March, the stationer John Stevenson was

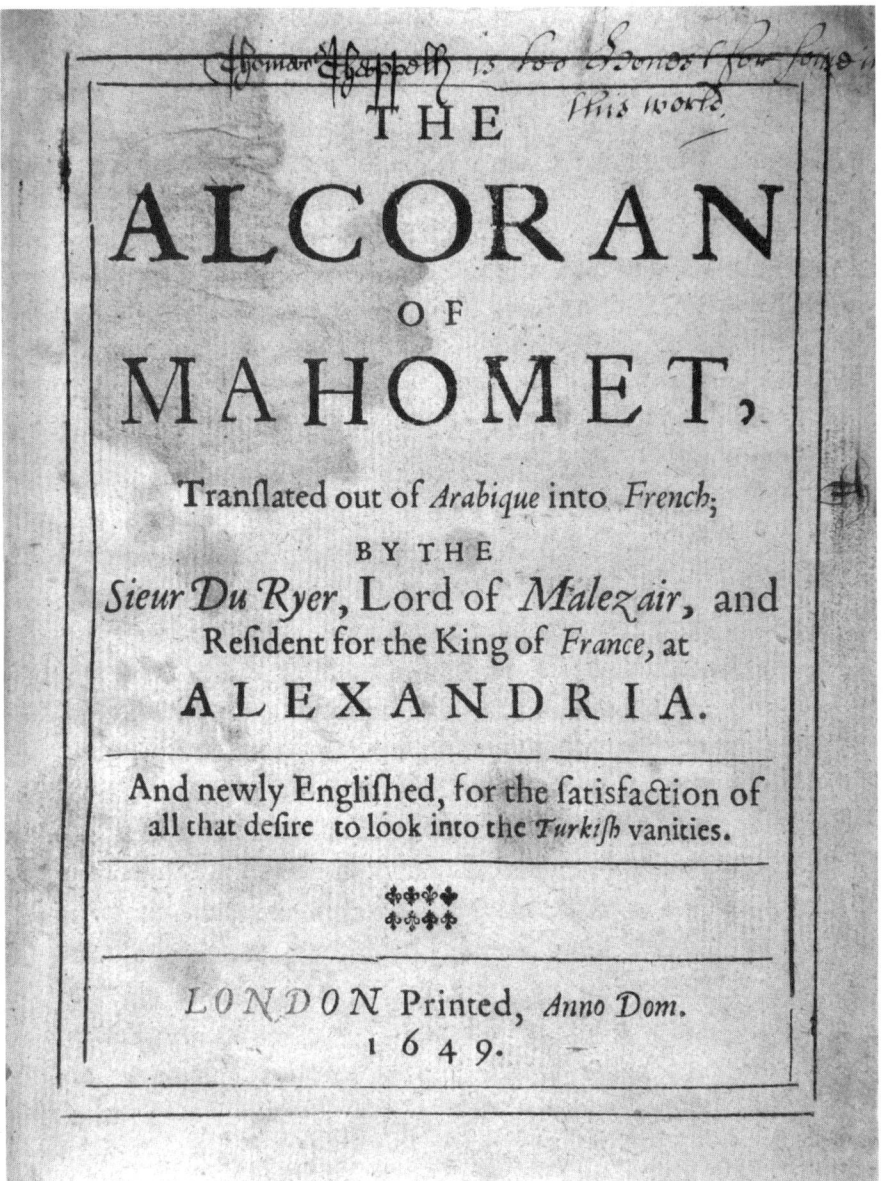

Figure 1. *The Alcoran of Mahomet* (1649), title page to the first English translation of the Qur'an
MacLean copy

summoned again, while 'Mr White, printer' was ordered to be discharged 'on giving security to be forthcoming'. White was, presumably, the printer who had been taken into custody between the 19th and 21st, though one cannot be certain. That same day another printer, one 'Thos. Ross' was ordered 'to be summoned to give an account for the printing of the Alcoran, which Stevenson, the stationer, received from him'. Thomas Ross was duly released 'with a monition not to meddle more with things of that nature' on 4 April.[89] While it is clear that someone with authority objected to the printing of an English translation of the Qur'an, it remains unclear exactly what those objections were, and why they were so easily passed over once the printers and Stevenson, the bookseller, had been examined. The question of who produced the translation seems not to have troubled the authorities, and the book was eventually published: George Thomason dated his copy of *The Alcoran of Mahomet* on 7 May—mere months after the execution of Charles I.[90]

The English *Alcoran* of 1649 was based on a French translation by André Du Ryer that had been published in 1647, and has long been thought to be the work of Alexander Ross. It appeared with a translation of Du Ryer's preface, an anonymous life of Muhammad, and a text signed by Ross that instructs the reader in how to read the Qur'an: 'A needful Caveat or Admonition, for them who desire to know what use may be made of, or if there be danger in reading the Alcoran' bears his signature. After pondering why an English translation has appeared, Ross offers a standard argument:

> Good Reader, the great Arabian Imposter now at last after a thousand years, is by the way of France arrived in England, and his Alcoran, or Gallimaufry of Errors (a brat as deformed as the Parent, and as full of heresies as his scald-head was of scurffe) hath learned to speak English. I suppose this piece is exposed by the Translator to the publike view, no otherwise then some Monster brought out of Africa, for people to gaze, not to dote upon; and as the sight of a Monster, or mishapen creature should induce the beholder to praise God, who hath not made him such; so should the reading of this Alcoran excite us both to blesse Gods goodnesse towards us in this land, who injoy the glorious light of the Gospell.[91]

Ross relies on a well-worn argument that understanding Islam could only encourage greater piety and patriotism among Protestant English readers. No reader could approach the source of Islamic belief, Ross emphasized, except with hostility and disdain. Yet at the same time, Ross argues that reading the *Alcoran* will enable Christians to refute Islam in its own terms, 'to cut off the head of this Goliath with his own sword'.[92] Ross later wrote *Pansebeia: or, A View of All the Religions in the World* (1653), a much-reprinted study of comparative religions that, according to Ziad Elmarsafy, 'prompted a paradigm shift according to which the validity of religions other than Christianity became increasingly acceptable in seventeenth-century England'.[93]

The *Alcoran* of 1649 proved so influential that 'Qur'an', 'Mahomet', and other terms and phrases associated with Islam started to appear in poems, plays, and sermons. The allusions were erratic and sometimes inappropriate, but English writers were eager to show their knowledge of Islam, and their ridicule of it. Still, the translation offered easy access to the text of the Qur'an, and careful readers could at least learn of its teachings and, perhaps, discover what it did not teach. Richard Baxter read the text carefully and, in his *The Reasons of the Christian Religion* (1667), found occasion to describe 'the Religion of Mahumetans'.[94] He admitted finding 'much good' in Islam especially in the Qur'anic affirmation that 'Christ is the Word of God, and a great Prophet, and the Writings of the Apostles true'. But Baxter continued in Ross's vein, also calling the Qur'an 'a Rhapsody of Nonsence and Confusion'.[95] Keen to defend his religion, he did not reflect on whether Christ as the word of God was part of that 'Confusion'. Other theologians also relied on Ross, although some started reading more broadly in the field to familiarize themselves with the traditions of Islam that assisted in the interpretation of the Qur'an. The only English writers willing to take the Qur'an on its own terms, and to approach it from its own premises rather than through the Christian prism, were George Fox and Henry Stubbe. They alone were prepared to concede theological legitimacy to the Qur'an and to Islam.[96]

One aspect of Islam that was deeply admired, especially by travellers into the Ottoman world, was Islam's iconoclastic strain—a feature that made for congruity between the Sunni Islam of the Ottomans and North Africans and the Protestant British. Both visitors and armchair wanderers praised the Ottomans for not worshipping idols, as Catholics did. There were also numerous features of Islamic culture and civilization that writers and visitors could not help admiring: kindness to animals, the prohibition on duelling, opposition to the idleness of plays, the obedience of Muslim women, respect for discipline and law, and grudgingly, Islam's ability to win converts peacefully.

At the same time, one aspect about the Islamic world that writers described endlessly was the harem. For many, the harem was an integral part of the religion of the Muslims: it was not a cultural but a theological component. In the early 1600s, the Venetian representative in Istanbul, Ottaviano Bon, composed a detailed description of the harem, thereby whetting the appetites of Euro-Christians for information about the libidinous world of Islam.[97] Even a pious Anglican minister such as William Biddulph, writing in that same decade, could not resist describing the possibilities for sexual affairs that were available for European men living in Islamic lands—which T. S., an English captive in Algiers later in the century, allegedly fulfilled, thereby confirming the image of the Muslim woman as deceptive, adulterous, and sexually voracious.[98] Sir Thomas Herbert was honest enough to admit his inability to describe the harem of the Shah,[99] but Paul Rycaut offered a detailed account without ever setting foot inside one. Having lived in Izmir for years, Rycaut felt that he possessed enough authority to describe what he had never seen: 'And though I ingeniously confess my acquaintance there (as all other my conversation with Women in *Turky*) is but strange, and unfamiliar; yet not to be guilty of this discourtesie, I shall to the best of my information write a short account of these Captivated Ladies.'[100] Well into the modern period, the veil and the harem have continued to provide Europeans with 'a fantasy [that] dangled the promise of exotic and erotic experiences', as Judy Mabro puts it.[101]

Perhaps the best presentation of the teachings and practices of Islam appear in the account by Joseph Pitts, who learned about Islam from within. Having been captured by North African pirates, Pitts converted to Islam and lived in Algiers for nearly two decades. He undertook the pilgrimage to Mecca with his master, and wrote about the whole experience in a manner that combined personal narrative with a less chauvinistic attitude than earlier captives. Pitts presented information from a detached perspective, describing in detail all aspects of Islamic faith and piety, and not uniformly condemnatory: he corrected other writers' mistakes and praised the fervour of the Muslims in fulfilling their religious duties. As for many other writers before and after him—including Ross—Islamic submission to the will of God was a foil for Christian irresponsibility and looseness. The fact that admiration for such piety came from a man who had been a slave of the Muslims could not but have added poignancy to his description.[102]

With the hindsight of history, Pitts' account can be seen to be pivotal in the English understanding of Islam. It was written by a non-scholar without access to the tomes of orientalist learning. But Pitts, a mere mariner, always cautiously, corrected the doyens. After living among Muslims for fourteen years, he realized that understanding Islam could not be achieved by mere reading and study. And although he read what he could find about Islam and Islamic lands upon his return to Exeter, the authoritativeness of his voice derived from having been part of the Muslim community—having eaten, travelled, served, prayed, and conversed with, and among, Muslims. His book shows, for the very first time in English, that learning about Muslims and Islam required proficiency in languages, adaptation to custom, integration into religious culture, and some humility. It is notable that Pitts challenged hostile arguments advanced by the formidable Humphrey Prideaux and authoritative French travellers. Their observations, he announced, were either inaccurate because they had never visited or lived in any Islamic country, or because they presumed to interpret without understanding Islamic history, social habits, or regional peculiarities.[103] Had Pitts been a distinguished man of wealth or status, his text might have more forcibly encouraged a perspective that relied on approaching the different culture on its own terms just as he, a captive, had been forced to do. Only by approaching religious difference without preconceptions, rather than through the à priori of Christian certitude and English triumphalism, can there be both understanding and criticism.

By way of conclusion

From the medieval period on, Western Latin Christendom had defined and known itself 'above all through its vexed relations with religious "others": not only pagans and heretics, but Jews, Muslims and the various Christians belonging to the Eastern Churches'.[104] In the case of early modern Britain, the pagans had been long converted—despite missionary attempts in the 1650s to convert the Welsh in their 'darke corners'[105]—and the Jews had been expelled long ago—though a small number was readmitted in 1655. In terms of religious identity, then, national self-definition was left largely with the Muslims who were ever seen in English writings against the backdrop of the Crusades[106] and of the landings of 'Barbary' corsairs on English, Welsh, and Irish shores. At the same time, the new avenues of trade, commerce, and diplomacy, along with the 'rediscovery' of 'Arabicke' lore and the introduction of new material cultures from the Orient, forced Britons to re-evaluate the age-old image of hostility and conflict. By the end of the seventeenth century, Muslims, with their intellectual and religious legacies, had become an important factor in British imagination, theology, and society.

In this respect, the encounter with Indian Islam is important because of its differences from meetings with Muslims elsewhere. Englishmen arrived there by the land route at about the same time that they started sailing regularly into the Mediterranean. In the Mediterranean, they encountered a strident Islam that was in confrontation with western and central European Christendom. In India and other parts of South-East Asia, however, Islam had not taken form as anti-Christian militarism, though the violence of the Portuguese was never forgotten: as appears in one of the most harrowing descriptions of their sixteenth-century invasion of the western coast of India.[107] Nevertheless, and despite confrontations with the Dutch and other Europeans, the English never faced large-scale Christian–Muslim wars on the magnitude of those in the Ottoman–Habsburg theatre. Although the majority population of the subcontinent was not Muslim, British traders, consuls, and ambassadors dealt with governors and local rulers, and so were engaged largely, though not exclusively, with Muslims. British impressions about religions in the region were inevitably confused, given the diversity in Hindu traditions, Islamic-Hindu hybridity, and an Islam that, at the court of Shah Akbar and his descendants, was deistic and syncretic, though not disseminated beyond a small group at the court. The 'Din-i-Ilahi' or 'Divine Faith' that Shah Akbar formulated in the early 1580s, must have been quite confusing to English observers, especially since, in the words of the *Jahangirnama*, 'there was room for practitioners of various sects and beliefs, both true and imperfect... [and Akbar] conversed with the good of every group, every religion, and every sect and gave his attentions to each in accordance with their station and ability to understand'.[108] The British experience of Islam in India and Persia— whence the Mughals derived much of their cultural identity—was markedly not confrontational in the manner of Levantine, Anatolian, and North African Islam. In Surat, Agra, and Aceh, the English were seen as yet another European community arriving with its marketable wares, not as Christians whose ancestors had once sought to conquer the lands of Middle

Eastern Muslims, and whose Spanish, Portuguese, and French coreligionists were in possession of colonies from Santa Cruz to Melilla.

The association between 'Islam' and the Ottomans, including their regencies in North Africa, largely defined Islam for early modern Britons as a religion in conflict with Christendom. Even though no Muslims founded colonies near Penzance or Bristol or Dartmouth, as the Spanish, French, and later British did on the North African coast, and even though it had been European Christian crusaders who had invaded the Middle East, and even though it was Iberian Christians who expelled the Moriscos in a manner that no similar expulsions of indigenous Christians occurred anywhere in the Islamic Mediterranean, the religion of Islam still appeared to be driven by an aggressive ideology.[109] One can only speculate what attitudes toward Islam might have developed had Britons only encountered it in the Persian-Indian region, without the legacy of holy wars, without the threats of piracy, and in an environment dominated by trade and profit.

2

First Diplomatic Exchanges

Queen Elizabeth and personal diplomacy

The story of Britain and the Islamic world in the early modern era is by no means a love story. But neither is it a story of remorseless hostility and unending conflict. Indeed, as we argue throughout this book, relations between early modern Britain and the Islamic nations with which it became increasingly involved—Morocco, and the Ottoman, Safavid, and Mughal Empires—were far more complex, dynamic, and subject to regular sea-changes than can be accounted for by simple explanations. Yet it remains notable that at no time during this period did religious difference constitute an insurmountable obstacle to trade, politics, or diplomatic negotiation. Wars were typically fought most brutally within, not between, faiths: Sunni Ottomans battled the Shi'ite Safavids, Protestants fought Roman Catholics, and devastated central Europe. This is not a love story, then, but it is a story that emphatically gives the lie to those who would see Islamic countries and the West as locked into a history of inevitable conflict.[1]

This chapter charts the origins of English diplomatic contacts with the Islamic world beginning with the correspondence that Queen Elizabeth (r. 1558–1603) personally conducted with Muslim leaders. The nature and range of Elizabeth's letters to and from Muslim leaders was unprecedented and unequalled. Her epistolary exchanges with the Sa'adian sherif of Marrakesh, Mulay Ahmad al-Mansur (r. 1578–1603), shows how, in al-Mansur's eyes, England's imperial virgin was hardly imperial at all. In England, Elizabeth built a mythology of her own international importance which poets, painters, and panegyrists dutifully elaborated and broadcast. This was a mythology that proliferated after her death, raising her to semi-divine heights of Marian veneration and imminent imperial power.[2] Elsewhere in the world, however, Elizabeth and her insular realm were simply not that important. In his *True and Strange Discourse,* published the year Elizabeth died, Henry Timberlake reported being stopped two years previously at the city gates of Jerusalem where he was refused admission by the Ottoman guards who 'knowe not what you meane by the worde Englishman'.[3]

For his part, James I (r. 1603–25) was no writer of personal letters to Muslim rulers, and his policy of peace with Spain not only ended England's strategic alliances with Morocco, but also directly altered the ways that British shipping behaved in the Islamic Mediterranean.[4] If Elizabeth never directly condoned what many called piracy among her sea-going subjects, neither did she do much to discourage those who were successful at it. James tried to change all that, denying mariners with reputations for illegal activities the right of return. Central to this policy was the common fear that mariners who had served on foreign or pirate ships had most likely been contaminated by Islam. Several returning sailors were caught and, to considerable publicity in broadsides and ale-house gossip, duly hanged from the docks at Wapping, where their bodies were repeatedly drowned and revealed with the shift in the tide: a grim warning to all returning mariners. Inadvertently, however, James's policy also produced a folk hero in the form of Captain John Ward, an English-born pirate, whose sumptuous marble palace in Tunis, described by the Scottish travel writer William Lithgow, was the material reward of several successful years seizing, looting, and ransoming off smaller ships flying any flag whatsoever. Moralizing broadsides, and even Robert Daborne's play, *A Christian Turn'd Turke* (1612), which punitively stages Ward's violent death when it was known he was still alive, contributed to, rather than detracted from, Ward's reputation as a popular rogue-hero. A champion of free trade, Ward's name survived in ballads well into the nineteenth century.[5]

Indeed, from James onwards, the Stuart monarchs who followed seemed less eager than Elizabeth to maintain such direct and personal epistolary relations with Muslim rulers. The merchant elites and statesmen had taken over the business of diplomacy, even as the ambassadors and consuls, who were paid by the merchant companies, asserted relative autonomy over the diplomacy of business.

The story, then, begins with Elizabeth's diplomatic alliances with the great Islamic nations for commercial and strategic ends. To secure direct trade with the eastern ports of the Mediterranean, it made a great deal of sense for Elizabeth to seek strong ties with Morocco—source of crucial

1585 Elizabeth, Queene of England, France and Ireland, Defen-
dresse of the Catholicke Faith, and Protectrix of the libertie
of the vnited Prouinces of the Netherlands.

ELIZABETHA ANGLIÆ REGINA.

When God by grace had me aduanc't vnto my regall state,
(Which till this time I ruled haue in peace most fortunate)
To serue him, and my subiects good to seeke, it was my care:
And those that forced were to flie by meanes of bloody warre,
'Gainst them by Spaniards made, I did most willingly relieue,
And with a feruent zeale to them all aid and comfort giue,
And by what meanes I could deuise, my mind I alwaies bent,
Their imminent decay and danger great for to preuent.
And to that end protectrix of their country I became,
Defending them with all my power (to my eternall fame)
Wherein no feare of Spanish force ere could my courage quaile,
Nor in my resolution good, make me in ought to faile.

Figure 2. Queen Elizabeth 1 (r. 1558–1603), from Edward Grimseston, *A Generall Historie of the Netherlands* (1609)
From the James Ford Bell Library, University of Minnesota, Minneapolis, Minnesota

leathers, sugar, saltpetre, and gold—and with the Ottomans. Politically, these alliances made a great deal of sense too, given Elizabeth's rivalries with Spain and France. Although trading contacts between the English and Muslim peoples can be traced back before the late sixteenth century, it was during Elizabeth's reign that, encouraged by crown policy and an aggressive community of entrepreneurial merchants, English relations with Muslim states put religion aside and flourished in unprecedented ways. Elizabeth herself helped put England on the map of international affairs, in part by maintaining an active personal correspondence with kings of Morocco, such as al-Mansur and his predecessor, 'Abd al-Malik (r. 1576–78), with Ottoman sultans such as Mehmed III (r. 1595–1603), and with the immensely powerful women of the Ottoman harem such as Safiye, Mehmed's mother. Elizabeth also had direct dealings with the duke of Muscovy known as Ivan the 'terrible'—she ignored his proposal of marriage—and for a time entertained ambitions to establish direct trade with Persia and even China via a north-east sea passage and a trans-Caucasian route.[6] What we learn from Elizabeth's letters of state to Muslim rulers is that she was actively, personally, and shrewdly engaged in matters of international diplomacy, with mercantile and strategic interests ever to the fore.

Examples of letters exchanged between Elizabeth, the Ottoman sultans, and the powerful women of the harem were first made public by Richard Hakluyt in the 1598–1600 edition of his *Principal Navigations*. Although scholarly translations and texts of additional letters exchanged between Elizabeth and women of the Ottoman court were published by Susan Skilliter in the 1960s, these fascinating letters have only recently begun to attract attention despite their importance as the only occasion on which a Muslim queen corresponded with an English ruler.[7] These letters establish personal contact while exploring mutual interests between England and the Ottoman Empire. Elizabeth's status as a Protestant queen proved useful, since her religion allied her with Muslim rulers against Catholic nations, while her gender meant she posed little threat to male authority. At the same time, her evident status as a monarch appealed to the powerful women of the Ottoman court in a historical moment when their own authority was in the ascendant.[8]

In one of her earliest letters to Murad III (r. 1574–95) written in 1579, Elizabeth established common ground against Catholic nations by calling herself 'the most invincible and most mighty defender of the Christian faith against all kinde of idolatries'.[9] For their part, Ottoman sultans considered

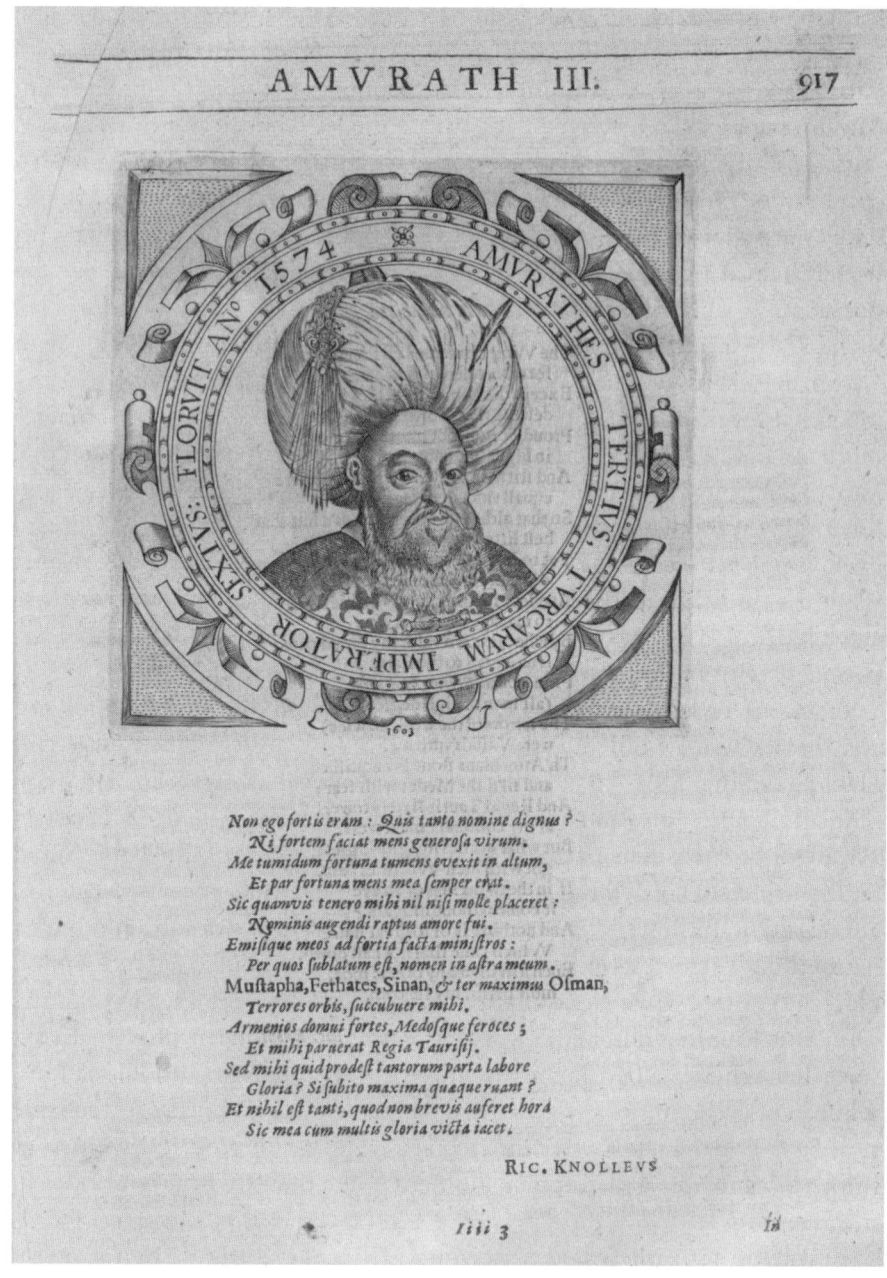

Figure 3. Sultan Murad III (r. 1574–95), from Richard Knolles, *The Generall Historie of the Turkes* (1603)
From the James Ford Bell Library, University of Minnesota, Minneapolis, Minnesota

themselves to be *padishahs*, kings of kings and indeed rulers of the world. Consequently they did not make diplomatic visits, nor did they post resident ambassadors abroad, nor did they engage in the diplomatic rhetoric of mutuality and reciprocity. By the late sixteenth century, Ottoman court protocol insisted on formal displays of submission and obedience for ambassadors, and other forms of representatives from non-Muslim states. These rituals were formulated in *kanun-names* based on ancient Oghuz tales, and were influenced by Byzantine practices. Other kings should come to them, taking 'the road of submission to the Padishah of the House of Osman', as was said of Elizabeth by the Ottoman historian Mustapha ibn Ibrahim Safi.[10]

By contrast, three extant letters from Safiye to Elizabeth are especially revealing since they vary between a formal letter of 1593, a veritable 'showpiece of rhetoric' in Skilliter's phrase, to two later 'personal letters' from 1599.[11] Composed in reply to Elizabeth's request that Edward Barton be granted full ambassadorial status, Safiye's 1593 letter—made famous from Hakluyt's publication—is a costly and exquisite work of calligraphic art that is 'composed in a very involved and flowery rhyming prose with many poetical comparisons'. Several keywords are written in gold leaf, while the whole has been 'liberally flecked with gold'.[12] More than half of the text is given over to 'established formulas of Imperial letters', such as the praise it lavishes on Elizabeth for having sent 'a special letter, full of marvels, whose paper was more fragrant than pure camphor and ambergris and its ink than finest musk, notifying indescribable and immeasurable consideration and love towards (me) Her well-wisher'.[13] Although Elizabeth's response has not survived, Richard Wrag—who witnessed 'the pompe & solemnitie' of the ceremony at which it was delivered on 17 October—reports that Elizabeth had sent Safiye 'a jewel of her majesties picture, set with some rubies and diamants, 3 great pieces of gilt plate, 10 garments of cloth of gold, a very fine case of glasse bottles silver & gilt with 2 pieces of fine Holland'. According to Wrag, Safiye was so delighted with her presents 'that she sent to know of the ambassador what present he thought she might return that would most delight her majestie'. Having received Barton's reply, Wrag continues, Safiye sent Elizabeth 'an upper gowne of cloth of gold very rich, an under gowne of cloth of silver, and a girdle of Turkie worke, rich and faire, with a letter of gratification, which for the rarenesse of the stile, because you may be acquainted with it, I have at the end of this discourse hereunto annexed'.[14] Safiye's gifts and letter were sent overland in March 1594 and presented at a ceremony held at Greenwich on 10 August.[15]

Safiye's 1593 'letter of gratification' is nevertheless a formal document of state. It opens with praise of God and the Prophet, and catalogues Sultan Murad's many titles and claims to power. Yet it does not lose sight of the fact it is being written 'on the part of the mother of Sultan Murad Khan's son', that is, Safiye herself, whose consequent status as '*Khasseki*'—the mother of the heir—gave her considerable influence in the affairs of the empire. Having listed the many territories over which Murad holds dominion, the letter carefully turns from him to Elizabeth in an illuminating exegesis of the gendered character of the power relations that were at stake in this Anglo-Ottoman correspondence:

> the shadow of God, the protector of faith and state, Khan Murad [is] the support of Christian womanhood...who follow the Messiah, bearer of the marks of pomp and majesty, trailing the skirts of glory and power, she who is obeyed of the princes, cradle of chastity and continence, ruler of the realm of England, crowned lady and woman of Mary's way—may her last moments be concluded with good and may she obtain that which she desires![16]

Having established that Sultan Murad protects Christian women, Safiye thanks Elizabeth for the gifts and her letter, then ends by requesting that Elizabeth continue to write directly to her so that 'I can repeatedly mention Her Highness's gentility and praise at the footdust of His Majesty, the fortunate and felicitious Padishah'.[17]

Two later surviving letters to Elizabeth from Safiye suggest that a curious form of intimacy developed between these two women, despite distance and differences of religion and culture. Following the death of Sultan Murad in 1595, Safiye became the Valide Sultan, mother of the sultan, and even more powerful than before. Her letters to Elizabeth of 1599 concerning the renewal of trading agreements are considerably less formal, more personal and intimate. Unlike the beautiful and elegantly styled letter of 1593, which had most likely been composed by one Paulo Mariani, a Venetian merchant,[18] Safiye's letters of 1599 are 'extremely primitive and crude in appearance and...style', probably having been written, according to John Sanderson at least, by 'som woman in the seraglio'.[19] In the 1599 letters, then, we may hear something closer to Safiye's own voice, uncluttered with rhetorical formalities:

> Your letter has arrived and reached (us); whatsoever you said became known to us. God willing, action will be taken according to what you said. Be of good heart in this respect! We do not cease from admonishing our son, His Majesty

the Padishah, and from telling him: 'Do act according to the treaty!' God willing, may you not suffer in this respect![20]

Although it is impossible to know for certain, it is difficult to imagine that Safiye's pleading on Elizabeth's behalf made no difference. Finding diplomatic favour at the Ottoman court was no small achievement for a queen of a remote Atlantic island. The sultans—Murad III and Mehmed III—with whom Elizabeth and her agents had direct dealings, were rulers of a massively powerful imperial civilization and military state that many held to be the terror and scourge of Christendom. The Elizabethans held some land in Ireland, claimed parts of France, and had not yet built any settlements in the New World: they were not an emergent imperial force such as the Spaniards or French, and therefore were not taken too seriously by Ottoman statesmen. All the same, the Ottoman sultans allowed increasing numbers of British merchants to take up residence in major centres of trade—Aleppo, Izmir, and Istanbul—while the Ottoman regencies of Algiers, Tunis, and Tripoli developed communities of expatriated English, Irish, and Scottish mariners, and captives or former captives who, for one reason or another, had not gone home. There were many such men—and a few women—by the start of the seventeenth century, who crossed cultures and left records of doing so. Even so, the influence of English culture on Ottoman culture remained relatively negligible during the sixteenth and seventeenth centuries.

Queen Elizabeth I and Mulay Ahmad al-Mansur

Numerous letters from al-Mansur to Elizabeth have survived, along with an account by his court scribe and historian, 'Abd al-Aziz al-Fishtali (1549–1621). These previously unknown Arabic sources provide the most extensive contemporary view of Queen Elizabeth from outside Anglo- and Euro-centric vantage points. Indeed, they probably provide the only detailed commentary about any European ruler in non-European sources of the sixteenth century. The royal correspondence and al-Fishtali's writings disclose the first developed friendship between a Muslim and a Christian monarch in the early modern period. These documents also reveal a view of Elizabeth that differs greatly from that to be found in the English and European records.

Upon acceding to the Moroccan throne in August 1578, following victory at the battle of Wadi al-Makhazin (Alcazar), Mulay Ahmad al-Mansur had little reason to notice or court the English queen. Actually, he looked askance at her since a contingent of English and Irish Catholic soldiers, led by Thomas Stuckley, had joined King Sebastian and fought against him in battle. Furthermore, Elizabeth's coffers were not as replete as they needed to be to make England a powerful nation. When an English ambassador arrived in Marrakesh to congratulate al-Mansur on his victory and accession to the throne, he brought presents that, compared with those from Portugal, were considered so insignificant that al-Fishtali did not even bother to mention them. The Portuguese 'magnificent present was beyond calculation', wrote al-Fishtali, 'and people wondered at the one who gave it. The present was brought into the gate of Fez on coaches and carriages... People flocked to see the present like butterflies.'[21] But as soon as al-Mansur found himself having to manoeuvre between the Ottoman and Spanish superpowers that were trying to conquer his kingdom, he turned, just as his predecessors had done, to countries such as France, Holland, and England for possible assistance. All were enemies of Spain, and needed access to the natural resources that only Morocco could provide—chiefly saltpetre for manufacturing gunpowder, but also gold, sugar, and leather. None proved more cooperative than England, whose queen found herself confronted by the formidable power of Spain. In the dangerous years after her excommunication in 1570, and until the very end of her reign, Elizabeth was much in need of an ally such as al-Mansur, especially since she saw before her a determined adversary, Philip II, whose vast New World resources of gold and silver were matched by his antipathy to the Protestant heresy.

On 23 June 1580, al-Mansur sent Elizabeth a letter that opens with five lines of honorific titles, praising her as the greatest among those who follow the 'religion of Christ'. Al-Mansur wrote with eloquence and flattery, insisting on the 'evident love'—*al-hubb al-sarih*—between him and 'sultana Isabel': she was 'the majesty in the lands of Christ, the sultana Isabel, may God grant her all good and continue her good health'. Al-Mansur promised that English merchants in his dominions would receive all the help they needed: 'As you are doing the best to facilitate our affairs there [in England],' he continued, 'so will we do the same for you here.'[22] Such friendship became crucial for Elizabeth a few months later in September 1580, once Philip II had annexed Portugal, and after Don Antonio, who had proclaimed himself king of Portugal on 26 August 1580, fled to England seeking her support. Elizabeth realized that tensions with Spain were destined to increase since Philip II could not look kindly on her harbouring the Portuguese claimant. Al-Fishtali, monitoring the situation from Marrakesh, commented on the flight of Don Antonio and confirmed Elizabeth's need for an alliance with al-Mansur. The Portuguese claimant, he wrote, had 'fled to Elizabeth of the lands of England, Izabil, where he was well received, and she rolled up her sleeves to help him. But then she realized that she could only rebuild what had been destroyed, and repair what had been damaged, with the help of the Prince of the Faithful, al-Mansur, who extended his support from across the sea.'[23]

Both Elizabeth and Don Antonio realized that the support of the newly enthroned Moroccan ruler would prove crucial for confronting Spain— a support that al-Mansur was not unwilling to extend. Promptly, the Moroccan ruler called for expanding trade and establishing diplomatic cooperation with England. By 1583, when advising Elizabeth about her political options with regard to Spain, Lord Burghley suggested that an alliance with Morocco could well 'serve your Majesty'.[24] Elizabeth had already rejected the Duke of Anjou's suit of marriage, an action that had alienated the French and encouraged them to mend fences with Spain. Elizabeth knew she needed extra-European support. Formal diplomatic and commercial agreements with the Ottomans had been in place since 1582, but strategic interests in the western Mediterranean and Atlantic required strong cooperation with Morocco. In July 1585, she granted the letters patent for establishing the Barbary Company to coordinate trade to the North African coast.[25] Morocco, moreover, was emerging as a desirable market for English cloth, and Elizabeth was eager to strengthen all ties, especially since her forces had failed to defeat the Duke of Palma in the Netherlands, leaving the Spanish army just a channel away. The menace was such that, in February 1587, she ordered the execution of Mary Queen of Scots, thereby inviting revenge by Philip II, who was building a large fleet. Beset by dangers on all sides, Elizabeth turned to al-Mansur, dispatching a Portuguese agent, Matias Becudo, to Marrakesh in hopes of convincing him to cooperate with her. Accompanied by English merchants residing in Marrakesh, the Portuguese envoy requested al-Mansur grant the English a seaport in Morocco from which they might divert Spanish ships from their intended attack on England.[26] Al-Mansur refused, temporizing lest the Euro-Christian balance of power change. Nevertheless, in March 1588, he issued a royal edict protecting all English traders, travellers, and residents in his kingdom.[27]

England's victory over the Spanish Armada in the summer of 1588 prompted al-Mansur for the first time to view Elizabeth as a viable military and diplomatic ally. He now recognized the role she could play in his plans for the re-conquest of Spain and in Euro-Moroccan cooperation. To him, Elizabeth was now a means to an end: while she fought Spain to defend her island, she opened up the possibility for him to liberate al-Andalus from 'the tyrant of Castile', as he called Philip II. With such a goal in mind, al-Mansur encouraged the Andalusian exiles to attack Spanish-held Ceuta, which, as his scribe recorded, they nearly conquered.[28] He also strengthened his fleet, his 'ships of jihad'—*marakib jihadiyya*—for the 'conquest of the land of al-Andalus'. His plan was to 'cross to al-Andalus by sea with the soldiers of God and Islam to re-establish the roots of faith and to liberate it from the hands of unbelief'.[29] As far as al-Mansur was concerned, Elizabeth had opened the door to Europe. Mulay al-Mansur was now ready to take his rightful place on the European stage.

In such an anti-Spanish, pro-English mood, al-Fishtali addressed a letter to the people of Sus, on whose 'tribal elements' al-Mansur's army relied strongly.[30] In the letter, al-Fishtali shared with them the happy news about the Spanish naval defeat, described the English victory under the 'sultana Isabel', and then represented the advantages which the Anglo-Spanish conflict had brought to al-Mansur, to Morocco in particular, and to Muslims in general. The letter shows that al-Mansur and his scribe fully understood the religious causes of the conflict between England and Spain, the piratical attacks by England on the Spanish New World fleet, and events before and during the Armada's attack. Despite living in landlocked Marrakesh, al-Mansur knew exactly what Elizabeth had achieved, and how that achievement could serve his own goals. At the same time, the letter proclaims God to be on the side of England's queen: the difference between her Christianity and Spain's was known to him, and its relevance understood. Also, the scribe was well informed about the course of the sea battle: how a storm had first ravaged the Spanish fleet, following which the English fell on it and destroyed it. What was important for al-Fishtali and the Marrakesh court in all this European religious and military rivalry was that Elizabeth was worthy of praise, despite being a Christian. Religious difference with England was less important than political, ideological, and military cooperation. Indeed, God Himself seemed to authorize such cooperation—having supported Elizabeth against Philip—for the benefit of al-Mansur's Islamic objectives.

Toward the end of 1588, al-Mansur received an ambassador from Don Antonio who 'asked the King of Fez for 300,000 crowns'.[31] Al-Mansur was now willing to join the Anglo-Portuguese alliance against Spain, but as a 'hostage or surety', he asked for Don Antonio's son—a tactic that Queen Elizabeth herself had suggested earlier that year.[32] Don Antonio agreed and sent his son, Don Christobal, who left England on 10 November 1588. As al-Fishtali wrote:

> Don Antonio saved himself by fleeing to Elizabeth of the land Nigaleetra. She welcomed him and gave him shelter and rolled up her sleeves to help him. But then he looked around and saw that only the hand of the Prince of the Faithful could build what had been destroyed and mend the cracks... and that he [Don Antonio] could not build his fort without him who gave him pickaxes. He needed [al-Mansur's] imamate swords and spears, so he wrote to him, and stretched his hand of need from behind the sees, and sent his son from the lands of Langalteer, imploring and begging.[33]

To welcome him upon his arrival in Morocco in January 1589, Mulay al-Mansur ordered his son Abu Faris to meet the Portuguese hostage.[34] Abu Faris sent the most senior Portuguese convert under his command, al-Qa'id Mahmud, who led Don Christobal and his entourage from Asila via Fez to Marrakesh, where great festivities were held in his honour.[35] Ironically, Don Christobal landed in Asila, where Don Sebastian had landed ten years earlier on his fateful journey to defeat and death. The son of the Portuguese *taghiya* (tyrant) was in Marrakesh, wrote al-Fishtali, seeking help from 'our swords, made triumphant by God, to regain his lost kingship... although our imamate swords with their sharp blades had earlier destroyed the edifice of his kingship [in the battle of Wadi al-Makhazin or Alcazar, Don Christobal knew] that only with our hands would he recuperate it'.[36]

Once al-Mansur had his hostage, he procrastinated. As months passed, Elizabeth grew frustrated and demanded Don Christobal's return to England since he had evidently become a captive in Morocco: so at least he described himself in a letter to Lord Burghley of 25 May 1590.[37] The attack on Lisbon the year before, which Elizabeth had hoped would replenish her coffers, had failed to do so. Elizabeth wrote to the Moroccan king, revealing, perhaps inadvertently, her helplessness. She was bitter that al-Mansur had ridiculed her letters—'*con mucha honra y humanidad*'—and had not even listened to her; she further complained that he had not sent her the money she needed to defend herself against Philip II, and that he was ignoring their friendship. Nor had he released British captives held in his kingdom, two of whom had already died. Unable to force his hand, and without any tempting prospect to dangle before him, Elizabeth nevertheless imagined she could threaten him. Should he continue to prevaricate, she wrote, she would complain about him to her powerful Muslim ally, Sultan Murad III in Istanbul. She could do nothing else but try to frighten al-Mansur with the might of the Ottomans: 'If you would not grant us what we so reasonably ask from you, we will have to pay less attention to your friendship. We know for sure also that the Great Turk, who treats our subjects with great favour and humanity, will not appreciate your maltreatment of them in order to please the Spaniards.'[38]

Elizabeth was clearly helpless. For years, she had been consolidating her relations with the Ottomans so much that by 1590 it was reported from Scotland that 'no Christian Prince ever had in the Turk suche great estimacion'.[39] Unfortunately, that consolidation had not translated into the naval assistance for which Elizabeth's ambassador in Istanbul had constantly pleaded. On 23 June 1590, al-Mansur replied to Elizabeth's letter by assuring her of his love, opening with pompous honorific titles to 'the firm-footed, of celestial light and knowledge, the great *sultana al-asila, al-mathila, al-athila, al-khatira* [true-blooded, exemplary, high-born, great], the famous, the possessor of England, sultana Isabel'—titles that al-Mansur applied to Muslims, too. For him, the Christian queen was as valued as a Muslim ruler,[40] and the praise he heaped on her was intended to assure her that he was preparing to send an envoy to her with the money promised to Don Antonio. However, al-Mansur wanted to make sure that Elizabeth was serious about supporting the anti-Spanish claimant and establishing a league with him. 'If you extend the military help you promised Don Antonio this year,' he continued, 'we shall send our envoy as soon as the "happy action" of conquering Sudan is finished. You and I,' he concluded, 'share the same goals.'[41]

The praise that al-Mansur used in this letter was part of a rhetorical tradition characteristic of Moroccan royal correspondence.[42] Indeed, the honorific titles that al-Mansur used in his official addresses to both Muslim and Christian rulers indicated exactly how he viewed them. In all communications with the Ottomans, al-Mansur refused to use any title for them other than 'sultans'; on rare occasions only did he address them as 'kings'.

Much as he may, or may not, have respected the Ottomans, they did not have the caliphal status of which he felt himself alone to be worthy: they were rulers whose authority derived from worldly power and not from the lineage of God's Prophet, as did his. In the case of Elizabeth, and since he wanted to honour her, he sometimes called her *malaka,* queen, and at other times, he called her *sultana.* Don Antonio was addressed in the same honorific formula as Sultana Isabel—at the same time as the Songhai Emperor, whom al-Mansur would soon defeat, was addressed as the mere 'leader of Kaghwa and its great one, its administrator and keeper' in the letter in which al-Mansur threatened him with invasion.[43] Christian monarchs who cooperated with him received more honour than did Muslim leaders who were seen to defy him. Throughout his correspondence with Elizabeth, al-Mansur never changed his attitude towards her: she was always honoured with the highest titles possible to a ruler—any ruler, Christian or Muslim.[44]

On 28 February 1591, a Moroccan army reached Niger across the Sahara, 135 days after leaving Marrakesh. Two weeks later, 13 March, the Moroccans defeated the Songhai army, after which the 'Sudan'—the Land of the Blacks—submitted and would henceforth send an annual tribute of 100,000 pieces of gold and 1,000 slaves to Marrakesh.[45] The wealth that al-Mansur gained from the invasion immediately attracted European traders. The Portuguese captive Antonio de Saldanha reported that Marrakesh soon teemed with English, French, Flemish, Italian, and Spanish merchants, each seeking al-Mansur's favour and approaching him with requests for monopolies.[46] Elizabeth swallowed her pride and wrote requesting help to build a front against Spain, reminding him that she had sold him the tents and the heavy weapons for the invasion of the Sudan.[47] Having ignored her earlier letter, and having delayed her messenger for two years, some time between January and March 1592,[48] al-Mansur finally replied, assuring Elizabeth that he paid the closest attention to her needs and interests 'both great and small'. Nonetheless, he ignored her demand both for money and for Don Antonio's son 'whom you had sent to us'. Instead, he explained that he had not been able to help because he had been conducting the invasion of '*al-mamlaka al-sudaniyya*'—the Sudanese kingdom.[49] He then instructed Elizabeth to fulfil her part of the deal in assisting Don Antonio—and if she found herself unable to 'give the ayde, then send us wourde'.[50] Either Elizabeth would cooperate or the whole agreement between her and al-Mansur over Don Antonio would collapse.

In another letter sent later in 1592, Mulay Ahmad promised to return Don Christobal to England, and assured Elizabeth that he was ever attentive to diplomatic relations with her. He declared that his conquest of 'Sudan' would increase his strength as well as hers, and thereby strengthen England. Just as her victory over the Spanish Armada had benefited him, he argued, so would his victory in Sudan prove beneficial to her—because the gold would enable him to finance the conquest of al-Andalus, 'to re-take the region from the hands of infidelity and to return the word of Islam to its youth and vigour'.[51] His newly won wealth would help him defeat her chief enemy. As tensions mounted between England and Spain, after a break in peace negotiations, Elizabeth knew, as did al-Mansur, that she would need his assistance should fighting break out in the Mediterranean or the Atlantic theatres. Her fleet would have to victual in Moroccan ports. Consequently, when Elizabeth authorized preparations for an attack on Cadiz, the Privy Council determined that 'Sir Edward Hoby should be sent to Morocco in case help in galleys, men, or victuals should be needed from there'.[52]

In early July 1596, the English fleet attacked Cadiz, 'the heart of Spain', as the Venetian ambassador called it.[53] Al-Mansur seized on the English attack as yet another Christian means to his Muslim goal. Having sent ships to participate in the attack,[54] he viewed the whole enterprise as the realization of a Moroccan objective that would be achieved by Anglo-Moroccan means. It was he, al-Mansur declared to his subjects, who had prodded Elizabeth to attack by providing her with the necessary metals for building cannons and preparing gunpowder. It was he who had turned her against Philip, and it was he who was now wreaking vengeance on the Spanish. Since Philip had invaded Morocco by means of al-Nasir the year before,[55] al-Mansur was now invading Iberia by means of Elizabeth. This explained why English traders were clandestinely providing him with all the 'ores for gallies, launces, muskettes, muskett arrowes, caleveres, poldaves, cordage for gallies, sorde blades, gret shott and such like'.[56]

Once again, al-Fishtali seized the opportunity to write about the attack, indicating just how carefully English affairs were being monitored in Morocco:

> The sky darkened with dissension against the tyrant of Qishtala, and the kings of the nations of the Christians attacked him like wild dogs. The most ferocious against him, and the one most daring in attacking his kingdoms and tightening the noose around him, was Isabella the sultana of the kingdoms of the lands of England. For Mulana the prince of the faithful [al-Mansur], had

lured her with his support and had sharpened her will against him [Philip II]: he showed her his willingness to help confront him [Philip II] by supplying her with copper to use in cannons, and saltpetre for ammunition which he permitted her to buy from his noble kingdoms. He also supplied her with metals, which were not found in her lands. With God helping him, he pitted her against the enemy of religion and, with God's help, and because of his [al-Mansur's] decisiveness, capable organization, and deep caution, he kept her focused on [Philip II], both on her own and with his help.

Al-Fishtali confirmed that al-Mansur, 'may God be with him, prepared for *jihad* against the enemy of religion to punish him for what he had done to Islam'.[57] He then praised his master for sending other ships against 'the Eternal Islands'—the Canaries—and engaging the Spaniards in battle: 'He continued, God support him, his attacks on the lands of infidelity and *shirk* [associating other deities with God], taking captives and goods from the Eternal Islands, which [his] fleet mangled with its teeth.'[58] Many observers had been convinced of Morocco's collusion in the attack on Cadiz, while the detailed information that al-Mansur possessed helps explain why he felt that he could manipulate events to his own end. With the weakening of Spain, the wealth of the Western Sudan, and England's need to use his ports, al-Mansur was confident that the 'swords' of Islam could now begin the conquest of al-Andalus.[59] His reputation was so celebrated around the Mediterranean that, in December 1596, a French delegation arrived in Morocco to negotiate with him about military and financial cooperation against Spain.[60]

Although al-Mansur never succeeded in his design of conquering Spain, a year after the attack on Cadiz, a reporter in Brussels still feared that the English would equip 200,000 Moors from Barbary to 'descend upon Spain'.[61] Later that year, an anonymous memo addressed to Secretary of State Sir Robert Cecil expressed the hope that the 'King of Moroko' would send 'som of his Mores to burne and spoyle the Spaniards corne adjoyning to their fortts and garisons in Barbarie'.[62] Throughout those tense years, and as rebellion in Ireland festered, Elizabeth realized that any attack against Spain, which was supporting the Irish Catholics, would need al-Mansur's assistance, since, on her own, she could not muster sufficient military might. The Irish rebellion of Hugh O'Neill was draining her military strength, and the Earl of Essex, who had been sent to quell it, had not been successful. Still, in May 1599, the Dutch States General turned to England for help releasing Dutch captives. The Dutch recognized the ties that bound the two countries and the 'creditt', as Elizabeth wrote to al-Mansur, 'which they suppose the correspondency that hath long ben betweene you and us doth cause us to have with you'.[63]

Such credit was known to English playwrights as well as to the general populace. In *The Fair Maid of the West, Part I* (c.1600–3),[64] Thomas Heywood confirmed how Florentine and other Italian merchants recognized the 'creditt' and turned to English Bess (as in reality they turned to Elizabeth) for help with the Moroccan ruler. There was wide recognition of the power and wealth of the Moors into which England had managed to tap. Heywood presents an English virgin, suitably named Elizabeth, arriving in Morocco, enchanting the Moroccan ruler, and then staying with her sweetheart, Spencer, in the kingdom. The couple are married in Fez by an English cleric whom Bess had saved from death for his audacity in travelling to Morocco to preach Christianity, and receive a magnificent dowry from the Moroccan ruler. In this respect, the play presents an English couple settling, not in Roanoke, where Sir Walter Raleigh's colonies had failed, but in the wealthy and fabulously exotic kingdom of Morocco. Writing at the end of the Elizabethan period, Heywood was certain that his country's trading and settlement future lay in North Africa rather than North America. His play was the first to present Moors not drawn from Italian or Spanish sources, as other plays about North Africa did; even the name of the Moorish ruler was derived from actual contemporary events,[65] unlike the names of previous Moors in plays by Marlowe, Peele, and Shakespeare. Heywood was observing the course of English navigation and expansion, and may well have drawn inspiration for his picaresque plot from the adventures of his countrymen and women. Heywood clearly understood who his queen's potential allies were.

During the visit of the Moroccan ambassador to London in 1600–1, al-Mansur secretly proposed to Elizabeth a joint operation to seize the Spanish possessions in the Americas. But Elizabeth seemed diffident about building an extensive overseas empire, since she was in need of well-trained troops to help her against Spain. She tried, quite underhandedly, to steal his elite force of Morisco warriors by enticing them to come to England and serve on her fleet. Al-Mansur, however, wanted to expand his kingdom, and in a letter of 1 May 1601, stated that he would underwrite a joint military venture with her only if the goal was not just to fight Spain but also to colonize the New World. Al-Mansur wanted assurances that, having defeated the Spaniards, Moroccans would populate the land—to the exclusion of the English. In a moment of imprudent exuberance, al-Mansur outlined his vision—that Islam would prevail in the Americas and the *mahdi* would be proclaimed from the two sides of the ocean. To ensure cooperation, al-Mansur informed Elizabeth that such a venture would bring her vast benefits that would help her launch her own imperial venture:

> And your high estate shall knowe that, in the inhabiting of those countries by us and yow, yow shall have a great benefite: first for that those countries of the East are adjoining to many Kinges Moores and infinite nations of our religion; and further, if your power and command shall be seene there with owre armie, all the Moores will joyne and confederate themselves—by the help of God—with us and yow.[66]

When Elizabeth did not offer assistance, al-Mansur became convinced that she was useless for his grand schemes. On 3 July 1602, he wrote repeating his honorific praise of the English queen, and expressed his continued eagerness for cooperation. In his address, however, he quibbled over her status: to 'the Sultana Isabel,' he wrote, 'whom we *like [to think]* that her station is still recognized' among her religious community—'*al-lati nuhibu an la yazalu qadruha mu'tamadan*' [emphasis added].[67] A few months later, in October, he signed an agreement for military cooperation with Spain against his arch enemy, the Ottoman Empire. Having negotiated with Elizabeth for nearly two decades, he had found that she never put her troops where she promised, nor allowed him to put his troops where he wanted. On her side, Elizabeth knew that she needed al-Mansur more than he needed her, and that his gold, armies, natural resources, and antipathy to Spain were crucial for the defence of her kingdom. In her last letter to him, just before her death on 3 April 1603, she informed him of the release of Moorish captives who had been held in England, and requested the release of Cornelis Jansz, her subject, born in Flushing. She then signed the letter as she had been signing since 1598: '*Vuestra hermana y pariente segun ley de corona ye ceptro*'—your sister and relative according to the law of crown and sceptre.[68]

Elizabeth and al-Mansur were two of a kind. Both lived in a highly charged religious context: Protestant Elizabeth feared Catholic Philip in the same way that Maliki Ahmad feared the Hanafi Ottoman Sultan, Murad III. Both were highly opinionated rulers, expecting obedience and flattery, but also relying on the insights of a small coterie, the Privy Council and Majlis al-Shura. Both were consolidating national identity in the face of outside danger, and both were strapped for money: Elizabeth sent her sea-dogs after the gold of the Spanish galleys, while al-Mansur sent his Morisco army into the Western Sudan in quest of gold and conquest. Both feared the plots and schemes of their kin who were supported by Spain: Elizabeth had to contend with Mary Tudor just as al-Mansur had to contend with his nephew, who was defeated and killed in 1595. Both monarchs wrote repeatedly to each other, and frequently exchanged envoys and ambassadors. To no other European monarch did al-Mansur write more letters of amity and admiration than to Queen Elizabeth.

At the same time, their correspondence shows how staunchly they recognized religious differences that they were, nevertheless, willing to abjure in order to achieve mutual political goals. Perhaps the fact that Protestant Elizabeth was fighting Catholic Spain attracted al-Mansur, who found Protestantism more appealing than the religion of Rome with its idolatry. Al-Fishtali mentioned both Luther and Calvin in *Manahil al-safa'*,[69] and the changes they had effected in Christendom, upon which al-Mansur would have looked favourably. In an age of religious persecution and bigotry, it is striking that neither monarch tried to subvert the other theologically or viewed cooperation as an avenue toward conversion. Furthermore, al-Mansur repeatedly praised Elizabeth as a Christian and used formal addresses that were not theologically exclusionary: instead of invoking God and the Prophet Muhammad, he opened his letters with an invocation of God and all His prophets—which would include Christ. Al-Mansur was not apprehensive about dealing with a Christian *sultana* because these relations were not overshadowed by Muslim weakness or fear. Islam was safe, and al-Mansur did not need to defend, promote, or force it.

That Elizabeth was a woman and queen never bothered Mulay al-Mansur in the manner that it drove John Knox to near insanity. It is important that al-Mansur allowed her name to be mentioned in his presence and read in the correspondence. Just a few years later in the Mughal court, Thomas Roe discovered that any mention of his king's name constituted an insult to the Indian potentate who thought very little of James I. But much as al-Mansur seemed to have respected Elizabeth, he never viewed her as a sister, nor did he view himself as her big brother. He never reciprocated with fraternal titles, perhaps because he viewed her queenship as outweighing her womanhood in a manner that she did not. While to her own countrymen she wanted to have the fortitude of a man, revealed by her speech before the Armada attack, to Mulay Ahmad, she wanted to be a sister in royalty and a sister who needed the support of a brother. Al-Mansur did not view Elizabeth through specifically gendered eyes. She was a *sultana*, less than himself in majesty, not because of womanhood but because of pedigree. She was admired and never vilified as a *taghiya* (tyrant), but she was never his equal.

To English theatre audiences, the figure of al-Mansur appeared as a formidable figure, commanding respect for his wealth, military strength, and political acumen. Between 1588 and 1603, the year in which he died, numerous plays were performed in England featuring powerful male Moorish protagonists. After the Elizabethan period, Moorish characters would never again play such important and complex roles as they did in *The Battle of Alcazar* (c.1589), *Titus Andronicus* (c.1591–2), *The Merchant of Venice* (c.1596), *Lust's Dominion* (c.1599–1600), *Othello* (c.1602), and *The Fair Maid of the West* (c.1600–3).[70] Peele's *The Battle of Alcazar* ends with al-Mansur, one of the protagonists, standing victorious over the bodies of the English and the Portuguese invaders. Heywood's Mullisheq resembles al-Mansur, but refashioned according to English fantasies. At a time when al-Mansur was dictating conditions to Queen Elizabeth, audiences would have been gratified by Heywood's theatrical reversal that showed the Moroccan ruler doting on English Bess and obeying her every wish and whim. The westward venture of ambitious, but initially unsuccessful Britons toward North America contrasted sharply with the prosperous venture into the single most enticing region for trade, travel, and inquiry in the early modern period: the Islamic Mediterranean.

As the *Susan Constant*, the *Godspeed*, and the *Discovery* reached Virginia in 1607, the *Mayflower* had long been sailing the Mediterranean Sea, carrying English traders and cargo to Istanbul, Algiers, and Cairo—some of the richest and most alluring cities in the world. If North America was for colonization, North Africa and the Levant were for trade, cultural exchange, political alliance, and military cooperation. Before there was Jamestown, there were Ma'moura and Marrakesh, Algiers and Istanbul; and before there was Pocahontas, there were Robert Shirley's Circassian wife, Lady Teresa Sampsonia Sherley, and William Hawkins' Armenian wife. And before a few dozen Britons arrived and survived among the Native Americans in 1607, there were hundreds among the Moors and the Turks.

King James and the Ottomans

For decades, and well into the eighteenth century, English and Moroccan envoys, rulers, and writers looked back at the cooperation between Elizabeth and al-Mansur and remembered them as monarchs who had been able to move beyond religious polarization toward mutually beneficial diplomatic and military cooperation. The Moroccans would long remember the Christian queen who had tried to re-configure alliances beyond religious differences. Nevertheless, Elizabeth was the first and last Christian ally that any Muslim ruler ever embraced. Her death marked a sea-change in diplomatic relations between England and the Islamic world: no subsequent monarch would play such a personally direct and active role in negotiations with Muslim rulers. From then on, it would be the ambassadors and officials of the trading companies who would set the agenda for Anglo-Islamic relations. James and the Stuart monarchs who followed him to the throne of what he was first to claim as Great Britain, did not engage in the same kind of vigorous and personal epistolary exchange with Muslim leaders that had served Elizabeth and her merchants so well. By 1603 the records kept by the Levant Company and Secretaries of State provide overwhelming evidence that commercial negotiations had already established enduring connections that would flourish in the decades to come, keeping Britain and the British firmly linked to the Islamic world via trade.

For his part, James sought peace with Spain and was certainly not going to take 'the road of submission' and write personal letters on perfumed stationery to the Ottomans or any other Muslim ruler the way his predecessor had done, but there is reason to believe that he continued to meddle in Ottoman affairs. It seems likely that James promoted the interests of one Stefan Bogdan, a nominal Protestant and pretender to the throne of Moldavia which, at that time, was an appointment in the control of the Ottomans. In 1601, Bogdan had appeared before Elizabeth asking for assistance to promote his dynastic claims to the throne of Moldavia. She sent him off with some funds and a letter ordering her ambassador in Istanbul, Henry Lello, to provide him protection and support. Years later, in 1607, he reappeared in London, still only a pretender, and went before James with a similar plea. Bogdan soon afterwards showed up in Istanbul with letters of support from James addressed to the sultan and to the resident ambassador,

Sir Thomas Glover. For the next several years, Glover put him up at the English house in Pera, feeding and protecting him at his own expense. By doing so, and by constantly lobbying on Bogdan's behalf, Glover jeopardized his prestige at the Ottoman court. When Bogdan's aspirations were finally dashed by the appointment of a rival, he swiftly converted to Islam and was generously rewarded with appointments within the Ottoman state. Glover, meanwhile, suddenly found himself at the centre of attacks from powerful enemies, both Muslim and Catholic. After the Grand Vezir threatened to execute Glover for his persistent interference in Ottoman affairs, the French ambassador joined in with accusations that Glover's secretary was a Spanish agent who had been passing on information that was detrimental to the peace of nations. In 1611, amidst other scandalous accusations, Glover was recalled to London and replaced by Sir Paul Pindar. Once back in London, and to the surprise of many, Glover was found innocent of any inappropriate behaviour, and rewarded for his services to the state, suggesting that he had been dutifully serving James all along.[71]

Although James notoriously avoided direct military intervention when Europe erupted into war in 1618, in the earlier years of his reign his foreign policy does appear to have included limited support for Protestant interests in south-east Europe. Although Bogdan turned out to be unreliable as regards his religious affiliation, the affair indicates how intriguing at the Ottoman court remained on James's agenda. Of equal importance, it also indicates the extent to which resident ambassadors such as Glover were becoming accustomed to exercising relative autonomy as agents between Britain and the Islamic world. The Elizabethan era of direct royal contact had given way to diplomacy via the trading companies and the resident ambassadors.

Irregular envoys: early Anglo-Safavid encounters

Not all Britons serving as ambassadors to Muslim courts necessarily represented the Crown, Protestant cause, or even the merchant communities of London. There were several British subjects in the pay of foreign states, including Islamic ones. For his diplomatic and military services—including missions to the Ottoman court—the Scots adventurer Walter Leslie (1606–67) was appointed Count of the Holy Roman Empire in 1637.[72] Some years earlier, Sir Anthony Shirley had begun his career as a peripatetic envoy for the Safavid Shah 'Abbas (r. 1588–1629) on missions to Russia, Portugal, France, and Holland, seeking alliances against the Ottomans. With his brother Robert, Anthony had first appeared at the Safavid court in 1598, even as Safavid-Ottoman relations were degenerating into the wars that would run from 1603 for the next few decades. Advocating a coalition between Persia and Christian states against the Ottomans, Anthony caught the attention of the shah who dispatched him as head of a delegation to forge just such alliances.

Although Anthony failed miserably in his negotiations on behalf of the Safavids, he would later undertake an embassy to Marrakesh for the Emperor Rudolf, and lead a disastrous naval campaign for the Spanish against the Ottomans. Robert, meanwhile, had stayed behind in Qazvin, loyal to the shah, who deployed him on a diplomatic mission to Spain in 1608. Having married into a noble family of Circassian Christians, Robert returned via England, where his first child was born. At Whitehall in 1611, he represented Shah 'Abbas before King James, and returned to Persia via the Cape and India. After a subsequent mission for 'Abbas to Spain in 1617, Robert and his family again returned to England for several years before Robert was denounced by a visiting Persian nobleman and sent back to Qazvin by Charles I. Dying shortly after arrival, Robert left his family destitute. Anthony too ended up ingloriously, living out his last years in Madrid, but not before leaving behind a popular reputation and something of a literary legacy that—in Britain at least—would prove more enduring than his failures as a diplomat.[73]

Before the Shirley brothers came onto the scene, the earliest Anglo-Safavid encounters had focused on trade rather than international diplomacy, and were typically inadvertent. During the mid sixteenth century, English merchants made various attempts to discover a north-east route that would enable them to capture the fabled wealth of Cathay. An expedition in 1553 failed to reach China, but did discover a viable sea passage that would enable direct trade with Russia. Two years later, the Muscovy Company was formally established with the twin goals of using that route to formalize the Russian trade while also investigating possible routes further east into Persia and Central Asia. The 1555 expedition fell foul of the weather and both of the English captains died at sea, but in 1557 the Muscovy Company tried again, this time sending the ships under the command of Anthony Jenkinson.[74]

By 1572, Jenkinson had made four expeditions on behalf of the Muscovy Company, including the first English embassy to Safavid Persia. Although

Figure 4. Shah 'Abbas, from Thomas Herbert, *A Relation of some Yeares Travaile* (1634)
From the James Ford Bell Library, University of Minnesota, Minneapolis, Minnesota

he facilitated commerce with Russia, Jenkinson had less success opening up trade with Persia and Central Asia.[75] His meeting with Shah Tahmasp (r. 1524–76) at Qazvin in 1562 could not have come at a worse moment. Tahmasp was entertaining an ambassador from Sultan Süleyman with whom he had just reached an agreement aimed at ending territorial disputes between the rival Muslim empires. Since English merchants hoped to avoid paying customs duties to the Ottomans by trading directly with the Persians, any overtures to an English envoy would jeopardize the peace. When finally granted an audience, Jenkinson reports that the shah quizzed him about religion before dismissing him abruptly, declaring: 'Oh thou unbeleever sayd he, we have no neede to have friendship with the unbelievers.' Tahmasp was known to be devout, but Jenkinson thought the pious rhetoric merely a ruse resulting from the Shah's fears that 'if hee did otherwise, and that the news thereof should come to the knowledge of the Turke, it should be a mean to break their new league and friendship'.[76] When it was expedient to do so, religious differences between Shi'ite Safavid and Sunni Ottoman could be put aside to exclude the infidel English.

Anglo-Safavid relations continued to be erratic throughout the reigns of Elizabeth and James, and involved a number of irregular and even self-appointed 'ambassadors'. Unlike Morocco and the Ottoman Empire, with their control over the Mediterranean littoral, the Safavid Empire held little strategic interest for Britons beyond trade, with the result that even diplomatic initiatives tended to be overwhelmed by commercial concerns. Although the overland trade route to Persia via Russia and the Caspian proved impractical and was more or less abandoned by 1581, projects to establish alternative overland routes to Persia and further east were eagerly pursued for the next few years.[77] In June of 1581, John Newberry arrived in Hormuz at the mouth of the Persian Gulf having travelled from Aleppo, along the Euphrates to Fallujah, then from Baghdad to Basra, and finally down the Gulf.[78] Newberry was the first English traveller to use this, the 'Great Caravan Desert Route', which, already known to the Venetians and Portuguese, would later become popular with many East India Company officials on their way to and from India.[79]

At the time of Newberry's arrival, Hormuz was jealously controlled by the Portuguese, who used their fort on the island to dominate all sea-borne trade between Europe, the Persian interior, and the Indian Ocean. 'In this city', reported a Venetian merchant of the time, 'there is very great trade for all sorts of spices, drugges, silke, cloth of silke, brocardo, and divers other sorts of marchandise come out of Persia: and amongst all other trades of merchandise, the trade of Horses is very great there, which they carry from thence into the Indies.'[80] After a stay lasting six weeks, during which time he was welcomed by the Portuguese governor but aroused the suspicions of a resident Venetian merchant, Newberry left Hormuz and travelled home overland through Persia, Armenia, and Anatolia. Back in London, Newberry was commissioned to return with a group of merchants belonging to the newly formed Turkey Company. The scheme involved leaving two merchants in Baghdad, two more in Basra, while Newberry, armed with letters from Queen Elizabeth to the Mughal emperor Akbar (r. 1556–1605) and the king of China, was to travel further east accompanied by Ralph Fitch.

This expedition, which set sail from London on 13 February 1583, was evidently well publicized at the time. Richard Hakluyt clearly knew of it since he asked Newberry to bring back a copy of Abu'l-Fida's famed *Geography*.[81] The news had also reached William Shakespeare, who alluded to the journey portentously in *Macbeth* when the First Witch curses the parsimonious sailor's wife whose 'husband's to Aleppo gone, master o' the Tiger'.[82] As it happened, storms did delay the *Tiger*'s departure, but the ship arrived safely at Syrian Tripoli by the end of April. Despite numerous setbacks, Newberry and Fitch eventually reached Agra where they met with Shah Akbar, though Fitch's account is rather evasive on the matter.[83] From Agra, Fitch continued east to Bengal, Burma, and the Moluccas, not returning to England until April 1591. Intent on reporting back to the Company officers who had sponsored the journey, Newberry headed west, intending 'to goe for Persia, and then for Aleppo or Constantinople', but disappeared under unknown circumstances.[84]

In January 1592, less than a year after Fitch arrived back in London, the Levant merchants secured a new charter that allowed their Company a unilateral claim to monopoly rights over trade 'by land, through the countries of the said grand signior into and from the East India lately discovered' by John Newberry and Ralph Fitch.[85] It was a rather grandiose gesture, since for all practical purposes, 'the English attempt to establish an overland trade route to the Persian Gulf' had been no more successful 'than had the route via the north-east passage and overland across Russia'.[86] But the very pretensions of the claim, duly approved by Lord Burghley on behalf of the English Crown, signalled just how important the Company officers were beginning to consider themselves to be, and how far they could rely on state support, even if only on paper. In the event, it would be more than two decades before there was any further attempt by any English merchants to enter into direct trade with Persia, and then it would on behalf of the East India Company.

English interest in establishing direct trade with Persia was all about raw silk. Producing finished cloth from raw silk had become a major industry during the early decades of the seventeenth century. Looking back from the 1630s, Thomas Munn observed 'a notable increase in our manufacture of winding and twisting only of forraign raw silk which within 35 years to my knowledge, did not employ more than 300 people in the city and suburbs of London, where at this present time it doth set on work above fourteen thousand souls'.[87] One of the great Levant Company merchants, Munn was doubtless prone to exaggeration, but his claim is supported by the sheer and steady increase in the quantities of raw silk brought into England during the years in question. Contemporary records show that imports of raw silk rose from about 12,000 pounds in 1560 to about 120,000 pounds in 1621, and then to 172,000 pounds in 1630, 200,000 pounds in 1634, and over 220,000 pounds in 1640.[88] Much of the profit made from this vast importation of raw silk came from the resale of finished Persian silk to western and central European countries with emerging silk industries of their own. And those profits could be increased if the raw silk could be imported directly from Persian ports, and if it could be exchanged for English wools rather than cash.

While the appeal of direct trade with Persia was obvious to some, to the officers and merchants of the Levant Company, it was clearly a bad idea that, if put into practice, would anger the Ottomans and thereby endanger English shipping in the Mediterranean. During his 1611 embassy to King James, Robert Shirley, on behalf of Shah 'Abbas, proposed establishing direct trade in Persian raw silk at cheaper rates, provided the English merchants were prepared to take the entire annual stock and pay cash for half of it. The Levant Company 'threw all its influence against the project and successfully scotched it'.[89] In 1615, however, the threat to the Levant merchants returned in the form of Richard Steel and John Crowther, agents of the East India Company, who arrived from Surat seeking to unload excess stocks of English broadcloth in exchange for Persian silk, plying their trade in ports along the Persian Gulf. Encouraged by Robert Shirley, Shah 'Abbas granted them permission. Within a year, English broadcloth was being shipped back from Surat to Jask in exchange for silk and, in short order, the East India Company had established additional factories in Shiraz, Isfahan, and Kerman.[90] Anglo-Safavid relations were further bolstered when, in 1622, the East India Company's fleet aided 'Abbas in his designs to take Hormuz from the Portuguese: in exchange, the English were permitted to settle at Gombroon (Bandar Abbas), and to trade from there without paying customs.[91]

The Anglo-Persian silk trade encouraged political diplomacy and ambassadorial activities that, as so often, subordinated religious differences to commercial and strategic goals. With the Portuguese out of the way and a new commercial link with the English firmly in place, Shah 'Abbas continued to press his case for a political alliance with European states against the Ottomans by offering a monopoly on the raw silk exported from Persian ports. Hoping to enlist the support of Spain in this regard, Robert Shirley had arrived in Madrid back in 1618 and stayed on for several years without success, before turning up once more in England in 1624. The East India Company officers in London were by no means favourably impressed by his proposals: they were well aware he had already made his offer to the Spanish, and there was considerable reluctance to invest in the whole of the raw silk coming out of Persia, since that would involve an enormous capital outlay. There were also doubts about whether Shirley was sufficiently authorized to make a binding contract. They were right. Shah 'Abbas had, it seemed, given up on his English-born emissary and dispatched another ambassador, Naqd 'Ali Beg, who reached London in February 1626.

The officers of the East India Company went out of their way to receive him with greater honour than Shirley, arranging for him to be brought to London in the king's coach. Realizing that a regrettable diplomatic incident was in the making that he wished to prevent, Sir John Finett, the king's master of ceremonies, arranged for Shirley to call on Naqd 'Ali Beg on the morning before the Persian was to be received by Charles at Whitehall. Finett left the following account of that meeting:

> Entring the Hall, (where he [Naqd 'Ali Beg] then was sitting in a chair on his legs double under him, after the Persian Posture) and affording no motion of respect to any of us, Sir *Robert Sherley* gave him a salutation, and sate downe on a stoole neer him, while my Lord of *Cleaveland* by an Interpreter signified, in three words, the cause of the ambassador *Sherleys* and his and our comming to him, but with little returne of regard from him, till I informing the Interpreter

(of the new Ambassador) what my Lords quality was, he let fall his Trust-up-leggs from his chaire, and made a kinde of respect to his Lordship. This done, Sir *Robert Sherley*, unfoulding his Letters, and (as the Persian use is in reverence to their King) first touching his eyes with them, next holding them over his head, and after kissing them, he presented them to the Ambassador, that he receiving them, might performe the like observance, when he suddenly rising out of his chaire, stept to Sir Robert Sherley, snatcht his Letters from him, toare them, and gave him a blow on the face with his Fist.[92]

The Persian ambassador did little to ingratiate himself with the English. While in London, Naqd 'Ali began an affair with a 'lewde strumpet' whom he tried to take back with him to Persia. Opposing this plan, London merchants determined to prosecute the 'Persians wench'. Amidst such goings on, Charles I found himself uncertain how to proceed, so he sent both Naqd 'Ali and Robert Shirley back to Persia in the company of his own ambassador, Sir Dodmore Cotton.[93] All three ambassadors missed the fleet with which they were supposed to sail, and did not leave London until March 1627, arriving on the west coast of India toward the end of November. Thomas Herbert, who accompanied the party, left a detailed account of the events of 29 November in the 1638 reprinted edition of his popular *Some Yeares Travels into Africa and Asia the Great*:

> The same day we came to an Anchor in *Swalley* roade, *Nogdi-Ally-beg* the Persian Ambassdor (Sir *Robert Sherley's* Antagonist) dyed; having desperately posioned himselfe; for 4 dayes, eating only Ophium: the *Mary* (where he dyed) gave him eleven great Ordnance, whose thundring Ecchoes solemniz'd his carrying ashoare: his sonne *Ebrahim-chan* got him conveighed to *Surrat* (10 miles thence) where they intombed him, not a stones cast from *Tom Coryat's* grave, knowne but by two poore stones, there resting till the resurrection.[94]

According to Herbert, the first Persian ambassador to England was so afraid of what would happen to him when he reported his failure to secure King Charles's support against the Ottomans, that suicide was the only option. 'Doubtlesse, *Nogdibeg*,' Herbert continued, 'had a guilty conscience, hee had very basely misbehav'd himselfe in England, and feared the extreame rigour of *Abbas* a just (but too severe) Master.' Not content to leave it there, Herbert elaborated on the punishment that Naqd 'Ali feared he would have received had he returned to Persia:

> *Nogdibeg*, (as we heard the King protest) if he had not prevented it, should first have been hackt in peeces, and then in the open market place burnt with dogs

turds, a perfume not fetcht from *Arabia*, a staine indeleble, branding with shame all his posterity. Returne we to the roade againe.[95]

A few weeks later, Cotton and the English party arrived at Gombroon, and duly set out overland in pursuit of a meeting with Shah 'Abbas, finally catching up with him in May at his summer house near the Caspian. After an initially cordial reception at Ashraf, however, Cotton and Shirley were ignored, most likely—according to Herbert—because of the hostility of the shah's favourite, one Muhammad 'Ali Beg. Cotton was not, however, sent away, but instructed to follow 'Abbas to Qazvin. Here, Muhammad 'Ali reported to Cotton that Shah 'Abbas had formally dismissed Robert Shirley from service for being old and troublesome. In shock, Shirley died on 13 July 1628: Dodmore Cotton died ten days later, most likely from dysentery.[96] And so with these three deaths, while the officers of the East India Company maintained vigorous interest in the region, formal Anglo-Safavid diplomatic relations entered a lull that would last until 1808, when Sir Harford Jones would be dispatched ambassador to the Qajar Shah Fat'h Ali (r. 1797–1834).[97]

Commerce before dominion: Jacobean-Mughal relations

That a contemporary traveller should have noticed how the first Persian ambassador to England happened to be buried next to the grave of Thomas Coryate, the first English tourist to reach India, suggests just how difficult it is to separate Anglo-Persian from Anglo-Indian relations in this period. It was a time of historical firsts.

Back in 1591, John Newberry and Ralph Fitch, having failed to explore commercial possibilities in Persia, travelled on to India and arrived in Agra with letters from Elizabeth addressed to the Mughal Shah Akbar (r. 1556-1605). The next Englishman to reach India overland, John Mildenhall, arrived at the imperial court in Agra some time in 1603, seeking trading concessions similar to those enjoyed by the Portuguese. According to his own account, he obtained written assurances from both Akbar and his heir—the future Shah Jahangir (r. 1605–27)—that his requests would all be met. Since he makes no mention of Akbar's death in October 1605, it is generally presumed that he set out on his return before then, but he had not arrived in England by June 1608, when letters he had sent ahead outlining the privileges he had obtained were read out before the officers of the East India Company. No one seemed very interested in Mildenhall's proposals, particularly since in 1607, the East India Company had already sent William Hawkins on the so-called 'third' voyage with formal letters from King James to the newly installed Mughal emperor, Jahangir. After various further endeavours—including an attempt to reach Persia via the Black Sea from Istanbul—Mildenhall returned to India where he died in 1614.[98]

From this point on, the story of diplomatic relations between England and the Mughal Empire is the story of the East India Company, a story that has been told and re-told many times. It is, in essence, the story of the origins of the British Empire, and a very complicated story it is too. As we have seen, a number of commercially minded English adventurers had travelled overland to India and been received at court. William Hawkins, however, may be named as the first Englishman to captain an English ship into an Indian port, and the first to become a resident envoy at the court of the Mughal emperor. Thomas Roe, who would study Hawkins' journal of his two-year residence in Agra before taking up his own post as the first royal ambassador in 1615, noted: 'For Hawkins I find him a vain fool.'[99] And so he may have been, but if so, his vanity was not without some justification. In August 1608, Hawkins brought the *Hector* to anchor off the mouth of the river Tapti, and set off for Surat, where he was well received by the governor, but informed that permanent trade would require the consent of the Emperor. In accordance with Company orders, he sent the *Hector* on to Bantam before travelling to Agra to negotiate on behalf of the English merchants. Arriving at the imperial court in April 1609, Hawkins immediately found favour with Jahangir, in no small part because he spoke Turkish. Honoured by Jahangir, who made him captain of a cavalry troop, Hawkins married a wealthy Armenian woman and spent the next two years living and intriguing at the Mughal court. Despite Jahangir's personal favour, however, Hawkins was constantly frustrated in his efforts to achieve trading privileges. The emperor himself was actively uninterested in commerce, so Hawkins faced the combined opposition of the Jesuits, the Portuguese, and Mukarrab Khan, the powerful minister in charge of trade in the Gujarat ports. When an English fleet commanded by Sir Henry Middleton arrived off Surat in September 1611, Hawkins applied for permission for them to trade, but was met with repeated equivocations that caused him to quit the court in November. Taking his wife with him, he joined

Figure 5. Muhammad Sadiqi Bichitr, *Jahangir Preferring a Sufi Shaikh to Kings*, from the St Petersburg album. Mughal dynasty, reign of Emperor Jahangir (1615–18). Freer Gallery of Art, Smithsonian Institution, Washington, DC: Purchase, F1942.15a

Middleton's voyage east to Bantam. He died on the return voyage just before reaching England.[100]

If Hawkins was the first resident envoy to the Mughal court, Middleton has the dubious honour of being the first English captain to use military force in pursuit of English trade in the region. Before reaching India, Middleton had put in at the Red Sea port of Mocha where he and several other Englishmen were seized and thrown into prison. Escaping after six months, he proceeded to Surat where, as we have already seen, his arrival in September 1611 led to a protracted series of delays while Mukarrab Khan equivocated over granting permission to trade. By February 1612, however, Middleton received orders to leave, which he did, but not without formulating plans to get his own back for the months of wasted time and the way he had been treated. Since weather conditions were unfavourable for sailing south and east to Bantam, Middleton returned to the Red Sea to seek revenge. Seizing all the Indian ships he met with, Middleton imposed a forced levy on all ships registered to Gujarat ports. Once the winds had changed, he set off in August for Sumatra, arriving in Bantam just before Christmas.[101]

Back in September 1612, shortly after Middleton left the Red Sea, Thomas Best arrived off the Gujarat coast armed with a formal letter from King James to Jahangir on behalf of the East India Company requesting permission to establish trade. Best and the English factors in Surat soon learned that Middleton's Red Sea revenge had been to their advantage. Rather than seeking reprisals, Mukarrab Khan and the Gujarati merchants realized how defenceless their own ships were and, in October, offered the English factors the right to trade at Surat in exchange for protection. While waiting for the *firman* confirming the agreement—it arrived in January 1613 but was never followed up with a formal treaty between James and Jahangir[102]—Best learned that the furious Portuguese had sent four warships from Goa to seize his two merchant vessels. During several skirmishes over the course of December, the English gunners defeated the Portuguese fleet. 'Thus,' Best noted in his journal, 'we partted from thes valient champians, that had vowed to do such famous accts, butt yett [were] content [to] give us over, with greatt shame and infamy redounding unto themselves.'[103] And so Best became the first English captain to win a naval action against a foreign fleet in the service of trade in the Indian Ocean.

Meanwhile, in September 1613, the Portuguese Viceroy in Goa, Jeronimo de Azevedo, thought to imitate Middleton by intimidating the Indians into expelling the English. His cunning plan was to seize the *Rahimi*, a Surat ship returning from the Red Sea, 'wherein was three millions of treasure'.[104] Unfortunately for the Portuguese, a great deal of the cargo on this ship happened to be owned by Jahangir's mother; on board were pilgrims returning from Mecca. Under such conditions, de Azevedo's plan was destined to backfire. In a rage, Jahangir shut down the Jesuit chapel, expelled the Portuguese from his lands and ordered Mukarrab Khan to raise an army and seize a Portuguese settlement. De Azevedo, in turn, prepared a fleet to attack Surat. Amidst protracted military arrangements, trade fell off: the native merchants in Surat could no longer sell to the Portuguese, and the resident English factors found that they had overestimated the quantity of broadcloth that the Indian market could take: as we saw, it would soon be shipped back to the Red Sea for sale in Persia. In October 1614, Nicholas Downton arrived from England with a fleet of four merchantmen and anchored in Swally Roads, the estuary leading into the port of Surat. In January 1615 the Portuguese fleet finally set sail from Goa, only to find that it was incapable of dislodging Downton's ships from their secure anchorage and was forced to retire. As a result of these activities, prices had fallen so far that Downton was able to fill one of his ships, aptly named the *Hope*, with a valuable cargo of indigo and calicoes for shipment to England. Thus the *Hope* became 'the first ship to reach England direct from an Indian port'.[105]

In India, diplomacy followed trade; though the English made it clear that they were prepared to promote their commercial interests by force if necessary. Sir Thomas Roe became the first formally appointed English diplomat to arrive at the Mughal court. Bearing formal letters from King James appointing him 'ambassadour to the Great Maghoore', Roe was entrusted with full 'commission to make and contract a league between His Majesty and his subjects for commerce and traffique in his dominions, and to procure and establish a factory for our nation in sundry parts'.[106] On his arrival in 1615, all the major conditions of subsequent Anglo-Indian relations were in place: English ships had reached Indian ports, successfully taken up arms against Portuguese attempts to blockade them, and returned with profitable cargoes. English emissaries had been welcomed at the Mughal court and learned that compliance with local customs stood some chance of success, provided it was backed up with a firm willingness to use armed force. In preparation for his embassy, Roe had studied the reports of Hawkins and others who had preceded him, and arrived fully confident that he understood how he ought to behave. Within days of arrival, he observed that an imperious manner was essential for success: 'I best knew that see yt, these men triumphe over such as yeeld, and are humble enough when they are held up.'[107] But recent events were against him. Hostilities between the Mughals and Portuguese had ended, but there was a strong faction at court keen to expel the English, headed by Jahangir's son, Prince Khurram, who had recently been appointed governor of Surat.[108] Nonetheless, and despite ill health, Roe set off for Ajmer, where Jahangir had established his court. On 22 December Roe was received outside the city by a reception committee that included 'the famous unwearied walker' Thomas Coryate who, Roe noted, 'on foote had passed most of Europe and Asya, and was now arrived in India, beeing but the beginning of his purposed travells'.[109] For his own part, Roe admitted that he had suffered ill health since arriving in India and had grown so thin that he was 'scarce a crowes dinner'.[110]

For the next fourteen months, Roe's health seldom improved as he dutifully waited on Jahangir seeking to establish a permanent English trading base in India. Jahangir continued to take delight in the company of Englishmen, but remained actively indifferent to dealing with commercial matters, leaving such things to ministers with their own personal agendas. As Roe's recent biographer puts it: 'Roe was repeatedly led to believe that his demands were on the point of signature when in fact there was never any intention of this happening.'[111] Throughout 1617, Roe followed the imperial court as Jahangir travelled to quell local uprisings, but by 1618 had clearly given up hope of achieving a formal permanent treaty. In August he announced his imminent return to England and received a letter from Jahangir to James promising

> to all the English marchants in all my dominions there been given freedome and residence; and I have confirmed by my woord that no subject of my kyngdomes shall bee so bould to doe any injurie or molestation to the sayd English, and that their goods and merchandise they may sell or traficque with according to their owne content... and that all their ships may come and goe to my ports wheresoever they choose at their owne will.[112]

These assurances were personal and contingent at best. Such a document lacked the status of a permanent treaty between the two states. However, if Roe failed to secure English trade in India, his descriptions of life at the Mughal court, published by Purchas in 1625, were among the earliest and most important documents to recast popular imaginings about the Mughal Empire in England. Like the reports composed by his chaplain, Edward

Terry, also published by Purchas, Roe's descriptive accounts were written with strong convictions of the superiority of English life and manners, but were nevertheless instrumental in shifting knowledge of India from the fabulous tales of Mandeville to accounts that at least were based on observed experience. Roe himself wanted to write a separate history of Mughal India, but recognized there was little point. He realized English audiences were not yet ready for accurate accounts of Mughal splendour and civility 'because the people are esteemed barbarous'.[113]

At about the same time that Roe returned to England, the East India Company entered a period of 'contraction and difficulty that was to last into the 1660s'.[114] So it is perhaps not so surprising that the reports Roe did leave behind, in which he documents his frustrations at being welcomed by Jahangir but not taken seriously by his ministers, should remind us of how Britain remained relatively insignificant to the Mughals until much later in the century. Once Charles II inherited factories in Bombay and Goa following his marriage to Catherine of Braganza, Britain would no longer be a remote power that could easily be ignored. The stage, to borrow one of Roe's favourite metaphors, would then be set for the violence and outrage that would distinguish British behaviour in the Indian sub-continent.

By way of conclusion

England's earliest relations with Islamic countries were in many ways the result of competition with the imperial might of Catholic Spain, both to the West across the Atlantic and in the East throughout the Mediterranean. After 1492, the year in which Ferdinand and Isabella expelled the Jews and Columbus first sailed to the West Indies, Spain emerged as the foremost Christian imperial power. English ships, consequently, took provision in Muslim ports along the North African coast. During the 1580s, increasing direct trade into the Mediterranean brought increasing contact and exchange between the English and the Muslim merchants and the Ottoman sultan in Istanbul, as well as rulers of Morocco, Algiers, Tunis, Libyan Tripoli, and the many islands, ports, and harbours under Ottoman control.

When Pope Pius V excommunicated Queen Elizabeth in 1570, it is most unlikely that anyone in Rome recognized that it left the Protestant queen free to pursue alliances with powerful Muslim rulers—just like other Catholic monarchs, especially from France, were pursuing. Having inherited the crown of a realm that was mightily in debt and fragmented by religious and regional differences, Elizabeth and her loyal ministers recognized that both problems could best be addressed by a strategic foreign policy. They also recognized that having amicable relations with the Islamic Mediterranean, both in the Maghrib and the Mashriq, allowed them avenues of trade and cooperation that Spain could not have. After all, the goal of Columbus's Spanish-funded venture across the Atlantic, as well as of the later Portuguese venture around the Cape of Good Hope, was to reach India and the wealth therein. Unable to sail into the eastern Mediterranean, the Iberians had to cross oceans. And so, Elizabeth and her English merchants, sailors, and investors seized the advantage of being able to reach the Ottoman, Safavid, and Mughal empires both by land and by sea, and established their commercial presence. Although the East India Company began sailing around the Cape of Good Hope after 1600, English traders continued to have the advantage of being able to buy and sell in Islamic regions that the Iberians would have found too dangerous to explore.

James I dutifully signed formal letters to promote trade into Islamic markets but, unlike Elizabeth, refused to engage in personal correspondence with Muslim heads of state. Although the circumstances of his seeming interest in Prince Bogdan remain unclear, James appears to have been committed to Protestant ascendancy rather than any other agenda, despite his avowedly pacific policy towards Spain. After ineffectual efforts to engage the Mughals, James did formally appoint Roe as an envoy to the Mughal court, but this mission, far from constituting the triumphant originary moment of British imperium, as it has sometimes been portrayed, was largely a failure.

Elizabeth's legacy—a critical mass of energetic statesmen and merchants at home who looked East, and well-established English factors abroad—meant that English investments in the Islamic world continued to grow and prosper in the absence of direct intervention by the Crown. Elizabeth had, as it were, prepared a highly successful exit strategy that left future negotiations in the hands of the merchant elites and their envoys.

3

British Factors, Governors, and Diplomats

Elizabeth's reign witnessed the beginning of chartered company trade with Morocco and the Levant; under James, trade expanded into Persia and India. London merchants concentrated on the nearer ports in the Mediterranean, with Izmir and Istanbul serving as major hubs. Further afield, fortified factories were being settled on the western coast of India; by 1639, the English had built their first fortified settlement in Madras. After the Restoration of Charles II in 1660, commerce expanded once again into the Atlantic and Indian Oceans, with the accelerated building of forts and the installation of East India Company presidents and councils; by 1700, there were ten English outposts in Guinea and twenty-three between Persia and China.[1] Britons imported cotton, silk, leather and hides, sugar, currants, saltpetre, wax, and drugs; in return, they exported finished products such as woollens, caps, paper, navigational supplies, munitions, and weapons; they also sent consumer goods, children's toys, kitchen utensils, even royal carriages to rulers in Morocco, Persia, and India. Although the English did not formally trade in slaves in the Mediterranean—notwithstanding a good number of Muslim captives in their possession in Tangier—they did not hesitate from owning slaves who were often bought or seized from the Portuguese, or from incursions into West Africa, or in the open Mediterranean market of Muslim men and women.[2]

To regulate trade, attempts were made to post resident factors, consuls, or ambassadors, whose tasks included facilitating business, protecting British merchants and cargoes from harassment, and ensuring lower tariffs and cordial treatment.[3] Such endeavours were fraught with difficulties and varied widely in nature, scope, and success. Between 1585 and 1597, the short-lived Barbary Company failed to control trade with Morocco, yet these were the very years when the Levant Company was successfully regulating transactions through its resident representatives in Istanbul, Aleppo, and later Izmir. By the end of the sixteenth century, there was a network of Britons resident in major port cities stretching from Algiers and Malta, to Genoa and Istanbul. In 1608, the Surat factory was started and by 1614, there were thirty-five factors living there, in Agra, 'and other places adjoining'.[4] By the end of the century, consuls were being regularly posted to Algiers, Tunis, and Libyan Tripoli, while commercial settlements in Bombay, Madras, and Bengal were being fortified and garrisoned with armed soldiers. Whatever the local conditions and circumstances, increasing numbers of Britons moved to Islamic countries in pursuit of profitable trade and maritime services, regularly finding that they had to fight their way against opposition from Dutch, Portuguese, and even Danish shipping in the Indian Ocean, and French competition in the Mediterranean. Across the three regions of the Islamic world, the earliest consuls and factors encountered widely different circumstances and challenges.

Figure 6. A panoramic view of the port of Libyan Tripoli, from John Ogilby, *Africa* (1670)
From the James Ford Bell Library, University of Minnesota, Minneapolis, Minnesota

Business and diplomacy: factors and interlopers, consuls and ambassadors

The first Britons to settle in the Islamic world were merchants or factors who travelled into the Mediterranean.[5] These men were by no means the imperious Britons of the nineteenth century, but rather, as Daniel Goffman puts it, 'marginal men, even cultural hybrids who prospered by learning to live with, rather than by trying to recast, the civilization with which they had to treat'.[6] They ventured on their own, some to buy and sell, others to become active in piracy and pillage, others—especially the dozen or so resident in Aleppo—to serve as intermediaries between traders from Central Asia and Western Europe. All of them were trying to turn a profit for themselves or their companies. In 1583, a medley of English factors, sailors, and mercenaries were already living in 'a house to themselves' in Libyan Tripoli[7]; while others were living in Algiers, Tunis, Ma'moura, Salé, Agadir, and elsewhere along the North African Mediterranean and the Atlantic coast of Morocco.[8] In the eastern Mediterranean and the Aegean, factors, consuls, and ambassadors settled in Alexandria, Jaffa, Acre, Sidon, Beirut, Syrian Tripoli, Iskenderun, Aleppo, Izmir, Istanbul, and Patras as well as numerous islands including Chios and Zante.[9] 'English house' is a term that appears frequently in the correspondence from Algiers to Basra, to Surat and Bengal, signifying the residence of factors as well as their operational base, a depot, where they stored, weighed, and packed trade goods.

Realizing the fortunes to be made from trading in foreign markets, London merchants established limited companies that were protected by royal charters. These charters ensured, in theory at least, that company members held monopoly rights over trade in certain areas while at the same time enjoying royal protection and approbation. The task of resident consuls, ambassadors, and factors was to ensure those rights and privileges were upheld, and to prevent interlopers. From the start, however, their responsibilities also included political intervention. During the 1570s and 1580s, William Harborne in Istanbul constantly entreated Sultan Murad III for naval support against the Spanish fleet.[10] Pleading that the Protestant religion was closer to Islam than the idol-worshipping Church of Rome, the earliest English ambassadors were often able to take a lead in religious and political disputes involving Christian communities under Ottoman control.

One of Edward Barton's first achievements on becoming ambassador to the Ottoman Empire in 1588 was to help restore Protestantism to Moldavia, where a Jesuit takeover had occurred. Barton also took part in the behind-the-scenes negotiations that led to the appointment of the Orthodox Patriarch in Istanbul. In 1595 he scandalized other European representatives by joining Sultan Murad's military expedition into Hungary.[11] Sir Thomas Glover, as we have already seen, also actively intervened in Moldavian politics. In the 1620s, Sir Thomas Roe kept up these activities, meddling in the ecclesiastical affairs of the Orthodox patriarchy in hopes of thwarting Jesuit attempts to install a pro-Catholic church leader.[12] Sir John Finch would later devote much of his energies to trying to upstage the French ambassador and the Venetian *bailo* while serving as ambassador at the Ottoman Porte in the mid 1670s.[13]

Among British agents, the first ambassadors in Istanbul were the most powerful and knew most about what was going on in their region. From Istanbul, they were not only able to scrutinize the affairs of the imperial metropolis, but were also able to keep an eye on activities throughout the empire's reach and beyond. By the time Roe settled in Istanbul in the 1620s, he was corresponding with factors in Isfahan and Surat, as well as fleet admirals and captains in the Mediterranean and the Persian Gulf, giving advice about negotiations with local rulers, the export and import of commodities, and the movements of rival European traders, and suggesting safe travel routes. His international reach stretched across three continents. And like Harborne before him, he offered advice to the monarch in London: noticing how important Algiers and Tunis had become for trade, and that earlier appointments had not been maintained, he importuned King James to appoint consuls to these ports.[14] As if to confirm Roe's insight, an anonymous correspondent residing in Algiers in 1622 compiled a list of reasons why it would be useful to have a 'Consull' there, foremost of which was 'To hinder the reprisal of ships, and makinge our menn slave'. A consul would also help prevent the defection of Britons to Islam and their joining the Barbary Corsairs: 'To hinder the retreat of Piratts, who would Leave their Kings service and betake themselves to robbing every bodye.' The consul would help ensure a welcoming harbour for 'ships to retire to in the strayghts, where they may be secured, furnisht and refresht'. And, most importantly, the consul would facilitate trade: his presence would be conducive 'for the benefit of trafficke'.[15]

The earliest consuls to Chios were Italians, while the earliest consuls to Crete were invariably natives of that island, suggesting that in the early stages of direct trade in the Mediterranean, consuls were appointed for pragmatic reasons—knowledge of local customs and languages, familiarity with the trading community—rather than place of birth.[16] Generally, factors and consuls ranged from greedy traders to career diplomats, from culturally savvy men to uncouth, corrupt, and incompetent scoundrels: 'arrant theeves against the Company as any theeves in Newgate', observed one East India Company correspondent in 1654.[17] Some worked closely with their fellow expatriates, some became petty tyrants, while others caused scandals by acting riotously and indecently, 'entering into houses of strangers and women, to the disturbance and disorder of our nation', complained a group of merchants in Surat in February 1617.[18] The East India Company records are full of references to the disciplining of factors, sometimes by the president and council in situ, sometimes by shipping the miscreants back to England in chains. Not all consuls were good at their jobs. Admiral Arthur Herbert in 1682 suspected that 'twice, if not thrice', wars had been fought because of the incompetence of a consul.[19]

Not all consuls lived in the cities they represented, and not all such postings were replaced when they became vacant. In March 1585, after Harborne had appointed John Tipton 'Consul of the English in Algier, Tunis, & Tripolis of Barbarie', the latter moved to Istanbul in 1591 and, after he was murdered at sea in 1595 or 1596, the post remained vacant until 1656.[20] Algiers provides a good test case for further anomalies, such as the fact there was not always clear proof that a Briton claiming to be a consul had any authority other than his own claim. In 1600, for instance, the Bey of Algiers complained to Queen Elizabeth that one John Audellay, 'who says he is your Majesty's Consul here' attacked a Venetian vessel, claimed it was Spanish, and then set fire to it 'when we Muslims were in the mosques at prayer...at midday with a great danger of setting fire to our Galleys... causing much scandal & indignation among the people of this city at the sight of such a criminal deed'.[21] Such embarrassing situations also occurred in other parts of the Islamic world, and even ambassadors were sometimes suspected of bearing invalid documents; such in 1654 was the case of Henry Bard in Persia.[22] In Morocco, where trade in gold, saltpetre, and sugar was both crucial and lucrative, surprisingly no consuls were appointed, but until the 1630s, John Harrison spent a quarter of a century representing British interests there—and left behind the first, and vast, archive about Morocco in English.

One of the many public relations tasks of such men was to ensure the exchange of royal portraits. In 1588, Englishmen in Marrakesh joined Moroccans to celebrate victory over the Spanish Armada by running down the streets with a portrait of their queen.[23] The scanty surviving evidence about how different cultures viewed different artistic expressions shows that English and European paintings were so admired that in Agra, Roe could not distinguish between the original he had given of King James I and the many copies made of it by local artists.[24] In India, where there was a very limited market for woollens, the sale of English paintings of battle and nature scenes proved lucrative.[25] As a result of these and other European paintings and painters, especially Portuguese Jesuits, Mughal miniatures started depicting Euro-Christian themes such as the Crucifixion and martyrdom, in a manner that is inimitable in the early modern English experience of Islamic civilizations.

Alongside the large number of ships' captains who informally reported to them, resident factors, consuls, and ambassadors were the best informed Britons about the Islamic regions they inhabited. Yet the consuls and factors serving in North Africa were different from those in the other two regions in one important regard: unlike their opposite numbers in Anatolia, the eastern Mediterranean, and India, they came under far less scrutiny from the central administration in London. Although they reported to the Secretary of State, there was no powerful company advising them on strategies, monitoring their activities and finances, or coordinating their policies. Consuls in Anatolia and India were appointed and paid by chartered companies that kept close watch over their expenditures: the letters from the factories in India clearly show how much both the company directors in London, as well as the monarch, determined legal, commercial, and punitive decisions. Such control was not practised in the Maghrib, even during the brief history of the Barbary Company, since its anomalous charter 'did not endow the Company with the usual machinery for its own government'.[26] In Algiers and Tunis, where London's authority held little influence, factors and consuls operated on their own initiative, interacting with the local populations quite differently from their counterparts elsewhere in the Islamic world, where there was massive financial commitment, royal investment in political and commercial alliances, and in India, wide-ranging naval presence. In 1629, for example, the English factors in Algiers lived unarmed in a house that was protected only by janissaries they hired and by the goodwill of the ruler; that same year in Bantam, the English maintained a fortified base: '12 pieces of ordinance mounted in and aboute the house; 23 factors and souldiers remaining there'.[27] Living conditions in Islamic lands differed according to region and the degree of British financial and military investment.

Other differences distinguish the Anglo-Islamic encounters of North Africa from those of the Ottoman Levant, or the Persian-Indian regions. The North African region was less plentiful in natural resources, precious metals, and hard currency. Although Morocco became rich in gold after the 1591 conquest of the Niger region, its industrial and agricultural productivity, like that of its neighbours, was negligible. The North African ports offered services for British ships sailing across to the Levant, and some trade, but they did not supply the massive amount of cotton, spices, silk, or luxury items found in Agra, Isfahan, and Izmir. This limitation may help explain why the Barbary Company died out, unlike the other companies. Further, North Africa was highly militarized, with naval forces that became enormously powerful between the end of the sixteenth and the second half of the seventeenth century. The regencies received constant assistance from the Ottoman admiralty, while the Moroccan ruler Zaidan ibn Ahmad al-Mansur (r. 1603–27) bought ships from the Netherlands to strengthen his fleet. Between 1609 and 1614, the arrival of hundreds of thousands of Moriscos—Christianized Muslims from Iberia—many of them trained on Spanish ships, boosted naval expertise from Agadir to Libyan Tripoli. Without treaties, British ships were exposed to attack and seizure. As the North African records repeatedly show, factors and consuls in this region spent much of their time negotiating for the release of their countrymen, and while they were eager to pursue business opportunities, they often found themselves restricted by the expenses they incurred in ransoming their countrymen.

Such responsibilities did not trouble factors and consuls in the Ottoman Levant or Persian-Indian region, where British ships or crews were unlikely to be taken captive. The Levant region was secured, to a large extent, by the Ottoman navy; at the beginning of the seventeenth century, any danger of piracy came from the English and other European interlopers. In the Indian Ocean and the Persian Gulf, East India Company captains were prepared to trade and to fight—and they did, but the enemy was not the Mughals, Persians, or Arabs, whose ships lacked offensive capability, but rather the

Portuguese and later the Dutch. In those waters Muslim-owned ships traded between neighbouring ports, but they were incapable of long distances or of defending themselves against European predations. As Giancarlo Casale has recently shown,[28] the Mughals possessed large merchant ships, fitted with defensive weapons, but they lacked ships such as those owned by Dutch and English trading companies that roamed the waters in search of prey. Gujarat and Malabar had once possessed armed fleets, but after being conquered by the Mughals, these had decayed. Armed with offensive weaponry, British ships were in very little danger of being captured by Mughals or other local seafarers. While hundreds of British ships were being seized by the 'Barbary' pirates, and their crews taken captive into Libyan Tripoli, Tunis, or Salé, very few were taken 'prisoners'—as they were termed in East India Company documents—in the Indian Ocean. Some were seized by the Portuguese and Dutch, but trading interests generally favoured the arrival of European shipping since it valuably supplemented native freight.

All the same, so well prepared for naval action were the British ships sent by the East India Company that, as early as 1614, William Edwards wrote from Gujarat to the Company governor that 'the people of this country of all sorts pretend to love us, so I am sure they fear us concerning their seas'.[29] Within a decade, the British were attacking local ships and holding them for ransom, or selling them off to regional rulers.[30] At the same time, they were not unwilling to hire themselves out to the Persians against the Portuguese, but, prudently, not against the Ottomans, who would then hit back at them in the eastern Mediterranean.[31] In 1628, a report by English factors confirmed that traders who use 'Moores' to transport their 'vent' by sea, will 'dare not make an enimie of soe powerfull a naccion as the English'.[32] Even as pirates from North Africa were seizing British ships, taking captives, and attacking coastal villages in Cornwall and Ireland, in the Indian Ocean it was the British who were doing the attacking. One result of the success of these maritime predations was the need to transform their outposts into small fort-towns. Already by the 1660s, Madras boasted fortifications, hospital, chapel, library, and burial grounds; by century's end, the East India Company had become a 'Politie of Civill & Military Power...administered justice, coined money, and exercised other functions of government'.[33] Its policy slowly developed into a strident imperial agenda resulting in the East India Act of 1813.

Very few Britons found themselves being seized by Muslims in the Indian Ocean. On occasion, local rulers would imprison diplomatic hostages to ensure that agreements were honoured, but these were released once the terms had been satisfied. Britons were not seized and sold off to local masters, as regularly happened in North Africa, sending consuls scurrying after them. The records of the East India Company contain detailed information about the whereabouts of Company employees, but there is nothing comparable to the hundreds of captured Britons that appear in the North African archive—long lists of names, ransom sums, places of origin, ships on which they were sailing, and other information. Nor was there in the Persian-Indian region the danger of 'Moores' or 'Banians' forcing Englishmen to convert. Britons believed, not necessarily correctly, that North African Muslims wanted to convert Christians and that they tortured captives into submission. No similar beliefs concerning the Mughals appear in East India Company records.

Such differences make the writings of the North African consuls especially important since they describe Britons negotiating from subordinate positions. Not that living in Istanbul or Fort St George did not pose difficulties, or that sailors in the Aegean or traders in Indian outposts did not face serious dangers. Totally ignorant of the Muslim prohibition on bell-ringing, for instance, the English residents of Surat provoked considerable public anger in 1617 by installing a bell in the turret of their house there.[34] And there were always dangers from Portuguese and Dutch fleets and pirates, not to mention divine judgement in the form of serious illnesses and famines.[35] Some prospective factors to the British outposts found that they could not cope with living conditions, fell sick, and returned home, broken, weak, and sometimes terminally ill—if they survived the six-month journey from Madras to Plymouth. Meanwhile, lacking company stipends, consuls in North Africa had to rely on their personal talents to make a living, sometimes against great odds. Without discretionary funds, they could not establish proper networks and facilities for conducting business. Nor could they rely on a head office for help, information, or coordination. From London, the officers of the East India Company organized the various factories under their control; they encouraged factors to lend each other money at times of need and to share trading goods, and sent ships for protection when needed. The East India Company ensured a degree of centralization that was totally missing from the business practices and lives of the uncoordinated and often envious factors working in North Africa. Of course, such centralization sometimes hindered the work of factors on the ground in India, who complained of too much unhelpful control from London, just as North African factors complained of total indifference.

Unlike representatives of the chartered companies who were required to submit regular reports to shareholders back in London, North African factors were under no such obligations,[36] though many did write home about commercial, social, and political events as well as living conditions.[37] In some respects, however, their lives were simplified by the fact that the Mediterranean region had a limited number of languages, along with a lingua franca—in which mariners and traders and converts and captives from many nationalities could dabble. Weights, measures, and coinage were familiar, especially since many of the currencies in the Ottoman Empire and North Africa were European. In the ports and markets of the Persian Gulf and Indian Ocean, however, there was a confusing multitude of languages. Both overseas agents and London-based officers of the East India Company faced the pressing need to learn as much as possible about the dozens of coins, weights, and measures that were in use—the correspondence is full of terms such as 'barrutt', 'catty', 'coem', 'corge', 'covad', 'pecul'.[38] And then there was a specialized vocabulary for drugs and spices,[39] not to mention the various names for cotton products—'cachaes', 'chintz', 'dutties', 'ginghams', 'longees', and a host of others.[40] For the merchants of the Indian Ocean, there was also an urgent need to understand the differing measures used for cloth, to keep abreast of constantly variable rates of exchange between local currencies, and to follow the latest news regarding the success or failure of new factories, and the activities of the ubiquitous, and dangerous, Catholic missionaries. Factors were told by London overseers to make 'discovery' of new markets.[41] In the Mediterranean, there could be no such disoveries since there was no alternative to Tetuan or Algiers or Alexandria: in South East Asia, there were vast coastlines that allowed for constant experimentation with new sites and goods. As a result, factories rapidly appeared and just as rapidly disappeared, sometimes forever (Lucknow in 1652, Petapoli in 1654), or were reactivated (Agra in 1656).[42] The Persian-Indian region was geographically much bigger than the North African coast, and held a larger, and wealthier population than any of the port cities from Tangier to Alexandria.

Yet a further characteristic of working in the Mediterranean that differentiated it from the Indian Ocean was that reasonably accurate maps of the Mediterranean were readily available, while the English had only confused maps of the Indian Ocean region—ships' captains constantly complained that countries were wrongly charted—which may be why Thomas Hyde wanted to translate 'Abulpheda' in 1675, 'the most exact of all Eastern geographers, whereby for the Eastern parts the errors of our maps would be deleted and amended'.[43] Nor was communication between ships in the vast Indian Ocean or Arabian Sea as reliable as in the Mediterranean: Thomas Kerridge, who later became the president of the Surat factory, wrote from Swally that he had found out about the movements of the *Dolphin* by 'inscriptions on stones' in the Cape of Good Hope.[44] Since the mortality rate in the long sea journey around the Cape to Mocha, Hormuz, Surat, or Java was so high, there was always fear that the information which sailors and captains and factors acquired during their stay there would not return with them. Traders to Persia, India, and Sumatra simply needed much more information than those in the well-sailed Mediterranean.

There were many new products coming out of South East Asia about which Britons needed to learn if they were to succeed in trading them:[45] again, language was crucial, and letters contain a vast range of new Arabic, Hindi, and Farsi words. Factors became so used to the foreign words, especially in letters among themselves and other agents in the region, that they sometimes wrote them without considering whether their London recipients could understand them.[46] Since copies of letters were always sent to London, one can only wonder what a cockney clerk understood by 'choukees' and 'bucksha'.[47] These foreign words indicate just how limited English was in coping with the new goods coming out of Persia and India, but one cannot help but suspect that the writers did not always understand them fully.[48]

The letters and reports by factors, consuls, ships' captains, and ambassadors from all regions of the Islamic world provided London administrators with detailed information about the politics, geography, customs, products, and styles of life to be found in the host regions. Their crude ethnographic observations were used by company officers to plan commercial strategies. Factors, consuls, and ambassadors understood the physical and mental world of their hosts from engaging them intimately in proscribed drinking bouts, listening to their strategies, counting the number of naval vessels in their harbours, negotiating for captives, arguing for compensation of stolen or sunken goods, and sometimes even debating differences in politics, religion, and social custom. And after finishing their daily duties, whether in Algiers or Agra, they wrote back to London, passing on petty anecdotes alongside sensitive insights, clichés mixed with perceptive analyses of local customs, gossip involving court intrigues, together with observations about commercial priorities.

Britons in the Islamic world: living conditions

Multinational cities such as Istanbul, Cairo, and even remote Aleppo, as well as Tunis, Tetuan, and Marrakesh had long been accustomed to accommodating foreign residents and travellers. In the Ottoman Levant, new arrivals found established neighbourhoods of expatriate communities, along with warehouses, and well-documented agreements and treaties that determined their duties and the extent of freedoms they could enjoy. The areas where foreign consuls and traders lived were often named after the nationalities that patronized them, or for their function: *khan al-ifranj,* the khan of the Franks in Cairo; the *khan al-jumruk,* the khan of the customs house in Aleppo; or the *zanqat al-qanasil,* the street of the consuls in Rabat. The former Genoese colony of Galata, across the Golden Horn from imperial Istanbul, was a centre of trade with Europe, and would remain so till the collapse of the Ottoman Empire. In this walled enclave, non-Muslim communities of Italians, Greeks, Jews, and Armenians were as conspicuous as the cramped warehouses where European merchants stockpiled merchandise for selling on to agents of the guilds who controlled retail. The celebrated seventeenth-century Ottoman travel writer, Evliya Çelebi, who repeatedly confirmed his piety by praising all things Muslim and regretting anything even remotely infidel, describes the streets littered with drunkards, but also commends the quality of its food and commodities, names eight of its most famous taverns and half a dozen of its best wines. He assessed the population at 200,000 infidels against 60,000 Muslims, an obvious exaggeration that nonetheless conveys the contemporary sense of Galata as 'an essentially Christian environment'.[49] Already by the beginning of the seventeenth century, the European diplomats and wealthy merchants had begun moving up the hill and building villas in Pera, away from the hustle and noise of the warehouses. Here the English built their lodgings and enjoyed exemptions from Ottoman laws regulating clothing and the consumption of wine.[50]

During the course of the century, Izmir would experience the dramatic transformation from an insignificant agricultural town into a bustling multicultural entrepôt where Armenians, Greeks, Jews, and Muslims came to trade with the Dutch and English merchants, whose consulates and warehouses stretching along the seafront were known as 'the Street of the Franks'.[51] In Izmir, as perhaps nowhere else in the Islamic Mediterranean, the Europeans who came to trade ended up dominating the forms and patterns of urban life:

> When we are in this Street, we seem to be in *Christendom*; they speak nothing but Italian, French, English or Dutch there... There one sees Capuchins, Jesuits, Recolets... They sing publickly in the Churches; they sing Psalms, preach, and perform Divine Service there without any trouble; but then they have not sufficient Regard to the *Mahometans*, for the Taverns are open all Hours, Day and Night.[52]

If Izmir developed in accordance with the social and religious needs of its multi-national trading population, further east, in Aleppo, life for the European merchants remained far more sober and restricted. The London merchant James Staper kept a house there for travelling Britons, but in 1603, the unfortunate William Martin was murdered in his bed by prowlers.[53] For safety and privacy, most Aleppo merchants and consuls lived together in the fortified *khan*, which, however comfortable, closed its gates after dark. Nonetheless, social life among the expatriate communities seems to have thrived: in Syrian Tripoli, Henry Maundrell reported that he was 'generously entertain'd' by 'Mr. Francis Hastings, the consul, and Mr. John Fisher, merchant; theirs being the only English house'.[54]

The first agents of the East India Company similarly rented and furnished houses from which they conducted business and where they entertained each other as well as visiting countrymen. Following Thomas Best's success at securing a *firman* permitting the English to maintain a resident colony of merchants at Surat in 1613, Thomas Aldworth founded the first 'English house'. Here the young merchant Christopher Farewell reported feeling

> as at home, in all respects well accommodated save lodging, which with brevity was very commodiously supplyed, by taking another house with an Orchard and pleasant walkes upon the roofe (after the Spanish and the Moorish building) to our rich content, having Chambers, Dyet, Servants, Coach and Horse with attendance of Indians called peones, for the way, and all at our honourable Masters charge except our Apparell.[55]

In short order John Oxwick set up a similar establishment in Broach, further north on the river Narbada. 'Having high and pleasant tarasses or walkes on the roofe, for domesticke recreation', Oxwick's house provided ideal hospitality, according to Farewell who stayed there in the final weeks of 1614 and recorded 'that in this pleasant place... we lived like lords, to the honour and profit of our honourable masters and to our owne hearts content'.[56] Half a century later, and away from the commercial bustle of Izmir, according to John Covel, Rycaut and 'several of our nation' had built themselves 'houses of retirement... for divertisement, especially in summer'.[57]

When Thomas Roe arrived in Agra with a formal appointment as ambassador to the Mughal court, his status required that he be housed at the expense of the local authorities, an arrangement that was bound to create problems. Stopping over in Burhanpur en route to Ajmer where Jahangir held his court, Roe—who was, as so often, suffering a bout of dysentery—was not a little offended to discover that he was expected to house his entire entourage of twenty persons, as well as cartloads of gifts for the emperor, in 'four roomes... no bigger than ovens... and so little that the goods of two cars would fill them all'.[58] Inadequate space was not to be the only inconvenience of living as a guest. Arriving in Ajmer, where he would spend the next eleven months, Roe discovered 'a base old citie, wherein is no house but of mudde', and 'almost no civill arts, but such as straggling Christians have lately taught'. He promptly complained that Jahangir 'allowes me but a house of mudd, which I was enforced to build halfe'. With the local factor, William Edwards, Roe rapidly extended his 'mudde wals' by adding 'upon canes, a doozen thatched roomes'. But even so, this arrangement had serious drawbacks: 'builte all of strawe sides and tops, it neither kept out wynd, nor rayne, to our infinite discomoditye, and wee were nightly afrayed of our lives, the fiers being soe common that to my remembrance no night did escape without some'.[59] Never one to brook an insult or even an inconvenience, Roe negotiated terms for future ambassadors to be accommodated in Surat with proper consideration of their importance, and was himself generously hosted during his last months. Edward Terry describes the luxurious summer houses with garden walks, fountains, and bathing-places that the wealthy merchants of Surat had built for themselves outside the city, and how 'in such a Garden house, with all those accommodations about it, my Lord Ambassadour lay with his company at *Surat*, the last three months before he left *East India*'.[60] Such residences were built according to Islamic models, opening inward, and including a *hamam*.

The earliest factors and consuls arriving in Morocco and the Ottoman regencies across North Africa would enjoy few of the comforts and pleasures of Surat, Pera, or Izmir until much later in the century. No North African city ever rivalled Aleppo in the number of its khans or their architectural splendour.[61] Factors and consuls newly arrived in North Africa, on the other hand, were obliged to stay on board ship until accommodation could be secured, spending their time anxiously pondering the safety of their luggage and personal effects, and worrying about possessions getting 'spoiled by the dampness of the Ship'.[62] After spending three nights on board the *Grafton* moored in Tangiers harbour, Samuel Pepys discovered that a further inconvenience of staying aboard a ship moored in a North African port was the way it instantly attracted airborne predators from the land. 'Infinitely bit with chinches tonight', he recorded on Monday, 17 August 1683. His battle with biting insects continued for days despite attempts 'to preserve myself against the chinches, as the lime, candles, removing my bed...but yet my neck and other places bit and eyes'.[63] Pepys did, at least, have the consolation of being recompensed by the admiralty, while a newly arriving consul would face not only the inconvenience of finding somewhere to live, but also the indignity of being forced to pay a far higher rent than regular merchants. Canny Maghribi landlords reckoned that consuls could afford to pay more and took advantage of them.[64] As a result, some consuls stayed in the Jewish quarters because of the availability of wine, commercial contacts, and multi-lingual associates—in the same manner that their counterparts in Persia stayed in the Armenian quarter of New Julfa outside Isfahan. In India, Britons settled into armed forts and towns that they themselves built—which were not replicated anywhere else in the Islamic world.

After the middle of the seventeenth century, Britons and other Europeans, especially the French, began to establish permanent domiciles, or *fonduks,* in major North African ports; at the same time that their counterparts were buying land and houses in Syrian Tripoli.[65] Later in the century, English consuls in Algiers and Tunis moved into large residences with spectacular views. They beautified their gardens, planting trees and vines and adding so many improvements and decorations that their 'Villas [were] delightful beyond Imagination'.[66] In the early 1700s, the French consul in Algiers had the most elegant house and garden, with a large lime tree and maples that provided pleasant shade from the sun. 'Couches are also placed in several Places, and in this delightful Dormitory, the generous

Owner, and his Guests, may enjoy the sweetest Repose.'[67] An Anglo-Moroccan treaty from the early eighteenth century emphasized that an English consul could live anywhere he wanted on Moroccan soil, and that he and his retinue should 'enjoy the free liberty of ye exercise of their Religion... [and] a decent place appointed for ye burial of their Dead to which no violence shall be offered'.[68]

In Ottoman Istanbul, Christian funerals and graveyards remained a feature from the city's Christian era. When Mehmed III's favourite Englishman, Edward Barton, died in 1597, he received a full state funeral and was buried on Heybeliada (Halki), one of the Prince's Islands in the Sea of Marmara, where Roe would take refuge from the plague in 1625. His gravestone can still be found in the Crimean War Cemetery at Üsüküdar.[69] In April 1612, following a funeral ceremony held 'in a large garden under a Cypresse tree' and attended by representatives of 'most nations in the world', Anne, Lady Glover 'was buried with very great solemnity, the like had not bin seene in that countrye, since the Turks conquered Constantinople'. Her tomb, 'of faire marble, built foure square almost the height of a man', was placed among 'the English graves', a site that was cleared in the nineteenth century to make Taksim Square.[70] While it is worth noting that not all ambassadors to the Ottomans who died in office were buried locally—Daniel Harvey's body was brought back to England aboard the *Centurion* in 1672[71]—this was a matter of choice and not a matter of Islamic law; burial sites were specifically designated for Christians, from Algiers to Aleppo, and from Ahmadabad to Swally.[72] A few gravestones still decorate the yard of the Anglican Church in Tunis. Given the vast number of dead among the Britons in India, the coastline received many a Christian: one of the duties of factors and agents was to record the names of the dead and report them to London.

Since Islam is tolerant of other religions of the Book, being a Christian was not in principle a great problem for English expatriates. In accordance with the 'Pact of Umar', the Ottomans did not permit new churches or synagogues to be constructed in Istanbul, but allowed those remaining from before their arrival in 1453 to continue functioning so long as they were maintained by their respective communities.[73] When churches fell into disrepair, however, they were liable to expropriation. In 1478, for example, the walled inner-city of Galata boasted no fewer than twenty-one churches—eleven Catholic, nine Greek, and one Armenian—but only two mosques. Following the great fire of 1696, the church of St Francis was converted into a mosque, leaving only six churches 'against some twelve mosques'.[74] In practice this policy meant that, when the Protestant English and Dutch arrived, they found all the available church buildings already occupied by Catholic and Eastern Orthodox communities, a state of affairs that often led to fierce disputes with the French and Venetian communities.

Elsewhere within the Ottoman Empire, the Islamic restriction on building new places for Christian worship was not always rigorously enforced. In 1616, the Armenian community of Aleppo proved themselves to be not only wealthy but also sufficiently well connected to build a new cathedral, Surp Karsunk.[75] Private chapels were attached to consular residences where the community assembled on a regular basis for worship, as the following report from Algiers in June 1675 demonstrates: 'The Protestants have also a place to preach & pray, wch is permformed in ye English consull's House by the severall Nations, English, German, Dutch.'[76] This was certainly an improvement on the 'Cellar' in Algiers where, in the early 1640s, Devereux Spratt preached to a community of 'three or fourscore' Protestant captives.[77] Unlike the Mashriq or Persia, the Maghrib boasted no active churches because they lacked a native Christian community. In Cairo, Izmir, and Aleppo, local Catholic and Uniate populations shared their places of worship with pious French and Venetian visitors. As the presence of the Capuchins and Jesuits grew and spread from Istanbul to Aleppo, from Mosul to Alexandria to Agra, priests were granted permission to build chapels. After Euro-Christian captives were brought to Meknes, permission was given by Mulay Muhammad al-Sheikh al-Asghar to Spanish priests to build chapels, schools, and mini infirmaries.[78]

While the English communities of Istanbul and Izmir boasted sizeable populations and those of Surat and—after 1662—Bombay grew considerably throughout our period, in North Africa, the nation remained very small. The number of residents in North Africa can only be estimated by the petitions supporting or complaining about specific consuls that were sent to the Secretary of State in London. And these, from Algiers as well as Tunis, never show more than a few dozen signatures.[79] At no point were there as many Britons in any of the North African cities as there were, for instance, French residents in Izmir in 1670.[80] When Sir John Finch prepared for his courtesy visit to Sultan Mehmed IV (r. 1648–87), he was accompanied by the staff of the embassy and all the English merchants in Istanbul and Izmir, 'altogether one hundred and twenty horsemen, fifty-five baggage-waggons'.[81]

No such display could ever have been staged in Tunis or Algiers. Nor was there much variety in social background, training, or occupation among the Britons who were there: at no point did any member of the peerage, for instance, go, or find himself posted, to North Africa. To assist the consul was the secretary, as well as one or two *Chancellier* who recorded legal agreements in the *Chancellaria*, and a translator or *dragoman*. These and the few resident merchants, some of whom may have begun their careers as pirates, paid a set fee to join the consul at his table in order to have access to English cuisine and to remain close to the sources of information and news, both locally and internationally. Perhaps this uniformity in the community created an inwardness that made some expatriates deeply conscious of being separated from 'Christendom'—a term that shows up often in their letters home.

Domestic conditions varied greatly. Factors and consuls were clearly not very keen on taking their families to outlandish places that were not yet well known in England. One result was that there were marriages to members of local Christian populations—Latin Catholic, Eastern Orthodox, Jacobite, Armenian, and Syriac. Trade agreements regularly included an article about such marriages and their aftermath. The ambassador, according to the Grant of Capitulations signed with the Safavid Shah Safi in 1629, should be ready to take responsibility for the issue of any Englishmen who married locally should the man die and leave children behind.[82] In Aleppo and other parts of the Levant, however, consuls discouraged such marriages for fear that the grooms would abandon their Anglican Christianity in favour of Orthodoxy or Catholicism, or for fear that they would settle permanently in the Ottoman Empire. The number of recorded cases of English and other European expatriates marrying Christian Ottoman women, however, is relatively small. Some merchants bought slaves for sexual services, while often maid servants were, or became, mistresses.[83] More common, however, was the practice of contracting a temporary marriage by presenting a document called a *kabin* before an Ottoman magistrate or *qadi*. Here would be set out the terms of whatever financial settlement had been agreed upon for taking care of the woman and any children when the merchant returned to his native country. William Biddulph described the practice:

> both at *Constantinople, Aleppo,* and other places of Turkey where there is trafficking and trading of Merchants, it is no rare matter for popish Christians of sundery other Countries to Cut Cabine (as they call it) that is: to take any

woman of that contrie where they sojourne, (Turkish women onely excepted, for it is death for a Christian to meddle with them) and when they have bought them, and enroled them in the *Cadies* booke, to use them as wives so long as they sojourne in that Country, and maintain them gallantly.[84]

The French ambassador, François Savary de Brèves, openly lived with an Ottoman Greek woman with whom he had three children during his stay in Istanbul (1589–1605).[85] Thomas Glover is also known to have been involved in such an arrangement until King James appointed him ambassador in 1606, at which point he paid off his first local wife, a Greek woman called Sophia with whom he had two children, and married an English wife.[86] Biddulph was outraged at Glover's behaviour, though curiously George Sandys, who knew and admired Glover, made no comment about the ambassador's temporary wife in his account of such relationships, which he described as 'a use, not prohibited but onely by our religion'.[87]

Marriage with Muslim women was against Qur'anic law, and only those Britons who were willing to convert to Islam could marry and subsequently settle down. Such prospects constituted the biggest danger that captives in North Africa faced, at least, according to their relatives back in England. Although there was very limited, if any, British interaction with Muslim women in North Africa, writings by ransomers and captives alike were dominated by tales of the wily sexuality of those women. What was truly destabilizing was the ease with which some sailors and traders were willing to abandon their Christian God in return for a wife, along with some kind of employment. Such marriages were always feared as indications of the weakening of Christianity; they also led to the loss of manpower in factories that sometimes suffered from a scarcity of workers. Although this fear dominated the North African experience, it appeared, though rarely, in India. When a consultation was held in Surat by President Kerridge on 20 February 1626, the first item for discussion concerned one John Leachland who had 'for some years past privately kept a woman of this country' and was 'refusing to put her away, in spite of all persuasions'. A debate ensued 'whether to dismiss him from the Company's service' but, as Kerridge reported, 'as this would only lead to his marrying her and forsaking his country and friends, it is resolved not to adopt this extreme course'.[88] There are no records about how such inter-religious affairs or marriages fared: unfortunately, there is no description of the marriage of Gabrial Lewis to 'the Moorish woman formerly belonging to Monsieur Marine' in Tangier in 1672, nor did Thomas Pellow, who married after his captivity and conversion to Islam in Morocco, include anything about his family life in the account he wrote after his return to England.[89]

Istanbul may have been the first Islamic city to accommodate an ambassadorial family when Thomas Glover arrived back from London with his new wife in 1606, and it is possible to measure the strength and prestige of Britain by the presence—or absence—of wives and children. By the second half of the century, factors in India began to feel secure: in 1651, Captain Jeremy Blackman, on his way to Surat, took 'his wife and son, with two men and two women servants'—but a wife was a privilege requiring Company approval.[90] Chaplain John Ovington reported that after the takeover of Bombay, the company sent out girls from England as wives for factors—but without much success.[91] But as British outposts grew stronger and more infrastructurally established, single women headed out from England in search of husbands.[92] Many of these women whose husbands died in foreign service never returned but re-married among the community, suggesting that life in the growing fort towns was not too inhospitable. Following the death in Tangier of an English convert to Islam in 1682, however, his wife was assisted in returning to her native England.[93] In 1712, the Dutch consul in Algiers brought gifts to the dey and the pasha and then settled 'with his Lady and a Large family of Children and Servants'.[94] In November of that same year, following the death of consul Robert Cole in Algiers, his family was well treated: 'The Pasha and Dey hath upon this occasion shewed the family the utmost Civility that could be expected.'[95] The East India Company correspondence repeatedly mentions women, wives, widows, and daughters in a manner that rarely obtains in the North African archive. Far fewer British women went to Algiers than to Aleppo or Surat.

While it was certainly the case, as Biddulph observed, that liaisons between Christian and Muslims were punishable by death, there seem to have been exceptional cases. The Levant Company accountant John Sanderson claims that Edward Barton, who had constructed a covered entrance to the English house in Pera 'for convayance of whores', became involved with the exiled Sultana of Fez.[96] After joining the Ottoman army in Hungary, a group of French mercenaries showed up in Galata and promptly 'sequestered a number of Muslim women in their private rooms' without punishment. In 1609, an inspection of the religious houses in Galata discovered that 'several of the monks of San Pietro had been immoderate with some Turk women who neighboured their garden'.[97] Fynes Moryson reported that 'at Constantinople the houses of Ambassadors being free from the search of magistrates very Turkes, yea the Janizaries guarding the persons and howses of these Ambassadors, will not stick to play the bawdes for a small reward'.[98] Flouting of sexual prohibitions seems to have been not uncommon, provided the right quantity of money was offered in the right place. In 1638, a Venetian merchant who was arraigned for keeping a Muslim woman in his house escaped by offering a bribe of 300 ducats.[99]

Although there were evident difficulties enforcing legislation designed to keep Christians and Muslims apart, stricter codes were gradually introduced. In 1677, the grand vezir Merzifonlu Kara Mustafa Pasha announced that any foreigners who married local women would automatically come under Ottoman authority. Immediately, the Levant Company issued an order forbidding its members such marriage.[100] In 1716, the French went to the extent of issuing a royal declaration that prohibited any Frenchman married to a Levantine from engaging in trade, and deprived any Frenchman resident in the factories who did so marry of the right to trade or continue living in the factory.[101] A decade later, Frenchmen were prohibited from marrying even French women who had been born overseas.[102] Formally, at least, there were no such attempts to tighten controls on sexual conduct in the North African factories, suggesting that the problem never arose or was resolved in other ways. Although some Britons clearly engaged in illicit relations, they exposed themselves to severe punishment were they to be discovered.[103] Yet there is no record of Britons marrying local women in North Africa, as was the case in the Levant.[104] In the absence of native Christians in the Maghrib, there could be no marriage between Christian merchants and local Muslim women, while the danger of conducting an illicit affair across the religious divide was demonstrated by the execution in Libyan Tripoli of a merchant from Messina.[105]

Throughout their trading in the Islamic world, factors and consuls had to rely on local help: in Ottoman-held regions, they hired janissaries to help them, in the same manner that local servants, such as 'Mahomet and this Turk Nigebey', worked for Edward Connock in 1617.[106] Ship's ledgers indicate that 'Indians', 'Arabians', 'Moors', and 'Turks' were occasionally, and advantageously, hired by the East India Company, but not very frequently. On shore, throughout the dispersed factories of India, there was always need for local help including porters, letter-carriers (*pattamars*), translators, not to mention accountants and brokers who were 'skilled in the rates and value of all the commodities in India'.[107] In North Africa, where there were many Christian captives, consuls and their families often found themselves relying on them for help with household duties, gardening, shopping, and protection. Joseph Morgan reported that such captives were paid a 'Piastre per Moon'.[108] Sometimes groups of merchants brought their own cooks and secretaries from England, waiting to hire translators locally, often from among the communities of European converts to Islam. Consuls who knew Arabic or Turkish could dispense with translators, but unlike the French, the British never developed an institution for training translators to serve in their overseas outposts: not, at least, in the Mediterranean region, though by 1652, 'many youths' had been to India to train and serve in 'the writing office'.[109] As early as 1614, Thomas Aldworth and William Biddulph (the merchant) had urged that factors sent to Agra be familiar with Turkish or Persian; by the end of the century, in September 1698, the professor of Arabic at Oxford, Edward Hyde, was reminded by the archbishop of Canterbury of his promise to 'instruct and breed up some young man in the knowledge of the Oriental tongues, as they are in modern use; that there may be a succession of such as may serve the public'.[110] Nothing ever came of the plan, perhaps because Hyde could not count on the support of ecclesiastical orders to finance the project. The lack of linguistic versatility often forced consuls to commission translations of letters and communications—for which they had to pay exorbitant fees, as Jezreel Jones, Britain's factor in Morocco in the early eighteenth century, complained.[111]

In the North-African Mediterranean, once the trading season of three or four months was over, and the weather permitted ships to sail safely away, the British nations had little to do except play cards, hunt, or explore the local regions. Cultural interests were limited. With a few exceptions from Tangier during the British presence there, when plays were sometimes performed as John Luke reported in his diary, letters home from consuls and factors in North Africa are conspicuously free from requests for books: nor do they mention any cultural activities, music, or even worship. Living conditions were evidently bleak. Residents appear to have been short of cash, constantly having to budget in order to pay for essential services, bribes, and supplies. In India, by way of contrast, there was a larger community supported by financially astute company officials. In their fort-towns, factors had opportunity for reading, and references to the books that were sent to the East India Company factors include suitably pious tomes such as the Bible, the Book of Common Prayer, and Foxe's *Book of Martyrs*. Such works must have helped maintain the faith of Anglo-Protestants who were living amidst Portuguese, French, and Venetian Catholics. In a letter from Mocha dated 1611, Lawrence Fenell mentioned 'singing books' and a 'book of declination', but there is no mention of English literary material—poems or plays.[112] A copy of Isaac Walton's massive *Biblia Sacra Polyglotta* was sent out to Surat in 1660 in the hope that 'the Gospell may be propogated and made knowne'.[113] There were far more Company agents in India than in North Africa and, as in Aleppo, many of them were well educated and in need of books. Factors in India read works by Hobbes and Seneca,[114] while William Methwold, President in Surat from 1633 to 1639, was a scholar who had assisted Purchas in compiling *Hakluytus Posthumus*.[115] Some factors were also skilled musicians who provided entertainment; curiously, Muslim governors and rulers from Salé to Istanbul and Agra seem to have been attracted by western instruments and the sounds they made. In 1599, Thomas Dallam's mechanical organ attracted Mehmed III; in 1613, Jahangir enjoyed listening to the virginals that were played by one Lawes (who later died in Agra), tried to play a coronet, ordered six made similar to it ('proved not good'), and wanted to hire an English musician named Robert to become a member of his court.[116] In 1679, two musicians, a trumpeter and a violinist, were killed during a Dutch attack on Bengal.[117] There are no references to music in the North African archives—although during the 1670s there were musical and dramatic activities in Tangier for the 3–4,000 residents.

For some expatriates, natural history and archaeology provided intellectual amusement and social legitimacy, especially following the establishment of the Royal Society, which provided a venue for reporting discoveries of new and exotic species. In 1666, Paul Rycaut was elected Fellow of the Royal Society and issued with a list of 'Inquiries for Turky' that he took with him the following spring. It required him to answer questions on a host of topics such as the plague, opium, mummies, seedless grapes, earthquakes, tanning, inscriptions, and acqueducts.[118] John Verney spent a good deal of his time in Aleppo collecting seeds and plants to send home for experimental planting on the family estates.[119] There was also opportunity for visiting classical ruins and collecting manuscripts and old coins. There is no indication that British consuls or factors in the Maghrib ever became interested in searching for classical statuary, as Roe had done, although the French often bargained with the Moroccan ruler Mulay Ismail to acquire such objects.[120] Especially in the Levant, consuls became collectors and connoisseurs of rare objects which they avidly bought or pilfered. In 1621, Roe scoured Istanbul for Christian manuscripts, though he admitted to Lord Arundel that the French ambassador had found only very few, of Tertullian and Chrysostom.[121] Archbishop Laud nurtured interest in Arabic, Greek, Hebrew, and Syriac manuscripts for studying early Christian history: the Laudian collection of manuscripts at Oxford owes its beginnings to Edward Pocock, chaplain in Aleppo, where he studied Arabic with a local Syrian, and the first Laudian professor of Arabic at the university.[122] On returning from Izmir to England in 1703, William Raye donated his collection of over two thousand coins and medals to the Bodleian. Thomas Laxton's extensive collection of gold, silver, and brass medals collected in the same area was sold off in London after his death in 1714.[123]

Most Mediterranean agents and visitors generally pursued less intellectual and more muscular, pleasures. Rycaut reported that the English community in Izmir hunted with local greyhounds as well as a pack of beagles brought from home, 'and every Saturday could be found coursing on the empty plain to the south of the city'.[124] While visiting Aleppo, the chaplain Henry Teonge reported how the English community there would set out into the countryside for 'duck-hunting, fishing, shooting, handball, cricket, scrofilo, etc'.[125] Travelling in the 1670s, Cornelis de Bruyn was amused at the hunting habits of the English in Aleppo, which included 'the election of a master huntsman'.[126] The forests outside Tunis and Meknes were full of game, which provided not only sport and fresh meat but also a chance to reconnoitre regions seldom visited by Europeans. Everywhere, hunting was the most attractive entertainment as consuls and merchants joined the locals, even sometimes high officials, in the pursuit of game. But there was danger in such ventures. In 1693 consul Thomas Baker was confined to his bed after being attacked by a boar;[127] evidently, he liked to go in summer 'into the Country'.[128]

Writing to a friend at Exeter College in March 1698, Henry Maundrell gave a pious—and perhaps not entirely accurate—version of life among the English in Aleppo, comparing it to that of an Oxford college:

> As for our living amongst them [Turks], it is with all possible quiet and safety, and that's all we desire, their conversation being not in the least entertaining. Our delights are among ourselves; and here being more than forty of us, we

never want a most friendly and pleasant conversation. Our way of life resembles, in some measure, the academical. We live in separate squares, shut up every night after the manner of colleges. We begin the day constantly, as you do, with prayers; and have our set times for business, meals, and recreations. In the winter we hunt in the most delightful campaign twice a week; and in the summer go as often to divert our selves under our tents, with bowling and other exercises.[129]

How credible this description of an English Platonic academy of traders in the midst of the Islamic world is, is unclear. But piety was a common topic in the correspondence of factors and chaplains. Religious anxiety seems to have been stronger among those living in the Islamic Mediterranean and Levant, and their London sponsors, than in the Far East. Ottoman Islam was both strident and attractive, and Britons were known to convert and settle down from Santa Cruz to Istanbul. Letters and reports from the Mediterranean regularly refer to 'renegades' from all the European nations, including Britain. William Lithgow's report of dining in Tunis with the renegade pirate, John Ward, likely caused anxiety or excitement among readers who dreaded or admired the allure of Islam.[130] When an Italian convert welcomed Captain Towerton in Mocha in 1612 in his house, however, there was no exclamation against the heinousness of his conversion:[131] adopting Islam was rare and less common among Britons in Arabian and Indian waters than in the regions closer to home.[132]

There was always urgency regarding religious duties, and letters from South East Asia most often intoned piety. 'Mr. Camden,' Captain John Saris opened a letter of 23 November 1612, 'let not the men work on the sabbath day.' The two Englishmen who had died, 'ministered great comfort to us all,' wrote Ralph Preston in January 1614 from Ahmedabad, 'which I pray God give us grace to make use of to His glory and our own spiritual comfort.'[133] The Civil Wars of mid century generated religious confrontations among expatriates. In the Mediterranean, personal rivalries tended to supersede religious differences, since consuls there could not afford disunity in the face of a conversionist Islam,[134] but in India, intense Royalist–Parliamentary factionalism broke out from religious differences. In Madras, the staunch Royalist James Martin was a thorn in the side of the community. In 1652, he 'contrasted the Protestant faith unfavourably with the Papists,' described 'Generall Cromwell' as 'a cowardly fellow', insulted Cromwell's wife comparing her to 'the stone or excrescence of a fruite called a cadjew' [cashew], and never desisted for two years. Charges were eventually brought against him for maintaining 'evil and blasphemous doctrines in religion', after which he was to be 'removed from his command, as an enemy to God, the Parliament, and the Company'. He died before the sentence took effect.[135] At the Restoration, the Anglican Church reinforced itself. By 1663, there was a small library in Surat that included 'the holy bible in the languages, which are much esteemed by those that are learned amongst these people'. Next to the books was 'a large table... adorned with Moses and Aaron holding the two tables containeing the ten commandments [and] a the top, in triangles, God's name wrote in as many of these Eastern languages as can bee procured, as Arabick, Persian, etc'.[136] Curiously, there was no representation of Christ but, as the chaplain, John Ovington, observed about the chapel in the President's house in Surat, there was no 'figure of any living creature in it, for avoiding all occasion of offence to the Moors, who are well pleased with the innocence of our worship'. Such accommodation to local conditions may have led to the condemnation by the historians of the Society of the Propagation of the Gospel in 1900 that the English traders in India were 'long neglectful of religion', so much so that the 'first Governor of Bengal degenerated into an avowed Pagan'.[137]

'Paganism' and frivolity were ever present in India. Following the departure of President William Methwold from Surat in 1639, a magnificent banquet was held, with music and local dancing girls.[138] In India the English first learnt to drink tea, though it would not be imported into England until 1660, as Pepys noted in his diary on 25 September. Here too they first learned about Shiraz wine, and fruits that were imported from Persia. Doubtless, there were times of jollity that were never reported in letters to Company officials, so an account of entertainments in the English factory in Madras by a travelling Iranian delegate in 1685 provides an interesting perspective. Muhammad Hussain Beg, who was sent by the Safavid ruler to Thailand, admired the military discipline he witnessed, and praised the governor's fair treatment of merchants, whether Portuguese 'Franks' or Hindus. But when celebrations started for the accession of James II to the throne, the Persian was stunned: women appeared, 'whose faces beam like the sun and round like the moon, hidden with veils of modesty'. As the evening progressed, much dancing and hugging followed, to the displeasure of the ambassador, who enjoyed the food and drink, but thought very little of the open mixing of men with women. The celebration may not have been commonplace as it was in honour of the new king, but in the eyes of a Muslim observer, it was an extravagant night.[139] Such activities, with the enormous amount of eating and drinking must have contributed significantly to the high mortality rate, by far higher than among the frugal and impecunious North African consulates.

Life in the factories presented peculiar difficulties. Apart from the dangers of travel which claimed many lives, debilitating illnesses took their toll. Merchants bound for Aleppo feared having to put in at the port of Iskenderun, which was notorious for its 'pestilent air', as Fynes Moryson termed it.[140] Christopher Farewell, who travelled out to India in 1613, noted that on the seven-month voyage, they 'lost onely one man, who came sicke of an Ague out of England', but in Surat 'here quickly they began to dye faster of fluxes and Feavers'.[141] The French traveller, Jean-Baptist Tavernier, observed that anyone able to live there for more than two or three years would 'do well to stay there; for them to betake themselves to a good air, is to hazard their Lives'. He noted that 'Mr. *Philips*, the *English* Consul', is the only one known to have lived there for more than twenty years, perhaps 'he was a brisk merry Man, and of an excellent temper of Body'.[142] In January 1669, John Verney wrote home describing how 'staying there only 5 days I cacht—or rather Scanderoon diseases catcht me—& continued upon me for 3 months, changing the collour of my flesh to that yellownesse, which is customary for that desease'. Six months later he reported how the plague had struck Aleppo and 'swept away . . . 150,000 people'.[143] Although no more common than at home, outbreaks of the plague must have seemed more frightening to many because of the perceived unwillingness of Muslims to take any precautions against it. In 1713 eighty-two of the one hundred Frenchmen living in the Levant died from plague, although in 1675, not a single Briton died of the plague that ravaged Izmir that year.[144] Consuls had the grim task of reporting back to London about plagues and other epidemics; a task they dutifully performed.[145] Although there was no fear of the plague in India—at least letters home are silent on this matter—famines ravaged various regions, and British factors faced problems if no ships arrived with provisions from England or Iran.

And there were also man-made dangers: robbery and local hostility were by no means uncommon. Those living in the Maghrib faced the greatest risk of mob violence following attacks by British pirates, and later the British fleet on their country's ships and ports. In 1626, the Algerian dey imprisoned the consul along with all the merchants in the city and seized 1,000 dollars, because one of his ships had been attacked by British pirates.[146] On 20 October 1676, consul Samuel Martin reported from Tunis that he had been dragged by four 'Grand Chous & carryed aboard a shipp in the Roade, I knew not if it was to hang or Drowne Mee, my house at home was Rifled, & seazed on, my ffamily turned Into ye street not being allowed the Conveniency of a Lodging'.[147] A year later, on 26 Jan 1677, Martin's replacement consul in Tunis, Francis Baker, along with two merchants, Francis Barrington and Benjamin Steele, were seized by the bey and imprisoned, having found themselves, along with the French consul, caught in the middle of the bey's wars with his brother.[148] A quarter of a century later, in 1708, the consul in Tunis, John Goddard, described how he was being 'ill treated' by local authorities:

> Murat Bey forced me to lend him tenn thousand Dollars—Ibrahim Bey ordered me in Chain's to worke with the slaves on the Castle Walls till I had paid $1800 for damage her Majty Subjects did at Goletta, by Burning a French Tartan. Mahoment Dey Imprisoned me three days.[149]

That local rulers often forced loans on the consuls occurred widely, from Tunis to Surat. Such debts, which often went unpaid, were cause of despair;[150] perhaps it was the pressure of such debts that eventually drove Goddard mad. He died, 'non compos mentis', in 1711 and would be remembered for years to come for having been 'seized with a raging Lunacy of such a nature as (in the Opinion of two learned Christians residing there) will be utterly incurable'.[151] Clearly, some consuls paid a heavy price for the responsibilities and exigencies of their service to their country. In 1719 after British ships had taken Algerian captives, the wives and families of the captives invaded the consul's house, 'clamouring for their husbands, some for their children; he [the consul] is called ill names in the streets'.[152] Consuls in North Africa always had to have exit strategies for times of danger.

A further drawback, facing merchants and consuls in North Africa particularly, was the uncertainty about whether their letters home, telling of their committed service to their country and its trade, ever reached their destination. Ships carrying letters could sink or, in times of war, be seized by the enemy: hence the habit of keeping and sending duplicates. But the most depressing anxiety was the fear that they were no longer remembered back home in Britain. They often found themselves sending letters but not receiving any answers, resulting in a feeling of being cut off from their own country and the rest of the world.[153] By the summer of 1667, young John Verney had been two and a half years in Aleppo without receiving a single letter from his family, and was suffering from depression; 'my respects', he ended one of his letters, 'to those of my relations that have not forgotten me'.[154] Nor was young Verney alone in his sense of being abandoned. 'Tis now a yeare', wrote Benjamin Loddington in Algiers on 5 March 1692, 'since I received a Letter from your Lordship' [Nottingham].[155] For agents in North Africa, there was not much urgency for information since there was no centralizing authority in London seeking to keep track of finances and personnel. As a result, North African factors and consuls had no need for a network of correspondents—unlike East India Company agents, whose letters reveal a vast network stretching across continents and seas. The North African archive rarely, if ever, includes a letter to other outposts in the Mediterranean, or anywhere except London, which was the destination of all letters. In the Persian-Indian region, factors regularly communicated with each other directly while, at the same time, officials in London micromanaged commercial, political, and military affairs. Company officials scrutinized incoming letters, reviewed invoices, and checked carefully through shipping inventories. They also dictated instructions concerning who was permitted to return home, what punishment was to be inflicted on interlopers, private traders, or ships' captains who were caught transporting non-Company cargo,[156] and what military action the agents should undertake. London also forced resolutions of personal conflicts, determined areas of jurisdiction, and the number of factors, and was not unwilling to turn a blind eye when presidents cheated—for instance, sending saltpetre under the name of indigo in order to avoid paying customs at Burhanpur.[157] The Company urged factors and agents to keep each other abreast of developments in their regions: factors in Isfahan wrote to the President and Council in Surat in November 1654 reporting how the English in Aleppo were 'much molested' and that there was no redress from Istanbul.[158] The Company urged writers always to copy letters and other documents to London. Operations in the Indian-Persian region were extensive: nothing in the early English archive about North Africa or the Ottoman Levant can compare with the complexity and coordination of the East India Company.

Britons in the Islamic World: Working Conditions

Physical dangers and psychological pressures were not the only challenges facing Britons living and working in Islamic countries. To be successful, merchants, factors, and consuls needed to be assertive: 'If a man', wrote Thomas Thomson, consul in Tunis, 'does not show some Spirit among these people at his first arrival he is ever after esteemed a Gallina amongst them.'[159] Other consuls relied on friendship: Robert Cole used to drink coffee with the Algerian dey and watch him take 'his Opium little pill'.[160] Carefully, he listened to what the dey divulged about the French king to whom he had sent fifteen horses, hoping in return to receive 250 'slaves out the galleys'.[161] Such friendships remained formal, with consuls obliged to relish the 'favor of kissing' the hand of the ruler; in India, East India Company representative Ralph Cartwright had to kiss the foot of the Mughal.[162] Wise consuls established good relations with the local magistrates, or *qadis*, who were often a good source of information, while also cultivating any Anglophone converts with access to sensitive documents. 'I have made it my business', wrote Robert Cole from Algiers in 1709, to befriend the court 'clark from whom I have procured sight of the deys letter to her majesties.'[163] Consuls needed informants, and someone like Jezreel Jones, who spent a good part of his life in North Africa, cultivated a network that provided him with information and news throughout the region.[164] While ambassador in Istanbul, Sir Robert Sutton so befriended his 'draghoman' that he was able to gain information about the 1711 Ottoman campaign against Russia.[165]

Consuls needed to know how to address rulers according to regional protocols, and to ensure that merchants and other fellow countrymen abided by local customs. The formal terminology to be used in greetings must have seemed excessively lengthy to some, but such preambles were very important in oral as well as written addresses. An extended opening to a letter showed respect and amicability; a letter with an abrupt opening, or still worse, without one at all, immediately signified to the court audience, as well as the recipient in Europe, hostility and conflict. Expatriates had to learn to remove their shoes when entering the *diwans* or other sites of Muslim assembly—just as other Muslims did. But with the growth of British power, such actions came to be considered demeaning. In April 1730, a ship's captain refused to take his 'shoose' off in the presence of the Tunisian bey, who promptly complained to his consul, who reported how 'in Public Audience he gave us very Abusive Language'.[166]

At the same time, consuls were expected to entertain local officials and members of the *diwan*, indicating that there were no restrictions about eating with Christians. Factors, too, were also expected to offer gifts on religious feast days—*Bairam* was especially important for the Ottomans just as *Nevruz* was in Aceh—as well as birthdays, and special events. Such gifts advertised British products, ingratiated the donors with the recipients, and tied commerce and culture together: cloth needed for special turbans was carried on British ships from India to North Africa.[167] They also catered to the whims of the rulers, transporting Friesland mares to Morocco, and English greyhounds, mastiffs, hens, lutes, and cutlery to Persia and India. Of course, no one could guarantee that gifts would achieve their aims. On 17 October 1692, Thomas Baker wrote that the cloth sent from London for giving to the governors of Tripoli was of colours they did not like, 'and the Violett and the Crimson in Graine were falce [false] Dyes'.[168] Such gifts sometimes showed the British incapable of matching the French in their adroit diplomacy. Gifts varied from the valuable—gold-rimmed pistols—to new consumer goods—such as 'green tea'.[169] When the givers were merchants and consuls, and not officially designated ambassadors, no reciprocity was expected; unless the ruler liked the consul and offered presents, he was not obliged to offer a gift in return. Nor were local potentates obliged to support consuls financially, as was the case with ambassadors to the Ottoman, Safavid, and Mughal Empires.[170] Since they already enjoyed access to uncountable wealth, Muslim emperors did not demand valuable gifts so much as strange exotica: Shah 'Abbas wanted turkeys and peacocks, which 'he never saw', reported Edward Connok from Isfahan in 1617.[171] Many surviving lists document the value of the gifts that consuls offered and for which they sought reimbursement from the trading Companies. These gifts were effectively bribes and were distributed not only to rulers and members of the *diwan*, but also to translators and pages, to the 'Cryer of the Town', the 'Watchmen', the pasha's coffee-maker, even to the common executioner.[172] And because they were bribes, consorts of rulers, often quite influential, were taken into account. In 1617 Roe reported how he was able to procure a firman to protect the English traders in Agra by appealing to one of the consorts,[173] just as, less than a century later, English merchants in Meknes appealed to the English-born queen to support them against the French.[174] Which is why many gifts were expensive: Thomas Baker in

Algiers paid out £35.17.6 at the 'Festival of Bairam', and the same sum at 'Corban'.[175] After the Algerian victory over Tunis in 1700, Robert Cole received 'all the ladies of the first rank, all which I entertained magnificently with fireworks, dancing on a stage and music both Moorish and Christian, with throwing in the square rich perfumes and sending them custard, cheesecake, sweetmeats and other toys'.[176]

Consuls in the Ottoman and the Mediterranean regions were responsible for ensuring their compatriots did not convert to Islam. An article in a treaty signed with Morocco required that the consul was to keep any convert-to-be in his custody for three days and try to dissuade him; if he failed, then he would acquiesce and set him free.[177] While very few Britons in India converted to Islam, some deserted their factory posts, or accepted service in local armies—just as in the early seventeenth century, Britons served in the Moroccan civil wars, and Sir Robert Shirley drilled the Shah's soldiers. And as happened later in the bastion of Tangier, from which English soldiers sometimes defected, so in Fort St George where, in 1653, President Baker noted that the local Nawab had lured six of the 'best soldiers as gunners in his army', and feared that others might abscond if threatened with disciplinary measures.[178] And, just as there was always the fear in England of children being 'spirited' or kidnapped, so in Surat, John Osborne and Richard Watson, being promised reward, 'speritted' twenty-three men in 1654 who, upon hearing of favourable conditions, agreed to enter 'the Kings pay and put [on] Moores habitt'.[179] The danger of assimilation, whether by conversion or employment, was paramount in the minds of factors and consuls in all parts of the Islamic world.

North African consuls did not have a specific number of years to serve, as tended to be the case in the Levant where appointments of three to five years were standard. Many stayed until they died, while others repeatedly importuned the Secretary of State to be relieved of their duties, sometimes to no avail. Uncertainty of income and length of service proved harmful because the consul, along with his staff and family, incurred numerous expenses in maintaining an open house for visiting compatriots. 'All the people that belongs to the English shipps in port are sent to my house & live at my Charge', wrote Samuel Martin from Algiers in October 1677, 'being 36 persons, who Eate mee more Bread in a Day then the Benefitt of My Employment have affoarded mee in a year.'[180] And it was not just bread that they needed, but 'Wine, Pickels, Cheese, ffruit', as John Goddard complained from Tunis in 1708.[181] Morgan noted that 'for as these Ministers never fail to offer an Apartment in their House to any creditable Stranger, so with the same generous Pleasure they receive any whom Misfortunes have brought hither'.[182] On 8 December 1707, Robert Cole complained that he had provided for three to five thousand men for seventy days when the fleet docked in Algiers for supplies: 'there is no other English house on the Place, but mine, and no proper places of entertainment, the Commanders, Gentlemen, Officers, boats crew and seamen resort freely to my house, where they all find a hearty reception at my Table, Kitchen, and Wine Cellar.'[183] It is worth bearing in mind that the cost of wine in Islamic countries was such that capitulations sometimes awarded consuls and ambassadors the right to make wine in their own houses.[184]

As already noted, there is very little correspondence between Algiers and Tunis, or Tripoli and Tetuan, a state of play that was quite different from the vast number of letters that have survived from other regions: Istanbul, Aleppo, Isfahan, Surat, Agra, and beyond. This lack of communication among North African factors may have caused occasional hostility, which without London oversight, often festered. On 7 May 1695, Benjamin Lodington complained to the Secretary of State that Thomas Baker, whom he despised, had employed an English renegade to undermine Lodington's efforts to establish good relations with the Ottoman authorities in Algiers.[185] Lodington also accused Baker of 'French tricks'—pocketing the money that was given him to offer in bribes and gifts to the beys in Tripoli, thereby delaying and even disrupting negotiations: 'In what manner & amongst Mr. Baker obtained friends & Credit att Tripoli is publiquely knowne; being called there Tomas il mariot or drunken Tom: himselfe confessing not to have stirrd out of his house in six months or butt once in a yeare, spending all that time in treating the Runnagadoes indiscreetly.'[186] Such quarrels occurred in other European consulates, too. In 1694, the French consul in Algiers complained about the incompetence, blasphemy, and debauchery of one of the factory employees.[187] Two years later, John Goodwin accused Robert Cole of employing a secretary, Daniel Skinner, who had fought on the side of the French.[188] Cole was also 'suspected to be much inclin'd to a Turbant, Circumcision, that Ceremony of most paine is already undergone, as I understand, by reason of unfortunate femal adventures'.[189] These accusations and counter accusations came to the attention of the king in London because there were clear cases of consuls forging self-addressed letters from the king intended to impress North African rulers.[190] The moral integrity and competence of the consuls was much in question.

Half a century later, there were similar doubts about a consul in Algiers who was so often drunk—'Night and Day drunk, and minds nothing but to please his own Inclination'—that the dey wrote to King George asking that he be removed.[191]

Consuls were charged with preventing interlopers, and coordinating with the accountants who monitored and audited Company finances. In the Maghrib, however, where trade was not controlled by Company regulations, consuls were chiefly burdened with the problems of piracy and captivity. Although they tried to ensure that British ships had up-to-date passes to prevent seizure and captivity, when any British ship was brought in as a prize, the consul had to intervene.[192] If the crew had been taken captive, the consul was responsible for gaining their release and providing them with assistance. Consuls were also responsible for ships arriving legally with trade goods. All governments imposed tariffs on imports, as well as a fee payable to the consul for facilitating the distribution and sale of the ship's merchandise. In 1675, after disgruntled merchants complained about the consular fee, the ambassador John Finch urged that an article be added to the intergovernmental capitulations, confirming it.[193] Among the consul's tasks was ensuring that import tariffs were kept sufficiently low for English products to be cheaper than products of rival countries. Tariffs invariably reflected political circumstances, and were liable to be re-negotiated after military conflicts. The price of defeat for North African rulers might not only be the destruction of their fleets and bombardment of their ports—actions that sometimes provoked local revolts in which they lost their lives or were forced into exile—but also the forced reduction of their custom duties and consequent loss of revenue.

The embassy to Istanbul of Sir John Finch, 1674–81

During the 1670s, an extraordinary group of Englishmen happened to be living in, and reporting home from, the major Ottoman cities of Istanbul and Izmir. When Sir John Finch arrived to take up his appointment as ambassador in 1674, he was accompanied by his life-long companion, Sir Thomas Baines. Already resident were the Company treasurer, Dudley North, and the chaplain, Dr John Covel, while Paul Rycaut had been serving as consul in Izmir since 1667. These were an incomparable group of well-educated and perceptive men who left behind an extensive written record—much of it unpublished—of first-hand knowledge derived from living and working with Muslims.

Still in his thirties, Dudley North (1641–91) was busily amassing the huge fortune that would inspire Macaulay—who otherwise loathed the North family—grudgingly to admit that he was 'one of the ablest men of his time'.[194] Having been apprenticed to a merchant based in Izmir in 1661, North had rapidly become fluent in the Turkish language and the Ottoman legal codes, thereby ingratiating himself with local merchants by seeming to have become one of them, while at the same time avoiding the risks that ignorance of legal procedures and dependence on interpreters could entail.[195] After moving to Istanbul, North quickly became the consummate private merchant banker, lending out money at 20–30 per cent despite laws against usury, while dealing in jewels and precious stones.[196] Appointed Treasurer to the Levant Company, he grew his beard and would sit on the floor wearing local costume when entertaining Turkish clients in a special room where, again in flagrant disregard for legal prohibitions, tobacco and wine were served. He understood that the best way to fleece the rich was to flatter and spoil them with trifles. Such was North's claim to understand the intricacies of Ottoman culture and society that he reckoned Rycaut's *Present State* to be 'very superficial'.[197]

Hardly less colourful, Dr John Covel had arrived from Christ's College, Cambridge—where Finch and Baines had met as students—back in 1670, with a special dispensation from Charles II that permitted him to retain 'all and singular the profits, dividends, stipends, emoluments, and dues belonging to his fellowship in as full and ample a manner to all intents and purposes as if he were actually resident in the College'.[198] Evidently well connected and well on his way to becoming wealthy, Covel was fascinated by the various heresies to be found among Orthodox and eastern Christians; he spent a good deal of his time collecting manuscripts and debating ecclesiastical and theological matters with Baines and others. His diary and letters home reveal a man who was fascinated by just about everything he saw that was strange, unusual, or in any way remarkable. He clearly enjoyed reporting novel discoveries and correcting common errors, instructing his father in 1674:

> what you commonly talk in England of the Turks not shunning the plague I assure you is true only in the mean people which is the same amongst both Jews Greeks & Armenians, they value it not halfe so much as wee do the small pox in England never shun one anothers company; only when they dye.[199]

Covel observed and reflected on the human drama unfolding before him, noting how the plague mostly killed the poor since they spent the summer months eating only cucumbers and 'Carpooses, which are a sort of water Melon gourd, and such kind of trash' with the result that they had little resistance.[200] Meanwhile, and it was no great surprise, he reported that 'most of the Court, City and Country Chelebys (rich men) have found more relish in good wine [than sherbet] and nothing is more familiar than wine & tobacco amongst them though both are forbidden... This grand Vizier himself for certain is drunk (takes his *keif* as they call it) almost every night.'[201] He also noticed and described local costumes and exotic flowers, splendid jewels and beautiful women, recipes for sherbet drinks and the layout of Ottoman tents; he enjoyed hunting, eating, drinking, and collecting seeds to send home for his father's garden.

Although Finch moved into the English house at Pera when there happened to be particularly interesting colleagues among his fellow expatriates, he spend most of his time in the company of Thomas Baines with whom he had lived since his undergraduate days at Cambridge. Theirs was, in Finch's own words, '*suave et irruptum animorum connubium*'—'a beautiful and unbroken marriage of souls',[202] and the contemporary record is surprisingly lacking in criticism, or even innuendo, concerning the precise nature of their relationship. In Pera, the two friends enjoyed evenings spent sitting on the terrace watching the birds that, once Finch had ordered the servants not to scare them away, would visit their garden. Perhaps Baines was thinking of such occasions in the opening stanza of his unpublished poem 'On Friendship':

> Come my Fidelia, let us smile
>   At the dull World, and in this Arbour
> Wee'l innocently sitt a while
>   Free from the Cares which Great ones harbour.[203]

Unfortunately, the real problem was that his appointment as England's ambassador meant that whatever he might have wished, Finch was necessarily involved in the 'cares' of the 'great ones'.

Even before arriving in Istanbul, Finch encountered his first diplomatic crisis. While still in transit aboard the *Centurion*, Finch arrived in Izmir to learn that an English ship, the *Mediterranean*, had been seized by a Genoese pirate sailing under a privateering commission from the Grand Duke of Tuscany. The problem was that the *Mediterranean* had been transporting a retiring Ottoman pasha back to Tunis. The pasha himself had been safely set ashore with some of his belongings near Libyan Tripoli before the ship was seized, but his wives and most of his belongings were taken. The Porte was furious, deeming liability to reside with the English, from whom reparations were being demanded. However, Finch and Baines had spent several years in Florence and were on sufficiently friendly terms with the Grand Duke for Finch to secure an order banishing the corsair and recuperating all the goods that had been seized.[204] Finch may have won his first diplomatic victory through the careful use of personal connections, but would encounter increasing difficulties in subsequent negotiations.

In late March 1674 when Finch and Baines reached Istanbul, the Ottoman government was generally well disposed towards the English. As Rycaut observed less than a year later: 'the honour and priviledge which Our Nation enjoyeth here, and security of our Persons and Estates under the Turkes... is beyond the Example of former times.'[205] Reasons were not hard to find. Charles had not objected when the Ottomans made use of English ships during their siege of Candia back in 1668, and as both Finch and Baines at different times pointed out, the Ottoman economy still relied heavily on the importation of English wool, tin, and lead.[206] Although this claim may have been in part a self-serving fiction, certain it is that Anglo-Ottoman relations in general had been in good shape since 1656 when Köprülü Mehmed Pasha was appointed Grand Vezir, and had continued so under his son, Ahmed Pasha,[207] despite the relative incompetence of the previous ambassador, Sir Daniel Harvey (1668–72). Nonetheless, Finch arrived at a time when the status quo was about to change with the appointment of Merzifonlu Kara Mustapha Pasha as Grand Vezir in the late autumn of 1676. Meanwhile, Sultan Mehmed IV (r. 1648–87) continued to keep court in Edirne (Adrianople) rather than Istanbul, and was generally disinterested in matters commercial or political, preferring to spend his time hunting. Facing Finch was the problem of the capitulations which had not been renewed since 1662. So it was that Finch's first task was to negotiate terms that would benefit his own reputation and serve the best interests of the English trading community, but nothing could happen until he had been formally invited to be received by Mehmed in Edirne. And that meant waiting.

For a little over a year, Finch had to wait for an occasion to visit Mehmed IV who, besides hunting, had matters other than trade with the English on his mind. His armies, commanded by Merzifonlu Kara Mustafa Pasha, were dealing with insurrections in Poland-Lithuania and Muscovy.[208] In Edirne, he was planning a festival the likes of which had not been seen in the Ottoman Empire since the circumcision celebrations for the future Mehmed III in 1582—for which the fireworks had been designed by an English captive, Edward Webbe. By the spring of 1675, preparations were in place and Mehmed solemnly declared that, starting on 14 May, there would be thirty-three days of celebrations in Edirne for the circumcision of his sons and the marriage of his daughter. Dignitaries from far and wide, including all foreign residents and ambassadors, were not only expected to attend but also to compete with each other in the lavishness of the gifts that they would bring. Commoners could also offer presents for the privilege of being circumcised at the same time. As Covel noted in his unpublished journal:

> I saw many 100es of them (there being about 2,000 in all the 13 nights) cut, and the Turkes would be so farre from hindring your seing, as they would make way for you. There were many of riper yeares, especially renegades that turn'd Turks. I saw an old man which they reported to be 53 yeares old, cut.

Covel reckoned that, balancing the costs of the festivities against the presents, Mehmed's month-long party made him a tidy profit of no less than two and a half million pounds sterling.[209]

In high style and with, no doubt, great expectations, Finch had set out for Edirne on 2 May. The English ambassadorial entourage included fifty-five baggage wagons, three spare horses, a coach and six, and a coach and four, while Finch and Baines travelled in 'a kind of double horse litter, used by the great men in Turkey, caryed by 4 mules, cover'd with fine wrought cloath'.[210] Travelling at the rate of about twenty miles a day, the journey—recorded in detail by Covel—took them nine days. On arrival outside the city, they were formally received by an advance party that, in Covel's words,

> provided 12 of the G. Signor's horses for my Lord and his attendance to mount and ride into city with all; they were all admirable good ones, and set out as rich as was possible. I left my own and took one of them, whose bridle, saddle, great stirrups, breast plate, buttock cloth, etc., were either all of beaten gold and silver, or else most richly embroyder'd. My Lord's horses furniture were set out with jewels and pearles most gloriously.[211]

If the costly trappings of the fine horses sent to convey the English party into town seemed a token that all would go well during the diplomatic negotiations that were preoccupying Finch, such expectations were swiftly dashed once it was discovered that the house they had been allocated 'was the damn'dest confounded place that ever mortall man was put into . . . not half big enough to hold half my Ld.'s family, a mere nest of fleas and cimici, and rats and mice, and stench'.[212] To make matters worse, Finch had barely found acceptable lodgings when he learned that he had not been formally invited to attend any of the celebrations which meant that, to preserve his dignity, he could not afford to be seen in public since that would make it known he was there but had been snubbed. Finch was, however, able to arrange a formal meeting with the Grand Vezir Köprülü Ahmed Pasha on 19 May at which all seems to have gone well, though he learned that ratifying the capitulations would have to wait until the festivities were finished. In the meantime, Covel and North wandered among the crowds and recorded the extraordinary sights and sounds of 'young Men dancing in the Habits of Women, with a thousand Jack-pudding Tricks' alongside 'Farces acted with several filthy Dialogues, and all kinds of Obscenity acted most naturally', as North put it.[213] Amidst the fun and games, Finch kept himself busy holding meetings with the representatives of other Christian nations, mostly with a view to resolving the problem of Jerusalem.

Ever since Jerusalem had come under Ottoman control, disputes there between various Christian factions had to be resolved by resolutions approved by the Ottoman court. Most recently, disagreements between the Latin and Greek churches had again erupted over rights to hold ceremonies within the Church of the Holy Sepulchre. In April 1673, the French ambassador, Charles-François de Nointel, had successfully included a clause in the French capitulations giving priority to the Latin friars, but later that same year it transpired that an influential Greek dragoman, Panayoti Nicusi, had already secured a claim for the Greek monks. Nicusi had, however, kept quiet rather than offend his delicate relations with certain German bankers whose interests he was promoting at the Porte. However, when Nicusi died in the autumn of 1673, the pro-Greek *firman* was revealed, leading to a feud in which two Greek monks were murdered. De Nointel blustered, declaring that they had died of old age, but requested financial assistance from France and Spain for bribes that would help forestall Greek interests in Edirne and Istanbul. By Easter 1674, delegations of Greek monks and Spanish Jesuits from Jerusalem had arrived in Edirne and were bustling about hoping to resolve the problem by handing out enormous bribes. Such was the situation when Finch arrived.[214]

Since Edward Barton's day, the English had taken the side of the Greeks because doing so formed an invaluable alliance against Spanish interests. In 1661, however, Charles II's first ambassador to the Porte, Heneage Finch, the Second Earl of Winchilsea (1661–68) had arrived with a different agenda. His formal Instructions included the usual clause requiring him to 'show all kindness and humanity to those of the Greek Church' and to counteract by any means the machinations of the Latin friars, 'especially such Jesuits and Friars as under religious pretences compass other ends'.[215] While there is some reason to suspect that he was under verbal instructions from Charles to favour the Catholics right from the start of his embassy, in 1663 Winchilsea received permission from the king to disregard the pro-Greek clause 'and thenceforth made the protection of the Roman Catholics an integral part of his programme'.[216] The pro-Greek clause was subsequently dropped from the Instructions issued to Daniel Harvey in 1668 and was also conspicuously absent from Finch's Instructions.[217]

Finch accordingly adopted an anti-Greek, pro-Latin policy from the start, refusing to assist the Greek Patriarch in 1674.[218] On arrival in Edirne, Finch offered to support the Latin Fathers by including a clause in the proposed capitulations and brokering a bribe of 150,000 dollars for them that was designed to prevent the Greeks holding Mass in the Church of the Holy Sepulchre. Before Finch could act on this, the Greeks had discovered the plot and appealed to Covel for help overturning the plan. Finch may have known that the House of Commons, which had reconvened in April 1675, was vigorously debating a Bill against Popery and concluded that this was not an occasion for being too compliant towards Rome.[219] For whatever reasons, Finch moderated his position and removed the clause from the proposed capitulations while promising to organize and support a separate *firman* guaranteeing Latin supremacy. At the same time, while waiting for the festivities to end so that he might pursue securing the capitulations, Finch took to making his presence known and generating goodwill by sending gifts to notables at the Ottoman court. Having learned that only Mehmed and the Grand Mufti kept to the prohibition on alcohol, Finch discreetly distributed bottles of fine wine 'which the Grandees at Court baptize by the name of English sherbett'. Mehmed himself received a great English mastiff that was reputed to kill wild bears.[220] In due course, word came that the draft capitulations had been approved, but no date could be set for him to be received by the Sultan and, until that had happened, the capitulations could not be formally signed and put into effect.

Although the terms of the capitulations had become more or less standardized by this time, Finch was especially keen to introduce a few minor but significant changes. In all previous agreements, the English monarch had been referred to as *kral*, or simply 'king', whereas the French monarchs were termed *padishah*, or 'king of kings'. So far, no previous English ambassador had managed to rectify this obvious insult to the court of St James, and Finch was optimistic that he had managed to achieve it. There were also new clauses concerning the legal status of English converts to Islam. Finch had also resisted pressure from the Ottoman treasurer to agree to an increase in the amount of customs payable on imports of English cloth, which had always been set at a competitive rate of 3 per cent.

The festivities in Edirne ended on 25 June, and while Finch waited to be called to meet Mehmed, plague broke out in the city. Leaving North behind to take care of any business that might arise, Finch and Baines with Covel and the rest of the English party moved a few miles out to the Greek village of Karaağaç on the Aradas river. A month later, Finch was finally summoned to present himself before the Sultan and, on 27 July, proceeded back into the plague-ravaged city where, after a rushed banquet and an abrupt formal meeting with Mehmed, he learned that neither Köprülü Ahmed Pasha nor the Sultan had read, let alone approved, the new articles in his draft capitulations. Arriving back in Karaağaç, Finch discovered that his landlady's daughter had died of the plague. Without delay, he and the other Englishmen moved into a field and spent the next four weeks living in tents. As the heat of August and the plague raged on with ever greater intensity, rumours arrived that the key articles had been approved but, since Köprülü Ahmed Pasha refused to take bribes, nothing could be done to speed matters up. Finally, on 8 September Finch received a signed copy of the capitulations, and noticed that while Charles was still only a *kral*, his other requests had gone through.[221] He also found that the Sultan had introduced an entirely unexpected clause: 'Wee doe grant that two ships lading of Figgs, Raisins, or Currants, may be yearly exported for the use of His Majesty's kitchin.'[222] Within a week, Finch had made his farewells and set off on the return journey to Pera, losing several servants to plague along the way.

If Finch was at all optimistic that, capitulations signed, future matters would all go his way from now on, he would soon find himself disappointed. In January 1676, he did successfully secure the Porte's approval when an English fleet under Sir John Narborough entered the bay at Libyan Tripoli and, setting fire to four men-of-war, forced the dey to release all English captives.[223] But this might have been the last real achievement of his stay in Istanbul. Certainly the disputes over precedence in Jerusalem dragged on, and Finch's attempts to intervene on behalf of the Latin friars proved futile: as late as March 1680 Finch reports that the matter was still unresolved.[224] Following the death of Köprülü Ahmed Pasha in the autumn of 1676, the new Grand Vezir—Merzifonlu Kara Mustafa Pasha—proved to be a thorn in the side of all Christian ambassadors. One of his first acts on being promoted was to effect a major Franco-Ottoman rupture by inviting the French ambassador to a meeting but refusing to allow him to sit, as was traditional, on a stool placed on the same platform on which the Vezir himself sat.[225] Unlike his predecessor, he was very keen to accept presents—and indeed often demanded them—but seldom delivered on any promises made to 'Franks'. He swiftly set about extracting as many fines—known as *avanias*—as possible from the English and other Christian nations trading within Ottoman regions. In 1677 he fined John Ashby, an English merchant, $4,000 in a dispute over a debt owed to Ashby of $3,000, leading the Company to complain to King Charles that such extortions were imposed on the English 'for noe other Reason then . . . the Vastnes of Our Trade'.[226] That same year he seized a shipload of newly minted coins that had been sent from England to Aleppo in order to have them assayed in hopes of finding their gold content inadequate; although the coins turned out to be better than they needed to be, the English were fined $12,500.[227] In 1679, Finch wrote to the Levant Company complaining that Kara Mustafa had come up with a new scheme for raising money. All 'foreign Ambassadors' would, on arrival, now be expected to pay '100 purses', or $50,000, and the Vezir expected 'to have presents every month' from all representatives of Christian nations.[228] But matters continued to deteriorate, and in May 1689 Finch was writing home reporting 'the most prodigious and perhaps the most dismall news that ever came from Turky', which was that Kara Mustafa had seized and suspended the English capitulations.[229] As if matters could not be worse for the English ambassador, in July that year the Pasha of Tunis who had been abducted back in 1674, brought a case against Finch for $100,000 that, he claimed, remained unpaid. Finch, hoping to clear this matter up before the arrival of his replacement, James Brydges, Baron Chandos, managed to delay judgment by insisting that the witnesses were all corrupt and that he would have to take the advice of King Charles.[230] Chandos eventually showed up in July 1681,[231] and by August Finch had received 'his Majesty's express declaration to the Vizir and Grand Signor that his ambassador should not pay an asper to the Bassa of Tunis'. 'But,' he recorded in his journal:

> now a stop was putt to my further acting, for on August the 16, I was taken with a tertian ague; but that which cutt off the thread of all my worldly happinesse and application to businesse was the malignant double tertian which seised, August the 22nd my dear friend Sir Thomas Baines, and on Monday the 5th of September brought him to his last end... expiring in my armes, and rendring his soul to Almighty God.[232]

Suffering from 'an irresistible torrent of grief' at Baines' death, Finch's 'tertian ague' intensified, only to be aggravated further by Kara Mustafa Pasha who 'sent two messengers to order me to weigh anchor and be gone'.[233] Despite his lingering illness, Finch managed to return home to England but died in November 1682. Finch and Baines are commemorated in an elaborate monument in the chapel at Christ's College, Cambridge.

By way of conclusion

The period under study witnessed the expansion of Britain's commercial and diplomatic presence to the farthest ends of the Islamic empires. It was an expansion that was undertaken by a vast number of factors and governors, consuls and ambassadors, sailors and clergymen, carpenters and apothecaries, surgeons and cooks, who reached regions their countrymen had never known before. Whether they were honest tradesmen, pirates, or both, intelligent diplomats or drunks, adroit accountants or sharp entrepreneurs, they persevered, driven by the need to establish gainful trade, often against hostile Europeans with better maps who had been there long before them. In North Africa, as well as in the Ottoman, Persian, and Indian regions, the Britons who traded, settled, bargained, fought, and sometimes died, were there in search of opportunities for employment and commerce, for themselves as well as their countrymen, that were not available to them at home, and, during continental wars, were denied them in Europe. Their lives and experiences helped shape the course and contours of British national identity.

At first, their commercial ventures took them into the Mediterranean and to the Moroccan and Ottoman spheres of power. In these regions, the status of the British residents varied, from precariousness in North Africa, to relative security and comfort in the Ottoman Levant. It is not unsafe to confirm that factors and consuls in North Africa did not enjoy themselves—so many letters include pleas for permission to return to England, which were rarely answered. In the Ottoman Levant, with Levant Company support, and with the need to have diplomatic representation in Istanbul, factors, consuls, and ambassadors fared better, and learned more about the culture, history, and society of the region than did their counterparts in North Africa. No resident in North Africa ever wrote or published anything about the region in the manner of Rycaut, Covell, and Smith. In Persia, after the Shirley brothers, there were emissaries and factors, but the wealth of India prevailed and directed most of the East India Company in the direction of the fort-towns that began to appear in, and dominate, various coastal zones. As ship-building improved, Britons sailed to the Mughal Empire at the same time that they continued to trek through Europe toward Aleppo and into central Asia. In Indian waters, the British began building vessels in their own shipyards, especially frigates, which were stronger than the local junks. The records from the Arabian Sea and the Indian region show an aggressive and assertive stance. Here battles were fought, but chiefly against the Portuguese and the Dutch. The East India Company sent instructions for military action, whenever there was need, unlike in the Mediterranean where ships belonging to the Levant Company continued to fall prey to North African attacks—until the intervention of the Cromwellian and subsequent fleets. The North Africans were much more ready to take up arms against the English than the imperial Mughals. From Morocco to Libya, local rulers repeatedly demanded munitions, cannons, and naval supplies, often in exchange for captives. Consuls in Algiers or Tripoli had the most onerous task of all Britons in the regions of Islam: that of pleading for the release of their captured countrymen.

Thousands of British factors and sailors, consuls, and governors, sold and transported anything that would turn them a profit, and kept detailed records of what was or was not marketable. In the ports where they established trading centres, and in the zones in between—especially the coastal areas between Surat and Hormuz, and from Madras to Bantam—they bribed and intimidated, kissed hands and prayed, fought and made allies. On one occasion, there was even discussion of taking an English woman to marry her to the ruler of Sumatra in order to secure trade; only the intervention of Church of England officials prevented the marriage of a Christian woman to a Muslim, and all the religious implications such a marriage for the sake of commerce could carry.[234] Britons endured flux, ague, and fever, as well as imprisonment, robbery, insults, and monsoons. As they carried ambergris and elephants' teeth, mangoes and tin, broadcloth and beavers' skins, precious stones and Bezoar stones and opium, they participated with the Dutch, the Portuguese, the French, the Venetians, the Danes, and the Spaniards in the internationalization of consumerism.

Very rarely did Britons develop plans to convert native Muslims. In the North American colonies, they earnestly sought to convert the native peoples, but in the factories of the Islamic world, they kept their religion to themselves, sometimes fearing for it. Whether in Izmir, Isfahan, or Madras, they were there to earn a living, grow rich, and if death spared them, return home, their fortunes made. At no point did they develop missionary projects like the Jesuits or Capuchins who were so effective that by 1724, they had succeeded in converting an entire community of Orthodox Greek to the Church of Rome. The ambassadors who strutted in Istanbul, the captives who cowered in Algeria, the clergymen who officiated in makeshift chapels, and the sailors and ships' captains who fought the Portuguese and Dutch in Indian and Persian Gulf waters, or the French in the Mediterranean: all had left home in search of wealth. As Sir Walter Raleigh had sought the gold of Eldorado, so his countrymen ventured in quest of the riches of the 'Land of Canaan'—in North Africa as in India.[235]

Many Britons never returned, leaving graves spread all around the shores and in the cities of the Islamic world. But it is no coincidence that the largest mausoleums commemorating Britain's dead, built in imitation of Indian Muslim custom, still stand in Surat where most of the earliest Anglo-Mughal trading took place.[236] In all of *Dar al-Islam*, there was nowhere more conducive to British swagger and rapacity, or British coercion through military shows of force. Unlike their countrymen in Aleppo or Istanbul, the British East India Company governors and presidents did not engage in largely peaceful commercial and diplomatic exchanges, as guests of a great empire. Rather, among the Mughals, they asserted themselves ruthlessly for the first time as imperial masters.

4
Captives

From the late sixteenth century onwards, tales of captives held by Muslims in North Africa were regularly published and often reprinted. Interest in such works continued judging from the numerous editions, translations from French and Spanish, and the composite collections that issued from the press at regular intervals. Although contemporary reports of life among the Muslims of North Africa sent home by resident consuls and factors greatly exceed the number of accounts by captives, these writings have never been edited or even properly calendared. Yet this vast body of manuscript material provides evidence of a very different attitude toward Muslims and Islamic culture from that conveyed by former captives. Hard-nosed businessmen serving in consular roles were eager to turn a profit, despite expressions of piety, and they worked with Muslims on Muslims' own terms. They were concerned with saleable commodities, available sea routes, military supplies, commercial and diplomatic services, and with recruiting intermediaries who would serve their interests at royal courts and in seaports. Their writings are factual and lack the melodrama of accounts by captives, who always presented themselves as suffering Christian heroes. Had consular writings become known to early modern readers, attitudes to Muslims and Islam would have been far less imbued with religious animosity and more tuned to the advantages of commercial cooperation. But, as we explore in this chapter, it was the captivity narrative, buttressed by sermons about returning Englishmen who had converted to Islam during captivity, which held the public imagination, and shaped the way generations of English men and women thought about Muslims and the Islamic world.

Throughout the Medieval period, Christians and Muslims took each other captive in the Mediterranean and European theatres of war. As a result, Muslim rulers, from Al-Andalus to Alexandria, instituted a group of emissaries, the *fakkakin*, to negotiate the release of coreligionists, at the same

Figure 7. 'The Triumph of a Christian that has renounced the Faith', from Jean Dumont, *Nouveau voyage du Levant* (A la Haye, 1694)
From the James Ford Bell Library, University of Minnesota, Minneapolis, Minnesota

time that the Catholic Church established the religious orders of the Most Holy Trinity, the Trinitarians (1198), and of Our Lady of Mercy, the Mercedarians (c.1218).[1] In France and Spain, these orders became both efficient and successful, continually receiving privileges from the monarchy to facilitate their work.[2] Military orders, such as the Knights of the Order of Saint Stephen, were established in Italy to fight Muslims and combat captivity.³ During the later fifteenth and early sixteenth century, as Spain and Portugal pushed into North Africa,⁴ followed in the seventeenth century by Britain and France, what Fernand Braudel called the 'little wars' between the Christian and the Islamic states of the Mediterranean took their toll on travellers, sailors, and merchants. Captivity became a crisis that would persistently preoccupy Christian and Muslim leaders and religious organizations, not to mention merchants, ships' captains, sailors, families of captives, clergymen, and jurists.

No religious orders were established in England to liberate captives, though as early as 1480, indulgences were 'issued to raise money to fight the Turks or to ransom captives'.⁵ Under Elizabeth I, England separated itself not only from the Catholic Church but also from those well-financed institutions that negotiated to ransom captives held by Muslims. This separation coincided with the beginnings of England's maritime and commercial expansion into the Mediterranean and the Atlantic, enterprises that resulted in the capture and enslavement of unprecedented numbers of English, Irish, Welsh, Cornish, and Scottish travellers, soldiers, and sailors by Muslim and Euro-Christian privateers and pirates. The vast majority of these early modern British captives were seized in the Mediterranean, with only a few incidents of captivity reported in Anatolia, Persia, or India. Although Sir Henry Middleton was famously taken captive in Mocha, most English captives were taken to ports such as Salé, Algiers, Tunis, and Libyan Tripoli, ports that were seldom under the complete control of Istanbul and therefore usually beyond the remit of diplomatic negotiation.⁶ Captivity produced embittered and angry Britons, who, in oral and written accounts, conveyed a hostile view of their Muslim captors and their religion to readers who were otherwise unfamiliar with Islam and Islamic civilization. These tales were full of violence, hatred, and humiliation. Public demand was such that tales of captivity in North Africa were regularly printed from the 1580s until the early eighteenth century⁷—more so, by far, than accounts of captivity in any other part of the world.

Britons held in North Africa converted to Islam and lived on, or died in captivity, unless they escaped or were ransomed and returned home. On return, some wrote about their experiences because, as Braudel suggested, their home governments encouraged them to do so in hopes that these accounts would alienate readers from the temptations of Islam. This was, after all, a time when 'men flocked from Christendom to Islam, which tempted them with visions of adventure and profit—and paid them to stay'.[8] Christian governments needed propaganda that demonized Muslims. English dramatists and preachers, as well as continental painters and hagiographers of early modern Spanish and Italian saints—St Raymond Nonnatus and St Serapion in particular—depicted, in prayer, on canvas and stage, in print, and from the pulpit, the brutality of Muslim pirates, especially those of 'Barbary', thereby seeming to prove that anti-Christian violence was inherent to Islam. 'Western governments' encouraged 'the recounting of captive 'horror stories' in order to convince their subjects of the dangers of any contact with Islam', Ellen G. Friedman has argued, confirming Braudel.[9]

In the process, the captivity narrative acquired distinctive features that developed and mutated unevenly, even as British relations with the Islamic world shifted and changed. It was not autobiography, but a story of enduring a physically and spiritually dangerous experience during which the captive was denied freedom and enticed to renounce God and country and to join the infidels. Numerous captives told how, upon return, friends asked them to write and publish their stories. Many apologized for their unpolished style and rough content, claiming that they only resorted to print because of community interest and pressure. Some captives circulated their accounts in manuscript, while others, especially illiterate sailors, talked to ghost-writers who subsequently published them.[10] Since most captives lacked formal education or religious instruction, editors often stepped in to improve the original, sometimes spicing it with classical allusions and Latin quotations. Meanwhile, orally transmitted stories about the Islamic world became common gossip in theatres and the ale houses of port cities as well as the corridors of parliamentary and royal power. By the late seventeenth century, when the British imperial imagination was increasingly stimulated by the newly acquired garrisons of Tangier and Bombay, the ideological bearings of captivity narratives shifted from warning of the dangers of Islam to celebrating the resourcefulness and ingenuity of captives who managed to escape. Captives started representing themselves as providers of intelligence that would be useful for future British occupation and domination. The nightmare of captivity became the dream of empire.

The history of captivity and of captivity accounts in England wielded the strongest influence on British understanding of Islam and Muslims in the early modern period. These stories, both authentic and fictional, reached all sectors of society, from king to pauper, and confirmed the hostile stereotypes about the 'Mahometans' that appeared in sermons and chronicles. More than any other experience, Mediterranean captivity defined the religion and the society of Muslims for Britons, as well as other Europeans and colonial Americans. That captivity was a consequence of the imperial onslaught of western powers on nascent Muslim commerce and navigation, rather than a product of structural opposition between Islam and Christianity, was never analysed in the oral and written narratives of the long-enduring Christians, heroically returned from the bagnios of Algiers.

The first English account of captivity appeared in Richard Hakluyt's *Principal Navigations* (1589). Hakluyt was sharp enough to realize that captives could provide valuable intelligence about a Muslim world that was still largely unknown to English society from reports by merchants and travellers. If anyone, Hakluyt should be credited for promoting this popular genre. He realized that English readers lacked information about the geographically expanding world being explored by Spanish, Portuguese, and French missionaries. From the Americas to the Levant, India, and Japan, there were Capuchins, Franciscans, and Jesuits who were sending back a constant stream of information about the societies and regions they visited, thereby providing their orders and governments with knowledge the English lacked. Hakluyt recognized that captivity was total immersion: captives who had lived with Libyans or been held in Alexandria, brought back knowledge of local societies as well as of languages, making them among the first in England to acquire the spoken, rather than classical forms of Arabic and Turkish.[11] For English readers of the time, these gripping stories provided the most vivid, but also intimidating, descriptions of North Africa, a region that had become enormously important for trade.

On returning home, some captives clearly met with suspicion, though we know very little about the ways English communities treated returning captives, since published accounts invariably end heroically, with escape or return, but not arrival. Most likely, family and fellow parishioners were unsure whether their kinsmen had been tainted by contact with Muslims, had converted willingly or under coercion, or even whether they might have served on ships that attacked Christians. Many had, indeed, been compelled to work for the enemy, sometimes as mariners aboard ships that attacked English shipping, and were consequently obliged to exonerate themselves in court. But some willingly signed on with their captors, who paid hard currency that could be saved up to buy freedom. While friends and relatives were usually welcoming, however suspicious they might have been, the evidence of printed sermons delivered upon the return of suspected renegades suggests that parish priests and bishops took a stern view.[12]

Thomas Pellow, held in Morocco for twenty-three years, admitted that there were 'some ill-natured People [who] think me so [Muslim] even to this Day'.[13] Because of such suspicions, captives shaped their stories to exonerate themselves, expressing pious gratitude that they were, as Pellow put it, back in 'Old England'.

Since captives wrote to assure audiences that they had remained pious Christians, they assume religiously and socially conservative attitudes. Without the festive processions that priests held for liberated captives in France,[14] and without pictures, canvases, tapestries, illustrations, altarpieces, or chapels dedicated to saints of redemption,[15] English captives relied on words and print to confirm their identity and allegiance. Captivity was humiliating, and as much as captives tried to celebrate heroism and defiance, their experiences never became the subject of formal public celebration: not a single play dramatized the plight of English captives in the manner that Cervantes or Lope de Vega portrayed Spanish captives. There were no special days dedicated to public thanksgiving and prayer for their safe return, nor were captives presented to the king to be touched—even though the Stuarts, like Elizabeth, loved to show their benevolence by healing scrofula.[16] Captivity was never made to serve the interests of church and state as it was in France. Stuart monarchs never adopted captivity as a royal cause; they left ransom and liberation to trading companies, parishes, individuals, and families, which may explain why English and Scottish captives were regularly ransomed, while redeemed Irish captives seldom appear in the records. When 'Turkish' pirates seized over 100 men, women, and children from Baltimore in June 1631, little effort was made to rescue any of them, though it is possible that two of the women were freed and returned in 1647.[17]

Surviving captivity narratives in English are all by and about men, some of whom had been captured while still very young.[18] Women were sometimes taken captive, but since relatively few were ever ransomed, the chances of their writing about their captivity were greatly reduced. It was not until 1757 that Elizabeth Marsh became the first English woman to write about being held captive in Morocco.[19] Although French redemptionists mention ransoming women as early as 1587, when Charles Pandon stated that he had freed from Tunisian captivity twenty 'honestes Dames' from Coutron, no similar references appear in English archives until much later when, in 1637, the following women were ransomed back to England:

The names of the women that were redeemed:
London: Mary Russell, Anne Bedford, Joan Gillions.
Dorchester: Jane Dawe.
Exeter: Rebecca Man.
Bristol: Grace Greenfield.
Bantry: Grace Marten.
Yo-hall: Margaret Bowles, Katharine Richards, Mary Batten.
Kingsaile: Elizabeth Renordan.[20]

In 1645, several women were seized by North African Corsairs in a raid on the coast of Cornwall, but nothing was documented about their names, conditions, or ransoms.[21] Later lists of ransomed captives mention only a handful of women, but these contain no information about how they had fared, whether they had been mistreated, or whether they had converted. In France, women captives were given priority over men, and Spanish accounts are full of references to ransomed women, both single and married.[22] No similar urgency appears in the records of English negotiations. We do not know the 'Christian' name of the only English woman of the time whose story of captivity has survived in any detail; she married Mulay Ismail and never returned to England.[23] In 1719, the daughter of an Irish count was taken captive to Algiers, but doubtless since she was Irish and Catholic, nothing was written about her in English, though a translation of a French account eventually appeared in 1735.[24]

English captivity accounts published between 1589 and the first quarter of the eighteenth century can be divided into two groups: those written before 1640 and those written after. The first group tell stories of sea battles, torture, slave labour, and resistance to conversion, followed by liberation, either by escape or ransom. They tend to be short and relatively lacking in detail about the captors' geography or ethnography, except when such details comment adversely upon the religion of the captors, or upon life in England and the captors' need for employment. More to the point, Elizabethan and Jacobean accounts testify to fortitude in religious language. Hence the regular use of the term 'redemption' with its heavy New Testament association: as Christ bought humanity back from sin by his sacrifice, so captives were bought back, either by the intervention of the monarch or by the charity of the community. Writers treated captivity as a fall into Islamic sin from which Christ redeemed them. With their general ignorance of Muslims and Islamic culture, and by reiterating platitudes about Muslims, works appearing before 1640 correspond to writings that

Braudel considered deliberately anti-Islamic. While they provided the first glimpses of some Mediterranean regions, they also introduced 'Turks' and 'Moors' as dangerous captors who destabilized faith by forcing conversion to Islam, and threatened the flow of British trade and commerce.

Captivity narratives changed around 1640. From that year on, most published accounts were longer, describing the natural and built environments as well as the cultural, religious, and social life of the captors. Captives began to represent themselves as explorers and adventurers, returning with new, reliable, and valuable information that could be put to good use by future merchants, diplomats, and ransomers. These accounts reveal the captives fighting back: showing that enterprising Englishmen could defeat the dangerous Muslims, either by outsmarting them or, more impressively, by furnishing information and calling for naval and military action. While the earlier captivity writers were fearful and confused, later writers presented themselves as heroic, daring, and possessed of plans to conquer. One captive, perhaps fictional, told how he became a leader of Muslims under his Ottoman master; others portrayed themselves in heroic escapades, outwitting their dull captors, while helping them in administration and military campaigns. Captives could display their native-born mettle among their Muslim captors. They showed how simple it was to assume North African identities and pretend to be Muslims, since Islam was merely a religion of ritual. Doing so enabled them to achieve military and social status, since their English skills were far superior to anything the natives possessed. Such postures testified to Christian perseverance and the workings of providential design—some even ended their stories with 'Amen' as if they were sermons.[25] Captives also started mapping cities and routes, and listing natural resources. They emphasized cultural and religious details, as well as the military and mental inferiority of those they called 'Mahometans'. Filled with descriptions of vast natural resources, from Barbary horses to gold, and showing how underdeveloped the Muslims were and how false their religion was, captivity narratives pointed toward the possibility—and the means—of British domination.

From 1640 on, captives became heroes of adventures that were also morality tales designed to affirm Anglo-Protestant values, virtues, and attitudes. As a result, not a single printed captivity account that appeared was by a Catholic. Indeed, it may well be that British Catholics were not ransomed any more than Huguenots were by their Catholic compatriots.[26] William Okeley was perhaps the only 'Puritan' to publish an account of captivity among Muslims: his *Eben-Ezer: Or, A Small Monument of Great Mercy* (1675) included some lines from George Herbert's 'Church Militant' that had had to be excised before *The Temple* could be given Anglican imprimatur.[27] Published captivity accounts told of the spiritual victories and providential escapes of Protestant heroes: accounts by Catholics or Quakers never saw the print shop.[28] Captivity accounts were weapons in the Anglican battle with, and victory over, North African Muslims with their tempting women, fine weather, and well-paid jobs. They were aimed at general readers and priced accordingly. Unlike the erudite, thick, and costly tomes written by scholars and orientalists, captivity accounts were easily accessible. These inspiring stories of heroism and faith furnished readers with the earliest descriptions of Islam, Muslim society, and the alluring dangers of the Islamic World—all couched in adventures by sea or land. They also illustrated how Britons might defeat Muslims theologically, and conquer them geographically.

1589–1640

The very first captivity narratives published in Europe were set in the Americas and described the New World and its populations. The Spanish account by Alvar Nunez Cabeza de Vaca (1542) about events in 1527–28, and the account by Hans Staden (1557) about events in 1554, both describe captivity in South America and illustrate the variety of captors and captives.[29] In his dedication to Emperor Charles V, de Vaca noted that his report conveyed information about the geography and peoples that future conquerors and settlers would encounter. Staden similarly described the customs and practices of the Tupi Indians, including a strong indictment of cannibalism, thereby producing one of the first empirically generated ethnographical studies of a society that would soon be completely destroyed. Notwithstanding their proto-colonial stance—Staden initially served in a fortified Portuguese outpost in Morocco—these authors had no need to demonize the American natives since they posed no threat to the superior technology, and horses, of the conquistadores. Accounts by English mariners seized by the Spanish in Mexico in the 1560s, 1570s, and 1580s that were published by Hakluyt, also furnished extensive information about peoples and regions. Captives such as Miles Philips and Job Hortop spent many years in slavery (1568–82 and 1568–91 respectively), after which they confirmed to their readers the wealth of the Spanish possessions and the advantages of English conquest.[30] While captives in the New World feared for their lives, they never feared that they would lose their identity: all were firmly assured of the superiority of their Christianity, or at least, so they liked to convey.

Such superiority was challenged by captivity among Muslims, which helps explain the virulent hostility towards Muslim captors. The first printed account of European captivity among Muslims, Bartolomeus Georgievits' *De Turcarum Ritu et Caeremoniis* (1544), was translated into English by Hugh Goughe under the title *The Ofspring of the house of Ottomanno* (1570). This influential account was composed following the Hungarian defeat by the Ottomans at Mohács in 1526 and the captivity of the author for thirteen years in Istanbul. Georgievits describes his suffering, but his primary aim is much more practical: 'He wishes to share what he has learned about Ottoman social and military custom', as Linda McJannet puts it, though much of his information followed earlier writers.[31] Another early text about captivity among the Muslims was the translation of Sebastian Munster's *A briefe collection and compendious extract of the straunge and memorable things* (1572) that reported about the power and superiority of the Ottomans over Christians, how they 'keepe their captives not onely in chaynes, but also with gyves upon their handes, as they leade them... The nighte is more heavie unto they, for then eyther they are shit [sic] up in strong holds, or els are compelled to suffer the filthy lust of those that have bought them.'[32] English readers could also have learned about captivity from the plays by Cervantes that were based on his five years of captivity in Algiers.[33] Although they have happy endings, these plays include scenes of Christian submission, defeat, and martyrdom. Captivity, on stage as in autobiography, illustrated both the power of the Ottoman Muslims and how dangerous they were.

The earliest English account of captivity concerns one John Foxe who, in 1563, was seized in the eastern Mediterranean. He spent the next fourteen years as a galley slave on ships based in Alexandria, until escaping with 266 other Christian captives. Throughout, the account treats Foxe's story as a religious experience, aiming 'to shew the ende of those, being in meere miserie, which continually doe call on God with a stedfast hope that he will deliver them, and with a sure faith that he can doe it'.[34] The escape demonstrates the Christian God's power to bring about seeming miracles. An impossibility made possible by God, Foxe's escape proved the might of 'our' God in contrast to the ineffectiveness of 'their's'. Religious polarization between Christianity and Islam was at the core of the captivity experience. Unlike captivity accounts among the Spaniards in Mexico, this story reveals very little about Alexandria, or about Muslims. It describes the fort where the captives were held and depicts, for the first time in English, real Muslims going about the brutal business of captivity. The very first image, therefore, that English readers had of Muslims encountering their compatriots was one imbued with danger, violence, and religious opposition—but ending in the ascendancy of the Christian Englishman. Similarly, Edward Webbe's *Rare and most wonderfull things* celebrated Christian fortitude and ascendancy. It appeared in 1590, a year after Hakluyt's first instalment and Webbe's return from Mediterranean slavery. The first captivity account to be printed in England as an autonomous work proved so popular that two further imprints, 'Newly enlarged', appeared within the year.[35] Webbe's story takes him from Russia to Persia, Egypt, Syria, Palestine, India, 'the land of Prester John', not to mention France and Italy. The narrative is unified by Webbe's description of the comparative horrors of his captivity, first under the 'Tartarians', later the Ottomans, and finally the Neapolitans. By writing this account, Webbe became the first Englishman to provide, in his own voice and words, a factual-fiction describing the Islamic world. His experience is framed in opposition to the world of the 'Turk' while, paradoxically, showing the advantages of serving the Ottomans over being held prisoner by the much crueller Catholic Neapolitans.

During the 1590s, stationers evidently thought that there was a market for captivity accounts framed as adventure stories involving marvellous events set in dangerous lands. The commercial success of Webbe's book may have inspired the next captivity account, *Strange and Wonderfull Things Happened to Richard Hasleton* (1595),[36] which reuses some of the same woodcuts that had appeared in Webbe. It also draws attention to the way captivity involved employment opportunities among the Muslims. Held captive among both the Spaniards and the Algerians from 1582 until 1593, Hasleton presents a sympathetic view of the Moors while attacking Catholics and the Inquisition, just as Miles Philips had described his theological confrontation with the Spanish Catholics of Mexico and the cruelty of the Inquisition. In the same way that England confronted the Armada, so Hasleton—a lone Protestant Englishman—defied the Inquisition. Believing himself to be the first Englishman to spend time in Algeria, Hasleton offers basic information about the social environment of his captors, their political hierarchy, their technological underdevelopment, their need for gunners, and perhaps most importantly, the rich natural resources of the land:

> I have seen among the dross of the iron, very perfect gold. Which they, perceiving me to behold, were very inquisitive to understand whether it were gold or any other metal of substance. But I told them it was but a kind of dross whereof we made colors for painting in England.[37]

The captive has discovered untapped sources of wealth for his compatriots—who had failed to find them in North America.

Hasleton's account is important for a number of reasons. It provides the earliest detailed description of captivity in North Africa, where the vast majority of British captivities will take place in the next century. And it also shows that, during the Elizabethan period at least, the fear of falling prey to Catholics was even more frightening than captivity among Muslims. Hasleton's account can also be examined, not only through the captive's words, written with all the ideological emphases that assisted captives to reintegrate in their community after their long absence, but also alongside a petition that Hasleton's wife presented on his behalf. How relatives viewed the experience of the captives and what they thought about the captors is generally difficult to figure out. Hasleton's wife's petition is consequently useful because it reveals the workings of the public imagination about captivity at the time of its occurrence. In order to evoke sympathy, the petition emphasizes that

> the said Richard haselton above nyne yearees passed was taken prisoner under the king of Argiere having ever since remained there as Captyve in most vyle slaverie and miserable bondage And is worse used becawse he will not forsake his faythe in Chryst and can not be redeemed from thence but by paying the some of one hindered powndes for his raunsom the which he and his wyfe having a great Chardge of Children depending upon there hand are no way able to pay unlesse they be charitablie holpen and relieved with the devotion of weldisposed people.[38]

In the published account, Hasleton displayed greater fear and hatred of Catholics than of Muslims, declared himself better treated by the latter than the former, and described being offered tempting propositions to stay among the Muslims, prosper, marry, grow rich, and settle in a grand house. Catholics threatened to take his life; Moors offered him a job and a better life. Spaniards tortured him, keeping him in solitary confinement for nearly a year—the first record of this kind of torture in captivity literature—while later, numerous Moors came to his cell to 'persuade' him to convert. Yet the petition composed in England reiterated hostile images of Muslims because, from the perspective of his wife and kin, the most dangerous of all threats was conversion and assimilation. The menace of Islam was not simply that it promoted false beliefs, but also that Muslims offered an accommodating social order that quickly absorbed newcomers, making them forget their homes. Islam could defeat Christianity.

James's accession to the throne in 1603 drastically changed Britain's relation with the Islamic world. Eager to placate the Spanish, the king curtailed diplomatic relations with the North African and Ottoman rulers. He also issued letters of marque encouraging mariners to seize Muslim ships and passengers. James did not realize that his short-sighted policy, along with his neglect of the navy, would bring ruin to many merchant ships in the Mediterranean and Atlantic. Even as he was adopting what often appeared to be a confrontational stance toward Muslim rulers, the naval capability of the North African states was growing and soon they were strong enough to attack the western coast of England and south-east Ireland. At the same time, pirates from England had become very active in the Mediterranean, often attacking European ships and taking them back to their haunts in Tunis, Algiers, or Ma'moura, where they closely cooperated with local authorities. Other English pirates attacked Ottoman ships, taking them to Leghorn or Cadiz to be sold along with the Muslim crewmen and passengers. Retaliatory North African attacks rose dramatically following the 1609 expulsion of the Moriscos from Spain, who brought their hosts new navigational skills along with hatred of Christians that did not always distinguish Protestant from Catholic, English from Spanish. Consequently, the number of English, Scottish, and other European ships that were seized by the corsairs rose significantly in the early seventeenth century.[39]

In 1614, William Davies, a barber-surgeon who served under the duke of Florence, published an account of his captivity serving in the Italian galleys, adding a description of 'many mayne Landes, Ilandes, Riuers, Cities, and townes, of the Christians and Infidels, the condition of the people, and the manner of their Countrey'.[40] With Davies, the captive assumes his new role of descriptive explorer and empirical writer, detailing a Mediterranean world that was still, to most English readers, as unknown as the Atlantic. Davis treats the Mediterranean as a sea of two religious civilizations and describes both with as much precision as he can muster—proving, however, better in furnishing information about the European than the North African coast. A year later, a Catholic Englishman writing under the name of 'Roberto Elliatta' (Robert Elliott) was taken captive to Tunisia, and wrote the first detailed account of that country—in Italian. Although his manuscript was not published, it shows how the captive was turning into an informer furnishing intelligence about the city and its defences, the various ethnicities and social groupings, and the naval strength of his captors. Invoking the spirit of the crusades, Elliott sought to inspire Christian princes to conquer the Tunisians: he exaggerated the wealth and natural resources of the land, the rivalries among the population, and Tunisian military mediocrity. In a passionate and sometimes lyrical tone, he was the first English captive to issue a call for military action against Muslims, advocating open conquest of Muslim land.[41]

Italian Catholic rulers were constantly battling North Africans, but Elliott wrote to encourage colonization, not just warfare. In retrospect, his account can be seen to mark the first transition in the goal of captivity writings: from recounting captivity by Muslims to proposing conquest of their lands. Even if his report ever reached England, which is unlikely since it was addressed to Elliott's Italian Catholic masters, it would have fallen on deaf ears. James had no interest in fighting in the Mediterranean knowing full well that the expelled Moriscos, who had settled in North African cities and were planning naval campaigns against the Iberians, were also hostile to the English who had helped the Spanish king complete the expulsion in 1614.[42] By 1616, a Salé pirate had sailed up the Thames and reached Leigh in Essex just a few miles above Southend, as Lord Carew wrote to Sir Thomas Roe.[43] In other letters, Carew expressed his fear that 'this next sommer they will seeke for purchase uppon the coasts of England and Ireland... Every day we hear of our shippes taken in the Levant by the Turkish piratts.'[44] In 1621, Sir Henry Mainwaring, who had been a pirate with the Tunisians before returning to serve in the British navy, reported that a battle had taken place between Ottoman and English ships in which six English ships were lost.[45] That same year, after repeated criticism from Parliament, James sent the fleet against Algiers hoping to free the captives.[46] This was the only military expedition of James's reign, and it was a disaster: not only had the Barbary corsairs grown stronger, but the navies of England and other European countries had grown weaker—a fact confirmed by the seventeenth-century Tunisian historian Ibn Abi Dinar. European Christians of the early seventeenth century, he wrote, did not send out large ships, as a result of which the privateers who sailed in frigates, were able to capture much booty.[47]

Until 1625, all accounts by captives were set in the Mediterranean—a region in which Britons were eagerly exploring new avenues for trade. But in that same year, Samuel Purchas's *Pilgrimes* introduced the first captivity account from the Red Sea—a region that was becoming important for East India Company merchants. In 1610, Sir Henry Middleton sailed with the East India Company's sixth voyage to the Far East via Mocha on the western coast of the Arabian peninsula.[48] Middleton tells how he and some of his men were taken captive, dragged off into the hinterlands of Yemen, and how they finally escaped. But Middleton had no anti-Muslim agenda: he met Muslims good and bad, and does not include a single biblical allusion or religious reference. The encounter for Middleton was commercial not religious. Believing himself the first Englishman to traverse Arabian sands—wrongly, he had been preceded by John Jourdain[49]—Middleton recorded nothing about the religious environment of his captivity. Instead, he described the cities and landscapes, and reported on the different temperature zones, since such information would be useful to cloth makers in England who were producing one of the chief exports. He also mentioned the tribes he met, the distances he travelled, the landscapes he crossed, and the treatment he and his fellow captives received—useful information to his Company about the south-western part of the Arabian Peninsula. There were no other accounts published about British captives in the Persian–Indian zone.

Middleton's report reflects the different sensibility and interests of Englishmen trading with India from those dealing in North Africa and the Levant. In Mediterranean ports, Islam posed an inescapable danger of conversion and co-option—hence the need to denounce it. But Middleton and others trading in Mocha, Surat, and Agra had little to say about Islam, because they saw danger coming instead from the Portuguese and Dutch. In the Red Sea and Indian Ocean, the enemy was other Christians. Captives returning from North Africa, however, bewailed the dangerous and alluring world of Islam, while also declaiming against their own government's lack of assistance to the hundreds of sailors and seamen held in North African captivity.

Such an anti-establishment strain helps explain why no captivity accounts were licensed to be published in England between 1625 and 1640, though between these years the number of British captives in North Africa reached the highest yet in Britain's history.[50] There were so many captives that families, especially women, were driven to actions unprecedented in English history. Wives of captives took to the streets and petitioned the king, Parliament, the Privy Council, and any body in authority for assistance, warning that if nothing was done about ransoming their sons and husbands, they might convert to Islam.[51] Fear of conversion dominated encounters with Mediterranean Muslims. Confirming that anxiety, in March 1627 two sermons were preached in Minehead concerning a returning captive who had converted to Islam in Algiers and was to be readmitted to the Church of England. The sermons said less about Algiers than the sinfulness of apostasy, and described how circumcision linked Islam with the horrors of Judaism. They also ignored the tension between the captive's relatives, who were forgiving and eager to reintegrate him, and the parish minister who was determined to penalize him for following 'so notorious a monster as Mahomet'.[52]

The beleaguered Charles I would not have approved of publishing captivity accounts that showed the brutality of the Muslims and, by the same token, the incompetence of his administration and navy. He had, after all, insisted on poundage and tonnage from a disgruntled Parliament that he subsequently dissolved, and faced numerous petitions on behalf of forgotten husbands and brothers in North Africa. And after spending huge amounts of money to build the unwieldy *Charles*, the biggest ship in the English docks, he suffered the indignity of hearing how, in June 1636, the 'Turks' had sailed '*not three leagues off the shore*' from Falmouth and captured fifty men.[53] Given his role as head of the church, Charles's failure to ransom his subjects reflected the failure of the church to redeem its flock; both Crown and church clearly hoped that someone else, private persons or other institutions, such as the Levant Company or Trinity House—the guild dedicated to the safety and welfare of mariners—would resolve the crisis.[54] Pressured to act, the king sent his fleet against Salé and ransomed hundreds of captives who reached England in September and October 1637. A Moroccan ambassador, who happened to be a Portuguese convert from Christianity, accompanied the returning captives, bringing with him expensive presents—Barbary horses with carefully crafted saddles and 'a great quantity of Barbary gold'. On arrival, he fell sick and was cared for by the king's physicians. Once he recovered, on 5 November, the City Captains led him from his residence in Wood Street to Whitehall amidst the Guy Fawkes festivities. At Temple, he and his entourage, with the ransomed captives in procession behind him, were met by a military band that accompanied him to his audience, which finished by six o'clock that evening. The letter he presented to King Charles was 'the best penned letter ever you read', wrote Anthony Mangy on 20 November.[55]

The liberation of captives from Salé in 1637 improved the king's standing in the eyes of the trading companies and their beleaguered sailors.[56] It was suspected, however, that many of the returning captives had converted to Islam, forcing Laud quickly to produce 'A Form of Penance and Reconciliation of a Renegado or Apostate from the Christian Religion to Turkism' (1637).[57] Church and Crown needed to be seen to be earnest about helping Anglican subjects, but neither archbishop or king was eager for printers to continue publishing lurid tales of Mediterranean captivity. Those returning Salé captives had shown just how weak the hold of God and country could be on English folk exposed to the allure of Islam in North Africa: nowhere else in the expanding world of English navigation and trade was this danger so great. In the Americas, English settlers were either destroying or converting the native peoples; in South East Asia, one or two disgruntled sailors converted to Islam, but the Muslims that British factors and seamen met in Surat or Aceh made no attempts to convert or proselytize. In a region of such vast religious diversity, religious assertiveness may not have been as possible as in the Mediterranean, where only two monotheisms had been competing for centuries. Only in the Mediterranean was captivity inextricably linked to conversion, since it was only here that Britons were 'turning Turk' in such alarming numbers.

1640–1727

In 1640, a captivity account was published—and republished in the same year. Francis Knight's *Relation of Seaven yeares Slaverie under the Turkes of Argeire* is the first English publication to frame the captivity narrative as a call for conquest. Knight's account openly advocates military action and conquest—perhaps elated at the fleet's success three years earlier in Salé. But, as with Robert Elliott's earlier call to arms, it fell on ears deafened, perhaps, by the looming threat of civil war. Knight's *Relation* would be the last captivity account by an Englishman to be published until after the Restoration. It provided the most detailed English account so far of Algiers, a region of increasing importance to British traders and seamen. With rising numbers of British ships sailing into the Mediterranean, more and more captives were being seized by corsairs from the regencies and Morocco. But there was no reliable information about the ports from which the corsairs launched their ships, or any up-to-date information about their naval or military organization. Knight describes seven years of captivity in Algiers (1631–38), providing information about the rivalries among the various populations, the sea battles he witnessed, the varied abilities of various Ottoman naval commanders, and the ports his ship visited or attacked. Having completed the autobiographical narrative, Knight devotes a 'Second Booke' to 'a Discription of Argeire, with its Originall, manner of Government, Increase, and present flourishing Estate'. Although it is unlikely that he knew of Robert Elliott's earlier account, Knight similarly presents readers with an intelligence document—he even supplies a sketch map of Algiers, showing the various forts protecting it and the shape of the harbour. His is also the first captivity account to portray the torture and whipping of a Christian captive in a vivid illustration.[58] Knight wrote his 'Discription' confidently: he had not been broken by captivity, but had escaped back to his homeland having learned about Muslim religious culture, its rituals, customs, and daily practices: 'so depraved as they have no good Custome amongst them . . . they wash and pray five times a day, and are very ceremonious in their laws; yet . . . they are sayd to commit Sodomie with all creatures, and tolerate all vices'.[59] This hostile image of Muslims justifies for Knight the seizure of the riches of Algiers, 'an Indies of mineral'. With this vast mineral wealth in sight, Knight eagerly promotes an English conquest of Algiers that he wants to join: 'Oh that I might live to be an actour in a Marshall way, to see her Conquest, they feare none so much as our English Nation, neither is it difficult or doubtfull, with a good fleete of shippes, and an Armie, of 3000. Souldiers on Land to plucke downe her pride.'[60] Unfortunately for Knight, his fellow countrymen were too preoccupied with domestic problems to follow his advice.

In 1641, the reverend Devereux Sprat was captured by the Algerians. Rather curiously for a Protestant minister, in writing about his encounters with Muslims, he praised his captor's submission to divine will. 'I was', he recorded, 'very sad' to discover himself sold off to a 'Musselman', but his master

> asked me the reason, and withall uttered these comfortable words, Deus Grande—which took such impression as strengthened my faith in God, considering thus with myself, Shall this Turkish Mahumitan teach me, who ame a Christian, my duty of faith and dependence upon God.[61]

Spratt's memoir went unpublished at the time: if a clergyman could be impressed by Islam, perhaps it was feared that weaker men might succumb. Parliament, meanwhile, turned to acknowledge its commitment to the captured seamen: in November 1641, an eighteen-member committee with some of the fiercest opponents to the king, passed 'An Act for the Reliefe of the Captives' that imposed duties on imports and exports to provide funds for redeeming those 'loving Subjects [who] have of late time been surprised and taken at Sea (as they were in their lawfull trading) by Turkish, Moorish and other Pirats'.[62] Support for Parliament came chiefly from the south and the east, regions where maritime initiatives were bringing in customs revenue, crucial for ransoming captives. Parliament needed to show that it especially cared about captives who might lose their Christianity if they were not ransomed. Later, under Oliver Cromwell, Parliament stepped up its campaign to alleviate the damage that Mediterranean piracy was having on English trade: the 1641 'Act' was renewed in 1650, twice in 1652 and again in 1653.[63] For a revolution of saints, protecting their compatriots from apostasy was crucial.

In 1647, the parliamentary agent in Algiers, Edmond Cason, succeeded in ransoming a large number of British captives. *A Relation of the whole proceedings concerning the Redemption of Captives* contained the first list published in England by Parliament of the names of ransomed captives and the prices that had been paid for them. Cason catalogues the names of ransomed people from all around the British archipelago and beyond: from Dublin to Dover, from London to Penzance, from Bristol to Dundee. If these captives returned to their hometowns, they took with them manifold stories about their experiences and spread them far and wide throughout the English-speaking world.[64] In homes and parishes, returning captives were spreading sensational information about Islam and Muslim women, about mosques and bagnios, about Ramadan and couscous. In the conversations that they must have had with friends and family, returning captives made Islam and Islamic culture both knowable and known.

The Restoration of Charles II heralded a shift in attitude toward captivity. The British fleet had grown stronger under the Republic and the Barbary corsairs no longer sailed to the shores of England, Scotland, Ireland, and Wales as frequently as they had done half a century earlier. Nonetheless, tales of captivity remained frightening and compelling, so much so that Samuel Pepys spent the afternoon of 8 February 1661 'telling stories of Algier and the manner of the life of Slaves there' with 'Captain Mootham and Mr. Dawes (who have been both slaves there)'. From such reliable witnesses, he learned

> of their condition there. As how they eat nothing but bread and water. At their redempcion, they pay so much for the water that they drink at the public fountaynes during their being slaves. How they are beat upon the soles of their feet and bellies at the Liberty of their *Padron*. How they are all night called into their master's Bagnard, and there they lie. How the poorest men do use their slaves best. How some rogues do live well, if they do endent to bring their masters in so much a week by their industry or theft; and then they are put to no other work at all. And theft there is counted no great crime at all.[65]

However distressing Pepys may have found such tales of his fellow countrymen's ill treatment in Algiers, the new king was very much like his father insofar as he was by no means eager to spend money redeeming them, so a new means had to be found for raising revenues for ransom. A few months after his return, Charles received a petition from Captain Thomas Gardiner to 'hold a lottery in England and Wales for three years, for ransom of English slaves at Tunis, Algiers, or in the Turkish galleys'.[66] In December a proposal was advanced that part of the money raised from the sale of the property of those not pardoned by the Act of Indemnity was to 'go towards the redemption of English seamen taken by the Turks and Moors', while another proposal urged that condemned criminals be 'exchanged for Christian slaves in Turkey'.[67]

Both private individuals and Parliament were seeking new ways to ransom captives. They were also seeking new sources of information about the captors. In 1666 a translation of a Spaniard's captivity account was published in London concerning events between 1641 and 1642. John Davies' translation of Emanuel D'Aranda's *The History of Algiers and it's Slavery* opens, like Knight's *Relation*, with a title-page illustration of a Christian slave being beaten. The text had appeared in French earlier that year and would be republished in France several times.[68] The account is packed with information about 'the Scituation, strength and government of the City' of Algiers, the most powerful of the North African states. But for the most part the book consists of fifty episodes giving the most extensive, and sometimes entertaining, description of the social, religious, and cultural life of Algiers to appear in English. There is nothing like this description of Muslim society and Christian-Muslim relations in English captivity literature. D'Aranda had grown deeply familiar with Algerian society and, unlike English authors who always wanted to emphasize their heroism and their Englishness, was not embarrassed to tell about the wavering, weakness, deceit, anguish, and even the conversion or martyrdom of his countrymen in captivity.

The acquisition of Tangier as part of Charles II's marriage settlement in 1662 stimulated considerable interest in the region and its Moorish legacy.[69] Tangier now served as a meeting place for Britons, Moors, Turks, and European allies of Britain. The bastion relied on the port of Asila for supplies, and encouraged North African ships to dock and sell their booty, 'with more [freedom] then to Christian strangers'.[70] Similar cooperation between Muslims and Christians appeared in French accounts of captivity. A French novel translated into English as *The Fair One of Tunis* (1674),[71] describes a Frenchman visiting Tunis, becoming a friend of the ruler, and falling in love with his sister. The French captive, Germain Moüette, writing about his captivity in Morocco, called for diplomacy and trade with his former captors. Having spent eleven years, with freedom from his mistress to roam around, the Frenchman wrote specifically about the conditions and treatment of captives—and also about the opportunities for commercial treaties. His *Relation de la Captivité du Sr. Moüette dans les Royaumes de Fez et de Maroc* (1682)[72] illustrates how captivity and trade could converge: it was published 'Avec Privilege du Roy'. Just as the English captivity narratives sought to inform, so Moüette included 'a treaty on commerce and a glossary of Arabic terms and regional geography, which would prove useful to merchants and ambassadors alike'.[73] British and other European captives in North Africa had become informers and informants.

It was in this context of adventure and informative entertainment that *The Adventures of (Mr T. S.) An English Merchant, Taken Prisoner by the Turks of Argier* appeared in 1670. Given the publication that year of two monumental folios—John Ogilby's *Africa*, and Richard Blome's competing *Geographical Description of the Four Parts of the World*—it is clear that geography, and Africa in particular, was very much on the mind of publishers. 'T. S.,' if he had ever existed, may well have died long since, and the work—with its tips on trade and navigation—was probably compiled by the 'A. Roberts' who dedicated the work to Sir Thomas Manley.[74] Also the victory of the British naval attack on Algiers in 1669 brought Muslims back to the picture, especially after the publication, 'by Authority', of *A True Relation of the Victory and Happy Success of a Squadron of His Majesties Fleet In the Mediterranean, Against the Pyrates of Algiers* (1670).[75] Eager to capitalize on public interest, publishers dug up and printed manuscripts of captivity and escape realizing that there were readers keen to learn about Anglo-Muslim encounters—especially tales with happy endings.

Although formally a captivity narrative, T. S.'s work called itself a book of 'Adventures' that took place in 1648. T. S. described the 'Land Countries of Africa' in considerable detail, bragged about the women he had seduced, commented on the quality of the hunting, boasted of the military experience he gained, and casually commented on the invaluable assistance he offered in counsel and combat to his Ottoman master—to the point that the latter eventually set him free. Along the way the account includes information of a navigational and logistical value—'3 Places in the Castles that are weak'.[76] It also offers extensive descriptions of the military infrastructure, the history, flora, and fauna, and the distinctions between local Arabs and their Ottoman masters. And it dwells in detail on that staple of captivity accounts—the methods of torture and execution practised by Muslims on innocent Christian bodies. But it also recalls Pepys' comment about rogues prospering by demonstrating how an ingenious captive could do rather well for himself. Algeria may have been a place of captivity, but it also offered tremendous opportunity where some of the people were affable, hospitable, courteous, kind, and very liberal. In short, T. S.'s report presented North Africa as a playing field for the self-realization of a virile and militarized English masculinity that imagined the future of the world was resting on its shoulders.

During the 1670s, the demand for tales of heroic English captives successfully coming to terms with their circumstances and outsmarting or manipulating their Muslim captors proved such that old manuscripts continued to be found and printed. No longer were the Barbary corsairs fearsome since Englishmen could outwit them and escape. And there was now a fleet that could bomb them with impunity. Thus it came about that a 1671 report tells of one Gilbert Young who had been captured, but then disguised himself and, with his knowledge of Arabic, was able to escape from his Moroccan captives.[77] In 1672 an account of Algerian captivity appeared under the generic title: *A True Relation of the Adventures of Mr. R. D. an English Merchant taken by the Turks of Argier in 1666*. Once again, the emphasis is on the Englishman's military prowess while he served the 'Turks'—and the admiration that he inspired among the Algerians by displays of his English valour and leadership.[78] That much of the pamphlet was copied verbatim from the *Adventures* of T. S. would have troubled neither publisher nor reader. The captivity tale did not simply relay the sufferings of a bread and water diet interrupted by occasional beatings on the soles of the feet. As the first British garrisons in North Africa and India were being populated by young men, stories of how earlier generations of Englishmen had overcome captivity helped generate fantasies of national pride and power that could only be fulfilled by overseas conquests.

In 1675, William Okeley's *Eben-ezer; or, a Small Monument of Great Mercy* appeared. This account of a heroic escape from Algerian captivity back in 1644 went on sale about the time that the British fleet bombed Libyan Tripoli into submission and enslaved the crews of a number of ships.[79] Like T. S.'s *Adventures*, Okeley's *Eben-ezer* was edited—'trimm[ed] and form [ed]'—and probably augmented by someone other than the alleged author. Although it was published with illustrations of 'Turks burning of a Frier' and 'Divers Cruelties', Okeley does not represent himself being humiliated by Muslim torture or forced into conversion. Rather than providing stories of adversity, he focuses on moments of opportunity and tolerance. He describes how he came to run a successful business selling tobacco, wine, and canvas clothing; how he participated in religious services led by the Reverend Devereux Spratt, a fellow captive, and how he became so friendly with his captor that he started viewing their relationship as a form of service. Life was good, even better than in England, and Okeley started to debate with himself about settling down in Algiers, reflecting that '*where-ever we are well is our Countrey, and all the World is Home to him that thrives all over the World*'.[80] He discovered that as long as he did not try to dispute religion with Muslims, they left him alone to worship, to make money, and to congregate with his compatriots and coreligionists. Okeley did not, however, want to live the rest of his live there, so he later built a boat and escaped with five other Englishmen. But Okeley's account does not leave the reader with too hostile an image of the Muslims. Okeley denounced Islam and 'Mohomot', but he also discovered that the followers of the Prophet were not necessarily as bad or brutal as many imagined.

Although the vast majority of captives continued to be held in North Africa, a few Britons were seized in other parts of the world. *A True and Perfect Account* tells of the escape of one 'Mr. Harrison' who had somehow managed to find himself enslaved in Izmir, of all places, for two years. His master was an old man, who had 'formerly been in *England*, and knew *Crowland* in *Lincoln-shire*, which he preferred before all other places in *England*'.[81] This is the only published narrative reporting captivity in a major Ottoman city, perhaps because ambassadors in Istanbul curtailed enslavement.[82] In 1681, the account of the captivity of Captain Robert Knox was published, astounding polite London society with descriptions of imprisonment in Ceylon of a group of English traders. Lavishly illustrated with cuts of the inhabitants and their customs, Knox's *An Historical Relation of the Island Ceylon, in the East Indies: Together with an Account of the Detaining in Captivity the Author and divers other Englishmen now Living there, and of the Author's Miraculous Escape* was an instant and international success that inspired descriptive passages in Daniel Defoe's *Robinson Crusoe* (1721) and attracted the attention of members of the Royal Society, notably Robert Hooke.[83] Knox described how he and other Englishmen were prevented from leaving the island following a misunderstanding over protocol, but were not treated as slaves—the East India Company records use 'prisoners'. Knox spent his captivity working a small farm and became a wealthy dealer in corn.[84] Curiously, despite living among them for nineteen years, Knox seems to have been oblivious to the fact that the local inhabitants were Muslims.

In 1682, the year of Knox's success, Adam Elliot published 'A Narrative of *My* Travails, Captivity *and* Escape from Salle, In the Kingdom of Fez', the story of his six-months captivity in Morocco back in 1670, in a tract designed to vindicate himself from the accusations of Titus Oates that he was 'a *Mahumetan*'. The visit of the Moroccan ambassador, Muhammad ibn Haddu, that very year may have piqued the interest of the reading public since Ibn Haddu was accompanied by a delegation that 'by a strange providence' included Elliot's former captor who, he was able to boast, 'before several persons of Quality and Reputation, attested the truth of all these things by me related'.[85] Following his return to England, Elliot noted that he had 'freely comply'd with any handsome invitation to relate it [story of his captivity]; for there is *a great pleasure* in remembring the great Dangers I have past' [emphasis added] at the hands of his 'Barbarous Masters'. Such pleasures evidently involved reporting how the captives were welcomed into Salé 'by several hundreds of idle rascally people and roguish Boys, who came out of the Town to meet us and welcomed us with horrid barbarous Shouts somewhat like the *Irish hub-bub*'.[86] Elliot claims he was paraded in the market and sold like an animal, confined to 'a large Cellar under the Street... called the Kings *Masmora*' where slaves were kept, and then purchased by '*Hamed Lucas* (who is Secretary of this present Embassy from the Emperor of *Fez* to his Majesty)'.[87] But then, and not untypical of an

Englishman, he employed his intelligence to outsmart his dull-witted captors. He claimed to be a relative of Lord Howard, who was then in Tangier, and resorted to flattery, passing 'Moorish Complement[s] upon' his captor. Nothing was easier than deceiving the Moors with a few well-chosen lies. Thanks to English cunning, his master started to treat him well, even inviting him to join him in his drinking bouts. Elliot entertained his master by singing jolly London songs, while plying him with wine—until he was able to escape to the Spanish presidio and from there back to England. Although he suffered at first, Elliot outsmarted his captor and turned the few months of his captivity into a period of merrymaking.

Elliot's account provided the first inside description of a Salé, a port that had grown notorious in the English imagination since it was the centre of Moroccan piracy. It appeared at a moment of increasing interest in Morocco, a country about which very little information had been available in print except for the outdated description by Leo Africanus published by John Pory back in 1600, and the variously translated material in editions of Purchas's *Hakluytus Posthumus* (1614, 1617).[88] Elliot catalogued details concerning the mix of peoples and cultures, noting the large number of Moriscos, and described the palace and night-life of his captor. His account suggests just how easy it was to outsmart and defeat Muslims: despite the humiliation of captivity, an enterprising Englishman could still prevail. Islam and Muslims were by no means unassailable, but rather quite easy to overcome. In 1685 another English-authored captivity account appeared that was also full of new information about Morocco. Thomas Phelps' *A True Account of the Captivity of Thomas Phelps at Machaness in Barbary* (1685) continued a trend set by Okeley and Elliot of reporting how, against all odds, a small group of heroic Englishmen bravely escape by ingenuity, stealth, and a generous measure of good luck. The full title of this small tract continues by informing potential readers how Phelps 'and others' also managed to destroy 'Two of the greatest *Pirat-Ships* belonging to the Kingdom, in the River of *Mamora*; upon the Thirteenth day of *June* 1685'. Details of time and place were evidently important for proving that this was no concocted story, but a verifiable report, telling of suffering and humiliation, followed by escape, victory, and revenge on the Moroccan ruler, 'this Monster of *Africk*'.[89] Along the way, Phelps provided descriptions of the landscape and various routes across it, as well as facts about local tribes and what was available to eat. Like T. S. before him, Phelps portrayed a land that was at once desert yet fertile, both empty and virgin, yet peopled by hostile people. Constructed from such paradoxes, the region was clearly an empty stage awaiting military occupation and economic exploitation. It may not have been a coincidence that Phelps celebrated victory over the Moroccans just a year after the Moroccans had retaken Tangier. Although they had left Tangier, Britons could still prevail over the Moors.

A similarly heroic escape is reported by Francis Brooks in his *Barbarian cruelty being a true history of the distressed condition of the Christian captives under the tyranny of Mully Ishmael, Emperor of Morocco* (1693). Brooks informs his readers what to expect should they ever happen to be captured and taken to Meknes. He also encouraged them to plead with King William and Queen Mary to help the 340 Britons being held there by Mulay Ismail. He provides a history of the wars waged by Ismail, with description of the land, its foods, its populations—noting differences in skin colour—and the horrific treatment of Christian captives and Moorish slaves alike. As the title intimates, no other text published in England about captivity demonizes the Moroccan potentate as much as *Barbarian Cruelty*. Still, with help from a kindly Moor, Brooks managed to escape: endurance, courage, and English intelligence once again ensured success. After learning that the Moor who helped him had been captured and executed, Brooks reports 'I was much grieved, knowing the poor *Moor*'s true-heartedness towards us'.[90] But at no point did he mention the Moor's name—he was a man who remained faceless, unidentifiable, and completely other—just like the religion and civilization of his Islamic land.

These accounts show that, as the century came to an end, readers wanted contemporary, living heroes. Accounts by ransomed, and thus un-heroic, captives were ignored: the stories of Abraham Browne, captured in 1655, and Joshua Gee, held captive from 1680 until 1687, simply went unpublished.[91] Nor did the detailed description of Morocco written by John Whitehead ever see the print shop. Seized in 1691 and ransomed eight years later, Whitehead was asked by the physician and collector Hans Sloane to write about his experience, and to include a survey of geography, flora, fauna, distances, and curiosities. But his was not the story of a victorious English hero, and so it remained unpublished—notwithstanding the fascinating scientific information it contained.[92] In this respect, English published material about North Africa remained far more limited in scope than the French—which included not only accounts by captives, but more informatively, accounts by ransomers, ambassadors, and clergymen. These men had a wider access to information than captives, since they negotiated, moved around the cities, travelled across the countryside, and some even knew Arabic, Turkish, or the lingua franca. There are no similar accounts by English writers. Nothing in English compares with *L'Estat Present de l'Empire de Maroc* (1694), the historical and social overview of Morocco by the French ambassador Pidou de St Olon; it was translated into English in 1695.[93] The first similar account by an English author would not appear until 1725 when, in *A Journey to Mequinez*, John Windus explained that Morocco was still a country 'very little known to us'.[94]

The most important account produced by a captive in early modern England is, without a doubt, Joseph Pitts' *A True and Faithful Account of the Religion and Manners of the Mohammetans* of 1704. Not only was it the longest English captivity account printed to date, but it also offered the most detailed information about the culture and religion of Muslims and Islam. As early as the first English account of captivity by John Foxe, dominant motifs had been to exaggerate the terror of the infidels, magnify their violence against Christians, portray faceless and nameless 'Turks' as the enemies of God—unlike French and Spanish accounts, English accounts rarely mentioned the names of captors and other Muslims—and praise national heroism and royal protection. Over a hundred years later, the approach to captivity and its genre had shifted. Pitts wrote an analysis, providing details about a culture and a religious world that no previous Englishman could claim ever to have known so well. Having converted to Islam, Pitts entered fully into the faith, devotion, ritual, and customary practices of Muslims. Despite acquiring an insider's understanding of Islam, Pitts understandably tried to write from the position of an outsider since, on his return, he was viewed suspiciously in his Devonshire village. He wrote about Muslims in a detached manner similar to that used by Hans Staden when describing the Tupi of the New World. Adopting an objective voice, Pitts provided an ethnographic, geographic, and historical account of Islam in North Africa and the Arabian holy sites.

Pitts travelled on the *hajj* to Mecca and Medina via Egypt and Arabia, later visiting Izmir from where he escaped. These journeys enabled him to offer extensive and highly detailed information about life among various societies of Muslims.[95] He described cultural and religious traits and customs that he had seen and, presumably, practised but which, he incessantly reminds his readers, he never really embraced. He was keen to establish differences from his captors, even when it meant exaggerating: he alleged that 'Turks' slept with their sisters, were needlessly punctilious about '*salah*', or daily worship, and shared peculiar habits with Catholics.[96] He reported popular lore, offering sayings and superstitions, and corrected stories about how Muhammad's tomb floated in mid air.[97] But Pitts remained confused, perhaps unconsciously, even years after returning to Exeter. As much as he wanted to emphasize that Muslims were an alien people—he called them 'poor ignorant Creatures'—he repeatedly slipped into using 'we' when describing them, indicating how much he had entered into the community and its ways of thinking.[98] In this respect, he recapitulated the tension that many captives, both English and continental, felt upon returning to their countries: they could not fully divest themselves of their Islamic past despite wanting to be fully integrated in their redeemed present. Thomas Pellow, who was captured in 1715 and spent a very long time in captivity, continued to enjoy his 'Favourite Dish Cuscassoe' after his return to England,[99] while a Danish former captive, Hark Olufs, continued to wear his Islamic clothing even in church.[100] Captivity changed Christians, and many a returning man, and no doubt woman, may well have found that old Islamic habits died hard.

After Pitts, two accounts appeared that imitated him by describing the society, religion, and history of Morocco—a region that had come to dominate British interests because of the colonies in Gibraltar and Majorca that were provisioned from Tetuan and Tangier. *An Account of South-West Barbary: Containing What is most Remarkable in the Territories of the King of Fez and Morocco* published in 1713 by Simon Ockley, Professor of Arabic at Cambridge, was purportedly based on an account by an anonymous captive who had been freed back in November 1698. Now that Britain could start boasting about ruling the waves following naval victories over France, captivity no longer projected a sense of national failure as it had a century before. Trade with North America began to rival North Africa, and ships turned west and away from the Mediterranean, thereby reducing the traffic near the ports of danger. Morocco remained important logistically, however, inspiring Ockley to edit a captive's manuscript containing such a vast amount of information about the region. Evidently, upon his return, and perhaps like Whitehead, this anonymous captive realized the value of what he had come to know. He described in great detail the country, both geographically and culturally, and offered speculative advice on military options. Like Phelps, he evoked a land waiting for, and in need of, colonial exploitation since 'through the Idleness and Ignorance of this People, their

Country in a great many places, which undoubtedly is one of the best Soils in the World, lays waste lie a Wilderness or Desart'.[101] Moreover, Britain's fleet was strong and could easily 'retake' Tangiers, which has been lost to the Moroccans in 1684. 'For if 1500 or 2000 Men were to go with 2 or 3 Men of War,' wrote the anonymous captive, 'and a Bomb-Ketch or 2, they might make themselves Masters of it in 24 Hours time: For upon the heaving of a Score of Bombs, not one Soul of the *Moors* wou'd stay within the Town, and then the Soldiers might Land at their Pleasure.'[102] Since 1640, when Francis Knight had proposed a full-scale conquest of Algiers, the English captivity account had been slowly shifting ground, never simply a call for revenge against the 'pirates', but ever more urgently a summons for conquest and domination.

In 1721, a delegation travelled to Meknes to ransom all the British captives there. Immediately on returning to England, one of the 'redeem'd Captives' wrote and published *A Description of the Nature of Slavery among the Moors* (1721). He included general information about the size and grandeur of Meknes, described his labours as a gardener planting 'Carnations, Tulips, and other Flowers',[103] and added the inevitable praise of freedom and lack of servitude enjoyed by subjects under the British monarchs. When the captives arrived back in England, William Berriman delivered a sermon of celebration on 4 December 1721, the theme of which was to praise the '*English Air*, and *English* Liberty' to which the captives had returned, and to ask them to 'remember how much you are indebted to the kind Interposition of our Sovereign Lord the King'.[104] Four years later, John Windus, a member of the delegation, published his *A Journey to Mequinez* (1725) describing the journey, the negotiations, and the city with Mulay Ismail's palaces. This was the first publication in English by a ransomer rather than a captive, and it was by an author who took some care over his facts. Windus consulted earlier French and Dutch writings and wrote in the voice of a diplomat. Both accounts of the 1721 embassy include lists of captives' names. Oddly, Windus's list is much less complete than the one that appears in *A Description*, which included the most precise list of names of captives ever published in England; it even catalogues the names of the ships and the exact dates when they were seized. Windus's interest was in displaying the range of information that he had gathered about the diplomatic and ceremonial etiquette in the Moroccan court. To him, the captives were not as important—much as he pitied the few English captives who had been left behind.

The anonymous *A Description* introduces a new motif to the captivity account: romance. While T. S. had recounted his alleged affairs with Muslim women in a robust and bawdy manner, here the author describes his romantic relationship with Moriama, the Portuguese wife of his master, in the sentimentalized language worthy of the *Arabian Nights,* which had begun to appear in English translation during the first decade of the century. He first becomes aware of her existence from her plaintive singing, and the next day, as chance would have it, proves to be 'a Day of Devotion' when his master, her husband, is away, and our narrator coyly recalls that he 'made Use of it to the best Advantage I could, which gave me entire Posession of the lovliest Creature under the Sun'. Yet another wily English captive has managed to outsmart the Moors, courting his master's wife right under his nose, but not for long. After 'several Meetings of this Kind', word comes that the king, Mulay Ismail, has demanded her for himself, and that she will be 'bury'd alive' once the wicked king has had his way with her. Her husband, 'Chagrin'd by the Loss of his beloved Wife, grew so enrag'd' that he took his anger out on our hero, beating him daily for no reason, and setting him to pull a cart 'in Concert with a Mule'. Shortly after this, our hero is redeemed, but utters not a single word about missing his 'dear Moraima...the Solacer of all my Afflictions'.[105] After all, on arriving back in England, he had to prove that he had forgotten everything about the temptations of Islam, including his love for a Christian captive.

From now on, romance became a fixed feature of captivity accounts. In 1720, Eliza Haywood had written *The Fair Captive* about a Spanish woman seized by the Ottomans.[106] Although the play does not dramatize the English experience as such, it brought Mediterranean captivity onto the London stage by way of romance. Six years later, Robert Chetwood's fictitious *The Voyages and Adventures of Captain Robert Boyle* confirmed that captivity had become simply, a tale of 'adventures'. It describes how Boyle fell in love with a captive 'English Lady' whose beauty far outshone the 'Moorish women', but who was married to a renegade. Being English, he was obviously smarter and more well informed than the loutish Moors or their heinous converts, and so replenished his master's garden with 'European seeds', repaired the fountains in the shape of 'Triton', and subsequently outsmarted his captor and eunuchs, escaping with Mrs Villars in a boat at night. While the anonymous *A Description* blended a love story with a documentary about the Moroccan capital, Captain Boyle's narrative showed little interest in anything other than the honourable rescue of a 'distressed maiden' with whom the English gentleman exchanged numerous polite letters, and whose poetical talents had captivated him:

> My Grief lies all within,
> And those external manners of Laments,
> Are meerly Shadows to the unseen Grief
> That swells with Silence in my tortur'd Soul.[107]

The captivity narrative had degenerated into as poor a romance as the verse.

By way of conclusion

From the Elizabethan until the Georgian periods, captivity accounts appeared regularly, with only a brief hiatus during the Civil Wars. Both written and oral, they constituted the most original information that English readers possessed about Muslims, Islam, and North Africa, by their own compatriots. Some accounts were reprinted quickly and often, others pirated or improved without the author's consent. Their popularity helped establish a genre that would survive for generations, influencing other accounts of captivity in North America and Guinea, and by US writing about North Africa at the end of the eighteenth century.[108]

The captivity narrative belongs to the history of British encounters with Islam in the Mediterranean, but not the Indian Ocean, Persian Gulf, or South East Asia. By the time Britons were regularly sailing into these regions, their ships were strong enough to repel piratical attacks. Moreover, East India Company orders were strict: as a Persian ambassador observed in the late 1680s, captains were ordered 'never to give up the ship. Even if it is impossible to defeat the enemy, the Franks will not submit to the humiliation of being taken prisoner. Thus they are prepared to set fire to their own ships and perish in the flames before they will surrender.'[109] In the western Mediterranean, however, sailors had sometimes been all too ready to surrender, while others resisted but were taken all the same. Captives who returned, as we have seen, were anxious about their reputation, and told self-serving stories of heroic Christian resistance and Muslim brutality in order to deflect accusations. In doing so they not only pandered to popular taste for exciting tales, but created an image of Muslims and their religion that was inimical and adversarial: no reader could leave a captivity account without a view of the Mediterranean Muslim as dangerous, tempting, or violent. As a further attempt to justify themselves, they furnished logistical information about ports, military preparedness, and terrain. By the end of the century, no reader could leave a captivity account without the firm belief that England could—and should—set out to conquer the captors and seize their lands. From the first account by Foxe, the narrative of captivity evolved into colonial projects of domination, and finally into romances, all of which aimed at rousing Britannia to action against the Muslim captors.

This development reflects the shift in the balance of power during the period. The British fleet was growing in strength and sophistication, but Britons still needed information about the regions where they were trading and, sometimes, bombing. With the growth of naval ambitions and achievements, more captivity accounts appeared providing cultural, military, and maritime intelligence. Captivity narratives performed a task similar to the ethnographic geographies describing other regions of English colonial settlement. In much the same way that reports about North America by settlers, traders, and clergymen provided knowledge that inspired and facilitated colonial domination, so tales of Mediterranean captivity projected fantasies of conquest in North Africa. But they were fantasies that turned into goals: in 1728, Daniel Defoe, who claimed to have been captured by the Algerians, published *A Plan of the English Commerce* in which he called for a multinational force of Europeans to colonize all of North Africa in order to take possession of its 'Corn, Salt, Wool, Horses, Wax, Honey, Corall, Copper... Provisions of sundry Kinds'.[110] As in North America, so too in North Africa.

5

The Peoples of the Islamic Empires

While travelling or trading in Islamic lands, early modern Britons met people from different ethnicities, religions, and races; some they admired, some they served, and some they feared. Unlike the emergent European states that often sought to achieve internal uniformity by expelling ethnic or denominational minorities whether Jewish, Protestant, or Catholic, the Ottoman, Safavid, and Mughal Empires were heterogeneous. Amidst the racial and religious mixture, Britons often discovered themselves in situations that would have been inconceivable at home. In the 1580s, for example, John Sanderson found himself travelling through the Levant with 'a Jew, Turke, and Christians' for servants;[1] arriving in Baghdad, George Manwaring saw merchants from 'the East Indies, Armenians, Persians, Turks, and Venetians, and many Jews'.[2] Such gatherings might have been possible in Thomas More's *Utopia*—but not in the England of the early seventeenth century. The Islamic world differed spectacularly from the Christian one, therefore, not only because of the Muslim majority, but also because of the obvious presence of other religions and peoples unfamiliar to Western eyes.

Of the various communities that Britons met during their travels in the Islamic Empires, the eastern Christians and the Jews stood out, though there was also interest in Shi'ites, Armenians, and Mughals. Unlike meetings with American Indians about whom little had been known, eastern Christians and Jews conjured up a vast range of scriptural images as well as Graeco-Roman allusions. In travelling to North America, Britons arrived in a land without a known history, a space of the future where colonists would forge new beginnings; the Islamic lands were of the past, where Britons witnessed the biblical and classical texts come alive. And as the myth of Prester John slowly died[3]—of a Christian monarch ruling over a vast Christian population somewhere in the east—knowledge of Christians in the midst of the Empire became immediately important, especially when, arriving in Izmir, Jerusalem, or Alexandria, Britons found themselves face to face with real and thriving subjects of a Muslim sultan. Eastern Christians and Jews were figures from the Bible enacted in the midst of Islam, and Britons discovered that they could not describe the Islamic Empire without taking into account the existence of these communities, who, especially at the start, proved both useful and helpful. Nor could they dismiss Islam's extension of a protected and well-defined space for these non-Muslim People of the Book—a space that Catholics and Protestants in Western Europe, Anglicans and Puritans in the United Kingdom and Ireland, did not extend even to each other.

Encountering communities of eastern Christians and Jews posed a serious challenge to Britons for, had these communities appeared in London or Edinburgh, they would have been most fervently, and forcefully, converted to Christianity. Yet in the various Islamic metropolitan centres, they seemed to prosper and were completely indifferent, except in rare cases, to English Christianity. In facing this unusual, and often uncomfortable, reality, Britons adopted the strategy of using these two communities as a cudgel with which to beat Islam. Particularly in texts that were intended for the press back home, writers described these communities, and the Holy Land, as victims of the 'terrible Turks', even when they saw before them permanent legal and religious protection that arose not from the whim of the ruler, but from Qur'anic law. As for the land, writers and cartographers pushed it into the biblical past, with maps depicting an eschatological landscape, not the contemporary Ottoman *eyalat* (province). British writers assured their readers that the peoples of the Bible, eastern Christians and Jews, as well as the land of the Bible, were enduring persecution and discrimination by the 'Mahometans'—thereby giving their own presence a higher goal than mere trade: converting those communities to 'true' Protestant Christianity, and taking possession of the land where Christ had once walked. Such challenges of conversion, conquest, and primacy were quite different from what the English faced in their encounter with the various indigenous populations of North America, who were defeated, decimated, and then displaced. Among the Muslims, eastern Christians and Jews were legitimate subjects who could not be bullied, fought, or dominated.

It bears noting that from the start, the British were at a great disadvantage in the range of information they possessed about the peoples of the Islamic

Empires, in contrast with what other Europeans had. Particularly in the eastern Mediterranean, where the first English commercial ventures into the Islamic world took place, they were superseded by the French. Long before the English arrived on the scene, there had been Jesuit, Capuchin, and Franciscan missionaries living among the different communities to be found in Islamic lands. They learned local languages, acquired local habits, ate local foods, and they wrote home to their ecclesiastical superiors, in letters, *relations,* and travelogues that described those they were trying to convert.[4] Nor were the English capitulations with the Ottomans like those of France which, from 1569 on, allowed for French religious orders to establish schools, infirmaries, and even chapels. Decades before the first English consul arrived in Aleppo, the Venetians and French had established consulates there—in 1548 and 1562 respectively. When it came to eastern travel and trade, the English were well behind other European nationals.[5] But they will make rapid headway, and by the end of our period, will have established themselves in a foremost position.

The Christians of Islam

Britons came across many communities of native-born Christians, especially in the main cities of the Ottoman Levant, Alexandria and Aleppo, Jerusalem and Isfahan. The largest groups of eastern Christians that the English came to know, whether in the Islamic dominions or in London, belonged to the Greek-speaking patriarchate of Constantinople and the Arabic-speaking patriarchates of Antioch and Jerusalem. The English discovered that among the 'Turks' lived the largest Christian minority in a non-Christian empire of the early modern world—and that this minority had been in continuous existence since the beginning of Christianity.

Interest in eastern Christians was stimulated by Greek students, scholars, and even charlatans visiting England. These Christians arriving in England were welcomed for preferring the Anglo-Protestant faith to French Catholicism. But many Greeks travelled to England for practical reasons that had little or nothing to do with religious belief. In October 1581, one Lucas Argenter was given permission to 'gather the devotion of good people within the City, towards ransoming his wife and children, prisoners in Turkey'. Lucas was able to reach the Privy Council with his appeal after the Queen had taken pity on him and commended him to the bishop of

London. Since collections at the Spital sermons after Easter were designed to help ransom English captives, the bishop as well as the mayor was told to encourage people to assist this man who had come to England with 'good testimonials', and therefore was not a fraud, as others might have been. Some years later, 'certain poor Hungarians', who had won the queen's heart, were 'permitted to gather the charitable alms for their ransom at the sermons at St. Paul's, and the several churches within the City'. A decade later, in May 1595, another petitioner appeared in London, the Hungarian Caspar Camroni, and two decades later, in January 1615, another Greek called Anastatius Ralapolus came 'into these parts of Christendom, craving the alms of charitable people for the delivery of his parents out of a miserable thraldom into which they had fallen by the tyranny of the Turks'.[6] When Moldavian princes fled from the Ottomans, they sometimes sought 'succour under English protection at *Constantinople*, being Protestants, or at least willing to admit to our reformation', noted Thomas Gainsford in 1618.[7] Later, consuls in Anatolia tried to help captured eastern Christians escape, despite incurring a grave risk. The chaplain, Thomas Smith, recounted the tale of how a Russian boy who escaped from captivity in Izmir was taken in by the English ambassador, who gave him a peruke and his livery. Once the boy mastered English, he roamed Istanbul confidently.[8]

European Protestants considered eastern Christians to have been part of the eastern Roman Empire which had 'forfeited its claim to be considered a part of Christendom from its demise as a sovereign state in 1453' following the capture of Istanbul by the Ottomans.[9] Such a position was confirmed in article nineteen of the Thirty-Nine Articles (1563) which stated that 'the Churches of Jerusalem, Alexandria, and Antioch, have erred'. But some writers preferred the Roman image of the 'Merry Greek', without the medieval praise of Greek women's beauty, which, according to Edward Gibbon, had been among the reasons for the Crusades.[10] The 'Merry Greek' image, however, soon disappeared, as Britons wondered whether the eastern Christians preserved ancient Christianity or constituted a debased form. Orthodoxy was, perhaps, slightly less horrifying than Catholicism, but still exhibited 'barbarous Ignorance', since its 'best garments [are] so plighted with errours, and layd up unhandsomely with wrinckles'.[11] As early as 1553 during a visit to a Greek Church, one Englishman was deeply offended that nobody knelt during communion, but politely explained: 'Wherefore least I should offend any man, I leave it unwritten.'[12] Eastern Christians did not really resemble Christians at all and were communities who needed to be converted since, like the Russian Orthodox, they seemed ignorant of theology and doctrine, knowing no Latin or 'European decorum'.[13]

But once English trading factories arrived in Izmir and Aleppo and other Islamic cities with sizeable Christian populations, they began thinking that eastern Christians were followers of the early churches who thereby shared the Anglicans' adoption of the first Councils: they could thus become allies against Rome. William Bedwell praised the 'Arabs' for saying 'nothing about [the Catholic doctrine of] purgatory'.[14] Soon after, in the mid 1620s, a Greek printing press was sent from London to Istanbul to produce easily accessible reading material for the Greek congregations.[15] In that decade, Archbishop Laud negotiated with the Greek Patriarch of Istanbul, Cyril Lukaris, for the admission of a number of Greek students to Oxford University.[16] Once at Oxford, Laud and others hoped, they would embrace Anglicanism, though there is no evidence that any ever did. In 1637, John Evelyn, while a Fellow Commoner at Balliol, met 'one *Nathaniel* Conopios out of Greece sent into England by the famous Patriarch *Cyrill*, (whom the Jesuits murdered)'. Conopios was evidently strong in his native faith since Evelyn notes he later became 'Bishop of *Smyrna* and then (I think,) Patriarch of *Alexandria*'. Evelyn also tells us that Conopios 'was the first that I ever saw drink *Caffè*, not heard of then in England', and this very likely is the earliest record of coffee being made and drunk in England.[17]

Although no alliance between the Anglican and Orthodox churches ever came about—the only tangible result of the exchange was Lukaris's gift of the Codex Alexandrinus to Charles I—British travellers could not separate their interest in the Greeks and other eastern Christians from the rivalry with Rome and the desire to advance Protestantism. Despite the defeat and execution of 'Protestant Patriarch' Lukaris, which was partly the result of Protestant–Catholic rivalry, and the numerous treatises in Greek and Arabic attacking Protestant belief, Britons continued to hope for the conversion of these misguided Christians.[18] After the Restoration of 1660, numerous translations into Arabic and Turkish of Anglican texts appeared, including Edward Pocock's 1660 translation of Hugo Grotius's *De veritate del'religionis Christianae*.[19] In 1674, Pococke's translation of the *Book of Common Prayer* into Arabic, along with the catechism of the Anglican Church, was distributed in limited numbers. It encouraged worshippers, presumably in Aleppo or Alexandria, to pray for the safety of 'sultan' Charles II.[20] In 1692, a Greek College was established at Oxford. Modelled, perhaps, after the

Greek College of 1576 and the Maronite College of 1584 in Rome, it soon failed when the Greek patriarchs forbade students to attend because of the dangers of the 'irregular life' there.[21] While the Greeks may have been willing to study at Anglican institutions, they certainly did not want to become English in their customs and habits.

For factors in Istanbul or Izmir, eastern Greek Christians were of vital economic interest because their ranks provided the translators and intermediaries who facilitated trade with the Ottoman Empire. Converting the Greek Orthodox to Anglicanism was deemed the surest means to secure their commitment to England and their support of British commercial interests. At the same time, the factors in residence, who mixed daily with the Muslim administration and population, could not but see the co-option of this minority, as possibly also of the Jews, as a means to fight and weaken the Ottomans. Some factors conceived of the Greek-speaking Christians as possible fifth columnists who, with English military, financial, and logistical help, could subvert the Muslims, even though they had lived for generations alongside the Muslim majority. Such manipulation of Christian minorities in the Ottoman Levant was not restricted to the English alone. Describing a visit to the Maronites of Mount Lebanon in 1596, the Italian papal envoy, Girolamo Dandini, hoped they 'would throw off their Turbans and put on Hats instead, and turn their Arms against the Turks'.[22] At the beginning of the seventeenth century, the Florentines supported the Druze prince of Lebanon, Fakhr al-Din II, hoping he would fight the Ottomans and prepare for a western invasion.[23] While French Jesuit missionaries, who lived for long periods of time in the Levant, did not subscribe to such ideas of military crusades,[24] some travellers and zealous Englishmen, without the missions that could conquer souls and win allegiance, regularly thought of militarism. In 1662, it was reported in London that people living in the Morea had written to King Charles II 'inviting him to make war against the Agarens in the Morea. Within the Kingdom itself there are 20,000 Christians able to bear arms and the Turks are in all only 8,000. Promise the whole Kingdom of Morea will make themselves subject to Charles II.'[25] In 1675 an ingenious idea was proposed: there were thousands of Greek Christians in Crete and the Morea, all suffering under the Ottomans. They were industrious, 'very laborious, great herdsmen, and make much oil, wine, wax, cotton, and silk'. So, the best help that could be extended to them was to send them off to Virginia and Jamaica, regions that were 'wanting only people'. 'They only desire the free exercise of their religion, and enough land to maintain them.'[26] In the New World, it was argued, they would strengthen British control over a region that was being contested by the Dutch, French, and Spanish. Owing allegiance to the English in gratitude for transporting them, these Greeks would defy these interlopers. The plan came to nothing.

Attempts to militarize the eastern Christians proved fruitless, but were not simply a quaint preoccupation of a few eccentric writers in the Levant so much as elements of a confused political agenda.[27] Although none of the militaristic fantasies ever came to anything, English consuls and clergymen continued to promise eastern Christians royal support—specifically to prevent them from falling into the arms of Catholic missionaries, who, with large funds, were successfully turning Eastern Christians into Uniates, allies of the Church of Rome.[28] Such conversions worried pious Protestants. John Covel was devastated when an 'English Apothecary of my intimate Acquaintance Married a Greek Woman, and both of them were made Papists by the importunity of the Dominicans their Neighbours'. Fortunately, the man later repented and 'return'd to our Communion again and died in it'.[29]

But, in their eagerness to advance a united eastern Christian front against Muslims and Catholics, English writers failed to recognize how fissured those Christian communities were: Armenian, Coptic, Maronite, Melchite Orthodox, Greek Catholic, and Syriac Nestorians were all quite distinct. Nor did the English realize how much they resented attempts by western Christians to convert them. An Arabic account of the 'holy land' written at the end of the sixteenth century by an Orthodox priest denounced the Protestants and presumably '*haratiqa*', or heretics, who were beginning to appear in Jerusalem.[30] Eastern Christians, Muslims, and Jews shared geography, languages, and culture, whatever their differences in religion and views of history. And difference did not necessarily polarize them or threaten their survival with the implications of contamination that the Huguenots, for instance, felt in France after associating with Catholics.[31] Sandys noted how Greek women in Gaza adopted local customs, covering 'their faces, dying their hands black; and are apparelled like the *Moores* of *Cairo*'.[32] Ephraim Pagitt noted that the Christians living in Jerusalem 'mingled with Turkes and others'.[33] Paul Rycaut observed that in 'the *Morea*... *Turks* intermingle with' Christians, often living 'in the same Street, and sometimes under the same Roof; their Children play, and are bred up together, and have almost the same Manners and Customs with them, and have little different besides their Religion'. As a result, Christian women had little difficulty accepting Muslims as husbands.[34] The hostility to Muslims expressed by European travellers and missionaries was not always borne out in the daily relations between local Christians and Muslims. English residents in the Ottoman Empire failed to recognize that the Orthodox residents of Crete must have felt gratitude to the Ottomans for expelling the Venetians and then protecting the return of an Orthodox patriarchate after half a millennium.[35]

Ottoman society was multi-religious and the various communities met openly in the marketplaces, the ports, the ships, the courts, the hospitals, the coffee houses, and the bathhouses. Interaction could sometimes take curious and remarkable forms. Aaron Hill noticed that Greek churches were commonly ornamented with paintings of the Virgin 'which, you may observe, the *Eastern Nations* always represent a *Blackamore*'.[36] Muslims and Christians shared holy sites and practices. Corneille le Bruyn noticed that Christians and 'Arabians' in Palestine venerated the site that they both called 'Bon Ladron', the 'Borough of the Good Thief, who was crucified with Jesus Christ'.[37] Hill commented on the curious fact that Armenians and Muslims adopted the same 'postures, when at Prayers...cross-legg'd'.[38] Thomas Smith was struck by the behaviour of a 'Turk' of Istanbul who was eager to ensure that the money he was about to offer in *zakat*—the alms-giving to which Muslims were obliged—was not tainted, so he turned to 'an English Merchant' to 'change such a number of Dollars'.[39] Although it was not always the case, an Englishman could be relied on when fulfilling religious duties.

Numerous English writers could not help noticing various modes of social harmony among the different religious communities. Such harmony was deeply disturbing since it challenged the general belief that Islam was violently opposed to Christianity, that Muslims were obliged to persecute Christians, and that the Mahometans were the present terror of the world. And so, whether denouncing or pitying the Christians of Islam, English writers began to emphasize how these Christians should be viewed as fellow Christians under tyrannical Muslim rule. The constant fear of Ottoman power in the period under study was crucial in framing the views that English writers and readers held about the eastern Christians: chroniclers who never visited the East as well as long-term residents like Paul Rycaut could not separate them from the imperial and religious threat of the Ottomans. Because they had conquered lands that once belonged to a united Christendom, the Ottomans were characterized by Rycaut as 'a Whirl-wind from the East' who had 'like Locusts over-spread the Face of

Asia'.[40] Anti-Ottoman and anti-Islamic invective took shape and substance from the threat to fellow Christians. Just under a century earlier, a treatise published in 1595 called on God to 'deface the enemies of his Gospell' who were persecuting his flock in Eastern Europe.[41] When, in the 1670s, Thomas Smith came to write about the demise of the seven churches of Asia mentioned in the Book of Revelation, lamenting the plight of Levantine Christians could only mean denouncing Ottoman cruelty. George Meriton was not the first or last to lament how the 'great Turk' had turned 'St. Sophia [into] a Mosche'.[42]

The Ottoman treatment of Christians and Jews should be viewed amidst expanding global contacts between Britons and peoples of different religions and ethnicities. But such geographical expansion did not produce a parallel enlargement in British self-examination and scrutiny. Observing other societies did not lead Britons to a better understanding or a critique of their own habitual beliefs about, attitudes towards, and practices regarding members of other religions. In 1612, William Lithgow denounced the Ottomans as well as Catholics for harassing British and Armenian pilgrims on their way to Jerusalem, at a time when the largest population expulsion of Christianized Muslims was taking place in Spain.[43] Lithgow did not think about the friars, monks, and 6,000 Christians who, thanks to Ottoman policy and Qur'anic injunction, were able to celebrate Easter in the very centre of Islamic Jerusalem.[44] Nor did he or other writers compare the treatment of Christians and Jews by the Ottomans with the violence that those forging British colonies were inflicting upon native peoples in the New World. Standard accounts by Knolles and Rycaut relentlessly detail incidents of Muslim cruelty to Christians without ever reflecting on the brutalities being committed by their own Anglican coreligionists. Knolles, whose popular magnum opus of 1603 loudly denounced the treatment of Christians by the 'Turks', remained completely oblivious to the persecution of Catholics in Elizabethan England, ignoring the gruesome execution of priests and alleged conspirators at Tyburn. Descriptions of eastern Christians by Protestant Englishmen might well have been different had they been written by Catholics who might not have shared the fears and prejudices of their Protestant compatriots. Two of the major French writers about the East—Jean Chardin and Jean-Baptiste Tavernier—were Huguenots who described the conditions of the Christians of Islam favourably, especially after the Revocation of the Edict of Nantes in 1685 that led to the expulsion of over half a million French Protestants from their homes.

It is difficult to know whether the traders and clergymen who described the eastern Christians and their 'plight' under the Muslims felt challenged in their own cultural and religious principles. They did not travel into the Islamic world in order to learn about different cultures and societies, or to see how differences might enlighten them and their readers. Rather, they were in Izmir or Aleppo or Isfahan in the service of fiercely competitive trading companies with one single goal: profit. And so, even when they noted interesting, admirable, or startling differences in the society of the Muslims, they did not think them necessarily applicable, or comparable, with their own English Protestant society. And so it was that no Anglo-Protestant writer commented, for instance, on the fact that Christian sites and shrines had been physically preserved under Islam, while not a single mosque had remained standing in Spain during the *reconquista*. In England, the monasteries were gutted under Henry VIII, statuary in Anglican cathedrals was defaced, organs smashed, and gilded altars, choir stalls, and stained-glass windows were all destroyed in the name of Protestant reform. Although often sceptical about Catholic authentication, Fynes Moryson described numerous Christian holy places. His account documents the rich continuity of Christian worship in Palestine: nine monasteries in Jerusalem alone,[45] along with gold-gilded churches, 'stately and rich' in the midst of Ottoman lands.[46] Moryson, who had good reason to dislike the Ottomans for the rough treatment he often received, was impressed when visiting the Mount of Olives to notice how they 'give such reverence to the monuments of Christ living on earth, as they are much offended with Christians, if they creepe not on their knees, and with their shooes off to this and like monuments'.[47] Muslims respected Christian sites better than zealous Protestants, and they joined pilgrims to the Church of the Nativity with a conviction that he, a stolid Englishman, could not share. Sandys claimed that '*Mahometan* pilgrims' venerated '*Calvary*, or the Sepulcher' of Christ; Peter Heylyn, credulously echoing him, stated that Muslims, on their way to pilgrimage in Mecca, visited the 'Sepulcher of *Christ*'.[48] Although the Church of the Holy Sepulchre was not venerated by Muslims, visitors and subsequent writers commonly believed it was.

Although unwilling to contrast Ottoman treatment of Christians with the ways European Christians treated Muslims and native peoples from Virginia to the Caribbean, English and other European writers could hardly avoid commenting favourably on Islamic toleration. Sebastian Munster, in a 1572 English translation, confirmed that 'the Turkes compel no man to the denial of his religion' which explains 'the diverse sects of people ... found amongst the Turkes, al whiche do reverrence and honour God after their peculiar rites and customes'.[49] Coming from societies where even different denominations were not accepted—the wars of religion in France, the Thirty Years War, and the English Civil Wars were all products of inter-Christian differences—English and other European writers wondered at the acceptance that Muslims accorded the religions and the communities of the Book. And they were surprised at how Muslims offered 'Almes, not only to Turkes, but also to Christians',[50] while Islamic jurists deliberated on appropriate business relations with 'the traders from among the Christians and the Jews in the lands of the Muslims'.[51] Sir Thomas Roe did not really know how to comment on the legacy of Akbar who 'gave grant to all sortes of men to become Christians' and about his son, Jahangir, who opened one of his letters to King James I by wishing the latter well because 'you strongly defend the law of the Maiestie of Ihesus, which God make yet more flourishing'.[52] Jahangir's court was a site of open toleration, inspired by the peculiar form of Islam that Akbar had introduced—and which John Fletcher vainly struggled to represent in his play, *The Island Princess* (c.1619–21). The 1665 English translation of Pietro della Valle's *Travels*, which had taken place between 1614 and 1626, emphasized how 'all Religions are tolerated' in the Mughal Empire, and how every man was 'happy and safe in the profession of any Religion'.[53] In the Islamic empires, Christians and Jews were protected by the laws of Islam at a time when English law strictly prohibited business dealings with Jews, let alone granting them residence rights: symptomatically, Cromwell's successful proposal to admit some Jews to England in 1655 generated stiff and bigoted resistance. In May 1661, Henry Oldenburg observed that 'German and Hungarian Christians' are willing 'to live under ye Turk, because of liberty of conscience'.[54] '*Egypt*,' wrote an anonymous author in 1712, is

> one of the most ancient Conquests of the *Arabians*; nevertheless, after so many Revolutions, and so many Ages, the *Cophtic* and *Greek Christians* exercise their Religion there to this day. The *Mahometans* did not root *Christianity* out of *Spain*: and to speak of our own time, 'tis well known that *Christianity* is tolerated amongst the *Turks*, upon very hard and uneasy Conditions indeed; altho in some Places, as at *Scio* and *Athens*, the *Greeks* exercise the Ceremonys of their Religion, with as much liberty at least, as they could in the Dominions of the *Venetians*.[55]

Islam's relative toleration allowed Euro-Christian pilgrims, traders, and chaplains to travel freely and to write about what they saw. Although the latitude that Muslim authorities showed to Christian visitors may often have been attained by bribery, there was clear toleration that allowed for Christian presence, both native and foreign, in a manner not possible for Muslims in England. While some English writers invoked the Ottoman, Islamic model when challenging religious persecution at home, no legal change was instituted in Britain until the nineteenth century. There were no parliamentary debates to change English law so that situations of toleration which obtained among the Ottomans could obtain in the United Kingdom.[56] Moryson met a Spanish woman who had been living in the Church of the Holy Sepulchre in Jerusalem for seven years. She had arrived in 1589 to 'expiate her sinnes' and simply stayed on at a time when she, a Papist, would not have found a Catholic church in England, militant and exuberant after the defeat of the Spanish Armada.[57] Sandys was amazed to witness 'a thousand Christians, men, women, and children', celebrating Easter Sunday 'with joyfull clamors, according to their severall customes'.[58] T. B., while travelling with twelve other Englishmen from Aleppo to Jerusalem in 1669, came across two 'French-men that live a Hermits life' on Mount Lebanon.[59]

Although Muslims rejected doctrines central to Christian belief, they accepted Christians. Sometimes Muslims may even have accepted the validity of Christian worship. Rycaut was perplexed when the Ottomans asked the Greek and Armenian Patriarchs 'to pray against' the plague, since it indicated that Muslims accepted Christians prayed to the same God—an acceptance that Rycaut would have been hard put to find in the archbishop of Canterbury who granted the imprimatur to his book.[60] John Locke confronted the same conundrum when arguing reasons for excluding Jews and Muslims from the magistrate's power while retaining that power over Christian Dissenters. He maintained that the magistrate held authority over 'indifferent' matters among both his Christian and his 'Mahometan' subjects. But this authority, as it applied to the latter group, remained theoretical in Locke's argument, since the magistrate was urged not to use it because he should not ever indicate approval of the teachings of a non-Christian religion. It would not only be ridiculous but also anti-Christian, explained Locke, if the magistrate, at a time of national calamity, were to order his Muslim subjects to pray to Allah for the removal of that calamity. Such an order, which the magistrate could make, should not be made, concluded Locke, because it would give Christian legitimacy to a non-Christian belief.[61] While Ottomans recognized Christian and Jewish worship, Anglicans were not willing to grant such recognition, even theoretically. Locke later changed his views, and accepted the principle of allowing non-Christian beliefs in the British state, but his was not a majority position.[62]

John Covel lived in the Ottoman Levant at about the same time as his fellow clergyman, Thomas Smith (1670–79), but these two were strikingly different in their attitudes towards and representations of local people, including eastern Christians. Where Smith saw the empty half of the glass, Covel saw the full half. Covel liked drinking with Ottomans, soon discovering that the best way to escape the plague was to join his companions in 'drame of the bottle'.[63] He enjoyed taking part in local ceremonies and festivities, which invariably involved Christians, Jews, and Muslims. He emphasized the civility with which he was always treated, and the cooperation among Muslims, Greeks, and other Christians, not only socially, but also religiously. He noticed how the communities had much in common, reporting how the village of 'Bobbas-cui' was named after an old Turk who was subsequently buried in St Nicholas' church: 'When we went into it to see his tomb we met another old Turk, who had brought three candles, and presented them to an old [Christian] woman that looks after it, and shews it to strangers.'[64] Near Adrianople, he found a town where wine was sold to Greeks and Armenians, sometimes '200 or 300 persons'. 'The Turkes,' continued Covel, 'observe the same freedome, or rather take much more.'[65] As long as there was wine, there was general conviviality. The Christian vintner in the town, who was also the 'Parson', kept the wine in the church, and was so popular that when his daughter died, 'about 500 Greekes came to her buryall'.[66] On 15 August, the day of the Assumption of the Virgin, some 'gossips' mixed water with clay after which 'infinites of people, Turkes, Jewes, and Christians' join together to 'tumble in the mire' in the belief that their ailments would be cured by the '$Παναγία$ [Panagia], as they call her'.[67] Religious barriers fell before the commonality of culture, taste, and sometimes political necessity. Eastern Christians certainly lived better among Muslims than the Dissenters in Restoration England did among their fellow countrymen; which may explain why Covel's diary remained unpublished, while Smith's morose observations on the 'Seven Churches' was promptly given imprimatur.

The English were more interested in eastern Christians than in other Christian minorities, but that interest was directed at conversion. Eastern Christians were anti-Catholic at a time when Catholics in England and

Scotland were considered subversive and dangerous. Should they be won over, eastern Christians would form a sizeable community that could off-balance Catholics. Perhaps with Arabic Anglican publications and student scholarships to Anglican bastions like Oxford, they could be made to see the Protestant light and then return to their communities to effect ideological change. At the same time, eastern Christians could be co-opted to fight against the Ottomans. But English policymakers were worried by the way that the Catholic French had established themselves in the region through alliances with the large community of Maronites who were faithful to Rome, and through successfully converting other eastern Christians. These protégés of Britain's chief rival in the region could turn into a commercial and diplomatic asset that the British did not have. The eastern Christians were consequently imagined by English writers to be victims of Ottoman oppression, eager to ally themselves with the English to battle the Turks, and equally eager to convert to Anglicanism. They were, in this view, a means to an English end.

Eastern Christians and the Holy Land

Early modern English attitudes toward eastern Christians were largely shaped by their view of the region that, as Edmund Bohun wrote in 1691, was 'now commonly called the Holy Land, and in the Hands of the Turks ever since the year 1517'.[68] For the first generations of travelling clergymen and pious consuls, Palestine, 'the proper and adæquate name of the whole Countrey',[69] was of paramount importance 'because here was wrought the work of our salvation'.[70] Knowing that the land where Christ had walked was controlled by Muslims generated both anger and frustration. Anglo-Protestants did not regard the region with the sacramental veneration of Catholics; but neither did they see it as a region of commercial opportunity. When Lewes Roberts catalogued important commercial centres in 1637, Palestine was insignificant, meriting very brief mention: serious trade passed through Izmir, Aleppo, and Alexandria.[71] Nevertheless, when pious English visitors strolled in Jerusalem or climbed Mount Tabor, they felt that the land belonged to them, since they were Christians who possessed biblical revelation and redemption. Traders and travellers who visited Palestine could not but see themselves opposed to the Ottoman Muslims occupying Palestine.

Among the most important influences on the English and European imaginings of Palestine were the maps and commentaries of Abraham Ortelius' atlas that first appeared in 1570. There is little doubt that Ortelius' map established in the minds of Euro-Christian viewers an indelible image of a biblical Palestine which no amount of Islamic or Ottoman presence could change. Palestine was the Palestine of the Bible and thus the Palestine of Christians. The history of Palestine cartography in the early modern period, and perhaps of later periods, remains inextricably dependent on the eschatological thinking of Ortelius. As Kenneth Nebenzahl has stated, Ortelius' map of Palestine became the 'prototype for the modern cartography of the Holy Land', while Jerry Brotton confirms that the way in which Ortelius created and presented geographical information has continued 'to influence the field of geography even today'.[72] Indeed, between 1570 and 1624, the *Theatrum* appeared in Latin, Spanish, English, French, Dutch, Italian, and German editions. Those which Ortelius himself produced, from 1570 to 1595 (he died in 1598), saw an increase in the number of maps from 53 to 147: but at no point was there a single map of contemporary Palestine.

The *Theatrum Orbis Terrarum* presented a vast and politically savvy image of the world that combined cartography with up-to-date ethnographic, economic, and political knowledge. Ortelius was only too aware that while Spanish readers—like Philip II to whom the project is dedicated— would scrutinize his representation of the Spanish-occupied Netherlands, there were also men in his native Antwerp who had ventured to the ends of the earth in search of trade, who wanted details about contemporary matters. As a result, when depicting Islamic regions, he usually referred readers to recent books and events. The 1606 English translation of the *Theatrum*, for instance, declares that 'all that whole tract of *Asia* comprehended between the great river *Tigris*, the Persian gulfe ... and the Caspian sea, is now in these our daies possessed by the *Sophies*, the Kings of *Persia*'.[73] But not a word will be found about the historical Persians and Babylonians familiar from the Hebrew Scriptures. Similarly, in the case of the Ottoman Empire, readers are referred to books describing 'the greatnesse that now it is of, whereby it is fearfull to all nations round about',[74] where emphasis falls on the word 'now' since Ortelius described events up to the year 1566. When writing about 'Barbary', Ortelius describes people with specific complexions, talents and abilities, noting that the 'people generally of this whole country are of a brownish or tawny complexion. They which dwell in cities, are very ingenious in Architecture and such like Mathematicall inventions.'[75] For Ortelius, contemporary historical conditions were an essential part of cartography even if, as in the case of the New World, history had started less than eighty years before the *Theatrum*, which is perhaps why there are no references to native Americans.

The emphasis on recent and relevant information underpinned all the maps and discussions in Ortelius' atlas—except in the case of Palestine. Taken from the German mapmaker Tileman Stella, Ortelius' Palestine was the only map in the atlas representing spiritual rather than geographical space. The book of Joshua (18: 4–5, 9) tells how, after the conquest of the east bank of the Jordan river, the Israelite leader ordered 'three men of each tribe... to walk through the land [of Canaan] and describe it... and divide it into seven parts'. For Ortelius, Palestine had been mapped in biblical times and therefore its cartographic finality was a matter of divine authority. In mapping Palestine, Ortelius revered Old Testament geography for being changeless: no amount of history, conquest, religious transformation, or even empirical evidence could alter divine decree. In the second edition of the *Theatrum*, Ortelius introduced another map of Palestine by Christian Schrot, and in the third edition of 1584, he replaced Stella's map with a further version derived from the 1570 'wall map of Peter Laicksteen (fl. ca. 1556-1570) and Christian Sgrothen (*c.*1532–1608)'.[76] The inaccuracy of this latter map surpasses even the inaccuracy of Stella's.[77]

By including maps of Palestine that emphasized religious rather than geographical space, Ortelius invited readers to suspend disbelief, to replace truth with faith, and to shift their thoughts from geography to eschatology. There was nothing about Palestine 'in these our daies' except its religious history. Palestine, for Ortelius, was a predicate of Toranic history and New Testament imprints: religious belief determined cartography. This attitude to Palestine erased past and current history: the land had nothing to do with its present mix of eastern Christians and Turks, Jews and Arabs, and everything to do with biblical accounts and prophetic expectations. It was an attitude entirely different from that of Arabic Muslim writers and cartographers, some of whom drew on Judaic and Christian tradition, for whom the region combined all monotheistic history with the contemporary landscape, people, flora and fauna, local saints, and holy men.[78] The Ortelian attitude, on the other hand, enabled an English traveller like Laurence Aldersey to visit 'the Cities of Jerusalem, and Tripolis' of Syria in 1581, and describe the biblical sites without a single word about the living inhabitants;[79] it made possible the numerous plans and diagrams of biblical sites in the Holy Land that illustrate Sandys' *Relation* in which they represent a Palestine entirely vacant of people;[80] and it allowed Samuel Purchas, despite his avowed emphasis on recent travel, to include maps of 'Canaan' showing the supposed route of the Israelite exodus.[81] In his *Pisgah-Sight of Palestine*, the 'worthy Doctor Fuller' described the 'History of the Old and New Testament acted thereon', with only minimal allusions to contemporary events and sites. Although his descriptions purported to provide readers with a reliable guide to the inns between Aleppo and Damascus—'Amongst these *Canes* or *Turkish Innes*, *Marra* and *Cotefey* are most beautifull, the latter, little inferiour to the *old Exchange in London*'—his map offers a geography of faith not travel.[82] When Peter Heylyn wrote about Palestine in 1652, he used the present tense about 'Samaria', 'Iudea', and 'Peraea' as if they were part of current Ottoman administrative divisions.[83] In 1669, T. B. moved from one holy site to another, without ever noticing that there was life going on around him. He was visiting and describing a Palestine of the scriptures, sometimes coloured by Crusader memories, but never the Palestine of the Byzantines, the Umayyads, or the many Islamic dynasties that had built the cities, especially Jerusalem.[84] Published in 1693, Robert Morden's *Geography Rectified* claimed to represent the 'Accurate Observations and Discoveries of Modern Authors'. But when it came to Palestine, or rather 'Canaan', as he termed it, his map showed the land divided among the twelve tribes of Israel. Such a map provided no information about the contemporary land as promised on the titlepage, but rather served to confirm biblical faith since it showed a land that was 'now a fearful Monument of Divine Vengeance, a sad distant Mirror for all other like sinful Countries to view their Destiny by'.[85] When Henry Maundrell travelled through Palestine in 1697, he recalled the glory of his crusading ancestors, hoping that the liberation of the holy land would be forthcoming.[86]

This return to the biblical past when representing and thinking about Palestine ran counter to the prevailing interest in chorography, presented in such influential works as John Stow's *Survay of London* (1598) and John Speed's *Theatre of the Empire of Great Britaine* (1611). While the English were taking 'effective and visual and conceptual possession of the physical kingdom in which they lived', as Richard Helgerson put it,[87] they continued to view Palestine and other parts of the Ottoman Empire as lands defined by the classical and biblical narratives. Centuries of Arab-Islamic history and development in these regions were simply erased from account. Cartwright had no interest in anything that had happened since classical and biblical times. And if and when contemporary circumstances were to be credited, they had to be grim. Archbishop George Abbot stated how travellers described Palestine's barrenness, which had resulted from God cursing it 'together with the *Jewes*, the Inhabitants of it', but it was a barrenness that Arab travellers never saw since, on the contrary, they noticed abundance and fertility.[88] But English travellers could only see the ruins of time in a region that would only be redeemed by the removal of the infidels, and the return of Christianity, most assuredly in its Anglican version.

Figure 8. 'A Merchant Jewe', from Nicolas de Nicolay, *The Navigations into Turkie* (1585)
MacLean copy

Jews in the Islamic empires

Although there were Jews, many of them Marranos, living in Elizabethan England, it was not until the admission of a small number in the mid 1650s that they were able to live and practise their religion openly. While travellers and diplomats might have been familiar with some of the Jews who were living in London, knowledge of and attitudes towards Jews were mostly derived from biblical tradition, stage caricature, and diatribes in sermons. But in North Africa and the rest of the Ottoman Empire, Britons met an active and entrepreneurial community. The first ambassadors in Istanbul sought Jews out for assistance—Edward Barton praised them for furnishing him with correct information about the Armada attack.[89] John Sanderson wrote warmly about the Jews he met in the Islamic world: in company with a group of eight Jews, he travelled from Istanbul to Damascus and Jerusalem, meeting little interference from the local inhabitants along the way.[90] William Lithgow described staying 'within the Towne making merry with our Hebraick friends', just a few years after Sandys had declared that 'no citie is without them throughout the *Grand Signiors* dominions'.[91] In 1650, when Manasseh ben Israel petitioned the English Parliament to allow Jews to be admitted, he confirmed their presence throughout the Islamic world from Morocco to Persia.[92] Jews were visible, from the small seaport of Tangiers, which boasted 'several Synagogues', to Isfahan and beyond.[93] Some of these communities were large: '160000 persons' in Salonica and Istanbul alone, according to Peter Heylyn writing in 1652.[94]

The 'Jews of Islam', as Bernard Lewis called them,[95] offered advice, assistance, and housing to Britons, but they pursued their own interests, which could be contrary to British designs. As a result, views ranged from sympathy and careful observation to denunciation and bigotry. As a young man, Archbishop George Abbot, who never left England, managed to write *A Briefe Description of the whole World* (1599), which proved to be extremely popular. The Jews of Persia, he reported, were so well treated under Shah 'Abbas (r. 1587–1627) that they thought him the Messiah.[96] Travellers to the Holy Land, on the other hand, often felt anger and hostility towards the large and thriving Jewish community there, since they were deemed to be prospering despite their unwillingness to accept the Messiah. Sandys vituperated against their 'savage tones' and 'fantasticall gestures' during worship, 'weaving with their bodies, and often jumping up-right (as in the manner in daunces)'.[97] 'His blood be upon us and our Children,' quoted the reverend Lancelot Addison from Matthew 27: 25 to justify why the Moroccans 'Hector'd' over the Jews.[98]

Islamic tolerance allowed Jews to flourish and integrate, some to 'growe rich by their witts, or rather frauds' as Fynes Moryson observed of the Jewish community of the Ottoman Levant.[99] When the Shirley brothers crossed into Persia, they were accompanied by a number of Jews who often pointed out the biblical significance of specific locations.[100] Jewish women were known to be very active in the Ottoman court where they sold European make-up and traded in jewels.[101] This Jewish success in commerce and in polity doubtless provoked envy, and may help explain the eagerness of some English travellers to emphasize Jewish suffering and persecution: things were not, after all, that good. William Biddulph and Peter Heylyn both noted that Christians living in the Ottoman Empire vented their anger on the Jews, throwing stones at them during Passion Week.[102] Jews could not but pay for their apostasy: even the Persians denounced and punished them for rejecting Christ, according to the author of *The fatal and final Extirpation and Destruction of the Jews out of the Empire of Persia, begun in 1663*.[103] Other writers emphasized their poverty and consequent need for charitable donations from coreligionists in 'Poland, Lithuania, and other parts of Europe'. In 1656, there was so much need among the Jews that they were willing to accept money from European Christians, chiefly Dutch, in order to pay off the debts they had incurred as a result of high Ottoman taxation. It was a Christian responsibility to help them, explained the Baptist minister Henry Jessey, since doing so helped prepare the 'Way for their Deliverance'—their final conversion to Christianity.[104]

While some Anglo-Protestants eagerly anticipated the conversion of the Jews, others continued to be concerned about their ability to coexist with other religions. Britons living in India might well have been confused to discover that 'Frank and Jew' worshipped 'in one congregation' at Jahangir's court,[105] but there were very few Jews living in India so references to them are minimal. In Palestine, Sandys noted how Jews and Muslims shared religious customs, such as throwing stones at the tomb of Absalom for rebelling against David.[106] He also noted, that Muslims and Jews had much in common, such as 'circumcision, detestation of Images, abstinency from swines-flesh, and divers other ceremonies'.[107] To many, the coexistence of and similarities between Jews and Muslims proved deeply worrisome, causing many to oppose readmitting them to England. Fears that the Jews, if readmitted, might proselytize unwary Christians persisted from the debates of the 1650s until well after John Toland's call for Jewish naturalization in 1713 and after.[108]

Muslims, however, did not seem to fear for their religion, openly allowing Jews to live, work, and worship among them. In 1655, while the Protestant Waldensians were being massacred by Catholic troops—provoking John Milton's bitter lament—Jews were enjoying autonomy of self-expression. Sandys observed that they still used 'the Spanish tongue and Hebrew character', more than a century after their expulsion from Spain and settlement in the Islamic Mediterranean.[109] In North Africa, Jews lived apart from Muslims in their 'Juderia', as Lancelot Addison observed, but they were very much part of the region's economic and legal activity.[110] Addison, an Anglican clergyman writing in 1670, well may have wondered how Muslims accepted Jews in their midst at a time when his church was busy persecuting dissenting Englishmen in line with the Clarendon Code.[111] In Morocco, another English writer noted that the Jews of Islam separated themselves from 'European-Jews' who were chiefly Dutch: while the latter Jews were adapting to their Christian environments and selling 'Swines-Flesh' and drinking wine, the 'Moorish-Jews' were strict about dietary laws, and excommunicated their coreligionists—until the English intervened on the side of the Europeans.[112] Jews integrated with Islamic culture without losing their religion—and Muslims tolerated such hybridity. When, at the end of the eighteenth century, a Moroccan Jew settled in England and scandalously married an English actress, Leah Wells, she had great difficulty distinguishing his Jewishness from his Moorishness when writing her memoirs.[113]

Much as they travelled and traded with Jews in the Islamic world, English writers could not separate them from biblical history. Henry Blount wondered about the Ten Lost Tribes,[114] a topic that had fascinated travellers since the days of Marco Polo and Sir John Mandeville. By mid century, Persian Jews were believed to have travelled via 'Tartaria' to become the ancestors of the Native Americans.[115] Thomas Fuller speculated about where they were 'probably extent at this day'.[116] As late as 1709, Aaron Hill was still trying to discover what happened to the '*Ten Tribes* of *Israel*, which were carried away *Captive*, by *Shalmanezer, King* of *Assyria*'.[117] At home, other Britons, safe in their pulpits or universities, devised schemes of 'Restauration', hoping that Jews would convert to Christianity and become

England's surrogate fighters, spearheading Protestant opposition to the Ottomans.[118] Others actively tried to convert them. In 1610, John Harrison, representing the Barbary Company in Morocco, became the first English missionary to live with the Jews and then write tracts designed to convert them.[119] In 1611, he left Morocco for England, accompanied by Samuel Pallache, Mulay Zaydan's Jewish envoy to the States-General. Pallache introduced Harrison to the large Jewish community in Amsterdam. The sight of such an active community inflamed Harrison's zeal: in 1613 and again in 1619, he published *The Messiah Alreadie Come*, a tract aiming '*to convince the Jewes, of their palpable, and more then miserable blindnesse*'.[120]

The presence of large numbers of Jews in the Ottoman regions became well-known to English readers in the late 1660s with the rise and fall of Sabbatai Sevi, a self-proclaimed messiah whose movement attracted Jews from Gaza to Istanbul. Sevi's escapades were widely reported in London and showed the extensiveness of the Jewish presence in Islamic lands. His huge following unleashed English fantasies about Jews mobilizing armies to fight the Ottomans and taking possession of 'Meka' and 'the Arabians Countrey' since it was believed that 'the Great Turk had a dream that an Israelite had taken the Crown from his head'.[121] Other tracts proclaimed that the Ten Tribes would reappear and march from Salé toward Marrakesh, and from Persia toward Jerusalem.[122] Paul Rycaut, an Englishman with first-hand experience of the Sabbatarian movement, described how 'all the Cities of *Turkie*, where the Jews inhabited, were full of expectation of the Messiah, no Trade or course of gain was followed'.[123] Rycaut followed the news about Sevi from Izmir to Salonica, collecting copies of the letters that were exchanged between Sevi and his followers. Relying on Rycaut's account, John Evelyn included Sevi among the *Three Late Famous Imposters* (1669) after the false messiah had converted to Islam in Istanbul. Whatever Sevi's legacy, it alerted English readers to the strong presence of Jews in the Levant, and the fervency of their religion in the midst of Islam.[124]

When Britons began settling Tangier in the early 1660s, Jews joined them, only to find that deputy-governor Colonel John Fitzgerald had been cautioned against allowing them into the outpost: 'you must have a watchful eye over the Jews, if you suffer any.'[125] Such fears continued as English merchants became increasingly aware of how influential the local Jewish community could be in regional commerce. Although a Jewish interpreter, Solomon Pariente, served the English governors of Tangier, an order to banish Jews was issued in 1677. Despite the rebuff, some returned a few years later, but Colonel Percy Kirke ordered that they should 'lodge in tents outside the walls'.[126] In 1682, fears that Jews and Muslims would influence the Christian outpost were confirmed by reports that 'three soldiers, who have lately deserted and turned Moors, have been inveighed and enticed thereunto by the too great freedome, which hath been afforded of them conversing with the Moors and Jews'.[127]

In 1675, the resident English consul in Algiers described the local Jewish community:

> The Jewes whereof there are two sorts, the Natives consisting of 13 thousand families wch for ye most part are handy craftmen, & brokers, the other Christian Jews, soe called because they are bred up in Spayne, Portugall, & Italy, and goes habiled like the people of the country from whence they came, these are for ye most part Marchants & cunning fellowes.[128]

Jews were active from Mediterranean to Atlantic ports. At the end of the seventeenth century, an anonymous author described their role in trade. '*Sancta Cruce*' [Agadir], he wrote, 'is a Town of no great Extent; yet the Merchants and *Jews* there drive a considerable Trade,' while '*Sophia* [Safi]... is a better Town of Trade than *Sancta Cruce*, maintained as well by Christian Merchants as *Jews*, who have several Ships consigned them both from *England*, *Holland*, and *France*.'[129] In 1704, Jewish traders moved from Morocco to Gibraltar after the British had seized the Spanish outpost. In 1711, the British asked the Moroccan ruler for 'Lime Brick and Tyles' for Gibraltar, whereupon he insisted that, despite injunctions against giving 'materially for the Christians to Fortifie themselves', he would do so provided the British permitted 'all sorts of Merchants as well Moors as Jews' to trade freely in Gibraltar.[130] In December 1715, Captain George Paddon paused in Gibraltar on his way to take up an ambassadorial appointment in Morocco. Discovering the large Jewish community there, he wrote home suggesting that they should be treated as diplomatic captives until their coreligionists ransomed the Britons being held in Morocco.[131] Paddon's plan was doomed from the start since the Jews were protected by Mulay Ismail in a manner that was not yet possible in England: three years earlier, the Act for the Naturalization of Continental Protestants had been repealed under pressure from Tory politicians and mob agitation.[132] If foreign Protestants could not be accepted as subjects, neither could Jews. But the situation was slowly beginning to change: by 1725, the Jewish community in Gibraltar had grown to 111 men and 26 women.[133]

Figure 9. 'A Merchant of Armenia,' from Nicolas de Nicolay, *The Navigations into Turkie* (1585)
MacLean copy

British writers were seldom happy about the wide-ranging presence of Jews, and were alarmed at the way they seemed to flaunt their faith. In North Africa and the Mediterranean east, however, they were obliged to deal with Jews on the Jews' own terms since the Jews were protected by Qur'anic law. The Jews who settled in England after 1655—such as Antonio Fernandez Carvajal, Mendez de Costa, David Abrabanell Dormido, the Abendana Brothers, and others—were all from European Christendom as their Spanish or Portuguese names reveal.[134] These were not the Jews of Islam.

The Armenians of Islam

Unlike the French, English Protestants could not make league with eastern Catholic Christians, and were consequently thwarted in their evangelical endeavours. French travellers and missionaries, however, were widely mobile, with access to monasteries and churches from the Morea to Iraq, from Syria down to Egypt. The Jesuits even received royal and ecclesiastical support from their order, enabling them, in the frightened imagination of an English report from 1581, to win over and convert no less than 'the Grand Signior's mother, wife, and sister to the Romish religion'.[135] Meanwhile, English visitors to the Levant remained few, and the number of them who wrote was even fewer; on average only fifteen Britons travelled to Palestine annually between 1583 and 1632, and their knowledge of the region's religious and historical diversity remained limited.[136] Beyond brief mentions by Biddulph and Sandys, there is very little English writing of the period about the Maronites of Lebanon. The Copts excited some interest after the visit to London of the multi-lingual Josephus Barbatus,[137] but since Egypt seemed dominated by French merchants, English travellers largely ignored them.

Besides Greek and Arab Orthodox Christians, the English mostly dealt with Armenians. In 1582 Hakluyt included 'Harton an Armenian' in the list of 'late travaylers', though his voyages had taken place in 1300.[138] In 1608, Marcus Abraham, 'a pore Christian merchant borne in Armenia under the Dominion of the Turk', petitioned the Court of Alderman in London for financial assistance.[139] A year later, in the Mughal court, William Hawkins married the daughter of a 'Christian Armenian, and of the Race of the most ancient Christians'.[140] A few years later, also in India, Captain Robert Coverte, learned of an Armenian Christian who had 'turned More'.[141] Sandys often mentioned meeting Armenians, both in Jerusalem and Bethlehem, though their numbers were very small.[142]

Commerce was largely responsible for Anglo-Armenian relations. Following initial contacts through Jenkinson and the Shirley Brothers, formal trade into Persia started up in 1613, and English merchants were granted licenses in 1617 and 1629 to trade in silk. Upon arrival, the English lodged, as did other European factors, in the Armenian neighbourhoods. The Armenians were commercially versatile, and provided the English, and other Europeans, with translators and local assistance.[143] But the English and the Armenians were rivals—both wishing to dominate regional trade—so English observers were not always complimentary about them. William Gibson, the factor in Persia from 1632 until 1637, described the 'baseness of that nation in all manner of degrees... unfaithfull in work and deede'.[144] In 1651, English merchants in Isfahan discovered that the Armenians had flooded the market with cloth they had brought from Aleppo; similar events had earlier taken place in Delhi.[145] Rivalry, however, did not prevent some English residents from marrying Armenian women, or from being buried in Armenian cemeteries.[146] Armenians, were, after all, Christians, and although some had joined the Catholic Church, they led 'pious and just lives and conversations as becomes the Professors of the Gospel'.[147] But money was money. In 1651, Armenian merchants sailing from Izmir to Leghorn with a lading of silk, were attacked and robbed by English ships.[148]

Shah 'Abbas admired the business acumen of his Armenian subjects, often sending them as emissaries to European capitals. Others served at regional courts, such as 'Margevelo', who, because he was 'loved dearly' by the local 'Bashawe', was able to help the Shirley brothers on numerous occasions.[149] The freedoms enjoyed by Armenians made English writers imagine that 'Abbas might be a crypto-Christian: 'it is said', wrote Hugh Lee to Thomas Wilson in April 1608, 'that the Persian King is to become a Christian.'[150] Because of the Shah's authority, wrote Ephraim Pagitt later in the century, neither Jews nor Muslims could 'abuse' Christians for celebrating Easter.[151] Indeed, French Catholic clergy were shown such 'great signes of affection' that they converted five Muslims to Christianity—for which 'Abbas severely punished them.[152] Armenians too were often subjected to persecution in the Safavid Empire. In 1609 'a thousand of these [Armenians] suffered martyrdome by bloudy *Abbas*'; half a century later local rulers, who 'mortally hate[d] the Christian Religion', were elated at the conversion of Armenians to Islam.[153] Following social and religious pressures, Armenians from the Isfahan suburb of New Julfa began trading beyond Persia. By the second half of the seventeenth century, they had spread throughout the Mediterranean basin, establishing factories in Marseilles, Amsterdam, and all the way north to London. East India Company records contain numerous references to Armenians whether they were visiting London, sailing on Company ships from Surat to Bandar Abbas, travelling to Aleppo, or simply trading in amber, silk, tobacco, cloth, and jewels.[154] Some reached Morocco, as the case of Bentura de Zary at the beginning of the eighteenth century shows (see next section). Others reached the Pacific Ocean, as the Iraqi priest, Hanna al-Mawsuli, reported in the late 1660s.[155] In 1688, the East India Company signed a treaty with 'the Armenian Nation', represented by one Khoja Phanoos Kalantar, who had been 'residing in London when he signed this treaty'.[156] In 1706, Armenian merchants were trading in Cadiz.[157]

Paul Rycaut described Armenians in the Ottoman Empire, while John Covel commented that in Izmir they were 'a most wretched, illiterate, ignorant sort of people'.[158] Other English writers, sometimes translating from French accounts, described their religious beliefs, but generally the Armenians did not generate as much concern as Orthodox eastern Christians since they did not live in areas that evoked biblical memory or anti-Islamic fervour. They also seemed integrated: Joseph Pitts patronized an Armenian barber in Izmir who had 'both Christians and Turks' for customers.[159] The Armenian community of New Julfa in Isfahan attained a level of financial and social success that impressed European visitors, having built 'over a score of churches' in the city, thirteen of which are still standing.[160] They were so integrated that East India Company records sometimes did not bother to mention that a person was Armenian, just Persian: so we find entries such as: 'Ovanes, a poore Persian'.[161] The English may even have secretly admired the Armenians of Islam. When Daniel Defoe's William the Quaker settled in Venice, he disguised himself as an Armenian, 'Signore Constantine Alexion of Isphahan'.[162] Defoe may have been inspired by the recent visit to London of an Armenian who had created quite a sensation: his name was Bentura de Zary, or so he claimed.

The Armenian ambassador from Morocco

Bentura de Zary, an Armenian from Morocco, was dispatched to Queen Anne's court as ambassador by a Muslim ruler, the Moroccan Mulay Ismail (r. 1673–1727). One important difference between Eastern and Western regimes is that Muslim rulers were willing to send Christian and Jewish subjects to represent them in Christian capitals. In October 1709, Mulay Ismail wrote to Queen Anne, announcing that he was dispatching one 'Bentura El Armenio [that is] Venturo the Armenian Merchant' to be his ambassador at her court.[163] Towards the end of April 1710, Bentura arrived in London, carrying a letter from Ismail that described him as *al-nusrani*, the

Christian, and *al-armani*, the Armenian.[164] Later, Bentura described himself simply as representing Mulay Ismail, calling Morocco 'my Country'.[165] We can at least partly glimpse Bentura's experiences in early modern England through the extraordinary letters that he wrote during his stay in London from 1710 until his death in 1716.

The surviving correspondence reveals in striking ways how diplomacy might be enacted, and neglected, when non-European emissaries were at issue. Bentura's stay in London was so protracted that he ended up dying there. Having been initially welcomed by Secretary of State, William Legge, first Earl of Dartmouth, Bentura not only waited for months to meet the Queen, but later endured years of virtual house arrest, held hostage in exchange for captive British seamen. Such diplomatic insults would have been unthinkable had it not been for the seeming strangeness of an Armenian Christian merchant representing a Muslim ruler. These were circumstances that soon became a source of lively gossip that was compounded by memories of earlier self-styled representatives from Eastern potentates who had turned out to be imposters. Yet the archival evidence confirms the authenticity of Bentura's embassy. He may have been a financially strapped merchant who was hoping to repair his fortunes, but there is no doubt that he was officially appointed by the Moroccan king. Mulay Ismail's letter to Queen Anne of June 1710 confirmed him with full authority to negotiate 'anything relating to a good Correspondence of Trade or Otherwise'.[166] Ismail was eager that his ambassador be officially received at court. While waiting for an audience with the Queen, Bentura rented a house on Dartmouth Street right in the political heart of London between the Houses of Parliament in Westminster and St James's Palace.

By mid December, eight months after arriving, Bentura had received no sign of his expected audience. On 16 December 1710, he wrote a letter in Spanish—with an English translation—to the Earl of Dartmouth, stating that he had been 'in the Court of the most Serene Queen of Great Brittain some months', and was eager to present his credentials 'that he may be no longer in Suspence'.[167] Four days later, Bentura was granted his request. On 20 December, he was 'conducted from his House by Sir Clement Cotterel, Master of the Ceremonies, in Her Majesty's Body-Coach to private Audience at St James's, where being introduc'd into the Queen's Presence by the Lord Dartmouth', he congratulated her on her recent victory over 'the Two Great Flowers of the Christian Messias, the Kings of France and Spain'.[168] Bentura's 'Harangue' before the Queen exhibited more the 'Politeness of an

European than an African Court', as the local press commented in surprise. And the court was obviously perplexed and not a little suspicious that a Christian was representing a Muslim ruler. After all, Bentura was a Christian whose rhetorical strategies differed from those of the royal Moroccan tradition: he had spoken of the 'influence of our Great Prophet'—without explaining which prophet, Jesus or Muhammad, he had in mind.[169]

Securing good relations between Morocco and Britain was clearly less important for Anne's government than it had been for Elizabeth's. For months after his official reception, Bentura was again ignored. Left to his own devices, Bentura soon discovered how expensive 'this Great Citty' could be, since he found himself engaged in a costly game of diplomatic gift exchange involving exotic animals. Bentura's mission was, in part, to obtain for Mulay Ismail some of Queen Anne's 'spotted', or fallow, deer. The Queen was a famous huntswoman, driving her chariot in the chase, as commemorated by Alexander Pope in *Windsor Forest*. Early in his stay, Bentura had bought a small herd, for which he hired Greek attendants.[170] In a very short time, he was lamenting how looking after these deer was costing him as much as 'a Troop of Horse in my Country'. On 21 March 1711, he complained to Dartmouth that his 'Purse' was 'Empty'.[171] Two years later, on 27 April 1713, Bentura mentions a lion and tiger brought from Morocco as a present to Queen Anne that were presumably still in his care. Managing such a menagerie of predators and prey in his London house must have presented quite a challenge, but fortunately Dartmouth succeeded in having the Lord Treasurer ordered to 'give the necessary Directions for bringing the Lyon and the Tyger to the Tower'.[172] Although exotic creatures were common diplomatic gifts at the time, there is no further record of these particular felines.

By 20 July 1711, Bentura appears to have completed his mission. Having found a ship that would take him directly to 'Barbary', he was ready to set sail. He wrote to Dartmouth asking for a letter from Queen Anne to Mulay Ismail, and pleaded for reimbursement of money he had spent during his stay in England.[173] On 8 August, he wrote to Muhammad Andaluz, a Spanish Morisco convert who served as secretary to Ismail,[174] telling him that he would be bringing forty-two deer—twenty of them gifts from the queen, and twenty-two that he had bought himself—10,000 Dutch tiles that were part of a business agreement with a French 'Friend Pillet of Salle', and a coach, 'an Extraordinary Invention to goe two Leagues an houre… [along] with other things For my master & my Mistress the Sultana'.[175]

But events conspired to thwart Bentura's plans. On 8 August, describing his preparations, he sounded a first note of alarm:

> I am much concerned at the News I heard at Court the other day, that my Masters ships had taken two ships belonging to Her Britannic Majesty's Subjects, it troubled me very much till I had some consolation from my Lord Dartmouth, That the captains had written to their Friends here, that my Master promised to restore them with their Lodeing and Men.[176]

Bentura had become a victim of historical circumstances. The British captives were not released, and the ship left with the spotted deer but without Bentura.

For the next five years, between 1711 and 1716, Bentura remained in London, little more than a hostage to fortune. Evidence suggests that he was regularly harassed, both directly and indirectly. His servants were arrested, breaching diplomatic immunity,[177] and rumours about him and his household were spread in the *Post Boy* and the *Gazette*.[178] The smear campaign questioned his legitimacy as a Moroccan representative, and there were even insinuations that he did not know Arabic.[179] In June 1712, Bentura dashed off a letter explaining that henceforth in his correspondence, he would sign his name in both Spanish and Arabic—and at the bottom of the letter to Erasmus Lewis, signed in Armenian![180] He continued to do so until the end. Despite Bentura's protests, the British government exacted its revenge for the Moroccan government's failure to release the captives. On 9 January 1713, Bentura was placed under house arrest. He wrote plaintively to Dartmouth, inquiring 'what Improvement the seizure of me can be to bring matters to a good Understanding and lasting Friendship between the two Nations?' At the top of the letter, he sounded a note of pathos: 'From two pair of Stairs at the messengers hous in Dartmouth streete Westminster.'[181]

Throughout his pleading with Dartmouth, Bentura had recourse to the concept of the 'Law of Nations', appealing to a supposedly shared code. His confinement, he wrote, contravened the 'Law of Nations: for by that Law my Lord the Persons of Embassadors have ever been sacred, even from Princes actually in Warr, with those from whom they are sent, and the late act of Parliament relating to Embassadors wch makes their Priviledges inviolable'. From his confinement, Bentura had kept himself apprised of the activities of Parliament, which was just a short walk away from Dartmouth Street. Since British ambassadors enjoyed their privileges abroad, he wrote, he should enjoy his privileges in Britain. He would have accepted confinement, he explained, had he himself done anything wrong or had the captives in Morocco enjoyed the same diplomatic status that he had. His confinement was an insult because it equated common British seamen with an ambassador. In this respect, Bentura's invocation of the 'Law of Nations' was intended to address his hosts in the language they understood best: a precise legal language that ensured the safety of British residents in host countries. Tactfully, Bentura wrote to congratulate the Queen on her victory in the war of the Spanish succession and the peace secured by the treaty of Utrecht.[182]

In a letter of May 1713, Bentura's rhetorical master-stoke was to present himself as a martyr caught between ungrateful governments:

> My Lord though I might complain of being a Prisoner allmost five Months, and detained so (as I conceive) contrary to the Laws & Customes of Nations, and of other Treatment too; Yet as I am a Christian, and ambitious of doing the best Services for Her Majesty, I shall not Repine at my own Restraint nor Usage, if your Lordship does thereby obtaine the End, which was to bring Matters to a good Understanding and lasting Friendship between the two Nations.[183]

Bentura's declaration that he was a Christian should have worked, though it may also have created confusion. The Armenians, after all, belonged to an autocephalous church of the monophysite belief, but from the sixteenth century on, they had been exposed to Catholic missionary activity.[184] Bentura may well have remained faithful to his Armenian creed, or he might have converted to Catholicism: his letters do not tell. An English captive in Morocco c.1706 mentioned that the number of Armenians there was small, and then explained that though they went to 'Mass with the Roman-Catholicks yet they differ from in their Practices at least, if not Principles; and seem so far to follow the abrogated Ceremonial Law, as to Celebrate the Feasts of New Moons, &c. at whose appearance they immediately mount their Houses and Sing a Psalm or some other Canticle'.[185] Whether Bentura subscribed to such practices is not mentioned, but Armenian fasting was more severe and lasted longer than that of Catholics, while their alleged 'Worshipping of the Moon', and emphasis on good deeds— 'the Merits and Vertue of their own good Works'—may have made them appealing to Muslims who respected fasting, used the moon for their calendar, and emphasized the importance of good deeds.[186]

Bentura was finally granted an audience with the Queen on the evening of 2 August. Anne thought it prudent to make some amends so she ordered that all the deer that had died should be replaced, and that 'two dozen of the largest china dishes that can be had' plus 'two large copper tea kitchens and a fine tea' be included in the gift to Ismail, who despite being a 'barbarian' needed to be humoured so he would release the sixty-nine British captives.[187] As far as she was concerned, the insult to the Moroccan ambassador and her flouting of the law of nations could be appeased with some kitchenware. The Peace of Utrecht ensured her of superiority over both enemies and allies. She dispatched George Padden to Ismail's court to negotiate a treaty, which was eventually signed in 1714.

When Mulay Ismail wrote to congratulate King George on his accession to the throne in April 1715, he mentioned that the news of the accession had been relayed to him by 'our Christian servant Bentura de Zari the Armenian, who is there [in England] by our authorization there with you and in your country'.[188] Although eager that the new king should uphold the treaty with Morocco that Queen Anne had signed, Mulay Ismail was not willing to forget the insults Bentura had endured. The kitchenware had not done the trick:

> We have heard also that your servants have failed to give to our Christian servant Bentura the aforementioned his due, and have harmed him and have not acknowledged that he is there with you only for the purpose of our blessed service. When your Christian servant Padden came to our seat made lofty by God (who is exalted) did we fall short with respect to him? Or did anything disagreeable happen to him? Ask him and he will tell you how we behaved towards him. We have authorized our servant Bentura to reside in the city of London to fulfil for us any purposes of ours.[189]

Evidently, the 'barbarian' abided by the laws of nations more attentively than the British monarch. And the 'barbarian' was perfectly confident in employing and protecting, to the extent he could, a Christian envoy to the lands of the Christians—in a manner that no British monarch would have contemplated for a non-Christian subject.[190]

And so, five years after first arriving in London, Bentura was still serving his Moroccan king from his house on Dartmouth Street. He died a year later, in 1716. Bentura, Armenian and Christian that he was, had served Ismail well, which encouraged his master to reproach George I about the incivility of his treatment. Bentura represents the opportunity that the Islamic world offered to Christians, whether they were Armenians, British,

French, or Italian: to cross boundaries between the two communities. His feet were in Christianity though his responsibility lay in Islam. His culture and cuisine were rooted in the Mediterranean—hence the very Middle Eastern habit of eating melon seeds to pass the time during his house arrest. His will of September 1716 lists among his possessions European clothes, 'One paire of Cloath Breeches Embroidered with Gold', but also 'Outlandish Bookes', 'One Silver Snuff Box', and also a 'Damask Table Clothes', and 'One Parrott'.[191] Despite the cultural mix, to his hosts he remained a Moroccan, and therefore when the Moroccans seized a British ship, he paid. That he was a Christian wearing breeches meant nothing to them. In the dominions of Islam, there was not so severe a division between cultures, national identities, and civilizations as there was in Britain. There is no equivalent to Bentura in the annals of early modern British history.

The Shi'ites

Since the Shi'ites chiefly inhabited Persia, the English learned of them almost by accident. As Mohammad Taghi Nezam-Mafi has observed, 'English travellers to Syria predated their successors in Persia by a century'—and they were well behind the Italians and the Portuguese.[192] As a result, English understanding of their religion was both belated and confused: an early account of the wars between the Ottomans and the Persians mentioned nothing about the Shi'ite tradition, explaining enmity solely on diplomatic grounds.[193] Not until the turn of the seventeenth century, following the celebrated exploits of the Shirley brothers, would knowledge of contemporary Persia become at all widely spread, bringing with it some sense of the religious divisions within Islam.

George Manwaring recognized how little the English knew of anything east of Syria. 'I will speak somewhat of Babilon', he wrote, 'because it is not commonly known to the Englishmen.'[194] What was unknown was the difference from the Ottomans that he observed but never fully understood: how the Persians swore by 'Mortasolee', and how on 'the day that Mortus Alee died, they will slash themselves over their arms and breasts with knives'.[195] Manwaring himelf knew little of religion, and was confused regarding Ashoura. Like others, he recognized that the Shi'ites were distinctive, but was not clear why or how. Anthony Jenkinson, the first

Englishman to mention Persian religion, thought they believed both Muhammad and Ali to be prophets, while Geffrey Ducket in 1574 explained that it was 'a little Lizard, who declared that it was Mahumets pleasure that Mortus Ali should be his successor. This Mortus Ali was a valiant man and slew Homer [Omar ibn al-Khattab] the Turkes prophet.'[196]

English travellers could not avoid noticing how important Ali was since they heard his name repeatedly invoked. They also learned of disagreements regarding the first caliphs. John Cartwright described travelling to

> *Cafe* a little village, where the bodies of *Aly*, whome the Persians honor, and his two sons *Hassan* and *Ossain* lye entombed: by whose sepulchers, it is in great credit, and is every vere [sic] visited by the Persians in all respects, after the same sort, that the Turks do visit the sepulchers of the three first successors *Abuchacher*, *Ottaman*, and *Omar*: yea the very Kings of Persia used to be crowned and girt with the sword in this place, where the *Caliph* was wont to keepe his residence as being the man that represented *Aly*, and occupied the chiefe roome *of their filthy & abominable priest-hood.*[197]

This historical synopsis is very confused, yet reflects how early seventeenth-century Englishmen were likely to blunder when dealing with Islamic belief and history. Like the Shirleys, Abbot compared the differences between the Shi'ite Persians and the Sunni Ottomans to those between 'Papists and Protestants',[198] but no one in England at the time used the terms Sunni or Shi'ite. They knew no more than Thomas Gainsford who declared that the difference between the two groups was only 'in the antiquity of their Rabby, and idle nicety'.[199] Richard Knolles had been able to glean a little about the Ottoman-Safavid divide from his various sources. The 'Persians', he reported, believed that 'none of the professors of the Mahometan religion should inherit the kingdom of heaven after death, but such as were the followers of *Haly*', and that they 'do commonly say, *Cursed bee* Ebubekir, Omer, *and* Osman, *and God be favourable to* Haly'.[200] But there was still much confusion: the Persians of the *Travailes of the three English Brothers* (1607) worshipped the sun, Christ, Muhammad, and Ali—all at the same time. All that Roe could report to the archbishop of Canterbury about the Persians in 1616 was that they were 'Moores or Mahumetans adhering to Aly (such is their King)'.[201] But as late as 1679, Launcelot Addison knew little if anything about them, claiming that Armenia and Persia were inhabited by 'Moors' who followed the 'Hambeli' (Sunni) tradition.[202]

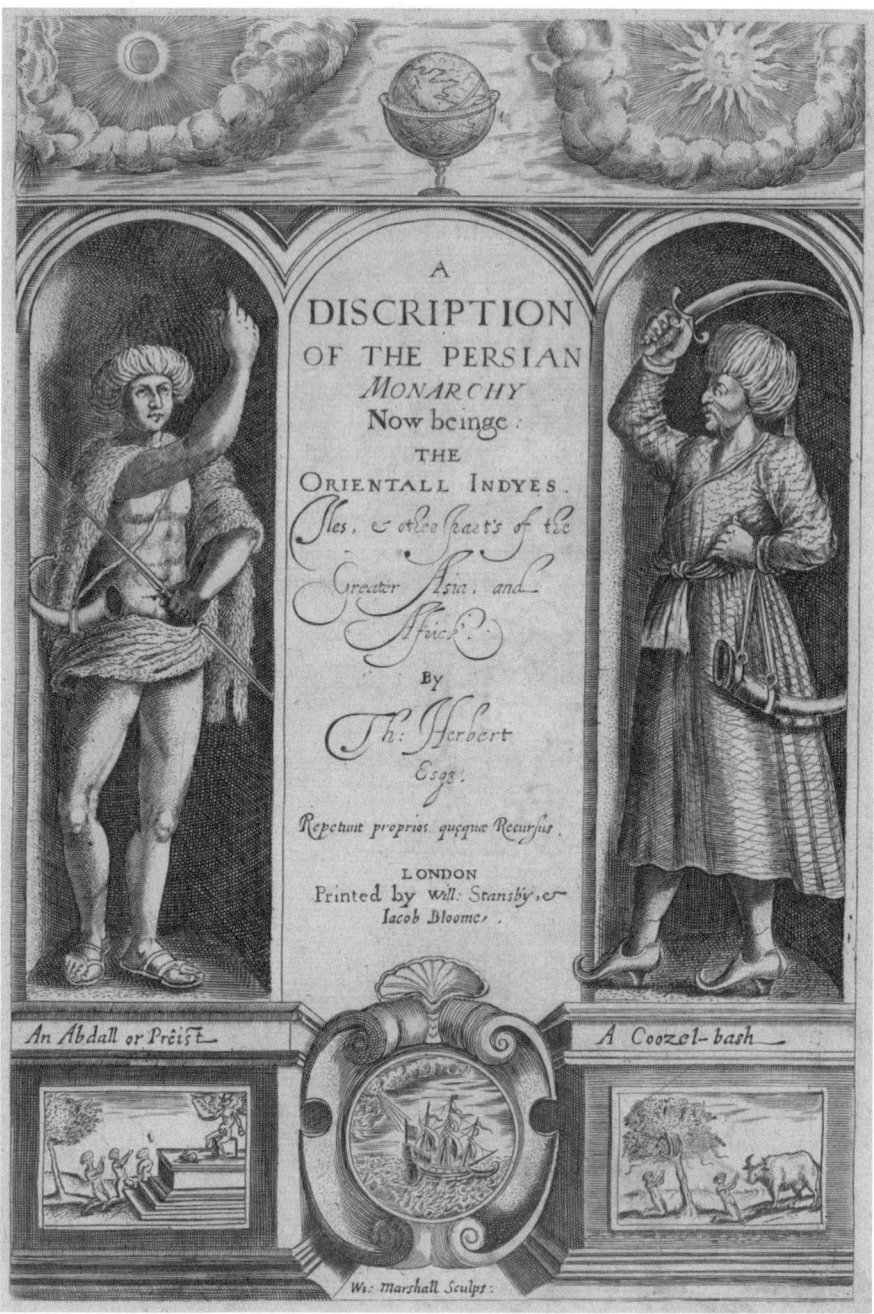

Figure 10. Types of Persians—an 'Abdall or Preist', and a 'Coozel-bash' (Kızılbaş or 'red head') warrior; William Marshall's engraved title page to Thomas Herbert, *A Relation of some Yeares Travaile* (1634)
From the James Ford Bell Library, University of Minnesota, Minneapolis, Minnesota

English merchants and factors took little notice of Shi'ite beliefs, even after East India Company factories were established in 1617 and 1622, and despite Thomas Herbert's detailed description of Persia being published in 1634. East India Company documents seldom refer to Persians as 'Mahometans,' using 'Persian' or 'More' instead, perhaps signalling awareness of Shi'ite difference.[203] English accounts of Persians and Ottomans differ considerably: while travellers among the Ottomans wrote extensively about religious doctrines, practices, hierarchy, rituals, and customs, accounts of Persia say little about religion. Herbert was unusual for discussing 'The Religion of the Persians', even referring to the distinctive principle of the *immamate*, or need for leadership, in Shi'ism. He also noted the commonly mentioned Shi'ite imprecations on the first three caliphs before 'Mortus Haly', and was the first to mention the addition of a phrase to the Islamic witness—that Ali is 'Vellilula' [*waliyy Allah*].[204] But Herbert managed to conjure up eight 'Commandments' that, though they curiously echo the Jewish Ten Commandments, he thought summarized Persian Islam: they ranged from '1. There is one God' all the way to '7. Cursed be the Slayer' and '8. Doe so to others as thou wouldest haue them doe to thee.'[205] Clearly Herbert understood less about Persian religion than he claimed, but his *Relation* generated considerable literary interest, inspiring John Denham's *The Sophy* (1641) and Robert Baron's *Mirza* (1642).

Paul Rycaut's account of the Ottomans and John Chardin's account of the Persians were composed, but not published, within a few years of each other. While Rycaut includes extensive information about Islam among the Ottomans, Chardin says very little about the religion of the Persians. Perhaps the Shi'ite tradition with its Sufi history, and the 'strong ethno-religious and tribal distinctions' of Persian society, kept Europeans at a distance.[206] As Rudolph Mattee has noted, citing Herbert, Persians purified the 'unclean' seats of the Englishman and his companions after their departure, while other Europeans met with 'instances of discriminatory treatment' as they tried to enter 'coffeehouses or public baths'.[207] On the other side, sixteenth-century Islamic scholars and jurists had clarified Ottoman religious claims as the empire had expanded to include power over other Muslims as well as define differences from the Safavids. English writers may well have been aware of different Islamic practices among the Shi'ites, but had little to say about those differences beyond what they picked up from general observation and hearsay. Chardin visited Persia twice but wrote only what he accidentally heard: at a puppet show, he noted that anyone leaving before making a payment was decried '*That he who steals away, is an Enemy to Ali*. As who should say among us, *An Enemy to God and his Saints*.'[208]

There were no manuscripts describing Shi'ism that English travellers could translate or read: the Laudian collection in Oxford has fewer Persian than Arabic or Turkish manuscripts. The English had no descriptions of the Shi'ites from which they could learn about jurisprudential and exegetical differences. Travellers did not dispute with Shi'ite scholars or, if they did, there is no record of them. No English visitor described the Shi'ite emphasis on the succession from the prophet Muhammad through Ali, Hasan, and Husein, nor any of the other distinctive Shi'ite doctrines. Such specificity only shows up in the writings of academic orientalists with access to manuscripts concerning the early history of Islam. Edward Pocock's translation of Abu al-Faraj in his *Specimen historiae Arabum* (1650) contains a brief discussion of Ali and his '*shi'a*', along with some explanatory notes.[209] But the book was in Arabic and Latin, and so had limited readership. And it was a historical rather than a theological survey. Having read Pococke, as well as numerous continental orientalists, Henry Stubbe presented a remarkable section on Ali in his manuscript 'The Rise and Progress of Mahometanism' (after 1671) in which he described Ali's important role defending Muhammad and in propagating Islam.[210] But Stubbe had nothing to say about Shi'ite theology, and his account was not published until 1911. Even in the eighteenth century, when David Jones wrote about the 'Sects of Mahomet' and described the 'Persians', he relied on a diatribe by the mufti of Istanbul as his main source. The result was a denunciation of Shi'ites for rejecting the three first caliphs, for excising verses from the Qur'an, for drinking wine, for being ruled by a 'King' who was their 'High Priest,' for 'frequenting Stews, and the Sties of deformed Lust', and for 'ravishing fair and chaste Wives from their Husbands embraces.'[211] Why Jones included such rant is unclear, but he may have lacked better sources.

The Persians differed from the Ottomans, and the English were interested in the difference between these two behemoths of Islam. Some even hoped, or at least the Shirleys did, to co-opt Persia into an alliance against the Ottomans. Most important was the financial question since, as Chardin confirmed: 'the *English* trade throughout their Empire free from all manner of Duties, and [the Persians] to pay them [the English] every Year fifty thousand Livres for a Service done fifty Years before; for which one may say, they were even then Superabundantly paid.'[212] With such incentives, it is hardly surprising that many in England admired the Persians more than the Ottomans.[213] But the Persians remained more remote than the Ottomans, and their religious culture and identity continued to be obscure: when Thomas Hyde, the most eminent Persianist in early modern England, turned to write about Persian religion, he composed a massive tome about Zoroastrianism.[214]

The Mughals

In their dealings with the Muslims of Persia and India, English envoys were, as might have been anticipated, prepared if not eager to put aside religious differences in the pursuit of common commercial and strategic goals, and their Muslim counterparts were generally in agreement on this. Even potentially tricky situations could be defused by goodwill and careful negotiation. In 1591, Edmund Barker reports how an English fleet captured a small vessel off Zanzibar. On board was 'a priest of theirs... a sherife,' or descendant of the Prophet, 'whom we used very curteously', with the result that the English fleet was supplied with 'two moneths victuals' as well as invaluable information regarding the hostile activities of the Portuguese in the region.[215] In 1602, the Muslim potentate Sultan Alauddin Riayat Syah (r. 1596-1604) of Aceh proved eager to find a religious connection with the first English merchants to land in Sumatra, asking them 'have you the Pslames of David extant among you?' On hearing that they did, Sultan Alauddin declared 'I and the rest of these nobles about me will sing a Psalme to God for your prosperitie, and so they did very solemnly.' He also sent valuable gifts and a letter, in Arabic, to Queen Elizabeth promising to make common enemy with the king of France.[216] Yet at other times and in different circumstances, the barrier between Christians and Muslims could be swiftly erected for diplomatic purposes: Anthony Jenkinson shrewdly recognized how Shah Tahmasp's pious outburst against an infidel Englishman was designed more to preserve a fragile alliance with the Ottoman ambassador than to insult an 'unbeleever'.

But if pragmatic interests typically displaced possible doctrinal disagreements, personal attitudes and misunderstandings frequently surface. Those who favoured the Shi'ite Safavids over the Sunni Ottomans, for example, urged their case by emphasizing how Shi'ism was based on claims of legitimate succession that more closely resembled the dynastic model of the English monarchy than the authority of the caliphate. Seeking to prove the superiority of the Persian state, Thomas Herbert appealed to English reverence for dynastic tradition when he observed that Shah 'Abbas derived his authority by 'true Discent from *Mortys-Ally*'.[217] 'The Persian praieth only to *Mahomet,* and *Mortus Ally,*' noted William Parry, while 'the Turke to those two, and three other that were *Mahomets* servants'. Both were 'damned Infidells, and Zodomiticall Mahomets', but at least the Persians followed family lineage and did not worship their servants.[218] Further east, the varieties of religious belief practised in India led to even greater confusion. In recording his travels in the Mughal Empire, for instance, Ralph Fitch formally distinguished Muslims from Hindus—or 'Moores and Gentiles'—but regularly collapsed the distinction into generalizations such as the following:

> heere be manie Moores and Gentiles. They have a very strange order among them, they worshippe a cowe, and esteeme much of the cowes doung to paint the walles of their houses.[219]

Clearly aware that Muslims and Hindus are not the same, Fitch had no interest in understanding the differences between them, but was rather intent on blending both into a common 'they' who occupy a shared 'strange order' in which religious practices are clearly idolatrous and smelly if not distinctly bestial.[220] For a clergyman such as Edward Terry, the imperative to disparage the beliefs of non-Christians was perhaps greater, but like Fitch, he resorted to accusations that are dismissive rather than substantial, and similarly collapsed any meaningful distinction between Muslims and Hindus into a general charge of irrational bestiality:

> It were easie to enlarge, but I will not cast away Inke and Paper in farther description of their stupid Idolatries. The summe is, that both Mahometans and Gentiles ground their opinions upon tradition, not Reason, and are content to perish with their Fore-fathers, out of a preposterous zeale, and loving perversnesse never ruminating on what they maintayne, like to uncleane beasts which chew not the Cud.[221]

Terry could, however, be more discriminating when it served his purposes. Of Muslims he notes that 'many amongst them, to the shame of us Christians...pray five times a day'.[222]

Although hardly less scornful of non-Christian beliefs than his chaplain, Sir Thomas Roe recorded some of the earliest detailed accounts of Islam in

India, though these too are marked by ambiguities, uncertainties, and contradictions. Writing in January 1616, Roe observed there to be 'Many religions, and in them many sects; *Moores* or *Mahumetans* adhering to Aly (such is the King)'.[223] Since the Mughal state was, nominally at least, Sunni, it is unclear whether Roe was confused or emphasizing the existence of 'many sects' of Shi'ite Muslims. As for Jahangir's personal beliefs, Roe revised his claim in a letter to Prince Charles dated in October of the same year, declaring:

> His religione of his owne invention; for hee envyes Mahomett, and wisely sees no reason why hee should not bee as great a prophett as hee, and therefore proffeseth him selfe so; and yet finds not (or confesseth not) that they are both imposturs in that kind. Hee hath found many disciples that flatter or follow him... The rest are circumcised Mahomatans.[224]

Roe knew no Persian, the language of the Mughal court, Arabic, or Turkish, so we can only surmise that confident declarations such as these were based on hearsay. Nonetheless, he felt sufficiently well informed to prepare a general history of religion in India that he sent in a letter to George Abbot, Archbishop of Canterbury, also dated October 1616. Here he tells how the 'descendants' of 'Temar the Great... brought in knowledge of Mahomett'. Employing an ingenious piece of false etymology, Roe says that the first followers of the Prophet were called 'Mogolls or cheefe of the circumcised', before continuing:

> Among the Mogolls ther are many strict Mahometans, many that follow Aly, his sonne-in-law, and other new risen prophetts, which have their *xeriffs*, *mulas*, and preists, their mosquies, religious votaries, washings, prayings, and ceremonyes infinite; and for penitenciaryes, no herecye in the world can show so strange examples, nor bragg of such voluntarie povertyes, punishments, sufferings and chastisements as these; all which are esteemed holy men, but of a mingled religion, not upright with their great prophett.

Despite his evident contempt, Roe concedes that 'the *molaes* of Mahomett know somewhat in philosophy and mathematiques, are great astrologers, and can talke of Areistotle, Euclyde, Averroes and other authors. The learned toong is Arab.'[225]

Later in his letter to Archbishop Abbot, Roe returns to his preoccupation with circumcision, and comments on the personal faith of the Mughal emperors. In this version, Akbar, Jahangir's father, considers himself equal to the Prophet. During Akbar's reign, he notes, the Jesuits arrived and first introduced their version of Christianity to the region and gained many converts. 'Ecbar-Shae him selfe', however, 'continued a Mahometan', yet 'considering that Mahomett was but a man... he thought hee might prove as good a prophett himselfe'. Reluctant to make this claim public, Akbar 'dyed in the formall profession of his sect'. On the other hand, Jahangir, 'beeing the issue of this new fancy, and never circumcised, bread up without any religion at all, continewes so to this hower, and is an atheist' who openly declares himself to be 'a greater prophett then Mahomett'. Further, Jahangir 'hath formed to him selfe a new law, mingled of all'. As a result, Jahangir welcomed 'Christians, Moores, Jewes' into his empire, and 'meddled not with their faith', declaring that since 'they came all in love... they lived under his safety and none should oppress them'.[226] For a diplomat such as Roe, discovering that an ecumenical policy held sway in a Muslim empire was doubtless of greater consequence than the emperor's bizarre personal beliefs and pretensions. Yet Roe eagerly sought to discover some providential assurances too, noting how 'of Christ he never utters any woord unreverently, nor any of all these sects, which is a woonderfull secreett woorking of Gods truth, and worthy observation'.[227] Perhaps he also derived comfort from the belief that here was a Muslim emperor who was 'never circumcised'.

By way of conclusion

In the early modern period, as Kenneth Parker has observed, the English began to realize that there were 'several different Orients: Turkey; Persia; Egypt; the Holy Land', and that these regions were inhabited by several kinds of people with distinct religions and specific cultural habits.[228] In general, and toward people who were geographically near, or at least religiously and culturally familiar, Britons felt a certain degree of missionary enthusiasm: Jews and eastern Christians, frequently encountered in the Levant and even in London, were prime for conversion in ways that the more remote Armenians and Shi'ites were not. Since Hebrew, Greek, and Arabic were taught at Oxford and Cambridge, many felt a sense of evangelical authority over members of the Jewish and Orthodox faiths. But as Britons saw more of those communities and noticed how they integrated into the Islamic empires without losing their faith, conversion seemed less feasible, even if it remained desirable.

On the London stage, few new parts for Jewish characters were written after the Restoration period, while eastern Christians simply never showed up. Elizabethan and Jacobean playwrights nominally set scenes in Greece, the Greek Mediterranean, and even Persia, but if we think about Shakespeare's *Pericles*, these were largely theatrical fictions and had little or nothing to do with contemporary eastern Christians. There are no plays featuring Armenian characters, not even as comic foreigners speaking broken English like the occasional post-1660 depictions of Jews and Turks. Yet the Levant, North Africa and even—in Dryden's *Aureng-Zebe*—India, proved popular settings since Muslim empires, populations, religion, and power continued to fascinate English dramatists and theatre audiences, at the same time that they attracted chartered companies and their heavily armed ships.

But British merchants, commercial agents, and clergymen met Jews, eastern Christians, Armenians, Safavids, and Mughals, in the context of global trade. Britons were crossing seas and mountains to sell their wares, to exchange goods, and to procure hard currency and precious metals. Their aims were to establish commercial monopolies and explore political alliances. As much as Britons may have sympathized with, or ridiculed, Jews and eastern Christians, they remained a means to Anglican ends: nothing changed in English perceptions to allow those religious communities to be treated on their own terms. Any assistance or friendship that Britons might have offered was aimed at bringing the minorities in the Ottoman Empire under the sway of Canterbury and making them useful for trade, diplomacy, and intelligence, in just the same way that French missionaries were trying to co-opt the Maronites and Armenians. In our period the British were not very successful, but by the nineteenth century British societies for converting Jews and the eastern Christians were firmly established throughout Palestine and Trans-Jordan. By 1917, the Balfour Declaration promised the Jews, in the hope that they would be converted, a homeland in what would be a British-mandated Palestine. At the same time, missionaries of the Church Mission Society set out to transform some eastern Orthodox Arabs into an Anglican congregation, and successfully turned many into *ta'ifat al-shillin*—the 'congregation of the shilling'—as their detractors taunted them. Conversion became an official instrument in the service of empire, and Canterbury an arm of the Foreign Office that, along with the French and other powers, would bring to an end the Islamic empire of the Ottomans.

6

Material Culture

On 12 August 1638, the French traveller Jean Baptiste Tavernier watched while a thousand janissaries from Cairo marched into the garrison at Aleppo to join the army of Sultan Murad IV (r. 1623–40) that was setting out to recapture Baghdad from the Safavids. He was much taken by the splendour of their colourful uniforms:

> Every one of them had Scarlet Breeches that reach'd down to their Ancles, with a *Turkie*-Robe of *English*-Cloth, and a Wast-coat of Calicut painted with several Colours.[1]

That '*English*-Cloth' would have been what the Ottomans called *çuka*, the hard-wearing broadcloth that had long been a staple of the English export trade. Those waistcoats made of colourfully printed heavyweight cotton, known first as 'Calicut', had most likely been carried across the Indian Ocean and through the Red Sea by English ships.[2]

Twenty-five years later, the young John Verney arrived in Aleppo where he would spend several years attempting—not very successfully—to make his fortune. In May 1663, John received a letter from Edmund, his brother back home in Buckinghamshire, requesting 'some silke waskots & shirts of the sort of linnen made where you are, a Turkish habit from head to foot, but not of cloth, because that's too common here. Let all', he continued, 'be neate & hansome, the Turbant cheifly.'[3] That curious stipulation, that he didn't want 'cloth, because that's too common here', suggests Edmund's desire to stand out, to dress differently from his friends who were already on the road to being connoisseurs of fabrics and styles imported from Islamic countries.

Material goods and exchanges

Since Paul Coles' important study of *The Ottoman Impact on Europe* of 1968, ways that trade in material goods from the Islamic world changed life in early modern Europe have become better understood. Currants and carpets, coffee and tobacco, silk and cotton, horses and weaponry, were all commodities that had wide cross-cultural circulation and influence. Wars and violent disputes did not cease, but as global commerce expanded, so diplomatic and strategic ties between Britain and the rulers of Islamic empires kept conflict at bay by negotiated settlements that ensured trade might flourish. The exportation of military supplies from Britain into the Islamic world—notably finished wool cloth for janissary coats, tin and bell-metal for canons and armaments, timbers for repairing the Algiers fleet, along with guns, gunpowder, sails, and masts—is a well-documented irony of such agreements. By the mid-seventeenth century, international trade had brought about massive changes to both European and Asian cultures, which now found themselves indelibly connected through a curious circuitry involving the exchange of consumer goods, precious metals, and commodities for war: tobacco, sugar, coffee and tea; currants, raisins, sweet wine and oil; cotton, wool and silk, both raw and finished; carpets and cushions; dyes, spices and drugs; jewels and precious stones; saltpetre for gunpowder, iron and tin for casting canons; horses for sport and war.

Even as those Ottoman troops were setting out to recapture Baghdad wearing uniforms made from materials manufactured in Britain, members of the landed and leisured classes in England were entertaining themselves by dressing up in 'Turkish habits'. This was a time when, spurred in part by the 'dramatic transformations in bullion flows... as a vast interpenetrating network of silver girdled the globe', unprecedented levels of economic integration were bringing about changing social habits and forms of self-representation throughout large parts of the world.[4] Imports from the Islamic world were changing the ways that people in England lived. Drinking coffee, imported from the Ottoman Empire, and tea, imported from the Far East, became national habits. Textiles—English wool, Persian silk, Turkey carpets, Indian cottons—were crucial commodities linking people in Britain with residents of the Islamic world that changed the ways people dressed themselves and how they decorated their houses. The intimate adoption of these commodities, their penetration into everyday lives, represents a largely unacknowledged relationship between Britain and the Muslim world. Domestic furnishings and styles of clothing were only part of the picture. In many ways, the widespread social changes constituting what has been called a 'shared consumer revolution' that was 'occurring simultaneously across vast regions of the globe', come into clearest focus on the worldwide spread of coffee and tobacco since, more than any other consumer goods, these were subjected to extensive moral and juridical anxieties in both Christian and Muslim states.[5] The reasons for those anxieties are perhaps not hard to find, for the consumption of these novel and addictive drugs swiftly and irrevocably introduced new patterns of economic, social, and cultural activity that challenged traditional ways of life, redesigned urban spaces, and opened up unprecedented forms of public encounter and sociability.

So although British views about Islam may not have been directly affected by these changes in culture and society that were due to Muslim influence, the new tastes and habits themselves represent a profound relationship, however hidden or forgotten, between East and West, the Islamic world and the European one. The other side of the coin was that Western imports such as tobacco led to controversy and Muslim scrutiny of Christian ways of life. In this chapter we show how the Islamic world too was transformed by commodities, consumption, and global trade.

Keith Thomas has argued that the increasing appearance and spread of consumer goods in early modern England was for many a cause of considerable anxiety since 'sixteenth-century moralists' agreed that 'it was wrong to covet clothes, diet, and possessions which were inappropriate to one's social position'. Christian tradition had long taught that riches were 'an impediment to salvation'.[6] The very pursuit of more than was needed was considered both a sin as well as a threat to the social order. In the early modern Ottoman world, however, a different system of values operated that Leslie Peirce calls the 'rule of ethical proportion'. Accumulation of material goods in excess of need was not a problem in itself, but the 'cardinal sins of materialism were the unseemly flaunting of one's wealth and the failure to honour the moral imperatives of philanthropy'.[7] Being rich was perfectly respectable so long as one acted with modesty and decorum, and made sure that one's patronage and charitable donations were as conspicuous as one's apparel and domestic furnishings. In both Christian and Muslim societies, of course, ethical ideals regarding wealth and material possessions were often contradicted by ingrained customs of honouring and emulating the wealthy, and that contradiction doubtless helped animate moral and economic controversies over novel imports such as tobacco, coffee, and cotton.

Whatever the traditionalists and moralists might have said, in commercial terms, the exchange of material goods between Britain and the Islamic world generally benefitted merchants, retailers, and consumers on all sides. In Britain, what has been aptly termed the 'Oriental Obsession' took root during our period initially as a craving for specific luxury goods as well as for objects whose aesthetic qualities advertised the oriental origins of their design and thereby increased their social value: lustre pottery, fine metalwork, porcelain tableware, printed textiles, Turkish and Persian carpets, wallpaper, embroidered cushions and curtains.[8] All such luxurious items would be subjected to satiric scorn by Richard Steele, but since the vogue for such costly objects fed an increasing appetite for comfortable living, we might also mention the simultaneous development of interest in, and taste for, Islamic designs, motifs, and practices in painting, bookbinding, sculpture, gardening, architecture, music, and literature.[9] In many instances—notably ceramics, carpets, and printed textiles—increasing demand inspired the domestic production of imitations: English-made carpets based on Turkish designs started to appear as early as the second half of the sixteenth century, but techniques for manufacturing fine porcelain and colour-fast printed cottons following oriental models would not appear until the mid-eighteenth century, by which time Manchester manufacturers were dominating the global market in the production of colour-fast printed calicos.[10] While pious moralists continued to rail against coffee houses and tobacco smoking, sometimes pointing to their dangerous associations with Islam, other commodities imported from the Islamic world were stripped of dangerous religious connotations and domesticated.

At the start of our period, the English were increasingly becoming addicted to sweetening their food with currants imported from Zante and the Morea, to such an extent that William Lithgow railed against those whose 'Liquourous lips' were threatening the national economy.[11] By 1700, 'coffee, tea and chocolate' could wittily be termed 'native drinks'.[12] This transformation of exotic imports into domesticated commodities underwrites the history of many of the material goods that came from the Islamic world and transformed English social life during the early modern period. Such changes generated debates about luxury and virtue, nation and economy, fashion and women. Coffee arrived with the stigma of being favoured by infidel Muslims. According to some, such as the ale-house keepers who saw their trade slipping off into the coffee houses, the 'Mahomettan berry' threatened Englishness: it reduced, or increased, sexual drives, was likely to encourage conversion to Islam, and was even said to be part of a Republican conspiracy of the 1650s to introduce Islam as a national religion. When Charles II ordered the coffee houses of London to be closed in 1675,[13] he may well have known that generations of Ottoman sultans had similarly sought to shut down these new urban spaces, where men of different ranks and degrees could meet and discuss dangerous ideas. In 1632, Murad IV famously led a particularly bloody campaign to close down coffee houses and punish those found inside.[14]

In this chapter, we consider some of the ways that material goods from the Islamic world were shaping how people in Britain lived their lives. Rather than attempt a comprehensive survey, we focus on four items of exchange—tobacco, calico, turbans, and horses—that signal the varied kinds of influence commerce with the Islamic world was having upon English social and cultural life, and indicate some of the various ways that importation, imitation, and domestication blunted the ever-present dangers of association with Islam. Since it was consumed in coffee houses, tobacco was reviled for having strong Islamic associations in English diatribes, while imported textiles were typically shorn of any religious connotations derived from their origins in Islamic design, materials, or production. We trace this ambivalence towards features of Islamic culture that were becoming increasingly familiar by examining how attitudes towards that principal symbol of Muslim identity—the turban—changed in significance as Britain extended its commercial reach globally, and Britons no longer feared the threat of the 'terrible Turks' as their forebears once had done. Finally, in turning to the matter of horses, we follow the lead of Donna Landry who has recently shown how a process of importation leading to domestic production and eventual naturalization, was radically transforming English equestrian culture. Bringing over hot-blooded Arabian, Turkish, and Barbary horses from the Ottoman Empire and North Africa led not only to the breeding of that English national icon the Thoroughbred, and to consequent changes in the ways such horses were trained and ridden, but also to the emergence of a vernacular idiom of sporting art that reached maturity with the work of George Stubbs.[15]

Tobacco

The history of tobacco as it moved between Britain and the Islamic world is mightily similar to, but also distinct from, the more familiar tale of coffee and the coffee houses of the early modern era. The economic difference between these two addictive substances, tobacco and coffee, is the direction and value of the trade, while the similarity arises from the way they both generated heated moral debates. While English critics of coffee damned it by association with the Islamic faith and dangers of tempting Christians to 'turn Turk,' the tobacco trade provided pious Muslims with ammunition against the infidel English. The first references to the English in North African Arabic sources appear in the context of the importation of tobacco from the New World. It came on English ships. It was English merchants who saw and exploited the market for this addictive New World herb that rapidly spread throughout Ottoman, Safavid, and Mughal cities and lands. The English were responsible for tobacco; the Muslims for coffee.

In England and the Islamic world, tobacco and coffee were similarly demonized on several counts, in addition to being considered distractions that impeded piety if nothing worse: they were clearly innovations; they were imported and thereby tainted by association with the alien cultures of their origins; they were luxurious consumables that encouraged idleness; and the places where they were bought and consumed were likely to be hotbeds of criminality, where social ranks were confused, debauchery encouraged, and seditious ideas openly expressed and propagated. Similar objections were brought against both coffee and tobacco in the Islamic world, where the religious objection was cast somewhat differently, since the pursuit of wealth for its own sake did not interfere with the journey to heaven. While managers of charitable foundations (*awqf*) invested in coffee houses to supply income for mosques, schools, and public bathhouses,[16] many pious Muslims disputed whether coffee and tobacco were acceptable, since they were so clearly 'innovations' that could not be accounted for in the Qur'an. What is striking, however, is that the introduction of these two commodities—coffee and tobacco—during the early modern era should have provoked such heated controversies as they did, whether voiced by Christian or Muslim, and that the disputes ran in what we might call a reverse parallel. Since tobacco had arrived in Britain before coffee, defences and objections that developed over smoking would reappear once coffee came on the scene. Similarly, in the Islamic world, the moral discourse generated over coffee was, in many regards, repeated with the subsequent arrival of tobacco.

Tobacco was viewed by Christian and Muslim alike as being someone else's fault, a foreign substance that should never have been permitted. The English first got it from the local population while they were settling James-Fort in Virginia, and were soon growing and exporting it wherever they could find markets. A quarter of a century after Sir Walter Raleigh is said to have brought tobacco to Europe, King James famously published his *Counter-Blaste to Tobacco* (1604) which deplores the introduction of smoking for being no more than 'an inconsiderate and childish affectation of Noveltie'. James's language of horror at this 'childish...Noveltie', resounds with the zeal of a jurist dwelling on the horrors of any godless 'innovation'. James thought that 'the barbarous *Indians*' had first started smoking tobacco as 'a Preservative, or Antidot against the Pockes'. He was not alone at the time in linking smoking with the pox by attributing both with New World origins, and concluded

> that as from them was first brought into Christendome, that most detestable disease, so from them likewise was brought this use of *Tobacco*, as a stinking and unsavorie Antidot, for so corrupted and execrable a Maladie, the stinkinge Suffumigation whereof they yet use against that disease, making so one canker or venime to eate out another.[17]

James must have been disappointed that his paternal advice did not stop the smoking habit from spreading throughout his realms. His curious ideas, however, may have encouraged popular belief that smoking tobacco was an alien and outlandish practice. In 1609, for instance, Samuel Rowlands blamed the tobacco-habit on the Moors:

> For all the broode of Black-a-moores,
> Will sweare I doe not erre,
> In taking this same worthy whiffe.[18]

This curious link in the English imagination between tobacco and North Africa was not uncommon: six years later, an English writer confirmed that the 'taking' of tobacco was widely prevalent in 'Barbary'.[19]

Richard Brathwaite also associated tobacco with Africa, warning readers that it was 'a late Negro's introduced fashion,/ Who brought his Drugs here

Figure 11. A Moor smoking; title page to Richard Brathwaite's *The Smoaking Age* (1617). By permission of the British Library; shelfmark C.40.b.20.
Copyright belongs to the British Library and further reproduction is prohibited

to corrupt our Nation'.[20] Where there might be a danger, it comes from overseas: never mind that it was English merchants who had brought tobacco into North Africa in the first place, initially via the Spanish colonies and later directly from Virginia. It is doubtless for this reason that the earliest written description of the English in Moroccan sources connects them with the use of this heinous herb called *tabigh*. Shortly after the invasion of sub-Saharan 'Bilad al-Sudan—modern-day Niger—in 1591, Muhammad al-Saghir al-Ifrani reported that the people of Sudan who herded elephants 'drank' tobacco, claiming it had medicinal benefits. And so it spread into Dar'a and Marrakesh and other parts of the Maghrib.[21] While physicians debated tobacco's potential uses, the *fatwas* of the jurists differed: some called for its prohibition while others called for its therapeutic use.

English merchants recognized the appeal of tobacco to Moroccan customers and started exporting it there in large quantities. As smoking spread among the population, jurists became increasingly concerned about this Christian—specifically English—marketing of tobacco and began denouncing the herb as an infidel innovation, deliberately introduced by the English to ruin Muslims. One seventeenth-century moralist argued that tobacco, like chess, distracted Muslims from performing their prayers and caused many sicknesses, including diabetes. 'For why do the English continue to use it and to claim that it causes no harm', he asked, unless they want Muslims to destroy their health and religion? He denounced tobacco since it was bought from people in 'the lands of the Christians, called the English, who were the first to introduce it to us'.[22] The English, continued the writer, live in a very cold region and their bodies are always damp, which is why they need to smoke in order to dry themselves up. But tobacco is bad for people in hot regions, even worse than wine, because it ruins the mind, and leads people into sin; it also diminishes the procreative drive, causes leprosy and trembling, and bores cavities in teeth which subsequently turn black. Tobacco turns the lion into a lamb.[23] The indictment of the English-sold tobacco concluded:

> I have been told by the traders, jurists, scholars and Sufi masters who travelled across lands and sailed the oceans and went on journeys that some [tobacco] is brought from the lands of the Christians and of the *rum* [Qur'anic name for Byzantines] while some other is brought from the lands of the Blacks and a few regions of the Maghrib. Some tobacco is grown in the lands of Islam ... That which is brought from the lands of the Christians is cooked and soaked in wine. A friend told me that an English ship brought [some tobacco] which was laced with pork fat.[24]

In 1604, Ahmad ibn Abi Mahilli, a Sufi rebel, became the first jurist openly to champion its use, and the first to introduce tobacco to Egypt.[25] It may well be that his failure as a messianic figure and his death after leading a failed revolt against the Moroccan ruler, led to the vilification of the herb he had championed. The association between tobacco and Christians, including the English, remained strong in Moroccan memory. In the mid seventeenth century, 'Abd al-Karim Lafqun denounced tobacco because smoking it 'is a characteristic of the *'ajam*... whom the Prophet told us not to emulate', adding: 'It was Christians who introduced it... [but it is] not a food which the Law allows us.'[26]

Despite these warnings, the Maghariba continued to smoke and to import tobacco from the English. Virginia tobacco became one of the most important commodities in the triangle of exchange between England, Virginia, and the Maghrib. By 1613, the demand in Moroccan cities for tobacco and opium had risen so much that it drew the attention of Jorge de Henin who was cataloguing imports into Morocco at the time. Although Henin did not specify their nationality, the merchants involved were likely to have been English, since he repeatedly mentions their sales of large amounts of hats, linen, cloth, and canvas.[27] Yet despite the increasing demand for tobacco in the region, North Africans continued to be among its most zealous opponents. In 1699, Moroccans and Tunisians who participated in carrying part of the *kiswa* of the *Ka'ba* through the streets of Cairo en route to Mecca, took to beating anybody who was seen smoking in the streets: for them the herb was a sacrilege to the sanctity of the pilgrimage, though these were extreme views. These zealots were eventually arrested by a janissary officer.[28]

Tobacco had been introduced by Christians, notably the English, who were responsible for bringing it into use within the Ottoman Empire.[29] This widely known fact encouraged extreme positions, including that of 'the Egyptian scholar Ibrahim al-Laqani (d. 1631/32) who viewed tobacco as a kind of Christian plot against Islam.'[30] An early Ottoman historian merely recorded how 'the English infidels brought it in the year 1009 [CE 1601] and sold it as a remedy for certain diseases of humidity', leaving readers to gather the inference.[31] The earliest attempts to ban the sale and use of tobacco by Muslim states, however, were not enacted because of the association with Christianity and England but in the name of moral rectitude and social order. The Ottoman Sultan Ahmed I (r. 1603–17) declared a ban on tobacco throughout the empire in 1611 from purely pious motives.

Similar Safavid and Mughal bans were announced in 1610 and 1617, but none of these early attempts to enact anti-tobacco laws proved enforceable.[32] In 1632, inspired by the reformist zeal of Mehmed Efendi Kadızade, the youthful Murad IV was the next sultan to attempt a ban on tobacco, declaring that smoking was a capital offence and personally visiting public places accompanied by janissaries to enact summary punishments on anyone caught smoking.[33] His new laws did not survive his death, though the French traveller Jean de Thevenot reports how, 'in imitation of his Uncle', Mehmed IV (r. 1648–87) 'caused two Men in one day to be Beheaded in the Streets of *Constantinople*, because they were smoking Tobacco'.[34]

But Ottoman attitudes were divided on the question of tobacco. Reflecting on these attempts to ban smoking in the later 1650s, Katib Çelebi opens with the tale of a ship's doctor who, after crossing the Atlantic, cured himself from a lymphatic disorder by inhaling the smoke from 'a kind of leaf' that he found on an island in the New World called 'Gineya'. Noticing that 'it did him good', the mariners loaded their ship up with the leaf 'and they all began to smoke. When the ship arrived in England, the habit spread, through France to the other lands.' 'It has', he continued, 'become a thing common to East and West, and no one has succeeded in suppressing it.'[35] As in his commentaries on coffee, opium, and other drugs, Katib Çelebi's aim here was neither to denounce nor defend tobacco, but to assemble and assess available knowledge. He correctly observes that tobacco first arrived in Turkey about 1601,[36] and that all attempts to suppress its use failed. He records how 'the eminent surgeon Ibrahim Efendi' spoke out against it, but 'the more he spoke, the more people persisted in smoking'. He recalls how Murad IV notoriously closed the coffee houses and banned smoking two weeks after the great fire that destroyed a fifth of Istanbul in 1632, and how the imperial ban was similarly unsuccessful:

> People being undeterred, the imperial anger necessitated the chastisement of those who, by smoking, committed the sin of disobedience to the imperial command. Gradually His Majesty's severity in suppression increased, and so did people's desire to smoke, in accordance with the saying, 'Men desire what is forbidden,' and many thousands of men were sent to the abode of nothingness.[37]

Since then, he reports, 'the late Baha'i Efendi' pronounced a *fatwa* that permitted smoking, and the habit 'is at present practised all over the habitable globe'. Such being the case, Katib Çelebi concludes that 'the most necessary and useful thing for the rulers of the Muslims to do is... farm out exclusive concessions to deal in tobacco-leaf... [since this] will yield 100 million aspers a year'.[38] Although the English had introduced tobacco, that was clearly no reason to allow them to continue profiting from the cravings of Ottoman subjects. Katib Çelebi was evidently not alone in this recognition: by 1700, the Ottoman market was supplied by a domestic product, grown widely throughout Macedonia, Anatolia, and northern Syria, 'supplemented with highly esteemed imports from Iran'. Within a century of its arrival, tobacco had become so cheap throughout the Ottoman world that smoking, despite its infidel origins, had replaced coffee drinking as 'the most affordable diversion of the Ottoman population'.[39]

The calico wars

The traditional English textile trades of the Tudor period were transformed by contact with the Islamic world. Both an increasing range and quantity of imported raw and finished materials, as well as developments in production and design techniques, brought work and wealth, comfort and colour, to the daily lives of Britons across the social ranks. Between 1590 and 1630, the number of women working in silk production within greater London was estimated to have risen from 300 to 14,000.[40] These women produced silk thread and cloth from raw silk that had been shipped in from the eastern Mediterranean. The stuff they made was then exported to Poland and other nations lacking silk industries of their own. Meanwhile, in Norfolk, skilled weavers were fabricating imitation Turkish and Persian carpets. The geometrical designs associated with Uşak, in western Anatolia, were especially favoured for personalized rugs bearing dynastic crests, such as the fine example at Boughton bearing the arms of the Dukes of Buccleuch.[41] Aristocrat and factory girl were brought together in this shared new world where Eastern textiles and designs imported from Islamic imperial civilizations became increasingly familiar elements of daily life up and down the social spectrum.

The story of how eastern materials, designs, and techniques altered life in England by transforming the English textile industries is too vast for us to survey fully here. We will focus on calico, since the story of this colourfully printed cotton cloth originally imported from Calicut took seventeenth-century England by storm, and it inspired subsequent technical developments that were central to both the growth of the British Empire and the Industrial Revolution. The London-based silk industries of Elizabethan times expanded massively during James's reign, but barely challenged the traditional dominance of the woollen sector. If our period begins with the established yet increasing importance of silk, it as surely ends with the massive impact of imported cotton, not only on trade but on domestic production and marketing methods. As Daniel Defoe wryly observed in 1712: 'Our wrought silks and our fine [woollen] stuffs submit to that noble usurpation of printed calico.'[42] English ships started carrying printed coloured cottons from India to Ottoman and Safavid ports almost as soon as they began operating in the Indian Ocean. Relatively small quantities of raw and finished cotton regularly arrived at English docks too, but coloured and printed cottons only started to appear during the second decade of the seventeenth century.[43] While the immediate rise in the quantity of finished Indian cottons brought into England fell off during the Gujarat famines of the early 1630s, the amounts imported thereafter more than trebled by the 1680s, when a 'storm of protest' against Indian cloth broke out that would inspire polemicists and satirists for the next forty years.[44]

What one historian has called a '"feverish" demand for indiennes', or painted Indian cottons, raged throughout the century and sparked off predictable controversies. Calico threatened domestic industries and was considered morally suspect since Eastern imports were invariably luxuries, and luxuries threatened traditional practices 'and hence... virtue itself'.[45] But demand and supply managed to outrun all objections. Indian printed cottons were not merely considered fashionable, they were also cheaper and of better quality in both material and design than anything the English were, as yet, capable of producing. European buyers in India ordered more of the same designs, originally Persian, as demand, supply, and profits continued to escalate. During the central decades, the growing market for colourful printed cottons inspired dyers and printers to explore new techniques for producing viable imitations at home, while weavers experimented with blending new fabrics from cotton, flax, and wool that would evade increasingly stringent taxes and controls on what kinds of material could and could not be used, produced, or sold in England. By the 1660s, East India Company merchants were setting up their own factories in India, paying much lower wages for better quality products than could be manufactured at home. The woollen manufacturers and the silk throwers of London maintained powerful lobbies against the many threats posed by calico, but the tale is also one of technical developments and trends in dyeing and printing, skills represented by guildsmen who brought their own interests into the fray. The story of weaving, dyeing, and printing in England continues well beyond our period. It leads directly to the inventions, associated with the names of James Hargreaves and Richard Arkwright, that made Manchester the centre of a global cotton industry that would clothe and enrich a global empire. And the story also reaches back to the Eastern origins of textile production.[46]

The printing of linen, calico, and other cotton stuffs is another eastern skill that was well established by the early seventeenth century.[47] In 1619 George Wood obtained a twenty-one year patent on printing and staining linen in colour, the first of its kind to be issued.[48] Although profitable large-scale domestic production had yet to begin, by century's end, it was the rapidly expanding importation of printed calicoes and silks from India that threatened the domestic silk and wool trades, and thereby sparked off the crisis. Rioting was followed by vigorous debates about trade and ethics, domestic versus foreign workers, ladies' fashions and morality. Attempts by the woollen manufacturers to ban the calico trade throughout the 1680s and 1690s generally fell foul of pressure from the East India Company, which was increasingly profiting from bringing cheaper printed calicoes and silks directly from India, many of them produced in the Company's own Indian factories, where materials and labour were inestimably cheaper than at home.[49] The battles continued well into the new century, with dyers and printers petitioning against attempts to prohibit the production and sale of English printed calicoes, and joining with colleagues in the wool trade to oppose the importation of calicoes printed in India. Silk manufacturers were equally enraged by East India Company merchants whose Indian workers were undercutting the costs of dyeing and printing finished cottons and silks.

The calico debates that raged between 1680 and 1720 centred on attempts to regulate trade, consumption, and production that clearly favoured the East India merchants. The published controversies ranged from serious disputes between advocates of free trade and stalwart defenders of traditional industries, to satirical attacks on women consumers and foreign manufacturers. This discourse was seldom marked by matters of religious belief or hostility, as had been the case with tobacco and coffee. Foreign enemies were most often those closer to home than India: the French who imposed frivolous fashions that were both costly and changeable, the Dutch whose ships competed in the Eastern trade: both competed in the manufacture of top-end finished textiles. In 1689, London silk manufacturers petitioning for protective legislation against the calico trade reminded their readers how 'the great Advantage that did arise by Silk to this Nation, consisted in Manufacturing' for export, and complained that recent imports of finished calicos and silks had brought unemployment to over 'Two hundred thousand Persons' who 'were comfortably maintained' by jobs weaving silk.[50] Defenders of the import trade, however, replied by blaming urban female customers, arguing that a prohibition on 'East-India' goods would simply create a clandestine trade bringing in exotic eastern fabrics through Turkey and Italy, by which means 'Foreigners will get a vast deal of Money which the *English* will pay, for the *English* Ladies will have them, by whatsoever means they are brought in'.[51]

Satires attacking prohibitions that would harm the East India Company regularly appeared under the pseudo-name of 'Prince Butler', who specialized in arousing indignation through ironic propositions and rhetorical reversals. Prince Butler revealed the startling possibility that calico had replaced silk as a status symbol: 'Had not a Hundred thousand Poor rather come to their Parishes for want of Work, and all the Land of *England* fall two years Purchase; then that the Cook-Maids should not be cloathed in *India* Silks, and the Ladies in Callicoes?'[52] Prince Butler also sought to stir fury against foreigners as well as domestic import duties, while at the very same time employing fiercely nationalistic rhetoric to defend imported goods. In *Five Queries Humbly Tender'd* [1696?] he ponders 'Why *East-India* Silks, *Bengals* and Printed *Callicoes*, that Pay Twenty per Cent Customs more than *Dutch* and *Italian* Silks, and Five times the Freight of *Dutch*, *French* and *Italian* Silks' have been prohibited. And he demands to know 'Why should Painted Callicoes from *India* be Prohibited, when We must in their Room Print *Dutch*, *French* or *German* Linnens, which will Cost the Nation Three Times the Price'.[53] In 1720, Richard Steele's satiric pen, also directed at fine ladies who simply had to have numerous expensive costumes from abroad, turned to those in India who were taking jobs from honest English folk, declaring that calico itself was an evil substance: 'A tawdery, Pie-spotted, flabby, ragged, low-priz'd thing call'd *Callicoe*: made the L...d knows where, by a parcel of *Heathens* and *Pagans*, that worship the Devil, and work for a Half-penny a day.'[54]

A Parliamentary Act of 1701, aiming to protect wool by prohibiting the importation of finished Indian cloth, proved impotent when confronted by the logics of commercial profits and market demands for oriental textiles.[55] In 1708 Daniel Defoe railed against the ways that fashions for eastern textiles had not simply changed the ways the English lived but threatened to confuse crucial class boundaries. Class-consciousness, as Defoe obsessively documents it for readers, was powerfully shaped for women as a discourse of textiles and their meanings, of clothes and their social values. From East to West, from chambermaid to fine lady, exotic fabrics made all the differences. The most infinite recesses of English life had been penetrated and decorated by foreign and oriental 'stuffs'. Defoe reported in horror how 'the Chints and painted Callicoes, which before were only made Use of for Carpets, Quits, &c. and to cloth Children or ordinary People, became now the dress of our Ladies.' '*Such is the power of a Mode*', he continued, that

> we saw our Persons of Quality dress'd in *Indian* Carpets, which but a few Years before their Chamber-Maids would have thought too ordinary for them; the Chints were advanc'd from lying on their Floors to their Backs, from the Foot-Cloth to the Petticoat... Nor was this all, but it crept into our Houses, our Closets, and Bed-Chambers, Curtains, Cushions, Chairs, and at last beds themselves were nothing but Callicoes.[56]

Eastern fabrics are not simply displayed on the body; they are increasingly used in large quantities by the very wealthy for decoration and interior design. In *Moll Flanders* and *Roxana,* Defoe elaborates on this 'noble usurpation of printed calico'. The novels evoke a world where 'silk' only appears in the form of 'silk-purses', those literal conveyers of wealth that signal achievement, desire, and status; a world where all purses are silk and where all silks are now purses carried about in a world dressed in calico and other fine woven clothes. Otherwise in *Moll*, silk exclusively appears in bulk form as a commodity, those great bundles of imported silk brocades that prove Moll's undoing.

While the market for silk remained ever powerful, the domestic demand for cheaper, printed calicoes that flaunted colourful, oriental patterns, continued to flourish and threaten the silk and woollen manufacturers. The 1701 Act had permitted the use of calicoes printed at home, but this provision only created legal loopholes for canny producers. In 1719 Defoe fired off yet another polemic against abuses in the calico trades:

> That the Printed and Painted Calicoes now worn or used in *Great Britain*, come under four Denominations, ALL pernicious and destructive to our

Trade, (viz.) such as being imported by the *Dutch,* are either printed in the *Indies* or in *Holland* and clandestinely run on Shore here, in spite of former Prohibition: OR such as being imported here by our own *East India Company,* and prohibited to be worn because printed in *India*, are pretended to be exported, but are privately run on Shore again and sold: OR such as being printed here, are enter'd and shipp'd for Exportation, in order to draw back the Duties on the Stamps, but are re-landed and sold here; and lastly, such as are printed here, and legally worn and used, and under the *Colour* of which ALL the other Frauds are practis'd and conceal'd.[57]

Revealing how goods being legally produced exclusively for export were finding their way back home, did little to prevent abuse. A later Act passed in 1721 that finally banned the use 'of all printed, painted or dyed calicoes' at home regardless of their origin, continued to allow them to be produced for the lucrative export market in the New World—where the trans-Atlantic slave trade had created a massive demand—and re-importation doubtless carried on much as Defoe describes it. The Act also permitted the dyeing and printing of linen, the export trade in which boomed, thanks to the cheap imported cotton being used to produce a blended cloth that could pass inspection as 'linen'.[58] By the time the 1721 Act was finally repealed in 1774, the London wool traders and silk manufacturers had lost ground to Lancashire, where commercial calico printing started up in 1764 and rapidly expanded through the rest of the century to become 'by far the largest branch of British commerce' throughout Britain's imperial age.[59] The story of how Manchester's cotton factories enriched the nation and clothed the world is a tale in the sagas of the British Empire and the Industrial Revolution.

What the calico story exemplifies is a pattern that we have already noticed, one that is repeated elsewhere in the history of how material goods from the Islamic east came to change life in England: importation, imitation, and invention, followed by domestication. As we will see, a variant form of this formula reappears with the importation of eastern horses, while the tale of the turban in England amply illustrates how domestication transformed this potent symbol of religious difference and military threat.

Turbans

In the early modern period, the turban served as a gauge of England's attitude to Islam. The Muslim headdress, chiefly associated with the Ottomans, became the most dominant, the most feared, and the most awe-inspiring symbol of Islam. While the scimitar and the crescent were familiar Islamic signs, the turban supplied preachers, theatre audiences, and engravers with the pre-eminent token of Muslim hegemony and power. Travel books, which often included a frontispiece portraying the divisions of the world and the empires of mankind, regularly portrayed Muslims wearing turbans. Indeed, the engraved portrait of the prophet 'Mahomet' included among the 'Lives, Actions, and Ends of certain notorious *Hereticks*' that concluded the second edition of Alexander Ross's *View of All Religions in the World* (1675) shows that seventeenth-century writers believed the turban to have been donned by the founder of Islam himself. Perhaps Ross had good reason. The Ottoman historian and traveller, Evliya Çelebi, recorded a vision of the Prophet wearing a turban 'formed of a white sash with twelve folds'.[60] Other English writers attributed its general use to a command of Sultan Mehmed following the conquest of Istanbul.[61] The turban, in other words, pointed both to the origins of Islam and to the breadth of contemporary Muslim domination. Turbans on Muslim figures provide a useful angle from which to study the Christian art and print culture of early modern England in its engagements and encounters with Islam. They were metonymic of Islam and its haughty power.

Artistic representations of the turban suggest two important patterns in England's changing perceptions of Islam: first, an attitude of engaged fascination that took shape at the late Tudor court leading to entertainments at which aristocrats and royalty took pride in wearing turbans and other Muslim dress. Alongside this trend, however, we can trace how the turban commonly encodes rivalry and antipathy resulting from commercial and religious fears. Shifts in these attitudes vacillated as the forces of English trade and faith combined in direct encounters with Muslims and the worlds they lived in. Drawings, paintings, and prints of turbans appearing in early-modern England were often based on actual familiarity with Muslim attire and custom rather than on types inherited from the iconography of the Crusades. The turbans were not imaginary fabrications or orientalist constructions, but accurate depictions that English men had seen, both in England, on the continent, and in the Islamic world. In this respect, they are not like the turbans that appear on Jewish figures and which, as Ivan Davidson Kalmar has carefully shown, belong to the orientalist representation of the biblical Jews.[62] In late medieval and early-modern painting, the turban most often appears in Italian and Flemish paintings on the heads of Biblical figures, male and female, and regularly features in paintings of the three magi.⁶³ A conflation of biblical and Islamic traditions appeared in the portrayal of the turban-clad Hagar whom the Bible, along with continental Arabists including Joseph Scaligar, identified as the mother of the 'Saracens'. Paintings of Hagar reflected the European perception of the bond-woman who had given rise to the Arabs, who in turn, gave rise to Islam.⁶⁴

Turbans were worn at the Tudor court. On Shrove Sunday in 1533, the youthful king Henry VIII, along with the Earl of Essex, hosted a banquet at Westminster 'for all the Ambassadours, whiche then wer here'. Henry and his companion presumably aimed to startle the foreign envoys when they 'came in appareled after Turkey fasshion, in long robes of Bawkin, powedered with gold, hattes on their heddes of Crimsoyn Velvet'.⁶⁵ In a painting of the king in 1537, Islamic interlacing patterns appear on both the king's gown and the curtain behind him.⁶⁶ Later in the century, Queen Elizabeth received a present from the Sultana in Istanbul consisting of a 'princely attire being after the Turkish fashion'.⁶⁷ Unfortunately, as Edward Barton noted, 'the attyre for the head', which the Queen had so much wanted, was 'imbeazelled' on the way.⁶⁸ The aristocratic taste for having fun by dressing up in oriental costumes continued with masques at the Jacobean court, and become part of the tradition of country-house theatricals still practised today.

Meanwhile, travelling Englishmen started returning from the Levant fully 'attired in Turkish dress complete with turban':⁶⁹ after all, whenever they went into the domains of Islam, they dressed in Muslim attire. The first engraving that survives of a Christian from Britain dressed in Muslim clothes and turban shows the Scottish traveller William Lithgow who visited the Levant in 1612.⁷⁰ 'I clad in Turkish manner,' wrote Henry Blount in his 1636 account of his *Voyage into the Levant*.⁷¹ For audiences at home, the turban was a token from a land beyond Christendom, a land that was becoming increasingly familiar by way of imported signs of Islam: on textiles and rugs, in the form of spices and the magnificent lines of 'Barbary' horses, by travellers sporting their moustaches 'turnde the Turky waye',⁷² as well as by the Saracen Head signs above inns and public houses that had been there since the Crusades.

Costume is historically important. Clothes in the early modern period were treated not as mere external accoutrement, but as integral to the religion and identity of the individual. And, as Amanda Wunder has succinctly stated, 'costume was a moral issue'.⁷³ With the Reformation and Counter-Reformation partition of Christendom into nation states, and at any meeting between Christendom and Islam, costume was an important indicator of national allegiance and religious affiliation, while it increasingly marked personal identity too. 'God hath many times', translated Robert Ashley from the Italian in 1637, 'made garments expresse his intentions, peradventure because they are in some sort a part of our selves.'[74] 'A Musulman', wrote John Trapp in 1647, is 'a believing Turk both within and without.'[75] The clothes and turban 'without' were as much a demonstration of Islam as the faith 'within'—both for the Christian and for the Muslim. A Morisco text of the early seventeenth century stated that 'Turbans are the crowns of the Arabs' and 'Turbans distinguish us from the polytheists and their hats'.[76] Clothes defined people, their rank, morality, and national and religious identity.

Inside the Ottoman Empire, the white turban distinguished Muslims from Jews and Christians. The Islamic empires were multi-religious with large Christian, Jewish, Zoroastrian, and Hindu populations who were formally integrated into social, cultural, and financial institutions. Islamic empires were also multi-ethnic, making it difficult, even for local rulers and administrators, to distinguish Muslims from non-Muslims. As a result, the white turban became the only external evidence and the most imposing demonstration of a convert to Islam. This Muslim turban was made 'like great globes, of callico ... hauing little copped caps on the top, of greene or red veluet', wrote George Sandys.[77] Those who wore such turbans were Muslims, for 'Christians use not white nor round' turbans, wrote Purchas in his *Pilgrimes*.[78] Jews, wrote William Biddulph, 'are knowne by their hatts: for they were accustomed to weare red hatts without brimmes'.[79] Headgear prevented confusion:

> They [Turks] cover their head with a Turbant, except those of the discent of Mahomet; they were altogether green: but the christians inhabiting among them, were no one colour, but as they please (except greene) but they are all clothed in long garments like the Turkes, & are not distinguished by any apparell they wear (of what profession soever they be) but only by the attire of their heads.[80]

The white turban constituted the dividing line between Muslim and non-Muslim. Consequently, when a Christian converted to Islam, he was circumcised—in accordance with Islamic practice—and turbaned—also in accordance with Islamic custom; though neither of these practices is Qur'anic. By replacing their Christian hats with Muslim turbans, converts demonstrated that they had renounced an identity founded on country of origin in favour of Muslim culture and custom. Clearly, the donning of the turban was as important to Muslims as circumcision: the latter ritual signified that the convert's admission to Islam was as irreversible as the physical change; wearing the turban meant that the convert fully entered the community of Islam. Sandys described Christians in the process of converting to Islam, noting specifically how they threw 'away of their bonnets' and received a 'change of rayments'.[81] English and continental writers emphasized the link between conversion, circumcision, and the turban. The playwright Robert Daborne dramatized John Ward's conversion by showing him donning the turban in preparation for circumcision.[82] The French traveller, Jean Dumont, whose work was published in English in 1696, included an illustration of a Christian convert to Islam sitting on a horse with a prominent white turban on his head followed by turbaned celebrators (Figure 7): 'As soon as he [the convert] has made a public Profession of his Faith by pronouncing these Words, they put a Turbant on his Head, and make him kiss the Alcoran.'[83] A Christian apostate to Islam, wrote John Trapp, is 'circumcised, and doe put on a new turbant, as a badge of a *Musulman* or right believer'.[84]

Linking conversion to Islam with the turban could be used to provoke anger and fear in England. The turban signalled all that was weak in Christendom and powerful in Islam. As a result, the more Muslims gave prominence to the turban, the more Christians feared it. The turban identified the Englishman who wore it as a compatriot who had chosen to separate himself from the community and join the unbelievers. Everyone knew that the turban had to be earned—it was not given gratuitously but required a public declaration of faith as well as a complete change of religious and cultural practices that deliberately and consciously betrayed previous allegiances. Donning a turban was a statement of radical change. That is why Sandys denounced Christian princes who were sometimes suffered by Muslims to don the white turban: the wearing of the Muslim turban was an 'apostaticall insinuation', he warned.[85] The French traveller Jean Baptiste Tavernier recounted an episode that shows the supreme importance which Muslims placed on the distinctiveness of the turban: when an Armenian merchant mistakenly put on a Muslim's turban, he was immediately forced to convert to Islam because the turban could not be worn except by a Muslim.[86] For both Christians and Muslims, clothes proclaimed the man, and the white turban distinguished between Englishman and Muslim, infidel and believer.

Anxiety over turbans intensified after North African pirates began to attack the British Isles, to abduct English men, women, and children from coastal villages and to terrorize the English Channel. Large numbers of English and European men, finding themselves without any hope of returning home, converted to Islam, and subsequently became prominent in North African affairs. In 1637, the Ambassador of Morocco, Alkaid Jaurar ben Abdella, visited England and was received with due pomp and ceremony. In the account written about him, mention was made that he was a Portuguese renegade: the portrait in the frontispiece shows him with a magnificently white turban on his head.[87] Clearly, there was enterprise, reward, and glory in converting to Islam and numerous Christians from England to Portugal to Italy were seizing the opportunity to don the turban. The previous year, Charles Fitz-Geffrey had preached that many of the corsairs attacking the English coast were renegade Englishmen eager to capture their co-nationals in order to convert them.[88]

During the course of the seventeenth century, the turbaned Englishman stopped being a contradiction in terms, and emerged as a real and ruthless adversary. The turban symbolized slavery and violence.[89] No example better reveals the extent of English religious anxieties over the implications of the turban than two sermons preached in 1628. In 1627, an English renegade returned to his native Somerset and went before his parish in order to reassume his former Christian faith. Aware of the heinousness of his deed and the danger of his predicament—apostasy, after all, was punishable by death—the man tried to justify his apostasy by stating that he had conformed to Islam only by his mouth and not his heart. Edward Kellet, who preached the first sermon on the occasion of that man's Christian readmission, was not impressed by that defence because the man had been captured in 'Turkish-guise' which 'apparrell proclaimed you to be a Turke'. 'You were seene and taken in... such an attire,' he thundered, 'as did discriminate you from a Christian.'[90] The difference between Christian and Muslim was not only in faith and creed, but in clothes. By casting 'away [his] hat' and donning the turban, the man had actually discarded Christianity and adopted Islam. There was therefore no question about his apostasy: the 'Turkish attire' was the 'Embleme of Apostacie, and witnesse of your wofull fall' confirmed Henry Byam in his afternoon sermon on the same occasion.[91] Both preachers on that March Sunday declared there was no excuse for the returning Englishman to have donned the turban: 'The Turkish Turbant was nastie in the cause, senceless in the use,' declaimed Kellet as he fulminated against the Muslim headdress. He also gave a history of its origin, showing how the turban was not really a symbol of Muslim power and allure but of a diseased skin. The turban, he told his congregation, had first been worn by the prophet 'Mahomet' because he was 'an unhandsome man' who suffered not only from 'a Scabbed head, but a Scald pate which occasioned himselfe (as some say) to weare a white Shash (woollen would have made his scald pate sorer) therefore his Turbant was of linnen)'. The turban was not evidence of the high culture of Islam nor was it a token of Islamic power: it was a sickly attire full of 'ridiculous folly'.[92] He who wore it degraded himself because he excluded himself from the prospect of Christian salvation. 'Thou hast changed, thy Habit and Vestmentes, in token, of change in Religion: thou hast denyed thy Faith. Thy sinne of being *Circumcised*, was a bloody sinne.'[93] Turban and circumcision went together: and as circumcision made impossible the salvation of man—in Christian eyes—so did the wearing of the turban and of Muslim clothes: 'How could you hope in this unsanctified habit to attaine heaven?' asked Byam.[94] The turban had sealed the man's spiritual doom, for no soul could enter the Christian kingdom of God unless it was dressed in English hat and breeches. No wonder that over a century later, Thomas Pellow, an Englishman who was forcibly converted to Islam in Morocco, refused to wear the 'Mahometan' dress: though he had converted to Islam, he rejected the clothes of Islam. Only after being jailed for forty days did he give in and wear the turban.[95]

Following the two sermons, the anonymous apostate was readmitted to his Christian community and his English clothes. But the English ecclesiastical system was both lax and inefficient in dealing with the hundreds of renegades who returned to England and who simply bypassed the church's authority and slipped into their pews while still, literally, Muslim. While consul in Smyrna, Paul Rycaut expressed horror at the ease with which English apostates reassumed their former religion: among Greek converts, he noted, there was a public expression of renouncing the adopted religion of Islam and confessing faith in Christianity. Since the turban demonstrated the convert's allegiance to Islam, casting it off demonstrated renunciation. In *The Present State of the Greek and Armenian Churches*, Rycaut described how Greek converts returning to Christianity 'confess Christ at that place where they have renounced him; and this they have resolutely performed by leaving off their Tulbants, and boldly presenting themselves in publick Assemblies'. Then 'being carried off to the Justice of the City or Province, they have not only by words owned the Christian Doctrine, but also trampled their *Turkish* Tulbants or Sashes under their Feet'.[96] The Armenian merchant mentioned by Tavernier, who had been forced to convert to Islam for accidentally putting on a turban while in a coffee house, decided a few years later to return to his original faith. So he went to 'where the *Basha* was sitting in Council with the Grandees of the Country, and getting as near the *Mufti* as he could, and throwing his Turbant in his face; *There Dog*, said he, *Thou wert the cause that I have worn it so long, of which I have repented.*' Reassuming Christianity necessitated the renunciation of the turban, though in the case of Tavernier's Armenian, it also cost him his life.[97] When Dorax in John Dryden's *Don Sebastian* (c.1689) converts back to Christianity, the stage direction reads '*Re-enter Dorax, having taken off his Turbant and put on a Peruque Hat and Crevat*' (4. 3. 380).[98] To a late seventeenth-century London audience, the meaning of this change of headdress would have been only too clear.

After the Restoration, however, the turban became no longer simply a feature of the distant realm of Islam and the wicked world of renegades. The 1650s had introduced coffee houses into England, and with coffee came the turban, since coffee house keepers often wore turbans as an advertising ploy. An illustration to 'A Broad-Side against Coffee: or, the Marriage of the Turk' (1672) shows a black man serving coffee to two Englishmen and to a big turbaned Turk with twirled moustaches (Figure 11).[99] As noted earlier, in 1663 Edmund Verney was keen to obtain an authentic turban via his brother in Aleppo, but wearing them except for special occasions seems still to have been an eccentricity that could provoke anxiety. In November 1666, Samuel Pepys was evidently surprised to find Sir Philip Howard 'dressing himself in his night-gown and Turban like a Turke; but one of the finest persons that I ever saw in my life'.[100] Clothing clearly continued to signal national and religious identity, yet John Evelyn was evidently pleased when, in October the next year, King Charles appeared at court in 'the *Eastern fashion* of Vest... after the *Persian* mode'. The King's aim, however, was not to encourage conversion to Islam, but rather to discourage the continued fashion for wearing extremely expensive French styles.[101] Unfortunately Evelyn does not specify what manner of head covering Charles wore with his 'Persian' waistcoat, but it would most likely not have been a turban. It is, however, important that Charles sought to challenge the supremacy of France's *haut couture* with Islam's: the best way to defeat the ascendancy of French dress in England was to introduce the powerful oriental dress of the Muslims.

The turban's declining power was declared in the 1670s, a decade in which the English fleet bombarded Algiers and Libyan Tripoli, and accelerated in 1683 when the Ottoman armies fell back from the gates of Vienna. In 1682, the Moroccan ambassador, Ahmad Ibn Haddu, arrived in London. John Evelyn's description of the visitor specifically noted his turban: 'The Ambassador had a string of pearls odly woven in his Turbant,' he wrote in his diary on 11 January 1682. A portrait of Ibn Haddu shows an elegantly imposing turban sitting above the proud face.[102] The reception of the ambassador in England was both elaborate and courteous, but a French report claims that King Charles, having learned that the English ambassador in Morocco had been humiliated by Mulay Isma'il, sought to humiliate ibn Haddu by obliging him to appear at court without turban or shoes.[103] Slowly but firmly, the turban was losing its power.

The Ottoman defeat of 1683 irreversibly transformed British attitudes towards Islam and the turban. The Scottish poet Alexander Tyler, writing to celebrate the victory at Vienna, denounced a Christian rebel count as an apostate who had vainly renounced 'the Truth for a Turbant'.[104] The turban now came to symbolize falsehood and ignorance. A quarter of a century later, while Alexander Pope and other writers were fashionably portrayed wearing turbans, Joseph Addison wrote of '*Ignorance* with a Turband upon her Head'.[105] From the once-formidable symbol of Islamic cultural and military hegemony, the turban had come to replace the hat of the dunce. Still there were those who did not agree:

> Some Persons are so bigoted, that a Native of Barbary, and a Brute, are with them synonymous Terms... Yet I am persuaded that were such Persons to converse unknowingly with Mahometans in a Christian Dress, they would look upon them to be just such Creatures as themselves, having the same Faculties and Dispositions; but did they wear a Turban, that alone would be abundantly sufficient to eclipse all the Beauties of their Deportment.[106]

Horses

The story of how English equestrian culture was transformed by the importation of blood-horses from the Islamic world, and of how that change was central to broader social, cultural, artistic, and even imperial developments, has recently been recounted in detail by Donna Landry in *Noble Brutes* (2008). The importation and subsequent breeding of horses known as Arabians, Barbs, and Turks to produce the English Thoroughbred is, as Landry demonstrates, only part of that story. The arrival of eastern bloodstock also introduced different attitudes towards horses as well as new ways of riding, feeding, training, thinking about, and representing them. These new practices accompanied wider social and cultural developments that continue to shape and define Englishness. Landry describes the elaboration of 'a rich verbal and visual record of obsession with the equine species' throughout the seventeenth and into the eighteenth centuries that, she argues, reveals 'how crucial horses were to formulating what emerged as English culture on the world stage'.[107] A conspicuous 'sign' of how the island nation was becoming 'a mercantile and imperial power' was the 'plethora of Eastern horses who had been acquired, by fair means or foul, from whom there issued forth a new equine breed, the English Thoroughbred'.[108] Once merely beasts of burden that were often brutally treated, horses came to be viewed as creatures of beauty and, above all, intelligence, as well as speed. Increasing familiarity with eastern bloodstock and their hybrid offspring meant that horses were no longer considered animate machines but animal companions who deserved, and responded to, kind and thoughtful treatment. Such was the impact of this new way of regarding and handling horses that 'in the later seventeenth and early eighteenth centuries', Landry claims, 'the horse began to figure as an idealized version of the human self'.[109]

Horses had, of course, served internationally as symbols of power and prestige long before the first Turkish, Barb, or Arabian horse ever set hoof to English soil. Throughout Europe and Asia, generations of princes and emperors had sent each other horses, and costly saddles and bridles, as diplomatic gifts. Since horsemanship was associated with nobility and the right to rule, such gifts proclaimed the power of their giver, while flattering the receiver. Ottoman emperors regularly dispatched 'Turkish horses of purest breed' to the Mughal court, while Henry VIII received 'gifts of Barbary horses from the Gonzaga family of Mantua'.[110] Henry's prime concern was to increase the size and strength of native horses so that they might carry heavily armed soldiers into battle.[111] Yet it was also during his reign that archival evidence first appears of 'Spanish, Neapolitan, and Barbary horses, who would themselves have contained Arabian or Turcoman blood' arriving into Britain. These duly brought speed, stamina and endurance to the new English experiments in 'multiracial cross-breeding'.[112]

Early English travellers were duly impressed by the legendary beauty and speed of the eastern horses they encountered in Islamic lands, often commenting on how feeding, handling, and stable management differed from European practices. Writing in the late 1590s, Fynes Moryson was among the first English travellers to remark upon how the appearance and performance of Turkish horses clearly resulted from the manner in which they were handled and kept. 'Their horses are very beautiful,' he observed, 'having their skinns shining which is caused by the horsedung which they lay under them first dryed into powder... they are very swift.'[113] Using dried manure for bedding would, of course, have proved highly impractical in lands with a wetter climate, such as England, but the ideal of eastern equine beauty had taken root in the English imagination and along with it, interest in different methods of horse management.

Admiration and desire for eastern horses was by no means entirely aesthetic. Travellers were regularly amazed by their evident intelligence and tractability, qualities that distinguished them radically from the rambunctious hairy ponies and great plodding cart-horses of home. Writing of equestrian practices among the Mughals, Edward Terry praised their 'excellent good skill in riding and managing of their well turn'd, high metald, choise horses, which are excellent good at mounting up, bounding and curvetting, and when they runne them at their full swiftest speed will stop them at a foots breadth'.[114] Like Moryson, Terry was struck by the obvious links between performance, appearance, and methods of handling: 'The hair upon their Horses (whom they keep plump and fat) is very short, soft and lyes sleek upon them, and I wonder not at it, they are kept so daintily, every Horse being allowed a man to dress and feed him, and to run by him when he is rode forth, and this is all his work.'[115] Terry was by no means alone in being struck by the way these horses were handled and trained 'daintily', with individualized care and affection, rather than the indifferent brutality common among European horsemen and grooms.

Ogier Ghiselin de Busbecq, the Flemish-born Habsburg ambassador to Istanbul in 1554–6, was perhaps the earliest observer to contrast the intimacy shared by Turks and their horses with the casual violence common throughout Europe. He records staying overnight in a caravanserai where only a low wall divided men from 'Camels, Horses, with other Cattel'. But, he continues, 'the *Turks*... so tye their Horses, that their Heads and Necks are above it, or at least may lean over it; and thus when their Masters are warming themselves at the Fire, or else are at Supper, they stand near them as Servants us'd to do; and sometimes they will take a piece of Bread or Apple, or whatsoever else is offered them, out of their Masters Hand.'[116] Busbecq so greatly admired the way that horses were treated with kindness, recognizing how it improved performance, that he returns to the topic in detail. He describes Ottoman horsemen behaving as if their horses were members of the family, and how the horses respond to such treatment. 'There is', he writes:

> no Creature so gentle as a *Turkish* Horse; nor more respectful to his Master, or the Groom that dresses him... they frequently sleek them down with their Hands, and never use any Cudgel to bang their Sides, but in cases of great necessity. This makes their Horses great Lovers of Mankind... But alas, our Christian-Grooms treat Horses at another-guess rate; they never think them rightly curried, till they thunder at them with their Voice, and let their Club or Horse-whip, as it were, dwell on their Sides... But the *Turks* love to have their Horses very gentle, that at a word of command they may fall down on their Knees, and in this posture receive their Riders.[117]

Busbecq's enthusiasm for the kindness with which the Ottomans trained and treated their horses 'even as Children' would have surprised his contemporary Europeans, but he cannot have been alone in recognizing the benefits of having a gentle horse who would kneel willingly rather than tremble from fear.

Englishmen living in the Islamic world developed unusually fond and affectionate relations with the horses they met there. The Levant Company accountant, John Sanderson, for example, may have exposed his commercial preoccupations when noting that his favourite horse, 'a Babilonian', on which he travelled to Aleppo from Istanbul in 1597 cost him '24 ducats gould', but his genuine affection for this horse is only too evident. He was, Sanderson writes:

> an excellent daple grai, very sadd [dark coloured], of a meane stature; rather too little for me, but the best, I am of opinion, that ever I shalbe master of. He would walke by me, licking my hand; stand still when I backed him; and kneele at my pleasure.[118]

For Sanderson, the reciprocal bond of affection between horse and 'master' was perhaps no more than yet another exotic feature of eastern difference, but in England at the time, others were eagerly breeding horses that might display just such differences. 'I have no one worldly delight that feedes my melancoly moste but the breeding of a horse,' wrote Sir Matthew Arundel to the Earl of Shrewsbury on 23 May 1597, 'and ther was no one horse in England I so wel lyked as your Lordships black Turk (myne own being ded I had of my Lord Treasorer) howbeit his lyttlenes did nothing please me... I kno he is a fyne horse and right jennett, otherwise you wold never have brought him over.'[119] Arundel does not detail which features of Shrewsbury's 'black Turk' he admired, but since he regrets the stallion's 'lyttlenes', we can presume that there were qualities other than size that he wished to breed for and hoped to find in his next season's foals. Earlier in the century, Henry VIII had received Barb racehorses for the royal stables from the Gonzaga family. What Arundel's letter instances, however, is one of the earliest pieces of evidence we have that private gentlemen were importing Turks on their own behalf before the sixteenth century had come to an end.

The great era of importing Arab, Barb, and Turkish horses to improve the native stock, however, did not get fully under way until the 1650s when, in Landry's words: 'English (and some Irish and Welsh and Scots) aristocrats, mere upstarts in the world economy where Eastern blood horses had been traded for centuries, began shopping the world.'[120] Oliver Cromwell himself proved specially keen on acquiring 'some good Arabian horses, to furnish England with a breed of that kind', according to a Levant Company commission sent in September 1657 to Sir Thomas Bendish, ambassador in Istanbul. Bendish was ordered 'to procure two at Constantinople, and send them to England, but let them be of the best kind'.[121] A similar commission was sent the same day to Henry Riley, consul in Aleppo, ordering him to 'enquire after two of the best breed, and, if possible, send them to us in England', and confidently assuring him that 'the ambassador will give you a licence'.[122]

While tracking the success of these specific ventures proves difficult, by the final decades of the seventeenth century the introduction of eastern horses and eastern bloodlines into England had brought new standards of speed and endurance to racing and hunting. Under Charles II's patronage of racing at Newmarket, the search for ever increasing speed in the newly anglicized Thoroughbred racehorse began to dominate English equestrian sports. Yet the desire to know and understand the origins of Arab, Barb, and Turkish horses continued unabated. Published in 1670, John Ogilby's compilation of previously published knowledge about Africa provides an indicative summary of contemporary interest in, and information about, exotic breeds. 'In several parts of *Africa*', he writes:

are an excellent breed of Horses, term'd by us *Barbs*, strong of Hoof, and extremely fleet: But the swiftest and most hardy either in *Africa* or *Asia*, are the *Arabian* Horse, so call'd because first broke by the Arabs from running Wild in the Woods... since when the *Arabs* have stock'd with them all *Asia*. The most assured proof of the celerity, is, when they can overtake the *Lant* or *Ostrich* in their Flight; if so, that Steed they value at a 1000. Duckets, or else Barter for 100. Camels.[123]

Ogilby clearly lacks the affection born of personal contact that we noted in Sanderson and others who had spent time among eastern horses, but his comparison of Arab horses with camels and ostriches emphasizes their speed, utility and exchange value, all qualities that make them both exotic and fit for envious admiration.

Being able to describe equine conformation had long been an essential ingredient of the educated gentleman's personal acquisitions: being English entailed being a knowledgeable horseman. Ogilby did not live long enough to witness the arrival in December 1684 of the 'three Turkish or Asian Horses... brought newly over, and now first shewed his Majestie', but he would doubtless have been just as fascinated by the sight of them as was John Evelyn who reported seeing them paraded in St James's Park:

> They were taken from a Bashaw at the seige of *Vienna* in Austria, the late famous raising that Leaguer: & with mine Eyes never did I behold so delicate a Creature as was one of them, of somwhat a bright bay... in all reguards beautifull & proportion'd to admiration, spiritous & prowd, nimble, making halt, turning with that sweiftnesse & in so small a compase as was incomparable, with all this so gentle & tractable, as called to mind what I remember *Busbequius* speaks of them; to the reproch of our Groomes in *Europ*.[124]

Nahum Tate's translation of Busbecq's *Letters* into English would not appear until 1694, though the *Letters* had been in circulation in the original Latin since 1581. Perhaps we should not be too surprised, therefore, that more than a century after Busbecq had condemned the cruel habits of 'our Christian-Grooms', Evelyn, confronted with authentic Ottoman horses, should feel the need to repeat his observations. Cruelty was still the norm in England, it would seem. But as Evelyn makes clear, great excitement and even awe were inspired by the splendid physique and effortless agility of eastern horses when they appeared in London. He summons a host of noble and expert witnesses including 'the King, Prince of Denmark, the Duke of Yorke, and severall of the Court Noble persons skilled in Horses', to confirm his opinion 'that there were never seene any horses in these parts, to be compared with them'.[125] The greatest connoisseurs of horseflesh known to Evelyn were, like him, struck by the combination of delicacy and strength, athletic ability and gentleness, high spirits and tractability displayed by horses schooled and handled in a manner different from those of western Europe. Not only the horses' physical properties, but also their characters and temperaments signified a superior regimen in which a sophisticated partnership between man and beast was called for. Not coercion, but intelligent and kindly sensitivity to another species produced a working relationship that was a thing of beauty in itself.

The horses Evelyn saw exhibited in St James's Park were not diplomatic gifts or commercial purchases, but spoils of war. The importation of eastern horses was in part linked with the desire to improve the quality of English cavalry mounts. Breeding for improvement for military purposes was a constant preoccupation amongst English gentlemen. However, during the later seventeenth and eighteenth centuries, mercantile success and even imperial ambition were conspicuously exhibited on the turf and the hunting field as well as in military manoeuvres. Ogilby's report of North African horses kept not for agricultural work or war, but for hunting, would have found a sympathetic audience among his countrymen:

> few of these Horses are in *Barbary*, but some are bred up in *Arabia*, and abundance in *Lybia*, not enured to Tillage, or Warres, but Hunting. They feed them daily twice with Camels Milk to keep them lusty and quick, but not too foggy: When the ranck Grass flourishes, they turn them into the Fields, but then they Ride them not: the *Lybian* Horse, hath a Body long, Ribs and Sides thick, and broad Breast strutting forth.[126]

The equestrian ideal was increasingly one conducive to sport, which could always be justified as keeping horses and men fit for war. Both battlefield and hunting field were now scenes of fast and agile movement, as in the East, not tests of brute strength or ponderous armoured clashes. Even here, in horse culture as entertainment as well as horse culture for war, exchanges with the Islamic east had effected changes that were profound and irreversible.

By way of conclusion

At the beginning of our period, England was still a globally inconsequential island nation distinguished by bad weather, monotonous food, and dull domestic appointments. The Islamic world, by contrast, possessed empires that were at the height of their power, glory, and splendour. If goods from the East changed forever the ways that the English lived their lives, furnished and decorated their houses, planted their gardens, bred and rode their horses, the nature and range of goods exported to Islamic countries on English ships served less benign purposes. English woollens clothed the Sultan's armies; tin from Cornish mines and 'bell-metal' from disbanded monasteries supplied the manufacturers of bullets and cannons; oak beams furnished the builders and repairers of the corsair fleets of North Africa. Merchants on both sides made considerable profits, but while Britons took increasing delight in the 'higher, more civilized way of life' made possible by luxury goods imported from the East,[127] Muslims found their libraries ransacked and their citizens addicted to tobacco, while on distant shores their religion was reviled and their costumes were parodied on stage and at fancy-dress parties. The insular backwardness or underdevelopment of the British Isles was undergoing rapid change. Yet the comparative barbarity and inconsequence of the English in Muslim eyes meant that commercial exchanges, however profitable for both sides, were far from equal. The inequality here is one of civilization rather than of culture.

Conclusion

British engagements with the three Islamic regions that we have described took place even as sailors and merchants were beginning their 'trafficks' into other parts of the world—North America and Russia, Japan, Madagascar, and the Bermudas. We have shown how the first chartered companies under Queen Elizabeth were directed at the Islamic world since it promised lucrative markets and rich natural resources. At a time when English merchants were unable to trade with Catholic neighbours in Europe, the Islamic empires offered vast and rewarding alternatives. Belatedly, the English finally began voyaging where the Portuguese, Venetians, Dutch, and French had already ventured.

We have also shown how, during the next century of Stuart ascendancy, British understanding of Islam and Muslims took shape in ways that were at once generalizing and often inaccurate, yet also regionally specific. At the risk of oversimplifying, these might be summarized as follows:

(1) The North African region of the western Mediterranean projected to English travellers, readers, and investors, the most confrontational and dangerous image of Islam and Muslims, and continued to do so throughout our period. The reasons were directly linked to piracy and the seizure of captives—activities that were eagerly pursued by Britons and other Europeans as well as by North African Muslims. This dangerous and hostile region, especially after the Moriscos arrived, was unavoidable for British ships trading to the wealthy cities of the Ottoman Levant. Even though English mariners and captains regularly avoided the dangers of being seized and taken captive, the English imagination—religious, literary, and historical—remained firmly in thrall to the reputation of the Barbary pirates, elevated to mythic status as perpetually fierce Muslims who abducted men and women and sought to convert them forcibly out of their Christian purity.

(2) In the Ottoman Levant, Britons met a different form of Islam, one that was imperial, tolerant, secure, and powerful. Here they encountered Muslims who controlled a vast and magnificent empire that continued expanding until 1669 when Crete, the last Ottoman conquest, was won over from the Venetians. In many ways this Islam, peopled by militaristic, assured, and proud Ottomans, served to intensify fears and anxieties. Islam continued to be closely associated with the figure of the 'Turk', not only because of Ottoman military prowess, but also because their empire controlled large biblical populations of Jews and Christians. In travelling into Ottoman-controlled lands, for the first time Britons met fellow Christians who were physically and religiously submissive to an Islamic state.

(3) The Persian-Indian region was also imperial in its splendour, wealth, and magnitude, yet unlike the North Africans and Ottomans, had no history of war with Christendom. Safavid and Mughal cultures were little known in England. Early European chronicles and histories of the Ottomans had been translated into English, but there were no similar works about the Safavids or Mughals. Although early travellers in the Persian-Indian arena sometimes found themselves confronting difficulties because of religious differences, they never encountered the level of danger and religious enmity that they met in regions closer to home. The earliest Britons to settle in India were most often confused by the wide variety of religions in the region, even by the varieties within Islam itself, but were never personally threatened as they were in North Africa.

Meanwhile, for Britons who only knew of Muslims and Islam from written sources, misunderstandings were bound to be numerous and widespread. Costly and learned works, whether based on other sources, such as Knolles's *Generall Historie*, or personal experience, such as Rycaut's *Present State*, as well as cheaper pamphlets reporting horrifying tales of captivity and forced conversion, all conspired to encourage English readers to imagine that Islam was a dangerous and militarized threat to godly Christians. Even Lancelot Addison, who lived in Morocco during the 1660s, claimed to have mastered the language, and who cited Arabic histories and religious sources, managed to produce *The Life and Death of Mahumed*, an account of Muslims and their prophet that was full of egregious errors, mistranslations, confusions, and blatant bigotry.[1] Such misleading texts, along with repeated accounts of captivity, consolidated the image of Islamic militarism and expansionism. Throughout the Mediterranean, from Izmir to Tangier, even to Atlantic Salé, Britons encountered Muslims who were as zealous as the proud followers of St George. The maritime confrontations and piracies that ensued, with both Britons and North Africans sinking each other's ships, attacking seaports, and seizing captives, led British writers, sailors, preachers, and state officials to create a generalized portrait of Islam as an aggressively violent religion peopled by sabre-wielding turbaned janissaries.

This point has been central to our discussion: that a large sector of British society could only think of Muslims and Islam by way of thinking about the thousands of compatriots held captive in Salé, Algiers, Tunis, and even Mocha, and of the imperial might of the Ottomans, of which piracy was a fearsome arm. The publication of dozens of accounts about battles with Turks and Moors, and of the captivity narratives of returning sailors, clergymen, and ship's captains, shaped how Britons conceived of Muslims. During the Elizabethan and Jacobean periods, England had had fewer dealings with the Islamic Mediterranean than France and Spain, and consequently had produced fewer original writings about Islam and Muslims. Yet Henry du Lisdam's *L'Esclavage du brave chevalier François de Vintimille*, France's first captivity account, only appeared in 1608, long after Marlowe's Tamburlaine had railed against the piratical renegades of Algiers (*Tamburlaine Pt I*, 3.3.55–58), and after England had produced seven of the ten captivity accounts to appear before 1640. As soon as the English began travelling and trading in the Islamic Mediterranean, and throughout our period, captivity narratives generated and sustained an inimical view of Muslims. Even after the decline of North African naval strength, accounts of captivity, compounded by the publication of the *Thousand and One Nights* at the beginning of the eighteenth century, continued to appear, with numerous plays and novels describing the salacious harems of the Moors and the danger of forcible conversion to Islam. Although very few British captives would be seized in the Georgian decades, the imagined danger continued unabated.[2]

But even as tales of captivity were being printed and narrated in dockside alehouses, a vast array of information was reaching London from resident agents, factors, and consuls about conditions inside the Islamic empires. Since neither the Safavids nor Mughals had past histories of war with European states, merchants and diplomats found themselves unencumbered by memories of past hostilities. They may not have understood the religions of the Persians and Indians, but it did not matter in the least. And since they made no attempts to convert Muslims to Christianity, nor were they enticed, or forced, to convert out of Christianity, religion never caused problems. Such, however, was not the case with the Dutch who, from

1619, attempted to convert Muslims by offering them government posts, or the French Catholics who tried converting the Armenian population of Persia—until Shah 'Abbas threatened that if the Armenians were to leave their religion, they would have to convert to Islam.[3] British attempts to convert Muslims and eastern Christians belong to a later age.

Differing encounters with different forms of Islam help explain the different colonial trajectories that developed in the course of the seventeenth century. In the Mediterranean, the conversionist zeal in the North African states and the relatively strong military and naval defences throughout the region prevented Britons from establishing outposts in the manner that the Portuguese, Spaniards, and French had done in earlier times. Even Tangier, once conceived as a stepping stone to the conquest of Africa, was relinquished in 1684 after constant Moroccan attacks. Britons realized that they would not be able to establish, much less defend, permanent footholds in the Islamic Mediterranean. In India and the Persian Gulf, however, conditions were less hostile. Initially encountering little by way of religious, military, or naval resistance, Britons quickly began establishing residential bases for trade that slowly but resolutely, developed into colonial settlements. At first, the British won over the local populations by presenting themselves as mere traders not colonists, as Sir Thomas Roe assured the Prince Sultan of Coronne.[4] But in 1616, they seized the island of Pulo Run ('Pooloroon') to serve as a base for trading in the Spice Islands. By 1619, they had established a fort there, and were planning more that would be protected by armed ships—there were to be 'five at Surat and four at Bantam, to procure trade of the Chinese'.[5] In 1639, they acquired the port of Madras and built Fort St George to protect it; in 1641, settlements in Bengal led to the establishment of a factory at Hugli; in 1668, the East India Company acquired Bengal from Charles II; and in 1686, English forces occupied Calcutta, followed, in 1687, by the new charter for the East India Company to raise money to maintain a military force. In 1690, a factory was established in Calcutta, and in 1698, Fort William was built to guard Calcutta. By the end of the seventeenth century, the East India Company had developed into a full-scale colonial enterprise, a 'Politie of Civill & Military Power... [that] administered justice, coined money, and exercised other functions of government'.[6] Its policy slowly developed into a strident imperial agenda that would bear fruit with the East India Act of 1813.

British foreign trade benefitted greatly from the openness of Islamic societies to foreigners. None of the Islamic empires ever expelled foreign

Christians as took place in Japan during the early seventeenth century.[7] But neither did a community of resident Muslim diplomats and merchants ever develop anywhere in Britain comparable to the settlements of Britons in Algiers, Istanbul, Hormuz, and Surat. Trade and travel took Muslims into the eastern Mediterranean, the Indian Ocean, all the way to the China Sea, but those same Muslims were not allowed into Britain or other European regions with the ease with which Europeans were able to travel, trade, settle, and even proselytize inside the Islamic empires. While Catholic priests would never have been able to preach or seek converts in London, they were able to convert eastern Christians in Aleppo. In 1023 AH (c.1714), the Algerian Dey, wrote to Queen Anne complaining that two of his cruisers had gone into Gibraltar harbour, whereupon 'the English threw Stones and Cursed and Spitt in the Faces of our Men being on shore and the Governour Detained our Captaine and gave them much trouble saying that they had English men on board their ships whereas when any of your Ships either men of Warr or Merchant men come here we give them esteem and respect'.[8] Neither Muslims nor Jews who were subjects of the Moroccan ruler were permitted to reside in Christian regions, not even the Gibraltar outpost: they could trade, but they had to 'depart with their effects' at the end of the day.[9] Yet large numbers of Britons were able to travel into the regions of Islam because Muslim rulers saw no reason to keep them, or other Europeans, out. Conspicuous in their distinctive hats and breeches, British and European visitors eventually began appearing in Mughal, Safavid, and Ottoman paintings and illuminations—without obvious animosity or religious vilification.[10]

In the course of their travels and residencies, factors, consuls, sailors, and merchants made friends with their local counterparts, sometimes seeking to turn a profit at the risk of defying Company regulations. One John Leigh, unwilling to leave his dissolved factory in Petapoli, took up 'building hummums or hot houses'.[11] Some so integrated into the local culture that they took home with them their turbans, coloured calicos, chess, Arabian and Turkmen horses, and servants. Some arrived home with pornographic literature from India, which was immediately consigned to the fire 'till they were burnt and turned into smoke', by the governor of the East India Company, who hoped such a display of displeasure 'would give satisfaction that such wicked spectacles are not fostered and maintained by any of the Company'.[12] Many Britons, not involved in the drudgery of business, reinvented themselves as men of oriental culture and leisure, notwithstanding their difficulties in the new geographies and among the new cultures and ethnicities and languages. At the same time, they imparted some of their cultural traits to their hosts: from English instrumental music to bear-baiting with much-admired English mastiffs, to clocks with Qur'anic verses in Arabic script. That several of the largest cities in India— Madras, Bombay, and Calcutta—developed from the East India presidencies that traded in textiles shows the enduring impact of British commercial presence on the region.[13] Had some of the correspondence and informal memoirs of these factors, agents, and governors been published in the seventeenth century, without the strictures that contemporary religious prejudices imposed, they would have conveyed cooperation and curiosity between Christians and Muslims.

Yet behind those Britons who lived among Muslims, eating and carousing with them, lurked the officials of the trading companies with their balance sheets, bills of exchange, and investment figures. Based in London, run by merchant elites ever in search of increased profits, and sponsored by monarchs greedy for customs revenues, the trading companies produced a new breed of bureaucrats with extensive commercial skills. These bureaucrats, particularly 'The Governor and Company of Merchants of London Trading into the East Indies', as they had been called by Queen Elizabeth, studied and centralized all the information they could get. They coordinated international trade by commissioning the most detailed maps and Portolan charts for their captains, paying for ocean-worthy ships that were armed with the most advanced weaponry, hiring sailors, caulkers, surgeons, and clergymen, resolving crises among factories and agencies, and directing the fleet to seize non-company English ships that were trading illegally. They interviewed returning employees for logistical information. They invited investment in maritime enterprises, an activity that often involved the wives and widows of employees and company officials. And most importantly, they kept a close eye on all financial activities by means of solicitors, bookkeepers, and auditors. From Algiers, Izmir, or Madras, consuls and factors wrote about dangers and festivities; they described Islamic traditions, languages, and histories. But in London, officials who read their reports paid little attention to cultural interaction. Their concern was to determine the trading priorities that the factors and agents should pursue. With their international perspective over multiple regions of British investment, and with up-to-date commercial information, maps, and military intelligence on their desks and in their archives, they identified new outposts to which agents should be sent. They balanced supply and demand through monitoring the export and import of goods, and experimented with commodities that could prove profitable, from calico to ambergris. From the letters and memoranda sent by company employees, they identified profitable goods and imported them thereby changing English culture forever. They also exported commodities across the Channel and across the Atlantic, thereby changing habits and customs in Spain and New England, in Morocco and the Caribbean.

By the time war broke out between France and Britain in 1689, the British fleet was docking and taking on victuals in Algiers and Tetuan, and not in Catholic Marseilles. Once Britain came into possession of Gibraltar (1704) and Minorca (1707), the North African regions assumed a crucial role in supplying these two outposts—which British consuls relentlessly pursued.[14] During times of famine in France and Britain, North African grain, corn, wheat, and other food supplies ensured the survival of fighting forces on the Continental theatre—especially since the price of grain in the European west was 'mostly higher than in the territories of the [Ottoman] Empire'.[15] Amidst the rivalry between Britain and France in the Mediterranean, Muslim rulers, from the beys and deys to the sultan in Istanbul, became directly involved in military supply and intervention. For a time, access to North African resources enabled Britain to hold on to its new Mediterranean outposts. But in the longer term it was trade with India that was rapidly producing the vast new wealth that transformed London's merchant elites into an imperial caste. By the end of the seventeenth century, the East India Company, with its monopoly on that trade and its formidable fleet, had eliminated both the Dutch and the Portuguese naval danger, while the French Companie des Indes, not founded until 1664, had never been a serious contender. At the dawn of a new century, from the Cape of Good Hope all the way east to Japan, the world belonged to the East India Company.

By now, the officers of the East India Company harboured no fantasies about converting their customers to Christianity, much as clergy on the ground might have. The commercial imperative had, of course, been there from the start in Hakluyt's 1599–1600 title with its additional emphasis on 'Traffiques'. Over two decades earlier, in 1566, Elizabeth had explained that her willingness to incorporate 'Merchants adventures' was intended 'for the glory of God, the honor and increase of the revenues of the Crowne, and the common utilitie of the whole Realme of England'.[16] Beyond pious rhetoric, what the 'glory of God' might have meant to a monarch whose accession was still contested remains unclear, but the national coffers needed those revenues, and the population needed employment, hence the urgent reasons for what Hakluyt had, all along, termed 'Navigations' and 'Discoveries'. So urgent was that need that a decade later, the queen was perfectly happy to invoke the 'one God' that united her Christian peoples with the Muslims, be they in the Ottoman Levant or in Persia, and who 'disposed of our affairs on earth that ech one should need the other', in order to ensure safe conduct for her trading and income-generating subjects.[17] Differences in religion were no reason for discouraging trade and profit: except with Roman Catholics. Unfortunately, the most egregious misnomer in the history of British colonial history and empire sank deep in English discourse thanks to Samuel Purchas, who called his trading and conquering countrymen 'pilgrims'. That the conquerors of North America and the settlers on the coasts of India might be considered 'pilgrims' inaccurately suggests that the British Empire was, in some sense, a product of Protestant piety and evangelism: that the *Mayflower* colonists were pilgrims on their way to salvation.

From the very start, and throughout the ensuing century, limited natural resources in England, overpopulated cities that could not support their citizens, economic instability, and religious persecution of Dissenters and Catholics, sent Englishmen and later Britons in search of livelihood across seas and oceans, in regions never before seen by their countrymen. Their interest in the regions of the Islamic world, as in other regions, was financial and entrepreneurial. Although Elizabeth and Hakluyt might have liked to convert the world to Christianity while that world was enriching English coffers, very rarely did later Britons develop plans to convert native 'Mahometans' in Istanbul, or 'Moors' in Algeria or Aceh. Whether in Izmir, Isfahan, or Madras, they were there to earn a living, grow rich, and if death spared them, return as prosperous retirees to Albion. The ambassadors who strutted in Istanbul, the captives who cowered in Algerian bagnios, the clergymen who officiated in the chapels of Madras and Surat, and the sailors and ship's captains who fought European rivals: all had sailed in search of wages, wealth, and resources. By the beginning of the Hanoverian period, the thousands of company officials in London and their determined investors preferred to anglicize rather than Christianize their Muslim customers. Only then would those customers, from Algiers to Agra, buy English tobacco, kitchenware, and guns, or wear English-manufactured cloth, drink ale, or enjoy English paintings. The Islamic regions had become markets for trade-serving multi-religious, multi-ethnic, and multi-linguistic clients. Ottomans, Mughals, and Safavids, native Christians, Jews, and Muslims, like Protestant New England colonists, continental Catholic Europeans, and Londoners themselves, were all being turned into consumers of British goods. And Muslims, like others, desired those goods, though the price is still being paid.

Notes

INTRODUCTION

1. John J. Pool, *Studies in Mohammedanism* (London, 1892), 395, 397. According to Pool, the first convert to Islam in England was a 'Mr. William Henry Quilliam, a solicitor' from Liverpool who converted to Islam after visiting Morocco in 1884; 395. On Quilliam and the Liverpool community, see Humayun Ansari, *'The Infidel Within': Muslims in Britain since 1800* (London, 2004), chapter 5.
2. TNA SP 12/240 fo. 28.
3. Christopher Hill, *The Century of Revolution, 1603–1714* (1961; rpt. London, 1974), 230; Charles de Secondat Montesquieu, *Persian Letters*, trans. C. J. Betts (Harmondsworth, 1973), 242; and see James Mather, *Pashas: Traders and Travellers in the Islamic World* (New Haven and London, 2009), 44–57.
4. See John Tolan, *Saracens: Islam in the Medieval European Imagination* (New York, 2002), xviii.
5. Donald F. Lach, *Asia in the Making of Europe. Volume I: The Age of Discovery* (Chicago, 1965). Lach's focus, however, is on Asia east-of-the Indus.
6. Prospero Alpino, *La Médecine des Égyptiens, 1581–1584*, trans. Raymond de Fenoyl, 2 vols. (Cairo, 1980), 2: 288.
7. J. Caille, 'Le commerce anglais avec le Maroc pendant la seconde moitie du XVI siècle', *Revue Africaine* 84 (1940): 186–219, especially 203–5.
8. Cecil T. Carr, ed., *Select Charters of Trading Companies, A.D. 1530–1707* (London, 1913), lviii–lix.
9. George Manwaring, 'A True Discourse of Sir Anthony Sherley's Travel into Persia', in Edward Denison Ross, ed., *Sir Anthony Sherley and his Persian Adventure* (London, 1933), 200, 212, 222.
10. Bennet Woodcroft, ed., *Appendix to Reference Index of Patentees of Inventions* (London, 1855), 9.
11. William Dalrymple, *White Mughals: Love and Betrayal in Eighteenth-Century India* (New York, 2002), 14–15.

12. See, for example, 'The Ceremonies used in Constantinople at the Coronation of Mehemet, the new great Turke, and Successor to Sultan Ibrahim his Father', *The Moderate Intelligencer* no. 215 (26 April –2 May 1649). There was a vast production of various forms of newspapers containing information about the Ottoman Empire: see, for instance, *Newes from divers countries as, from Spaine, Antwerpe, Collin, Venice, Rome, the Turke* (1597); *A coranto Relating diverse particulars concerning the newes out of Italy, Spaine, Turkey, Persia, Bohemia* (1622); and discussions in Dahl Folke, *A Bibliography of English Corantos and Periodical Newsbooks, 1620–1642* (London, 1952), and Gerald MacLean, 'Re-siting the Subject', in Amanda Gilroy and Wil Verhoeven, eds., *Epistolary Histories: Letters, Fiction, Culture* (Charlottesville, VA, 2000), 176–97.
13. On the Shirleys, see Mohammad Taghi Nezam-Mafi, 'Persian Recreations: Theatricality in Anglo-Persian Diplomatic History, 1599–1827' (PhD dissertation, Boston University, 1999), 1–136.
14. Muhammad Rabi' ibn Muhammad Ibrahim, *The Ship of Sulaiman*, trans. John O'Kane (London, 1972), 33.
15. See C. A. Bayly, *Imperial Meridian: The British Empire and the World, 1780–1830* (London, 1989), chapter 1.
16. See A. W. Lawrence, *Trade Castles and Forts of West Africa* (London, 1963), and Charles Fawcett, ed., *The English Factories in India, 1670–1677, vol. 4 (New Series) The Eastern Coast and Bay of Bengal* (Oxford, 1955), 1.
17. See P. J. Marshall, 'The English in Asia to 1700', in Nicholas Canny, ed., *The Oxford History of the British Empire, Volume 1: The Origins of Empire* (Oxford, 1998), 264–85, especially 280–3; and 'The British In Asia: Trade to Dominion, 1700–1765', in P. J. Marshall, ed., *The Oxford History of the British Empire, Volume 2: The Eighteenth Century* (Oxford, 1998), 487–507.
18. In 1679, Haji Muhammad invested 15,000 rupees through Mathias Vincent, chief Bengal Council; see Fawcett, ed., *English Factories . . 1670–1677*, 206.
19. Ibid., 192.
20. William Foster, ed., *The English Factories in India, 1655–1660* (Oxford, 1921), 314, 323–27; see also plans to use force against Persia, 338–47, and Bengal, 392; R. J. Barendse, *The Arabian Seas* (London and New York, 2002), 429.
21. See Miles Ogborn, *Indian Ink: Script and Print in the Making of the English East India Company* (Chicago, 2007).
22. See Nicholas Dew, *Orientalism in Louis XIV's France* (Oxford, 2010).
23. For Jenkinson, see Richard Hakluyt, *The Principal Navigations: Voyages, Traffiques and Discoveries of the English Nation* (1589; rpt. 8 vols. London, 1910), 2: 22; for Kerridge, see William Foster, ed., *Letters Received by the East India Company from its Servants in the East,* 6 vols. (London, 1896–1902), 4: 342.
24. See William Crooke's 'Introduction' to John Fryer, *A New Account of East India and Persia Being Nine Year's Travels, 1672–1681*, 3 vols. (London, 1909).
25. See Joan-Paul Rubiés, *Travel and Ethnology in the Renaissance: South India through European Eyes, 1250–1625* (Cambridge, 2000), 353, and see his 'Historical

Perspectives' in *Travellers and Cosmographers: Studies in the History of Early Modern Ethnology* (Aldershot, 2007). For the earliest writings on India, see the selections from Eldred, Newbery, Fitch, and others in J. Courtenay Locke, ed., *The First Englishmen in India* (London, 1930). Published in Calcutta in 1864 to commemorate the 250th anniversary of the appearance of Purchas's *Hakluytus Posthumus*, J. Talboys Wheeler's edition of *Early Travels in India* managed to remain entirely silent on the topic of Islam.

26. *King Charles His Letter to the Great Turk* (1642), sig A2v.
27. Charles Fawcett, ed., *The English Factories in India, 1678–1684*, vol. III (New Series) *Bombay, Surat, and Malabar Coast* (Oxford, 1954), 420.

CHAPTER 1

1. See Gustav Ungerer, *The Mediterranean Apprenticeship of British Slavery* (Madrid, 2008).
2. For a popular account of the first Englishman in Japan, see Giles Milton, *Samurai William: The Adventurer who Unlocked Japan* (New York, 2002).
3. John Philippson's *A briefe Chronicle of the foure principall Empyres. To witte, of Babilon, Persia, Grecia, and Rome* (1563) was reprinted as *The Key of Historie* (1627).
   Persia was also a land of cruel tyrants and beautiful princesses who featured in ballads and romances such as S. C., *The Famous and Delectable History of Clerocreton and Cloryana* (c. 1660), as well as dramas such as John Denham's *Sophy* (1642), Robert Baron's *Mirza* (1647), and Thomas Crown's *Darius, King of Persia* (1688). The Books of Esther and Daniel also presented a favourable image of the Persians, especially King Cyrus in his assistance to the Jews to rebuild the temple.
4. Guzman de Silva to Philip II, *CSP, Spanish, 1558–67*, 455 (23 July 1565).
5. *A forme to bee used in Common praier every Wednesdaie and Fridaie, within the citie and Dioces of Norwiche: to excite all godlie people to praie unto God for the deliverie of those christians, that are now invaded by the Turke* ([1565]), *A fourme to be used in common prayer every Wednesdaye and Fryedaye within the cittie and dioces of London, for the delivery of those Christians that are now invaded by the Turke* (1565), *A short forme of thanksgeving for the delyverie of the isle of Malta from the invasion and long siege thereof by the great armie of the Turkes* (1565). See also William Keatinge Clay, ed., *Liturgies and Occasional Forms of Prayer Set Forth in the Reign of Queen Elizabeth* (Cambridge, 1847), 519–23, 524–6, 532–3.
6. *A fourme to be used in common prayer every Sunday, Wednesday and Fryday for the preservation of those Christians and their Countreys that are now invaded by the Turke* ([1566]); and see *CSPD, 1547–1580*, 277 (10 August 1566).
7. Suraiya Faroqhi, 'Introduction,' *The Cambridge History of Turkey, Volume 3*, ed. Suraiya Faroqhi (Cambridge, 2006), 3.

8. John Sanderson, *The Travels of John Sanderson in the Levant 1584–1602*, ed. William Foster (London, 1931), 57.
9. George Sandys, *A Relation of a Journey begun An. Dom: 1610* (1615), 200.
10. See Alison Games, *The Web of Empire: English Cosmopolitanism in an Age of Expansion, 1560–1660* (New York, 2008), 74–9.
11. Henri de Castries, *Les Sources Inédites de L'histoire du Maroc... Archives et Bibliothèques D'Angleterre*, 3 vols. (Paris, 1918-35), 2: 143–4.
12. See Yaron Ben-Na'eh, 'Hebrew Printing Houses in the Ottoman Empire', in Gad Nassi, ed., *Jewish Journalism and Publishing Houses in the Ottoman Empire and Modern Turkey* (Istanbul, 2001), 35–82; *The Capitulations and Articles of Peace* (Constantinople, 1663); and Bruce Masters, *Christians and Jews in the Ottoman Arab World: The Roots of Sectarianism* (Cambridge, 2001), 112.
13. See T. S. Willan, 'Some Aspects of English Trade with the Levant in the Sixteenth Century', *English Historical Review* 70 (1955): 399–410, especially 400–1.
14. For Jenkinson's licence, see Hakluyt, *Principal Navigations: Voyages, Traffiques and Discoveries of the English Nation*. 1589; rpt. 8 vols. (London, 1910), 3: 36–8.
15. See Edhem Eldem, 'Capitulations and Western Trade', in Faroqhi, ed., *Cambridge History of Turkey*, 283–335.
16. See William Foster, *England's Quest of Eastern Trade* (1933; rpt. London, 1966), 32–8.
17. See R. W. Ferrier, 'The Terms and Conditions under which English Trade was Transacted with Safavid Persia', *Bulletin of the School of Oriental and African Studies* 49 (1986): 48–66.
18. Robert Morden, *Geography Rectified: Or, A Description of the World* (1680; rpt. 1693), 394.
19. For Jenkinson and Aldersey see Hakluyt, *Principal Navigations*, 1: 456, 3: 78; and see 'Leo Africanus' [Hasan ibn Muhammad al-Wazzan al-Fasi], *Della Descrittione dell'Africa* (Venice, 1550), and *A Geographical Historie of Africa*, trans. John Pory (1600).
20. Henry Timberlake, *A True and Strange Discourse of the Travailes of two English Pilgrimes* (1603); see Joan Taylor, *The Englishman, the Moor and the Holy City* (Stroud, 2006).
21. On Harrison, see *ODNB*.
22. TNA SP 16/373 fos. 144–5. Bradshaw was found guilty by the Privy Council and sent to jail, while Blake was praised: *CSPD, 1637–38*, 206.
23. Fynes Moryson, *An Itinerary Containing His Ten Yeeres Travell* (1617; rpt. 4 vols. Glasgow, 1907), 2: 94; Thomas Smith, *Remarks upon the Manners, Religion and Government of the Turks* (1678), 34, 54.
24. Foster, ed., *The English Factories in India, 1655–1660* (Oxford, 1921), 193.
25. Francis Brooks, *Barbarian Cruelty, Being A True History of the Distressed Condition of the Christian Captives* (1693).
26. See BL Add Ms 47028, fo. 14.

27. *The Arrivall and Intertainements of the Embassador, Alkaid Jaurar Ben Abdella, with his Associate, Mr. Robert Blake* (1637).
28. *Historical Manuscripts Commission Report on the Manuscripts of the Family of Gawdy* (London, 1885), 166.
29. Cited in Brian Vickers, ed., *Shakespeare: The Critical Heritage*, 6 vols. (London, 1974-81), 2: 29.
30. TNA SP 102/2 fo. 96.
31. Sanderson, *Travels*, 240; John Evelyn, *The History of the Three late famous Imposters* (1669), 34.
32. Norman Egbert McClure, ed., *The Letters of John Chamberlain*, 2 vols. (Philadelphia, PA, 1939), 1: 108 (15 October 1600).
33. Thomas Coryate, *Coryats Crudities 1611*, intro. William M. Schutte (London, 1978), 231.
34. See Charlotte Jirousek, 'Ottoman Influences in Western Dress', in Suraiya Faroqhi and Christoph Neumann, eds., *Ottoman Costumes: From Textile to Identity* (Istanbul, 2004), 231–51.
35. 'Abd al-Hadi al-Tazi, 'Muhammad ibn Haddu', *Academia* 2 (1985): 55–80.
36. Imtiaz Habib, *Black Lives in the English Archives, 1500-1677* (Aldershot, 2008), 274–368.
37. John Rawlins, *The Famous and Wonderful Recovery of a Ship of Bristol* (1622), in Daniel Vitkus, ed., *Piracy, Slavery and Redemption: English Captivity Narratives in North Africa, 1577–1704* (New York: 2001), 110; for the rite, see, ibid., 361–7.
38. See Nabil Matar, 'The Last Moors: Maghariba in Britain, 1700–1750', *Journal of Islamic Studies* 14 (2003): 37–58.
39. TNA SP 102/2 fo. 179. Joseph Pitts transliterated many Arabic and Turkish expressions, but he neither knew the difference between the two languages, nor how words and expressions were written. He transcribed what he heard, not what he read; for examples, see *True and Faithful Account of the Religion and Manners of the Mohammetans* (Exeter, 1704), 31, 38, 40, 41, 51–4, 57, 92. Thomas Pellow claims he started learning to write 'Arabick', *The History of the Long Captivity and Adventures of Thomas Pellow, in South-Barbary* (1739), 16.
40. TNA FO 113/1 fos. 18–9 (20 December 1600).
41. TNA SP 71/1 fos. 99, 193.
42. See Gerald MacLean, *Looking East: English Writing and the Ottoman Empire before 1800* (Basingstoke, 2007), chapter 4. On 'Cannary the Algier pirate', see *CSPD, 1686–87*, 176, 191, 204, 234.
43. *A True Declaration of the estate of the Colonie in Virginia* (1610).
44. See David Armitage, *The Ideological Origins of the British Empire* (Cambridge, 2000), and Games, *Web of Empire*, 9.
45. Jenkinson, in Hakluyt, *Principal Navigations*, 2: 21; Hawkins in Samuel Purchas, *Hakluytus Posthumus, or, Purchas His Pilgrimes* (1625; rpt. 20 vols. Glasgow, 1905–7), 3: 14; George Phillips, *The Present State of Tangier* (1676), 34. Hawkins

concludes his account with a detailed description of the 'wealth' of 'the great Mogol', Purchas, *Hakluytus Posthumus*, 3: 29–36.

46. For exceptions, see Dominque Meunier, *Le Consulat Anglais à Tetouan sou Anghtony Hatfeild [sic] (1717–1728)*, preface by Chantal de La Véronne (Tunis, 1980), and the journal of Thomas Baker, English Consul to Libyan Tripoli, 1677–85 examined in C. R. Pennell, ed., *Piracy and Diplomacy in Seventeenth-Century North Africa* (London and Toronto, 1989).
47. Joseph Morgan, *A Complete History of Algiers*, 2 vols. in one (1728): 2: 646.
48. TNA FO 113/1 fo. 119 (12 February 1624).
49. On the survival of captivity tropes from the early modern period, see Khalid Bekkaoui, *In Moorish Thralldom: Narratives by White Women Captives in North Africa* (Basingstoke, forthcoming), preface.
50. See Nabil Matar, *Islam in Britain, 1558–1685* (Cambridge, 1998), chapter 5.
51. *An Extract of several Letters Relating to the Great Charity and Usefulness of Printing the New Testament and Psalter in the Arabick Language* (1720; rpt. 1721), 7.
52. On More, see Matthew Dimmock, *Newe Turkes: Dramatizing Islam and the Ottomans in Early Modern England* (Aldershot, 2005), 25–32.
53. See George W. Forell, 'Luther and the War against the Turks', *Church History* 14 (1945): 256–71; Harvey Buchanan, 'Luther and the Turks 1519–1529', *Archiv für Reformationsgeschichte* 47 (1956): 145–60; Adam S. Francisco, *Martin Luther and Islam* (Leiden, 2007); Jacques Pannier, 'Calvin et les Turcs' [Mélanges], *Revue Historique* 180 (1937): 268–86.
54. Our thanks to Professor Tom Freeman for this date.
55. John Foxe, *The Acts and Monuments of John Foxe*, ed. George Townsend (1843–49; rpt, 8 vols., New York, 1965), 4: 122.
56. See Thomas Brightman, *A Revelation of the Apocalyps* (Amsterdam, 1611) and *A Most Comfortable Exposition of the Prophecie of Daniel* (Amsterdam[?], 1635); for European contexts, see Kenneth M. Setton, *Western Hostility to Islam and Prophecies of Turkish Doom* (Philadelphia, PA, 1992).
57. Among numerous studies of English millenarianism which refer to the 'Turks', see: R. Clouse, 'The Influence of John Henry Alistead on English Millenarian Thought in the Seventeenth Century' (PhD dissertation, State University of Iowa, 1963); Peter Toon, ed., *Puritans, the Millennium and the Future of Israel* (Cambridge and London, 1970); Katharine R. Firth, *The Apocalyptic Tradition in Reformation Britain, 1530–1645* (Oxford, 1979). On Milton's views of Islam, see Gerald MacLean, 'Milton, Islam and the Ottomans', in Sharon Achinstein and Elizabeth Sauer, eds., *Milton and Toleration* (Oxford, 2007), 284–98, and 'Milton Among the Muslims', in Andrew Hadfield and Matthew Dimmock, eds., *The Religions of the Book: Conflict and Co-Existence, 1400–1660* (Basingstoke, 2008), 180–94.
58. Scholarship on dramatic representations of 'Turks' and Moors has become extensive, but see Jack D'Amico, *The Moor in English Renaissance Drama* (Tampa, FL, 1991); Emily C. Bartels, *Spectacles of Strangeness: Imperialism,*

Alienation and Marlowe (Philadelphia, PA, 1993); Daniel J. Vitkus, *Turning Turk: English Theatre and the Multicultural Mediterranean, 1570–1630* (New York, 2003), and Vitkus, ed., *Three Turk Plays from Early Modern England* (New York, 2000); Jonathan Burton, *Traffic and Turning: Islam and English Drama, 1579–1624* (Newark, DE, 2005); Linda McJannet, *The Sultan Speaks: Dialogue in English Plays and Histories about the Ottoman Turks* (New York, 2006); and Lara Bovilsky, *Barbarous Play: Race on the English Renaissance Stage* (Minneapolis, MN, 2008). By contrast, Restoration plays set in the Islamic world such as Dryden's *Aureng-Zebe* (1676) remain relatively unexplored except in Bridget Orr's *Empire on the English Stage, 1660–1714* (Cambridge, 2007), chapter 3 especially. See also Michèle Longino, *Orientalism in French Classical Drama* (Cambridge, 2002).

59. See Anthony Parr, ed., *Three Renaissance Travel Plays* (1995; rpt. Manchester, 1999), 10–12.
60. William Painter, *The palace of pleasure beautified* (1566), fos. 107–12.
61. See Galina Yermolenko, ed., *Roxolana in History and Literature* (Aldershot, 2010).
62. *The Most Ancient and Famous History of the Renowned Prince Arthur* (1634), chapter XCVII.
63. On the popularity of itinerant print-sellers, see the contemporary image reproduced in David Woodward, *Maps as Prints in the Italian Renaissance* (London, 1996), 94.
64. On tapestries designed and woven between 1546 and 1554, see Lisa Jardine and Jerry Brotton, *Global Interests: Renaissance Art Between East and West* (London, 2000), 83–6; Jerry Brotton, 'Carthage and Tunis, *The Tempest* and Tapestries', in Peter Hulme and William H. Sherman, eds., *'The Tempest' and its Travels* (London, 2000), 132–7; and Javier Lobato Domínguez and Angel Martín Esteban, *Reales Alcazares de Sevilla* (Barcelona, 1998), 56–61.
65. Holland Cotter, 'The Splendor of Tapestries Both Opulent and Complex', *New York Times*, 15 March 2002, B33.
66. Torquato Tasso, *Godfrey of Bulloigne*, trans. Edward Fairfax (1600); a partial translation by Richard Carew had appeared in 1594. The tapestries depicting the story of Rinaldo and Armida are now at the Victoria and Albert Museum, London.
67. See Joan Allgrove McDowell, 'Elizabethan Embroidery at Hardwick Hall,' *Hali* 10: 4 (July–August 1988): 16–25.
68. See MacLean, *Looking East*, 27–31.
69. Matthew Dimmock, 'Britain and the Prophet Muhammad: Precedents and Paradigms', unpublished paper delivered at 'Britain and the Muslim World: Historical Perspectives' (University of Exeter, April 2009).
70. The National Gallery of Art, Washington, DC 'The Crucifixion' by the Umbrian Luca Signorelli (1445/50–1523) also shows soldiers flying the Turkish crescent surrounding the Cross.

71. See Peter Doyle, ed., *Butler's Lives of the Saints: October* (Collegeville, MN, 1996), 45.
72. Franklin Le Van Baumer, 'The Conception of Christendom in Renaissance England', *Journal of the History of Ideas* 6 (1945): 131–56; and see the same author's 'England, the Turk, and the Common Corps of Christendom', *American Historical Review* 50 (1944): 26–43.
73. See *A True Copy of a letter sent from Vienna, September the 2d, N. S. by an eminent English officer* (1683); *Count Taaffe's Letters from the Imperial Camp, to his Brother, the Earl of Carlingford here in London* (1684); *The bloody siege of Vienna: A Song* ([1688]). See also Janusz J. Tomiak, 'A British Poet's Account of the Raising of the Siege of Vienna in 1683', *Polish Review* 5 (1966): 66–74.
74. Joshua Gee, *The Trade and Navigation of Great-Britain Considered* (Glasgow, 1750), 9.
75. Antoine Geuffroy, *The order of the greate Turckes courte* (1542), sigs. Aii–Aiii.
76. *Mahometis Abdallae filii theologia dialogo explicata* ([Vienna? Nürnberg?] 1543); there is a copy in the Lambeth Palace Library, shelfmark C130.(W5).
77. See, for example, Thomas Lanquet, *Coopers Chronicle unto the late death of Queen Marie* (1560), 159–60.
78. Peter Heylyn, for example, claimed that 'Osman the fourth Caliph... got a sight of all Mahomets papers which he reduced into four Volumes, and divided into one hundred twenty and four Chapters' of the Qur'an; *Cosmographie in foure Bookes* (1652), bk. 3, 122. Even as late as 1671, it could be claimed that the Phoenix was still to be found in Arabia; see George Meriton, *A Geographical Description of the World* (1671), 164–5.
79. John Mandeville, *The Travels of John Mandeville* (New York, 1964), 95. The story involving the herd of swine has been traced back to a Pisan manuscript by Augusto Mancini, 'Per lo Studio della leggenda di Maometto in Occidente', *Rendiconti della R. Accademia Nazionale dei Lincei*, 6th series, 10 (Rome, 1934): 325–49.
80. Aaron Hill, *A Full and Just Account of the Present State of the Ottoman Empire* (1709), 46.
81. [Nathaniel Crouch], 'R. B.', *The Strange and Prodigious Religions, Customs, and Manners of Sundry Nations* (1683), 49. On 'Mahometan sodomy', see Nabil Matar, *Turks, Moors and Englishmen in the Age of Discovery* (New York, 1999), 114.
82. *Machumetis Saracenorum principis, eiúsque successorum vitae, ac doctrina, ipséque Alcoran... Haec omnia in unum volumen redacta sunt, opera & studio Theodori Bibliandri* (Basle, 1543); *L'Alcorano di Macometto, nel qual si contiene la dottrina, la vita, i costumi, et le leggi sue* ([Venice], 1547); *Alcoranus Mahometicus oder: Tuerckenglaub aus des Mahomets eygenem Buch genañt Alcoran* (Frankfurt am Mayn, 1604). See Ziad Elmarsafy, *The Englightenment Qur'an: The Politics of Translation and the Construction of Islam* (Oxford, 2009), 5–8.
83. Henry Smith, *Gods Arrow Against Atheists* (1593; rpt. 1604), 48. First published in 1593, this sermon was reprinted in 1604, 1607, 1609, 1611, 1614, 1617, 1618, 1622, 1628, 1631, 1632, 1637, 1656, 1657, 1675, and 1676.

84. Ibid., 50.
85. See Matthew Dimmock, ed., *William Percy's 'Mahomet and His Heaven'* (Aldershot, 2006).
86. William Bedwell, *Mohammedis Imposturae: that is, A Discovery of the Manifold Forgeries, Falshoods, and horrible impieties of the blasphemous Seducer Mohammed* (1615), sigs A2, A2v.
87. Alastair Hamilton, *William Bedwell The Arabist, 1563–1632* (Leiden, 1985), 66, 67.
88. See David Pailin, *Attitudes to Other Religions: Comparative Religion in Seventeenth- and Eighteenth-century Britain* (Manchester, 1984), 82.
89. *CSPD, 1649–50*, 42, 45–6, 59, 63, 70.
90. BL shelfmark E. 533.3. Previously, on 23 April, a work that does not seem to have been printed, was entered into the *Stationers' Registers*, entitled 'The generall history of the religion of the Turkes togither with the sumaries conteyning the birth life & death of their prophett Mahomitt'; Edward Arber, ed. *A Transcript of the Registers of the Worshipful Company of Stationers; from 1640–1708*, 3 vols. (London, 1913), 1: 317; and see G. J. Toomer, *Eastern Wisdome and Learning* (Oxford, 1996), 200–1.
91. *The Alcoran of Mahomet, Translated out of Arabique into French . . . And newly Englished, for the satisfaction of all that desire to look into the Turkish Vanities* (1649), sig. Dd7v; cited from the British Library copy, shelfmark BL 306.44.B.2.
92. Ibid., 411, sig. Ee2v.
93. Elmarsafy, *Enlightenment Qur'an*, 9. See also chapter 1 for a helpful survey of European translations of the Qur'an.
94. Richard Baxter, *The Reasons of the Christian Religion* (1667), 198–204.
95. Ibid., 203.
96. See James R. Jacob, *Henry Stubbe, Radical Protestantism and the Early Enlightenment* (Cambridge, 1983), and Nabil Matar, 'Some Notes on George Fox and Islam', *The Journal of the Friends' Historical Society* 55 (1989): 271–6.
97. The text was written between 1604 to 1607 while Bon was serving as the Venetian *bailo* in Istanbul. The first English translation appeared as *A Description of the Grand Signior's Seraglio*, trans. Robert Withers (1650; rpt. 1653).
98. See William Biddulph, *The Travels of certaine Englishmen into Africa, Asia, Troy, Bithnia, Thracia, and to the Blacke Sea* (1609), T. S., *The Adventures of (Mr T. S.) An English Merchant* (1670), and Gerald MacLean, *The Rise of Oriental Travel: English Visitors to the Ottoman Mediterranean, 1580–1720* (Basingstoke, 2004), parts 2 and 4.
99. T[homas] H[erbert], *A Relation of some Yeares Travaile, Begunne Anno 1626. Into Afrique and the greater Asia, especially the Territories of the Persian Monarchie: and some parts of the Orientall Indies, and Iles adjacent* (1634), 147.
100. Paul Rycaut, *The Present State of the Ottoman Empire* (1667; enlarged, 1670), 38.
101. Judy Mabro, *Veiled Half-Truths: Western Travellers' Perception of Middle Eastern Women* (London, 1996), 2.

102. See for example Pitts, *True and Faithful*, 12–13; reproduced in Vitkus, ed., *Piracy*, 233.
103. Pitts, *True and Faithful*, sig. A4, and see 61 and 69 for criticism of other writers; in Vitkus, ed. *Piracy*, 221, 262, 268.
104. Iain Macleod Higgins, 'Shades of the East: Orientalism, Religion, and Nation in Late Medieval Scottish Literature', *Journal of Medieval and Early Modern Studies* 38: 2 (2008): 197–228, this passage 205.
105. Christopher Hill, *The Century of Revolution* (1961; rpt. London, 1974), 145–6.
106. See Christopher Tyerman, *England and the Crusades, 1095–1588* (Chicago and London, 1988), chapter 13.
107. Zayn al-Din ibn 'Abd al-Aziz al-Malibari, *Tuhfat al-mujahidin fi ba'd akhbar al-urtughaliyin*, trans. Muhammad Husayn Nainar (Madras, 1942); for an early eighteenth-century account, see Hasan Taj al-Din, *The Islamic History of the Maldive Islands*, ed. Hikoichi Yajima, 2 vols. (Tokyo, 1984).
108. Wheeler M. Thackston, trans. and ed., *The Jahangirnama, Memoirs of Jahangir, Emperor of India* (New York and Oxford, 1999), 40.
109. For Muslim captives in Portugal, see Ahmad Bu Sharb, 'Mawarid al-Maghariba al-muqimin bi-l-Burtughal khilal al-qarn al-sadis 'ashar', *Majalat Kuliyat al-Adab wa-l 'Ulum al-Insaninyah* 19 (1994): 87–103 and his more detailed study, *Magharibah fi al-Burtughal* (Rabat, 1996); for Muslim captives in Malta, see the reference to 5,500 captives in Ahmad ibn Qasim al-Hajari, *Kitab Nair al-Din 'ala'l-Qawm al-Kafirin*, eds. and trans. P. S. Van Koningsveld et al. (Madrid, 1997), 83; for Muslim captives in British hands, see Nabil Matar, *Britain and Barbary, 1589–1689* (Gainesville, FL, 2005), chapter 4.

CHAPTER 2

1. See Samuel Huntington, *The Clash of Civilizations And the Remaking of World Order* (1997; rpt London, 2002), 207–12.
2. For a survey of the development of the image of Elizabeth, see Julia M. Walker, *The Elizabeth Icon, 1603–2003* (Basingstoke, 2004).
3. Henry Timberlake, Henry, *A True and Strange Discourse of the Travailes of two English Pilgrimes* (1603), 8.
4. See Nabil Matar, *Britain and Barbary, 1589–1689* (Gainesville, FL, 2005), 36–7.
5. See Gerald MacLean, *Looking East: English Writing and the Ottoman Empire before 1800* (Basingstoke, 2007), chapter 4.
6. See Gerald MacLean, 'East by North-East: The English among the Russians, 1553–1603', in Jyotsna Singh, ed., *A Companion to the Global Renaissance* (Oxford, 2009): 163–77.
7. See Richard Hakluyt, *The Principal Navigations: Voyages, Traffiques and Discoveries of the English Nation*. 1589; rpt. 8 vols. (London, 1910), 3: 52–72, 87–8, 4: 18–20; and Susan A. Skilliter, 'Three Letters from the Ottoman "Sultana"

Safiye to Queen Elizabeth I', in S. M. Stern, ed., *Documents from Islamic Chanceries* (Oxford, 1965), 119–57.
8. See Leslie Peirce, *The Imperial Harem: Women and Sovereignty in the Ottoman Empire* (Ithaca, NY, 1993).
9. Hakluyt, *Principal Navigations*, 3: 54.
10. Mustafa ibn Ibrahim Safi, *Zubdetu't-tevarih* (Beyazit Devlet Library, Istanbul University), fo. 32; trans. Geoffrey Lewis; cited from Gerald MacLean, *The Rise of Oriental Travel: English Visitors to the Ottoman Empire, 1580–1720* (Basingstoke, 2004), xii. On Ottoman diplomacy, see Palmira Brummett, 'A Kiss is Just a Kiss: Rituals of Submission along the East-West Divide', in Matthew Birchwood and Matthew Dimmock, eds., *Cultural Encounters Between East and West: 1453–1699* (Newcastle, 2005), 107–31, and Gerald MacLean, 'Performing at the Ottoman Porte in 1599: The Case of Henry Lello', in Ralf Hertel, ed., *Cultures at Play: Encounters with the East in the Early Modern Age* (Ashgate, forthcoming).
11. Skilliter, 'Three Letters', 122, 134.
12. The letter can be found at BL Ms Cott on Nero B.viii. fos. 61–3; similarly, a letter to Elizabeth from Sultan Mehmed of December 1599 is signed at the top with a fine *tuğra* in gold leaf; ibid., fo. 47; see Skilliter, 'Three Letters', 122, 121.
13. Ibid., 123, 132.
14. Richard Wrag in Hakluyt, *Principal Navigations*, 4: 1–18, this passage, 8. Skilliter points out that Wrag's catalogue of the gifts Elizabeth sent agrees with the inventory to be found in BL Ms Cotton Nero B.xi. fo. 124; 'Three Letters', 146 n. 25.
15. Ibid., 147.
16. Ibid., 131–2.
17. Ibid., 132–3.
18. Ibid., 147.
19. Ibid., 134, 151.
20. Ibid., 139. Bernadette Andrea presents an illuminating discussion of this exchange in *Women and Islam in Early Modern English Literature* (Cambridge, 2007), 12–29.
21. Abu Faris 'Abd al-'Aziz al-Fishtali, *Manahil al-safa' fi ma'athir mawalina al-shurafa'*, ed. 'Abd al-Karim Karim (Rabat, 1972), 49.
22. TNA SP 102/4 fo. 20.
23. Al-Fishtali, *Manahil al-safa'*, 101.
24. Quoted in J. N. Hillgarth, *The Mirror of Spain, 1500–1700* (Ann Arbor, MI, 2000), 366.
25. Henri De Castries, *Les Sources Inédites de L'histoire du Maroc... Archives et Bibliothèques D'Angleterre*. 3 vols. (Paris, 1918–35), 1: 455–7, 468–75.
26. António de Saldanha, *Cronica de Almançor, Sultao de Marrocos (1578–1603)*, ed. António Dias Fariha, trans. Leon Bourdon (Lisbon, 1997), chapter 47.
27. De Castries, *Les Sources.... D'Angleterre*, 1: 490–1.

28. Al-Fishtali, *Manahil al-safa'*, 96.
29. Ibid., 170.
30. Jamil M. Abun-Nasr, *A History of the Maghrib* (1971; rpt. Cambridge, 1993), 211.
31. *CSP, Foreign, January–July 1589*, 17. Al-Mansur's promises were treated as realities by European observers: in November 1588, it was reported from Antwerp that Don Antonio had actually been given by the Barbary king '100 ships'; Victor von Klarwill, ed., *The Fugger News-Letters, Second Series*, trans. L. S. R. Byrne (London, 1926), 183.
32. Henri de Castries, *Les Sources inédites de l'Histoire du Maroc, Dynastie Saadienne, Archives et Bibliothèques de France*, Series 1, 2 vols. (Paris, 1905–11), 1: 498–9.
33. Al-Fishtali, *Manahil al-safa'*, 101.
34. He had left by 10 November 1588: see Klarwill, ed., *Fugger News-Letters, Second Series*, 182.
35. Al-Fisthali, *Manahil al-safa'*, 101.
36. Abdallah Gannun, ed. *Rasa'il Sa'adiyya* (Tetuan, 1954), 165.
37. De Castries, *Les Sources . . . D'Angleterre*, 2: 34–39; *Calendar of Letters and State Papers . . . Archives of Simancas*, 4: 580–1.
38. De Castries, *Les Sources . . . D'Angleterre*, 2: 36, 38: 'Si no quisierdes conceder lo que con tanta razon os pedimos, allende que nos tendremos occasion de hazer tanto menos caso de vuestr'amistad, sabemos tambien de cierto qu'el Gran Turco, el qual usa de mucho favor y humanidad con nuestros vassalos, no tendra a bien que los maltrateys por dar contento a los Españoles.' Thanks to Anna Montoya for the translation.
39. *CSP, Scotland, 1589–1593*, 404. See also Francis Bacon, *Observations on a Libel*: 'he saith England is confederate with the great Turk', in *Works*, ed. James Spedding et al., 14 vols. (London, 1857–85), 8: 204.
40. See al-Fishtali, *Manahil al-safa'*, 187, where similar titles are applied to the Sultan of Mecca.
41. De Castries, *Les Sources . . . D'Angleterre*, 2: 18–20.
42. Not much research has been conducted on the rhetoric of Maghribian letters. See the brief discussion by Al-Tahir Muhammad Tuwat, *Adab al-rasa'il fi al-Maghrib al-Arabi* (Algiers, 1993), 258–69, and see Adrian Gully, *The Culture of Letter-Writing in Pre-Modern Islamic Society* (Edinburgh, 2008).
43. Quoted in Muhammad al-Gharbi, *Bidayat al-hukm al-Maghribi fi al-Sudan al-gharbi* (Baghdad, 1982), 667.
44. At the time, al-Mansur felt superior to Philip II. In the first letter al-Mansur sent to Philip after the Moroccan victory at Wadi al-Makhazen in March 1579, he addressed the Spanish king as 'the great sultan of status and place, of ancient blood and great deeds, the king of the Christian denomination and its great one, the centre of that circle, who has praiseworthy qualities, sultan don Philip son of the great sultans, known for their majesty': after all, Philip had become king of Portugal and its colonial possession, too: see Dario Cabanelas, 'Ortas

Cartas del Sultan de Marruecos Ahmad al-Mansur a Felipe II', *Miscelanea de Estudios Arabes y Hebraicos* 7 (1958), 13–14. By the late 1580s, however, with Spain in decline after the defeat of its armada, Philip II became the *taghiya*, as al-Fishtali confirmed.

45. See Nabil Matar, 'The Maliki Imperialism of Ahmad al-Mansur: The Moroccan Invasion of Sudan, 1591', in *Imperialisms*, ed. Elizabeth Sauer and Balchandra Rajan (New York, 2004), 147–61.
46. Saldanha, *Cronica*, chapter 96.
47. Ibrahim Harakat, *Al-Siyasah wa-l-Mujtama'fi al-'Asr al-Sa'di* (Al-Dar al-Bayda', 1987), 82.
48. It is not clear whether the month was Jamadi I or II. J. F. Hopkins, *Letters from Barbary, 1576–1774* (Oxford, 1982), 5, has January; De Castries has March.
49. TNA SP 102/4 fo. 30.
50. De Castries, *Les Sources ... D'Angleterre*, 2: 70.
51. Gannun, ed., *Rasa'il Sa'adiyya*, 59.
52. R. B. Wernham, *The Return of the Armadas* (Oxford, 1994), 108.
53. *CSPV, 1592–1603*, 216.
54. The Fugger informant stated that al-Mansur had sent 'five galleys from Barbary' to assist the English and had also given permission to the English fleet 'to put into Barbary and obtain provisions and other military stores'; Klarwill, ed., *Fugger News-Letters, Second Series*, 278. Another report alleged six thousand Barbary soldiers accompanied Don Antonio; de Castries, *Les Sources ... D'Angleterre*, 2: 94n. Actually, al-Mansur had sent three galleys which reached Cadiz on 25 June 1596: though they did not take part in the military action, they provided the English fleet with provisions and ammunition; see de Castries, *Les Sources D'Angleterre, 2: 229 n. 3*.
55. An-Nasir ibn Ghalib had escaped to Lisbon after the defeat of his father, Muhammad al-Mutawakkil, at the battle of Alcazar. In early 1595, an-Nasir crossed to the Spanish-controlled port of Melilla on the Moroccan Mediterranean coast with an army consisting of Morisco mercenaries and a number of political refugees from Morocco. The invasion proved unsuccessful: after two battles between an-Nasir and al-Mansur's son, ash-Sheikh al-Ma'mun, the invader was defeated and killed: see Richard L. Smith, *Ahmad Al-Mansur* (New York, 2006), 136–40.
56. De Castries, *Les Sources ... D'Angleterre*, 2: 103.
57. Al-Fishtali, *Manahil al-safa'*, 187. For a translation of the letter, see Nabil Matar, *Europe Through Arab Eyes, 1578–1727* (New York, 2009), 144–7.
58. Al-Fishtali, *Manahil al-safa'*, 197.
59. The Venetian ambassador in Spain reported the rumour that the English fleet carried arms to 'supply the Moreschi of Andalusia, who are ready to make a rising, and that, in order to support them, the English may very likely have opened communications with the Schereef [al-Mansur]', *CSPV, 1592–1603*, 216.
60. De Castries, *Les Sources ... D'Angleterre*, 2: 106.

61. Klarwill, ed., *Fugger News-Letters, Second Series*, 295.
62. De Castries, *Les Sources . . . D'Angleterre*, 2: 121.
63. Ibid., 2: 137.
64. Thomas Heywood, *The Fair Maid of the West, Parts I and II*, edited by Robert K. Turner (Lincoln, NE, 1967).
65. As Warner G. Rice pointed out, Heywood's Mullisheq could have derived from the names of any of three men who went by that name: 'The Moroccan Episode in Thomas Heywood's "The Fair Maid of the West"', *Philological Quarterly* 9 (1930): 131–40. Earlier, Shakespeare may have drawn on historical information: see Gustav Ungerer, "Portia and the Prince of Morocco", *Shakespeare Studies*, 31 (2003): 89–129; and Nabil Matar and Rudolph Stoeckel, 'Europe's Mediterranean Other: The Moor', in Andrew Hadfield and Paul Hammond, eds. *The Arden Critical Companions* (London, 2004), 230–52.
66. De Castries, *Les Sources . . . D'Angleterre*, 2: 208–9.
67. Ibid., 2: 210–11.
68. Ibid., 2: 221, see also 2: 131.
69. Al-Fishtali, *Manahil al-safa'*, 194.
70. For Moors on the Elizabethan stage, see D'Amico, *The Moor;* Matar, *Britain and Barbary*, chapter 1; and Emily Bartels, *Speaking of the Moor: from Alcazar to Othello* (Philadelphia, PA, 2008).
71. For this paragraph, see Laura Jane Fenella Coulter, 'The Involvement of the English Crown and its Embassy in Constantinople with Pretenders to the Throne of the principality of Moldavia between the years 1583 and 1620, with particular reference to the pretender Stefan Bogdan between 1590 and 1612' (PhD dissertation, University of London, 1993).
72. On Walter Leslie, see *ODNB*.
73. On the Shirleys, see Samuel Chew, *The Crescent and the Rose: Islam and England During the Renaissance* (New York, 1937), and R. M. Savory, 'The Sherley Myth', *Iran* 5 (1967): 73–81. Important contemporary accounts include Anthony Nixon, *The Three English Brothers* (1607), and the play by John Day, William Rowley, and George Wilkins, *The Travailes of The Three English Brothers* (1607).
74. See Hakluyt, *Principal Navigations*, 1: 318, 303; T. S. Willan, *The Early History of the Russia Company, 1553–1603* (1956; rpt. Manchester, 1968), 7–8; William Foster, *England's Quest of Eastern Trade* (1933; rpt. London, 1966), 8–13; and MacLean, 'East by North-East'.
75. See Roger Savory, *Iran under the Safavids* (Cambridge, 1980), 110–13.
76. Jenkinson, in E. Delmar Morgan and C. H. Coote, eds., *Early Voyages and Travels to Russia and Persia by Anthony Jenkinson and Other Englishmen*, 2 vols. (London, 1886), 1: 147, 148; and see Kurosh Meshkat, 'The Journey of Master Anthony Jenkinson to Persia (1562)' (MA thesis, University of Oslo, 2005), for detailed analysis of how this episode has been variously interpreted.

77. Subsequent attempts in the eighteenth century to revive the overland route through Russia were similarly abandoned: see Jonas Hanway, *An Historical Account of the British Trade over the Caspian Sea: with a Journal of Travels from London through Russia into Persia,* 4 vols. (London, 1753).
78. Newberry's account of his journey appeared in Purchas, *Hakluytus Posthumus, or, Purchas His Pilgrimes.* 1625; rpt. 20 vols. (Glasgow, 1905–7), 8: 449–81, and see Foster, *England's Quest,* 79–89.
79. See Douglas Carruthers, ed., *The Desert Route to India* (London, 1929), Introduction.
80. Hakluyt, *Principal Navigations,* 3: 204. This account by Caesar Frederick would form the basis for Ralph Fitch's later report of his journey, as recorded in Hakluyt, *Principal Navigations,* 3: 281–321. On Fitch see J. Horton Ryley, *Ralph Fitch, England's Pioneer to India* (London, 1899), and Michael Edwardes, *Ralph Fitch: Elizabethan in the Indies* (London, 1972).
81. Hakluyt, *Principal Navigations,* 3: 271: 'I have made very earnest inquirie both there [Tripoli] and here [Aleppo], for the booke of Cosmographie of Abilfada Ismael, but by no means can hear of it.' On Abu'l-Fida's reputation in Europe, see Toomer, *Eastern Wisedome and Learning: The Study of Arabic in Seventeenth Century England* (Oxford, 1996), 169–74.
82. *Macbeth,* 1. 3. 7.
83. Hakluyt, *Principal Navigations* 3: 289. See Edwardes, *Ralph Fitch,* 29–45 for a narrative account of the journey.
84. Hakluyt, *Principal Navigations,* 3: 290.
85. Alfred C. Wood, *A History of the Levant Company* (1935; rpt. London, 1964), 21.
86. Savory, *Iran,* 113.
87. Cited in Wood, *History,* 76.
88. Robert Brenner, *Merchants and Revolution: Commercial Change, Political Conflict, and London's Overseas Traders, 1550–1663* (Cambridge, 1993), 25, citing figures compiled by A. M. Willard, 'The Import Trade of London, 1600–1640' (PhD dissertation, University of London, 1956), appendix 2.
89. Wood, *History,* 48, and Foster, *England's Quest,* 297–8; and see C. H. Wilson, 'Cloth Production and International Competition in the Seventeenth Century', *EHR,* 2nd series, 13 (1960): 209–21.
90. See R. W. Ferrier, 'The Terms and Conditions under which English Trade was Transacted with Safavid Persia', *Bulletin of the School of Oriental and African Studies* 49 (1986): 48–66, and Rudolph Matthee, *The Politics of Trade in Safavid Iran: Silk for Silver, 1600–1730* (Cambridge, 1999), chapter 4.
91. See C. R. Boxer, 'Anglo-Portuguese Rivalry in the Persian Gulf, 1615–1635', in Edgar Prestage, ed., *Chapters in Anglo-Portuguese Relations* (Watford, 1935), 46–129. Willem Floor, 'The Dutch and the Persian Silk Trade', in Charles Melville, ed., *Safavid Persia: The History and Politics of an Islamic Society* (London, 1996), 323–68, provides a useful comparative analysis.

92. Sir John Finett, *Finetti Philoxenis: Som Choice Observations of Sir John Finett Knight, And Master of Ceremonies to the two last Kings*, ed. James Howell (1656), 174. See also Robert Stodart, *The Journal of Robert Stodart*, ed. E. Denison Ross (London, 1935), 14.
93. On Naqd 'Ali's affair, see Matar, *Europe*, 109, quoting BL East India Company Court Minutes, B/11, fos. 451 and 470. Dated 15 April 1626, Charles's 'Instructions' to Dodmore Cotton are transcribed in Stodart, *Journal*, 17–20, from original manuscript copies held in the Library of All Soul's College, Oxford at Owen Wynne Mss, XII: 144 and XXII: 84. See R. W. Ferrier, 'The European Diplomacy of Shah 'Abbas I and the First Persian Embassy to England', *Iran* 11 (1973): 75–92.
94. After the success of the 1634 edition, a revised and enlarged second edition appeared in 1638 and was reprinted, with further revisions and additional engraved illustrations, in 1665 and 1677. Quotations here are from *Some Yeares Travels into Africa and Asia the Great* (1638), 35, and do not appear in the earlier edition.
95. Ibid. Herbert's claim concerning Coryate's grave has been disputed; see Charles Nicholl, 'Field of Bones', *London Review of Books* (2 September 1999), accessed online 12 July 2009.
96. In addition to Herbert's account, see 'A Relation of Sir D. Cotton's Embassy', probably by Dr Henry Gooch, chaplain to the English in Persia, which offers a further contemporary report of the three deaths, transcribed in Stodart, *Journal*, 26–32, and see also William Foster's 'Introduction' to his edition of *Thomas Herbert, Travels in Persia 1627–1629* (London, 1928), especially xxiv–xxxi.
97. Denis Wright, 'Great Britain' in *Encyclopaedia Iranica*, ed. Ehsan Yarshater, Volume XI, Fascicle 2 (New York, 2002), 200–24; see 201–2.
98. Foster, *England's Quest of Eastern Trade*. 1933; rpt. (London, 1966), 173–82; and see Ram Chandra Prasad, *Early English Travellers in India* (1965; rpt. Delhi, 1980), 63–81.
99. BL Add Ms 6115 fo. 148, cited by Michael Strachan, *Sir Thomas Roe, 1581–1644: A Life* (London, 1989), 290 n. 32. Hawkins' journal can be found in William Foster, ed., *Early Travels in India, 1583–1619* (1921; rpt. Delhi, 1968) and Purchas, *Hakluytus Posthumus*, 3: 1–51.
100. Foster, *England's Quest*, 184–93.
101. Ibid., 194–7.
102. Ibid., 238–9; and see Marshall, 'The English in Asia', in Canny, ed., *Oxford History of the British Empire*: 1: 272.
103. Cited in Foster, *England's Quest*, 237–8; and see William Foster, ed., *The Voyage of Thomas Best to the East Indies, 1612–1614* (London, 1934).
104. William Foster, ed., *The Voyage of Nicholas Downton to the East Indies, 1614–1615* (1939; rpt. New Delhi, 1997), 3.
105. Ibid., xxviii, and see 80–123, and 155–9.

106. *Stow's Annals* (1615), cited in Thomas Roe, *The Embassy of Sir Thomas Roe to India, 1615–19*, ed. William Foster (1899; rev. 1926; rpt. New Delhi, 1990), xiii.
107. Roe, *Embassy*, 30. On Roe's imperious manner, see Richmond Barbour, *Before Orientalism: London's Theatre of the East* (Cambridge, 2003), 178–83, and MacLean, *Looking East*, 112–15.
108. Roe, *Embassy*, 27–8; and see Strachan, *Roe*, 75.
109. Roe, *Embassy*, 83.
110. Ibid., 115.
111. Strachan, *Roe*, 84.
112. TNA CO 77/1 fo. 67; printed in Roe, *Embassy*, 506–7.
113. Roe in Purchas, *Hakluytus Posthumus*, 4: 361; and see Kate Teltscher, *India Inscribed: European and British Writing on India 1600–1800* (Delhi, 1995), 20–8.
114. Marshall, 'English in Asia', 274.

CHAPTER 3

1. Nathaniel Crouch], 'R. B.,' *The English Acquisitions in Guinea and East-India* (London, 1700), title page.
2. Evidently, ad hoc slavery tempted some English mariners. In 1677, English sailors who had 'been several months on the coast of Guinea, where they took in 82 negroes and land them at Barbados except 6 or 7 that died in their passage. They sold them at good rates': *CSPD, 1676–77*, 246. Unlike the Dutch, however, the English obeyed the prohibition in Bengal and other parts of India not to 'purchase any slaves that were the children of Muhammadans', Fawcett, ed., *The English Factories in India, 1678–1684, vol.3 (New Series) Bombay, Surat, and Malabar Coast*. Oxford, 1954, 222. For the women, see John Luke, *Tangier at High Tide: The Journal of John Luke, 1670–1673*, ed. Helen Andrews Kaufman (Paris, 1958), 110 (entry for March 1672).
3. There was also the category of 'provider', a man officially designated by a Company or the Admiralty to facilitate trade in a port city: see *CSPD, 1656–57*, 273.
4. Foster, ed., *Letters Received by the East India Company from its Servants in the East*. 6 vols. London, 1896–1902. [volume 1 edited by Danvers], 2: 134.
5. See T. S. Willan, 'The Factor or Agent in Foreign Trade', chapter 1 of his *Studies in Elizabethan Foreign Trade* (1959; rpt. Manchester, 1968), 1–33, and James Mather, *Pashas: Traders and Travellers in the Islamic World*. New Haven and London, 2009, 72–102.
6. Daniel Goffman, *Britons in the Ottoman Empire, 1642–1660* (Seattle, WA, 1998), 24.
7. Richard Hakluyt, *The Principal Navigations: Voyages, Traffiques and Discoveries of the English Nation*. 1589; rpt. 8 vols. London, 1910, 3: 140.

8. On consuls in Aleppo, Alexandria, Istanbul and the Levant, see Niels Steensgaard, 'Consuls and Nations in the Levant from 1570–1650', *The Scandinavian Economic History Review* 15 (1967): 13–54.
9. See Gerald MacLean, *Looking East: English Writing and the Ottoman Empire before 1800* (Basingstoke, 2007), 73–4.
10. See Susan Skilliter, *William Harborne and the Trade with Turkey, 1578–1582* (Oxford, 1977), 82, 145.
11. Constantin Marinesco, 'Introduction', to E. D. Tappe, ed. *Documents concerning Rumanian History (1427–1601) collected from British Archives* (Hague, 1964), 8; William Biddulph, *The Travels of certaine Englishmen into Africa, Asia, Troy, Bithnia, Thracia, and to the Blacke Sea* (1609), 40; and Thomas Glover, 'The Journey of Edward Barton', in Purchas, *The Travels of certaine Englishmen into Africa, Asia, Troy, Bithnia, Thracia, and to the Blacke Sea* (1609), 8: 304–20.
12. See Michael Strachan, *Sir Thomas Roe, 1581–1644: A Life* (London, 1989), 170–5.
13. See G. F. Abbott, *Under the Turk in Constantinople: A Record of Sir John Finch's Embassy, 1674–1681* (London, 1920).
14. See Thomas Roe, *The Negotiations of Sir Thomas Roe in his Embassy to the Ottoman Porte from the Year 1621 to 1628 Inclusive* (London, 1740), 35; on the ambassadorial role more generally, see Mather, *Pashas*, 131–41.
15. TNA SP 71/1 fo. 116.
16. Alfred C. Wood, *A History of the Levant Company* (1935); rpt. London, 1964, 2.
17. William Foster, ed., *The English Factories in India, 1651–1654* (Oxford, 1915), 305.
18. Foster, ed., *Letters*, 5: 129.
19. TNA SP 71/2 fo. 243 (8 September 1682).
20. On Tipton, see Hakluyt, *Principal Navigations*, 3: 126; John Sanderson, *The Travels of John Sanderson in the Levant, 1584–1602*, ed. William Foster (London, 1931), 12; and Ali Tablit, 'Algerian-British Relations: 1585–1830', in Abduljelil Temimi and Mohammed-Salah Omri, eds., *Actes du Ier Congrés International sur: Le Grande Bretagne et le Maghreb: Etat de Recherche et contacts culturels* (Zaghouane, Tunisia, 2001), 197–212. On the Magharibi consuls, see Wood, *History*, 59–64.
21. TNA FO 113/1 fo. 20 (20 December 1600).
22. Foster, ed., *English Factories... 1651–1654*, 294.
23. Antonio Dias Farinha, ed., *Cronica de Almancor, Sultao de Marrocos (1578-1603), de Antonio de Saldanha*, trans. Leon Bourdon (Lisbon, 1997), 152.
24. Foster, ed., *Letters*, 3: 310.
25. Ibid., 3: 67–8. Massinger's *The Renegado* (1624), opens upon Tunisians flocking to stare at European paintings.
26. T. S. Willan, *Studies in Elizabethan Foreign Trade* (1959; rpt. Manchester, 1968), 185; Willan's study remains the best guide to the peculiarities of the Barbary Company.

27. William Foster, ed., *The English Factories in India, 1624–1629* (Oxford, 1909), 359.
28. Giancarlo Casale, *The Ottoman Age of Exploration* (Oxford and New York, 2010).
29. Foster, ed., *Letters*, 2: 246.
30. Foster, ed., *English Factories . . . 1624–1629*, 254, 262.
31. After East India Company ships seized Bandar Abbas for Persia in 1622, rumours spread that 'the Persians may be willing to employ the English ships in capturing Muskat' from the Portuguese; see ibid., 37, 43.
32. Ibid., 281.
33. Philip J. Stern, ''A Politie of Civill & Military Power': Political Thought and the Late Seventeenth-Century Foundation of the East India Company State', *Journal of British Studies*, 47: 2 (2008): 253–83, this passage 264.
34. See Foster, ed., *Letters*, 5: 152.
35. Some compassionately compared the famished 'natives of this country' with Jacob's sons, who 'with their whole famylyes dayley travell into forrain partes to seeck bread', William Foster, ed., *English Factories in India, 1630–1633* (Oxford, 1910), 135.
36. The one exception was Thomas Baker, consul in Libyan Tripoli; see C. R. Pennell, ed., *Piracy and Diplomacy in Seventeenth-Century North Africa: The Journal of Thomas Baker, English Consul in Tripoli, 1677–1685* (Rutherford, NJ, 1989), 217.
37. For a brief overview of resources for the study of British-North African relations in the National Archives, Kew, see Nabil Matar, www.hull.ac.uk/caravane/documents/sourcesmatar.pdfbar.
38. See the 'Description of the moneys, weights and measures which are current in the kingdom of Persia', sent to London in 1615 by Richard Steel; Foster, ed., *Letters*, 3: 176–8.
39. See Purchas, *Hakluytus Posthumus*, 3: 504–6.
40. William Foster, *The English Factories in India, 1661–1664* (Oxford, 1923), 252, 26, 85 (2), 187, 421, 163, 368. See each volume of Foster, ed., *Letters*, which includes a glossary of new vocabulary that entered, often temporarily, the English language.
41. Foster, ed., *English Factories . . . 1630–1633*, 161.
42. Foster, ed., *English Factories . . . 1651–1654*, 148–9 (Lucknow); 220 (Petaboli); Foster, ed., *English Factories . . . 1655–1660* (Agra), 303.
43. Foster, ed., *Letters*, 1: 313, 146; and see *CSPD, 1675–76*, 295, (entry for 14 September 1675).
44. Foster, ed., *English Factories . . . 1624–1629*, 35.
45. See, for example, instructions regarding indigo and vermillion, in Foster, ed., *Letters*, 4: 35 n. and 337 n. respectively.
46. See, for example, a short letter of 1631 by John Willoughby, in Foster, ed., *English Factories . . . 1630–1633*, 142, that casually refers to 'doulle', 'cahars', and 'doua'.

47. Ibid., 89.
48. One can only speculate why factors at Agra use the Hindi 'chappar', instead of thatched roof; or the Arabic 'cuttbah' instead of 'sermon'; or 'shraffage'; and why, in writing to London, the term 'xaroffs' was preferred to 'brokerage fee'; Foster, ed., *English Factories . . . 1624–1629*, 240, 354, 296.
49. See Edhem Eldem, 'Istanbul: From Imperial to Peripheralized Capital', in Edhem Eldem, Daniel Goffman and Bruce Masters, *The Ottoman City between East and West: Aleppo, Izmir, and Istanbul* (Cambridge, 1999), 135–206, this passage, 150.
50. Goffman, *Britons*, 34–5; and see Goffman, 'Izmir: From Village to Colonial Port City', in Eldem, Goffman and Masters, *Ottoman City*, 79–134.
51. Goffman, *Britons*, 38–9.
52. Joseph Pitton de Tournefort, *Relation d'un voyage du Levant*, 2 vols. (Lyons, 1727), 2: 375, 377, cited and translated in Goffman, 'Izmir', 94.
53. Biddulph, *Travels*, 59.
54. Henry Maundrell, *A Journey from Aleppo to Jerusalem in 1697*, introduction by David Howell (Beirut, 1963), 34.
55. C[hristopher] F[arewell], *An East-India Colation, or, A Discourse of Travels* (1633), 19.
56. Ibid., 32.
57. John Covel, 'Dr. Covel's Diary', in Theodore J. Bent, ed. *Early Voyages and Travels in the Levant* (London, 1893), 101–287, this passage 140.
58. Roe, *Embassy*, 69 n.
59. Ibid., 91, 116, 154–5.
60. Edward Terry, *A Voyage to East-India* (1655), 202.
61. 'The Europeans from their first establishment', Alexander Russell noted of the *khan al-jumruk* where English factors lived and worked in the middle of the eighteenth century, 'have been lodged in some of the principal khanes. Their houses are spacious and commodious; one house occupying the half, sometimes the whole of one side of the square. The piazza being walled up, large windows in the European fashion are made towards the court; the floors are neatly paved with stone, or marble; and the apartments enlarged, and handsomely fitted up. The warehouses are on the ground floor.' Russell, *The Natural History of Aleppo*, 2nd edn, 2 vols. (London, 1794), 1: 19–20.
62. TNA SP 71/22/III fo. 133 (28 August 1728).
63. Samuel Pepys, *The Tangier Papers of Samuel Pepys*, ed. Edwin Chappell (London, 1935), 17–18.
64. For a example from Tunis, see BL Add Ms 61536, fo. 50.
65. Farouk Hoblos, 'The European as Seen by the Inhabitants of the Syrian Coast during the Ottoman Period', in Bernard Heyberger and Carsten-Michael Walbiner, eds., *Les Européens vus par les Libanais à l'époque ottomane* (Beirut, 2002), 43–58, this passage 54.

66. Joseph Morgan, *A Compleat History of the Piratical States of Barbary* (London, 1750), 165.
67. Ibid.
68. TNA SP 71/15 fos. 44r–v (*c*.1703).
69. MacLean, *Oriental Travel*, 231 n. 26; on Roe's visit to Heybeliada, see Strachan, *Roe*, 178–9.
70. Richard Knolles, *The Generall Historie of the Turkes* (1603; rpt. 1638), 1313; and see Gerald MacLean, *The Rise of Oriental Travel: English Visitors to the Ottoman Empire, 1580–1720* (Basingstoke, 2004), 222–5 on the curious circumstances of Anne, Lady Glover's death.
71. On the repatriation of Harvey's corpse, see Covel, *Diary*, 154–5, and Captain Charles Wild's logbook of the journey of the *Centurion* at BL Ms Sloane 2439, especially fo. 26v. In 1789, the missionaries of St Vincent de Paul found a tombstone in Algiers of an English merchant, William Henry Ward, who had been buried on 4 May 1620; TNA FO 113/1 fo. 39.
72. Foster, ed., *Letters*, 3: 310, n.3; and see Foster, ed., *English Factories... 1651–1654*, 59.
73. See Bruce Masters, *Christians and Jews in the Ottoman Arab World: The Roots of Sectarianism* (Cambridge, 2001), 21–2.
74. Edhem Eldem, 'Istanbul: From Imperial to Peripheralized Capital', in Edhem Eldem, Daniel Goffman, and Bruce Masters, *The Ottoman City between East and West: Aleppo, Izmir, and Istanbul* (Cambridge, 1999), 149, 151.
75. Masters, 'Aleppo: The Ottman Empire's Caravan City', in Edhem, Goffman and Masters, *Ottoman City*, 38.
76. TNA SP 71/2 fo. 65v (10 June 1675).
77. William Okeley, *Eben-Ezer: Or, A Small Monument of Great Mercy* (1675), 24.
78. See the detailed study, with translations, of the Spanish missionary presence in Morocco, Badi'a al-Kharazi, *Tarikh al-kanisah al-nusraniyah fi-al-Maghrib al-Aqsa* (Rabat, 2007), 299–338, and Games, *Web of Empire*, chapter 7.
79. See, for instance, the petition from twelve 'Traders into the Mediteranian' (Tunis) on behalf of their choice consul, BL Add Ms 61536, fo. 80 (1710); another, on behalf of a rival, is from thirty-two signatories, ibid., fo. 84.
80. Sonia Anderson, *An English Consul in Turkey: Paul Rycaut at Smyrna, 1667–1678* (Oxford, 1989), quotes a French census listing '101 heads of household, 28 wives, 56 children, and 84 servants or slaves', 59.
81. G. F. Abbott, *Under the Turk in Constantinople: A Record of Sir John Finch's Embassy, 1674–1681* (London, 1920), 89.
82. J. C. Hurewitz, ed., *The Middle East and North Africa in World Politics: Volume 1 European Expansion, 1535–1914* (New Haven and London, 1975), Articles 17, 24.
83. Eric R. Dursteler, *Venetians in Constantinople: Nation, Identity, and Coexistence in the Early Modern Mediterranean* (Baltimore, MD, 2006), 95.
84. Biddulph, *Travels*, 81.
85. Dursteler, *Venetians*, 96.

86. See MacLean, *Oriental Travel*, 62–5.
87. George Sandys, *A Relation of a Journey begun An. Dom: 1610* (1615), 85.
88. Foster, ed., *English Factories . . . 1624–1629*, 119–20.
89. John Luke, *Tangier at High Tide: The Journal of John Luke, 1670–1673*, ed. Helen Andrews Kaufman (Paris, 1958), 102; Thomas Pellow, *The History of the Long Captivity and Adventures of Thomas Pellow, in South-Barbary* (London, 1739).
90. Foster, ed., *English Factories . . . 1651–1654*, 53.
91. John Ovington, *A Voyage to Surat in the Year 1689* (1696), 146–7.
92. Fawcett, ed., *English Factories . . . 1678–1684*, 4.
93. See William Franklin, *A Letter from Tangier concerning the death of Jonas Rowland, the renegade* (1682), broadsheet.
94. TNA SP 71/4 fo. 333 (14 June 1712).
95. TNA SP 71/4 fo. 433.
96. Sanderson, *Travels*, 10.
97. Dursteler, *Venetians*, 96.
98. Fynes Moryson, in Hughes, ed., *Shakespeare's Europe: A Survey of the Condition of Europe at the end of the Sixteenth Century, being Unpublished chapters of Fynes Moryson's Itinerary (1617)* (1903); rpt. New York, 1967, 68.
99. Dursteler, *Venetians*, 97.
100. Wood, *History*, 244.
101. François Charles-Roux, *Les Echelles de Syrie et de Palestine au dix-huitième siècle* (Paris, 1928), 26–7.
102. Ibid., 27 n. 1.
103. Curiously, the capitulations between Shah 'Abbas and the Netherlands of 17 November 1623 were less punitive: 'If any Netherlander should be found in the company of a woman, [Persian] officers shall not be empowered to apprehend that person but he shall be punished by his own chiefs after having been found guilty'—thereby leaving the punishment up to the Dutch consul; J. C. Hurewitz, ed., *The Middle East and North Africa in World Politics* (New Haven and London, 1975), 1: 18, Article 15. The practice was confirmed a century later in the 1708 capitulations with France; ibid., 1: 54.
104. See Dursteler, *Venetians*, 94–5.
105. TNA SP 71/22 fo. 71v.
106. Foster, ed., *Letters*, 5: 219.
107. Ovington, *Voyage to Surat*, 401.
108. Morgan, *Compleat History*, 224.
109. Foster, ed., *English Factories . . . 1651–1654*, 86. See also the 1660 reference to Surat in Foster, ed., *English Factories . . . 1655–1660*, 304. Every three years, the French sent six French children, aged 9–10, who were looked after by the Capuchins as they learned the oriental languages: Leila Sabbagh, *Al-jaliyat al-urubbiya fi bilad al-sham fi al-'ahd al-uthmani fi al-qarnayn al-sadis 'ashar wal sabi' 'ashar*, 2 vols. (Beirut, 1989), 2: 628–9; see also Marie de Testa and

Antoine Gautier, *Drogmans et diplomates européens auprès de la Porte ottomane* (Istanbul, 2003), 43–6.
110. Foster, ed., *Letters*, 2: 108; *CSPD, 1698*, 389.
111. TNA SP 71/15 fo. 189, for expenses between 1701 and 1704.
112. Foster, ed., *Letters*, 1: 115, 122. By contrast, Spaniards enjoyed light literature; see Irving A. Leonard, 'A Shipment of *comedias* to the Indies', *Hispanic Review* 2 (1934): 39–50.
113. Foster, ed., *English Factories . . . 1655–1660*, 324.
114. Ibid., 277.
115. H. G. Rawlinson, *British Beginnings in Western India, 1579–1657* (Oxford, 1920), 100.
116. The only English music that Saletians heard was the singing of the captive Adam Elliot, who entertained his master and friends with London ditties; but there is no reference to instruments: see Adam Elliot, *A Modest Vindication of Titus Oates the Salamanca-Doctor From Perjury* (1682), 12. For Dallam, see MacLean, *Oriental Travel*, 40–7; and for Jahangir, see Foster, ed., *Letters*, 1: 282.
117. Fawcett, ed., *English Factories . . . 1678–1684*, 207.
118. Anderson, *English Consul*, 210–11, and see Charles G. D. Littleton, 'Ancient Language and New Science: The Intellectual Life of Robert Boyle', in Alastair Hamilton, Maurits H. Van Den Boogert and Bart Westerweel, eds., *The Republic of Letters and the Levant* (Leiden, 2005), 151–73, esp. 164.
119. Frances Parthenope Verney and Margaret M. Verney, eds., *Memoirs of the Verney Family During the Seventeenth Century* (1892; rev. ed., 2 vols, London, 1907), 2: 265–8.
120. See the letter to the French agent in Paris (16–25 September 1699) referring to marble pieces, Philippe de Cossé Brissac, ed., *Les Sources Inédites de l'Histoire du Maroc: Archives et Bibliothèques de France-Dynastie Filalienne*, 6 vols. (Paris, 1953), 5: 424.
121. Roe, *Negotiations*, 16.
122. C. Wakefield, 'Arabic Manuscripts in the Bodleian Library: The Seventeenth-Century Collections', in Russell, ed., *'Arabick' Interest*, 128–46; Jan Schmidt, 'Between Author and Library Shelf: The Intriguing History of Some Middle Eastern Manuscripts Acquired by Public Collections in the Netherlands Prior to 1800', in Hamilton, et al., eds., *Republic of Letters*, 27–53.
123. Anderson, *English Consul*, 16–7.
124. Ibid., 14.
125. Teonge, *Diary*, 146.
126. M. Corneille le Bruyn, *A Voyage to the Levant*, trans. W. J. (London, 1702), 238.
127. TNA SP 71/14 fo. 535.
128. BL Add Ms 61536 fo. 74 (6 April 1710).
129. Maundrell, *Journey*, 198.

130. William Lithgow, *The Totall Discourse of The Rare Adventures and Painefull Peregrinations* (1632; rpt. Glasgow, 1906), 315.
131. Foster, ed., *Letters*, 1: 226–7.
132. At least one discontented mariner 'capitulated his soul to the devil by turning accursed Mahometan' while serving in the Indian Ocean; *CSP, Colonial Series, East Indies, China and Japan, 1513–1616*, 481 (6 November 1616). A century earlier, when the Portuguese conquered Goa, they 'punished the Christian renegades serving in the ranks of the Moors', but this may be unreliable since it continues by reporting that an embassy from Prester John arrived to encourage unity against the 'infidels'; ibid., 1 (6 June 1513).
133. Foster, ed., *Letters*, 1: 200, 2: 265.
134. See Goffman, *Britons*.
135. Foster, ed., *English Factories . . . 1651–1654*, 123, 248–9, 286.
136. Foster, ed., *English Factories . . . 1661–1664*, 212.
137. Ovington, *Voyage to Surat*, 404; C. F. Pascoe, *Two Hundred Years of the S.P.G.: An Historical Account of the Society for the Propagation of the Gospel in foreign Parts, 1701–1900* (London, 1901), 1: 471.
138. William Foster, ed., *The English Factories in India, 1637–1641* (Oxford, 1912), 16.
139. Muhammad Rabi' ibn Muhammad Ibrahim, *The Ship of Sulaiman*, trans. John O'Kane (London, 1972), 39; and see the discussion by Muzaffar Alam and Sanjay Subrahmanyam, *Indo-Persian Travels in the Age of Discoveries, 1400–1800* (Cambridge, 2007), 161–2.
140. Fynes Moryson, *An Itinerary Containing His Ten Yeeres Travell* (1617); rpt. 4 vols. Glasgow, 1907, 2: 69.
141. C[hristopher] F[arewell], *An East-India Colation, or, A Discourse of Travel*. (1633), 16.
142. Jean Baptiste Tavernier, *The Six Voyages of John Baptista Tavernier, Baron of Aubonne*, trans. John Phillips (1677), 55.
143. Verney and Verney, eds., *Memoirs*, 2: 267.
144. Sabbagh, *Al-jaliyat*, 2: 721; and Anderson, *English Consul*, 4–5.
145. From Libyan Tripoli in 1733, the consular communication reported the death from plague of 19 French Christians, 142 Christian slaves, 464 Jews, and 17,200 Turks and Moors; TNA 71/23/II fo. 183 (7 August 1733).
146. Roe, *Negotiations*, 604.
147. TNA SP 71/2 fo. 171 (20 October 1676).
148. A. M. Broadley, *The Last Punic War: Tunis Past and Present*, 2 vols. (Edinburgh and London, 1882), 2: 54.
149. BL Add Ms 61536 fo. 48 (9 March 1708).
150. Foster, ed., *Letters*, 5: 335.
151. BL Add Ms 61536 fo. 51 (25 October 1708). A memorandum of 1710 explains that Godard 'has by the ill Treatment & Imprisonment from that Government, been Lunatick for near two years'; ibid., fo. 76.
152. TNA FO 113/3 fo. 185 (14 August 1719).

153. See TNA SP 71/2 fo. 243 (8 September 1682).
154. Verney and Verney, eds., *Memoirs,* 2: 268, and see 2: 266.
155. TNA SP 71/22 fo. 112.
156. See the '"Act" by the President and Council of Surat against Private Trade, December 10, 1632', in Foster, ed., *English Factories . . . 1630–1633,* 248–9.
157. Ibid., 114; Foster, ed., *English Factories . . . 1655–1660,* 15.
158. Foster, *English Factories . . . 1651–1654,* 296.
159. TNA SP 71/27/III fo. 497 (16 April 1722).
160. TNA SP 71/3 fo. 657 (12 December 1695).
161. Ibid.
162. TNA SP 71/2 fo. 263 (23 December 1681). See also the reference in a letter to John Luke about having to 'kisse ye Governors hands who is brother in Law to Sid Gaylan', BL MS Sloane 3511 fo. 176 (21 November 1672); and see Christian Windler, 'Diplomatic history as a field for cultural analysis: Muslim-Christian relations in Tunis, 1700–1840', *The Historical Journal* 44 (2001): 79–106. Stanley Lane-Poole noted that the first consul to refuse to kiss the dey's hand was Archibald Campbell Fraser in 1767, *The Barbary Corsairs* (New York, 1890), 264. For Cartwright, see John Michael Archer, *Old Worlds: Egypt, Southwest Asia, India, and Russia in Early Modern English Writing* (Palo Alto, CA, 2001), 160.
163. BL Add Ms 61535 fo. 158 (30 December 1709).
164. A member of the Royal Society who was fluent in Arabic, Jones travelled to Morocco four times between 1699 and 1704; he died in 1731; *ODNB.*
165. Allan Cunningham, 'Dragomania: the Dragomans of the British Embassy of Turkey', *St Antony's Papers* 2 (1961): 81–100, this passage 83.
166. TNA FO 335/19 fo. 27 (29 April 1730).
167. Foster, ed., *Letters,* 4: 35.
168. TNA SP 71/3 fo. 439 (17 October 1691).
169. BL Add Ms 61493 fo. 7.
170. See Maya Jasonoff, 'Measured Reciprocity: English Ambassadorial Gift Exchange in the 17th and 18th Centuries', *Journal of Early Modern History* 9 (2005): 348–70.
171. Foster, ed., *Letters,* 6: 44, 117.
172. According to Thomas Baker, TNA SP 71/3 fo. 221 (April 1691).
173. Foster, ed., *Letters,* 6: 134.
174. See also Foster, ed., *Letters,* 4: 12.
175. TNA SP 71/31 fo. 295 (10 December 1694).
176. Quoted in John Selwyn Bromley, 'A Letter-Book of Robert Cole: British Consul-General at Algiers, 1694–1712', (1974) rpt. in *Corsairs and Navies, 1660–1760* (London: 1987), 29–42, this passage 36.
177. TNA SP 71/15 fo. 95.
178. Foster, ed., *English Factories . . . 1651–1654,* 154.

179. Ibid., 280. See *Ordinance of the Lords and Commons Assembled in Parliament, For the Apprehending and bringing to condign punishment, all such lewd persons as shall steale, sell, buy, inveighle, purloyne, convey, or receive any little Children. And for the strict and diligent search of all Ships and other Vessels on the River, or at the Downes* (1644).
180. TNA SP 71/22/I fo. 211.
181. Morgan, *Compleat History*, 135.
182. BL Add Ms 61536 fo. 51 (March 1708).
183. BL Add Ms 61535 fo. 97.
184. Hurewitz, ed., *Middle East*, 1: 35; see the capitulations of 1675 between England and the Ottoman Empire, 1: 34–41.
185. TNA SP 71/22/III fo. 38v.
186. Ibid., fos. 53–4.
187. Mohammed Touili, ed., *Correspondance des Consuls de France à Alger, 1642–1792* (Paris, 2001), 70 (1 August 1694).
188. TNA SP 71/27 fo. 66.
189. Ibid., fo. 89 (3 February 1696).
190. *CSPD, July 1 – Dec. 31, 1695*, 130–1.
191. TNA SP 71/11 fo. 249 (March 1746).
192. See TNA SP 71/3 fo. 214.
193. See Hurewitz, ed., *Middle East*, 1: 36.
194. Cited in *ODNB*.
195. Roger North, *The Life of the Honourable Sir Dudley North, Knt.*, ed. Montague North (London, 1744), 43–56.
196. Ibid., 61–2.
197. Ibid., 133.
198. John Covel. 'Dr. Covel's Diary', in Theodore J. Bent, ed., *Early Voyages and Travels in the Levant* (London, 189), ix.
199. BL Add Ms 22910 fo. 129.
200. Ibid.
201. Ibid., fos. 131, 132.
202. Abbott, *Under the Turk*, 41.
203. BL Add Ms 29921 fo. 79.
204. See Abbott, *Under the Turk*, 16–20.
205. Anderson, *English Consul*, 207, citing TNA SP 97/19 fo. 224.
206. *Historical Manuscripts Commission, Report on the Manuscripts of Allan George Finch*, 2 vols. (London, 1913), 1: 91, 148; hereafter '*HMC Finch Report*'.
207. See Goffman, *Britons*, 194–211.
208. See Caroline Finkel, *Osman's Dream: The Story of the Ottoman Empire, 1300–1923* (London, 2005), 273–6.
209. Covel, *Diary*, 209.
210. Covel, *Diary*, 171; and see Abbott, *Under the Turk*, 93.
211. Ibid., 189.

212. Ibid., 190.
213. Roger North, *The Life of the Honourable Sir Dudley North, Knt.* Ed. Montague North (London, 1744), 214.
214. See North, *Life*, 104–5, Abbott, *Under the Turk*, 116–22.
215. Abbott, *Under the Turk*, 120.
216. Abbott, *Under the Turk*, 121; citing *HMC Finch Report*, 1: 297, for the king's permission to ignore the earlier pro-Greek clause, dated 23 Dec 1663.
217. Abbott, *Under the Turk*, 122, citing Harvey's 'Instructions' at TNA SP 17/19 (3 August 1668), and noting that it reappears in 'Instructions to Chandos' in 1680, when anti-Catholicism is at its height.
218. See John Covel, *Some Account of the Present Greek Church* (Cambridge, 1720), lii.
219. *Journal of the House of Commons, Volume 9, 1667–1687*, 317–21.
220. Abbott, *Under the Turk*, 131–2, 181.
221. Ibid., 168–73.
222. Ibid., 170.
223. See *A Particular Narrative of the Burning of the Port of Tripoli . . . 14 Jan 1676* (Savoy, 1676), and [Narborough, John], *Articles of Peace & Commerce Between The Most Serene and Mighty Prince Charles II . . . And The Most Illustrious Lords, Halil Bashaw, Ibraim Dey* (1676).
224. *HMC Finch Report*, 2: 67.
225. See Abbott, *Under the Turk*, 196–9, and North, *Life*, 74–6.
226. Levant Company to Charles, cited Anderson, *English Consul*, 209. On the Ashby affair, see North, *Life*, 76–7, and Abbott, *Under the Turk*, 211–22.
227. North, *Life*, 83; on the Aleppo coins see generally ibid., 79–84, *HMC Finch Report*, 2: 143 (28 December 1677), and Abbott, *Under the Turk*, 227–45.
228. *HMC Finch Report*, 2: 62 (12–22 December 1679).
229. Ibid., 2: 72 (3–13 May 1680); and see North, *Life*, 90-2.
230. *HMC Finch Report*, 2: 80 (10–20 July 1680); and see North, *Life*, 93–8.
231. *HMC Finch Report*, 2: 116.
232. Ibid., 2: 162.
233. Ibid., 2: 163.
234. 'The King of Sumatra having desired one of His Majesty's subjects for a wife with sundry proffers of privileges to the issue, a gentleman of honorable parentage proposes his daughter, of most excellent parts for music, her needle and good discourse, as also very beautiful and personable. The kingdoms of Sumatra and Taprobane very eminent for antiquity amongst historiographers and known to be very powerful in shipping; debate whether it be beneficial to the [East India] Company, referred for consideration', *CSP, Colonial Series, East Indies, China and Japan, 1513–1616*, 335 (9–14 November 1614).
235. For 'land of Canaan' in India, see Foster, ed., *Letters*, 3: 337.
236. See Appendix I in H. G. Rawlinson, *British Beginnings in Western India, 1579–1657* (Oxford, 1920), 135–8 and the numerous photographs.

CHAPTER 4

1. In this discussion, the word 'captive' rather than 'slave' will be used. In the Arabic documents of North Africa, the former corresponds to '*asir*' and the latter to ''*abd*'. In North Africa, Europeans were captives not slaves.
2. In 1527 from François I, in 1552 from Henri II, in 1560 from François II, in 1566 from Charles IX, in 1602 from Henri IV, in 1618 from Louis XII, in 1650 from Louis XIV, and in 1716 from Louis XV; see Eugéne Plantet, ed. *Correspondance des Deys d'Alger avec la Cour de France, 1579–1833*, 2 vols. (Paris, 1889), 1: 407.
3. See Molly Greene, 'The Ottomans in the Mediterranean', in Virginia H. Aksan and Daniel Goffman, eds., *The Early Modern Ottomans: Remapping the Empire* (Cambridge, 2007), 104–17.
4. The Portuguese and Spanish conquests in Morocco are as follows: Ceuta 1415; Anfa 1469; Tangier 1471; Asila 1471; Al-Araish 1489; Melilla 1497; Agadir 1505; Al-Suwayra 1506; Asfi 1508; Azammur 1513; and Al-Jadidah 1514: see Jamil M. Abun-Nasr, *A History of the Maghrib In the Islamic Period.* 1971; rev. rpt. Cambridge, 1993, chapter 5.
5. *Indulgences issued to raise money to fight the Turks or to ransom captives* (1480).
6. See Purchas, *Hakluytus Posthumus, or, Purchas His Pilgrimes.* 1625; rpt. 20 vols. Glasgow, 1905–7, 3: 115–35, and Clements R. Markham, ed., *The Voyages of Sir James Lancaster, to the East Indies* (1877; rpt. New Delhi, 1998), 147–50.
7. See the chronological bibliography of publications on captivity in English in Nabil Matar, *Turks, Moors, and Englishmen in the Age of Discovery* (New York, 1999), Appendix I.
8. Fernand Braudel, *The Mediterranean and the Mediterranean World in the Age of Philip II*, trans Siân Reynolds, 2 vols. (1966; rpt., New York, 1972): 2: 799.
9. Ellen G. Friedman, 'Christian Captives at "Hard Labor" in Algiers, 16th–18th Centuries,' *International Journal of African Historical Studies* 13 (1980): 616–32; this passage 618.
10. So Simon Ockley regarding a manuscript he reprinted: 'I am entirely ignorant of the Name, Quality, and Circumstances of the Author [a former captive]: His Manuscript fell into my Hands accidentally some Years ago', *An Account of South-West Barbary* (London, 1713), xii. For ghost-written accounts, see for example, *News from Sally: Of A Strange Delivery of Foure English Captives* (1642). This phenomenon was not distinctive to England; see Antoine Galland, *Relation de L'Esclavage d'un Marchand de la Ville de Cassis, à Tunis* (Paris, 1810).
11. See, for example, Joseph Pitts, *A True and Faithful Account of the Religion and Manners of the Mohammetans* (Exeter, 1704): 'One thing I will desire of the Learned Reader, which is, that if the Arabick Words in any place be not rightly written, he will please to take notice, that I aim'd at the vulgar Sound of the Word, and writ as near, as I could, to their way of speaking it', sig. A4v; in

Daniel J. Vitkus, ed., *Piracy, Slavery and Redemption: English Captivity Narratives in North Africa, 1577–1704*, with an Introduction by Nabil Matar (New York, 2001), 221–2.

12. See Edward Kellet and Henry Byam, *A Returne from Argier. A Sermon Preached at Minhead* (1628).
13. Thomas Pellow, *The History of the Long Captivity and Adventures of Thomas Pellow, in South-Barbary* (London, 1739), 16.
14. Such processions were only held twice in England during our period, one in 1637 is mentioned later in this chapter, the other took place in 1721. The captives, wrote John Windus, 'went in Procession to St. *Paul's*, to return Thanks to Almighty God for their happy Deliverance, it was a Spectacle of less Pomp indeed, but of more solid and lasting Glory than a *Roman* Triumph', *A Journey to Mequinez, The Residence of the Present Emperor of Fez and Morocco* (London, 1725), 'Preface', sig. av. It is not clear whether the 150 captives who were released in 1675 went in a procession as 'they made haste to London and altogether intend to pay their obedience to his Majesty', *CSPD, 1675–76*, 12 (8 March 1675).
15. Gillian Lee Weiss, 'From Barbary to France: processions of redemption and early modern culturally identity', in Giulio Cipollone, ed., *La Liberazione dei 'Captivi' tra Christiantà e Islam* (Vatican, 2000), 789–806; and Gillian Lee Weiss, 'Back from Barbary: Captivity, Redemption and French Identity in the Seventeenth- and Eighteenth-Century Mediterranean' (PhD dissertation, Stanford University, 2002), chapter 2.
16. Weiss, 'Back from Barbary', chapter 3.
17. Although no Irish men are named, 'Ellen Hawkins' and 'Joane Bradbrook of Baltamore' appear on the list of those ransomed from Algiers in 1647: Edmond Cason, *A Relation of the whole proceedings concerning the Redemption of the Captives in Argier and Tunis* (1647), 18, 20. Among the list of those seized in 1631, there are 'Stephen Broadbrooke, wife and two children', and 'Old Hamkin, wife and daughter'; *CSP, Ireland, 1625–32*, 621 (10 July 1631). See Des Ekin, *The Stolen Village: Baltimore and the Barbary Pirates* (Dublin, 2006).
18. Children seldom appear, though nearly half of those seized from Baltimore in 1631 were children; see the list at *CSP, Ireland, 1625–32*, 621–2 (10 July 1631). Among those redeemed from Algiers in 1647, Cason lists 'Mary Weymouth, and her two children, James and John' and 'Bridget Randall and her son of London', *Relation*, 23. In 1721, Windus saw 'twenty eight *English* Boys' serving as attendants to Mulay Ismail; *Journey to Mequinez*, 104.
19. On Marsh, see Linda Colley, *The Ordeal of Elizabeth Marsh: A Woman in World History* (London, 2007), and Gerald MacLean, 'Slavery and Sensibility: A Historical Dilemma', in Brycchan Carey and Peter Kitson, eds., *Slavery and the Cultures of Abolition: Essays Marking the British Abolition Act of 1807* (Cambridge, 2007), 173–94.

20. Charles Pandon, *Copie D'Une Lettre Envoyee de Coutron en Calabre* (Lyons, 1587), 3; John Dunton, *A True Iournal of the Sally Fleet* (1637).
21. In 1645, seven Barbary ships landed in Cornwall. A brief description of this attack was written by Nehemiah Wallington: 'August 14, 1645. –Letters from Plymouth certify that the Turkish pirates, men of war, landed in Cornwall, about Foy, and that they have taken away two hundred and forty (of English Christians) of the Cornish men, women, and children, amongst which Mr. John Carew his daughter, that was cousin to Sir Alexander Carew that was beheaded, and some gentlewomen and others of note, and have carried them away; a very sad thing', *Historical Notices of Events Occurring Chiefly in the Reign of Charles I*, 2 vols. (London, 1869), 2: 266; and see *CSPV, 1643–47*, 209 (8 September 1645).
22. Weiss, 'Back from Barbary', chapter 2.
23. See Nabil Matar, *Britain and Barbary, 1589–1689* (Gainesville, FL, 2005), 99–102. Note the total indifference that Captain Braithwaite showed to an Irish woman who had been captured, married off in Morocco, then deserted, ibid., 104.
24. See François Comelin, Philemon de la Motte, and Joseph Bernard, *Voyage pour la Redemption des Captifs, Aux Royaumes D'Alger et de Tunis. Fait en 1720* (Paris, 1720), 26–42. Joseph Morgan's English translation appeared as *A Voyage to Algiers and Tunis, For the Redemption of Captives* (London, 1735), 14–36.
25. See Richard Hakluyt, *The Principal Navigations: Voyages, Traffiques and Discoveries of the English Nation*. 1589; rpt. 8 vols. (London, 1910), 3: 155; and Thomas Phelps, *A True Account of the Captivity of Thomas Phelps at Machaness in Barbary* (1685), 27, rpt. in Vitkus, ed., *Slavery*, 217.
26. Weiss, 'Back from Barbary', chapter 2. Huguenots were often enslaved on their compatriots' Catholic galleys: see Elias Neau's *Account of the Sufferings of the French Protestants* (1699).
27. 'Religion stands on Tip-toe in our Land, / Ready to pass to the *American Strand*; / When height of Malice, and Prodigious Lusts / Impudent sinning; Witchcrafts, and Distrusts, /(The Marks of future bane) shall fill our Cup / Unto the Brim, and make our Measure up, &c', William Okeley, *Eben-Ezer: Or, A Small Monument of Great Mercy appearing in the Miraculous Deliverance* (1675), sigs. A4v-B; see Izaak Walton, *The Lives of John Donne, Sir Henry Wotton, Richard Hooker, George Herbert, Robert Sanderson*, ed. George Saintsbury (London, 1973), 315.
28. Accounts by Robert Elliot, a Catholic, and Edward Coxere, a Quaker, were not published until the twentieth century: for Elliot see Jean Pignon, 'Un document inédit sur la Tunisie au début du XVII siècle', *Les Cahiers de Tunisie* 33 (1961): 109–219; and see E. H. W. Meyerstein, ed., *Adventures by Sea of Edward Coxere* (New York and London, 1946).

29. See Johann von Hans Staden, *The True Story of His Captivity 1557*, trans. and ed. Malcolm Letts (London, 1928), and Martin A. Favata and Jose B. Fernandez, eds., *The Account: Alvar Nunez Cabeza de Vaca's Relacion* (Houston, TX, 1993).
30. See Hakluyt, *Principal Navigations*, 6: 296–336 for Philips, and 6: 336–54 for Hortop.
31. Linda McJannet, 'The Translator as Emissary: Continental Works about the Ottomans in England', in Brinda Charry and Gitanjali Shahani, eds., *Emissaries in Early Modern Literature and Culture: Mediation, Transmission, Traffic, 1550–1700* (Aldershot, 2009), 147–66, this passage 155; and see Matthew Dimmock, *Newe Turkes: Dramatizing Islam and the Ottomans in Early Modern England* (Aldershot, 2005), 81–2.
32. Sebastian Munster, *A Briefe Collection and compendious extract of straunge and memorable things* (1572), 50.
33. English dramatists knew them from Massinger's *The Renegado* (1630); see Warner G. Rice, 'The Sources of Massinger's *The Renegado*', *Philological Quarterly* 11: 1 (1932): 65–75.
34. Hakluyt, *Principal Navigations*, 3: 40; rpt. in Vitkus, ed., *Piracy*, 60.
35. Edward Arber, ed., *Edward Webbe, Chief Master Gunner, His Travailes. 1590* (London, 1868), gives the following printing history: (1) London: by Ralph Blower for Thomas Pauier [1590]; (2) London: by A[bel]. J[effes]. for William Barley [1590], a reprint with six woodcuts added; (3) London: for William Wright, 1590, a second edition, Newly enlarged', 10. There were two subsequent reprints in 1592 and another in 1600.
36. As the *Short-Title Catalogue* shows, only one copy of the first imprint survives today, at the Marsh Library in Dublin. A copy of the second imprint survives at the Huntington Library, California: It was printed by 'A[bel]. I[effes]. for William Barley', the same team that produced Webbe. The first imprint was reproduced with modernized spelling by C. Raymond Beazley, *Voyages and Travels mainly during the 16th and 17th Centuries*, 2 vols. (1903; rpt. New York, 1964), 2: 151–85, and in Vitkus, ed., *Piracy*, 73–95.
37. Hasleton in Vitkus, ed., *Slavery*, 94.
38. Cited from Roslyn L. Knutson, 'Elizabethan Documents, Captivity Narratives, and the Market for Foreign History Plays', *English Literary History* 26 (1996): 102–10.
39. See David Delison Hebb, *Piracy and the English Government, 1616–1642* (Aldershot, 1994), 12–15; Ellen G. Friedman, *Spanish Captives in North Africa in the Early Modern Age* (Madison, WI, 1983), 3–4; and Matar, *Turks, Moors and Englishmen*, 71–81.
40. William Davies, *True Relation of the Travailes and most miserable Captivitie of William Davies, Barber-Surgion of London* (1614).
41. See Jean Pignon, 'Un document inédit sur la Tunisie au début du XVII siècle', *Les Cahiers de Tunisie* 33 (1961): 109–219.

42. See Nabil Matar, 'The 1609 Expulsion of the Moriscos in Early Modern British Thought', *Explorations in Renaissance Culture* 35 (2009): 132–49.
43. David Delison Hebb, *Piracy and the English Government, 1616–1642* (Aldershot, 1994), 20, citing TNA SP 14/90 fo. 24, Carew to Roe (June 1617).
44. Carew to Roe in John Maclean, ed., *Letters from George Lord Carew to Sir Thomas Roe, 1615–1617* (London, 1860), 61, 66, 111; see also 67, 77, 94.
45. *CSPD, 1619-23*, 273 (9 July 1621).
46. See Hebb, *Piracy*, 77–104, and I[ohn]. B[utton]., *Algiers Voyage in a Journall* (1621).
47. Ibn Abi Dinar, *Kitab al-Munis fi Akhbar Ifiqiyah wa Tunis*, ed. Muhammad Shammam (Beirut, 1993), 229; translation in Matar, *Europe through Arab Eyes*, 220.
48. Purchas, *Hakluytus Posthumous*, 3: 115–35.
49. John Jourdain, *The Journal of John Jourdain, 1608–1617*, ed. William Foster (Cambridge, 1905), 81–114.
50. Hebb argues that between 1622 and 1642, about 7,000 Britons were seized in the whole of North Africa, but by adding 'all the figures', he continued, the number would be 'approximately 400 ships and above 8000 persons', *Piracy*, 140.
51. Petitions warned about possible conversion, alongside letters describing forcible conversions, in the hope that ransom money would be raised: see, for instance, a letter of 28 July 1632 from Safi about Englishmen being forced 'to turne Moores'; also on 29 July: TNA 71/12 fos. 210, 211. One of the stock phrases was 'want of the spirituall foode of their soules' which made the captives vulnerable to Islam. On petitions, see Matar, *Britain and Barbary*, 81–4.
52. Kellet, *Returne from Argier*, 17; the other sermon by Henry Byam follows Kellet's.
53. *CSPD, 1635–36*, 15; *CSPD, 1636–37*, 4.
54. Such hopes were not entirely ungrounded: from 1634 there is a record of 'Mony Receved fro the Redeeming of the Captives in Marocos' that includes £100 from Sir George Sandys and £800 from Sir Nicolas Raynton, TNA SP 71/12 fo. 222; see also *CSPD, 1637–38*, 15.
55. *Historical Manuscripts Commission Report on the Manuscripts of the Family of Gawdy, formerly of Norfolk* (London, 1885), 166.
56. *CSPD, 1637*, 430 (20 September 1637).
57. See 'A Form of Penance and Reconciliation of a Renegado or Apostate from the Christian Religion to Turkism' (1637), in Vitkus, ed., *Piracy*, appendix 5.
58. Yet such descriptions of torture are unreliable, as Ellen G. Friedman notes of the period 1562 to 1769: 'it was a simple matter for redemptionists to obtain passports and certificates of safe conduct from the Algerian rulers . . . the evidence does not add up to a systematic pattern of purposeless brutality in Algiers. Such treatment was not the norm, but the exception'; 'Christian Captives', 629.

59. Francis Knight, *Relation of Seaven Yeares Slaverie under the Turks of Argeire* (1640), 50.
60. Ibid., 55.
61. T. Spratt, ed., *Autobiography of The Rev. Devereux Spratt* (London, 1886), 12.
62. 'An Act for the Relief of the Captives, taken by Turkish, Moorish, and other Pirates, and to prevent the taking of others in time to come'. Published in *An Act for the better Raising and Levying of Mariners, Sailers, and others* (1641) [Wing STC E1099A], sig. A4.
63. See *An Act for the Redemption of Captives* (1650), passed 26 March 1650; *An Act for continuation of the Act for redemption of Captives* (1652), passed 31 March, 1652; *An Act for continuation of the Act of redemption of captives* (1652), passed 21 December 1652; and *An Ordinance for continuation of one Act of Parliament entituled, An Act for Redemption of Captives* (1653), passed 24 December 1653.
64. Here is a summary of the numbers of captives and their home towns furnished by Cason: Poole 3; London 70; Dover 8; Liverpool 1; Plymouth 29; Southampton 4; Barnstable 18; Weymouth 11; Dartmouth 19; Baltarne 2; Epsom 8; Swansea 1; Edinburgh 3; Falmouth 1; Watchet 1; Folkestone 1; Dorchester 1; Worcester 1; Low 3; Fowey 5; Saltash 1; Sandwich 1; Rye 1; Sidmouth 1; Wareham 1; Youghall 11; Yarmouth 2; Ipswich 1; Dundee 1; Hull 1; Bristol 14; Chatham 2; Christchurch 1; Lyme 3; Newcastle 1; Exeter 1; Penzance 3; Milbrook 1; Seaborne 1: Edmond Cason, *A Relation of the whole proceedings concerning the Redemption of the Captives in Argier and Tunis* (1647), 17–24. Compare these captives and the range of their home towns with the procession of French captives 'from Marseille to Toulon, Avignon, Lyon, Bourgogne, Arle-Duc, Solieux, Avalon, Caphlis, Auxerre, Joigny and Paris', reported by Weiss, 'Back from Barbary', chapter 3.
65. Samuel Pepys, *The Diary of Samuel Pepys*, ed. Robert Latham and William Matthews, 11 vols. (Los Angeles and Berkeley, CA, 1970–83), 2: 33–4.
66. *CSPD, 1660–61*, 182 (7 August 1660).
67. *CSPD, 1660–61*, 405 (6 December 1660); *CSPD, Charles II: Addenda*, 505.
68. Emanuel D'Aranda, *Relation de la captivité et liberté du Sieur Emanuel d'Aranda, Jadis Esclave à Alger* (Brussels, 1662). French reprints appeared in 1657, 1662, 1665, and 1671. And see *The History of Algiers and It's Slavery*, trans. John Davies (1666).
69. The marriage stimulated geo-historical documents such as *A Description of Tangier, The Country and People Adjoyning* (1664), translated from a Spanish text, and Addison's *West Barbary* (1671), as well as numerous short pamphlets and fictional works, such as Elkanah Settle's *Empress of Morocco* (1673), Aphra Behn's *The Moor's Tragedy* (1676), John Dryden's *Don Sebastian* (1689), and a translation of a French novel, *The Amours of the Sultana of Barbary* (1689).
70. 'A Narrative of ye Voyage of Sir Tho: Allen begun the 15th August 1668', TNA SP 71/1 fo. 385.
71. Charles Cotton, trans., *The Fair One of Tunis* (1674).

72. Germain Moüette, *Relation de la Captivité du Sr. Moüette dans les Royaumes de Fez et de Maroc* (Paris, 1683).
73. Weiss, 'Back from Barbary,' 316.
74. T. S., *The Adventures of (Mr T. S.) An English Merchant, Taken Prisoner by the Turks of Argiers* (1670); see Gerald MacLean, *The Rise of Oriental Travel: English Visitors to the Ottoman Empire, 1580–1720* (Basingstoke, 2004), 177–219.
75. See also *A True and Perfect Relation of the Happy Successe & Victory Obtained against the Turks of Argiers at Bugia* (1671), and [Edward Spragge], *Articles of Peace & Commerce Between The Most Serene and Mighty Prince Charles II... And The Most Illustrious Lords, The Bashaw, Dai, Aga, and Governours of the Famous City and Kingdom of Algiers* (1677).
76. T. S., *Adventures*, 43.
77. TNA 29/441 fo. 213.
78. *A True Relation of the Adventures of Mr. R. D.* (1672).
79. On 16 January 1676, Narbrough wrote: 'I fired about (100) Shot into ye City of Tripoly amongst the Inhabitants. The 1st & 3rd of February I tooke & destroyed five Corne-Boats on ye Coast, to ye Eastward of Tripoly 20 Leagues: & Landed & burnt a Stacke of Wood & Timber, wch was for their building their New Ship, & some small Masts & Yards, & some Bags of Bread brought off, & two Guns spiked up.' The report continues: 'On the 10th of February, [we] tooke a Samberkeen in her Ballace 30 Leagues to ye Eastward of Tripoly, belonging to that Government;' TNA SP 71/22 fos. 131r–v, and fo. 131A. And see *Articles of Peace & Commerce Between The Most Serene and Mighty Prince Charles II... And The Most Illustrious Lords, The Bashaw, Dey, Aga, Divan, And Governours of the Noble City and Kingdom of Tripoli in Barbary* (1677).
80. Okeley, *Eben-ezer*, 46.
81. Thomas Overbury, *A True and Perfect Account of the Examination, Confession, Tryal, Condemnation, and Execution of Joan Perry* (1676), 18.
82. Elsewhere, however, matters were different: as late as 1726, at a market of Jewish and Christian slaves held in Aleppo, the wife of the English consul purchased Nestorian slaves, no doubt seeking to free them; see Bruce Masters, *Christians and Jews, in the Ottoman Arab World: The Roots of Sectarianism* (Cambridge, 2001), 47.
83. Thanks to a gift of a certain plant from Knox, Hooke was able to present a paper to the Society in December 1689 on a previously unrecognized variety of hemp, *cannabis indica*, which he declared had notable medicinal properties, commenting that Knox 'has so often experimented it himself, that there is no Cause of Fear, tho' possibly there may be of Laughter'. See Lisa Jardine, 'Hooke the Man: His Diary and His Health', in Jim Bennett, Michael Cooper, Michael Hunter, and Lisa Jardine, *London's Leonardo: The Life and Work of Robert Hooke* (Oxford, 2003), 206.
84. Robert Knox, *An Historical Relation of the Island Ceylon* (1681), 149.

85. Adam Elliot, *A Modest Vindication of Titus Oates the Salamanca-Doctor From Perjury* (1682), 19.
86. Ibid., 4, 6.
87. Ibid., 6, 7.
88. See 'Leo Africanus', *Geographical Historie of Africa;* Pory notes that the original was composed in 1526, 358.
89. Phelps, *True Account*, 9; in Vitkus, ed., *Piracy*, 204.
90. Francis Brooks, *Barbarian Cruelty* (1693), 113–4.
91. *Narrative of Joshua Gee of Boston, Mass.* (Hartford, CT, 1943); Stephen T. Riley, 'Abraham Browne's Captivity by the Barbary Pirates, 1655', in *Seafaring in Colonial Massachusetts* (Boston, MA, 1980), 31–42.
92. For Whitehead's account, see Matar, *Britain and Barbary*, appendix 3.
93. François Pidou de St Olon, *The Present State of the Empire of Morocco*, trans. Peter Motteux (1695). See also earlier French accounts: Pierre Dan, *Histoire de Barbarie et de ses corsairs* (Paris, 1637); Michel Auvry, *Le Miroir de la charité chrétiene* (Aix, 1663); François Comelin and Philémon de la Motte, *Etat des Royaumes de Barbarie, Tripoly, Tunis et Alger* (Rouen, 1703); Ahmed Farouk, ed., *Relation en forme du journal du voyage pour la rédemption des captifs* (St Denis, 2000).
94. Windus, *Journey to Mequinez*, 'Preface', sig. A5v.
95. Pitts was the first English writer to describe visiting Mecca and Medina, but not the first European. Vincent Le Blanc's *Les voyages fameux du Sieur Vincent Le Blanc* (Paris, 1648) recounts visiting the holy sites; see Francis Brooke's English version, *The World Surveyed; or the Famous Voyages and Travailes of V. Le Blanc* (1660). On Pitts, see also Humberto Garcia, 'Turning Turk, Turning Heretic: Joseph Pitts of Exeter and the Early Enlightenment, 1670–1740', in Gerald MacLean, ed., *Britain and the Muslim World: Historical Perspectives* (Newcastle, forthcoming).
96. On Pitts' concern for '*salah*', see *True and Faithful Account*, 35–44, 49, and for his comparisons between Muslims and Catholics, see 14, 50.
97. Ibid., sig. A5v.
98. Ibid., 73, and see 95.
99. Pellow, *History*, 386.
100. See Martin Rheinheimer, 'From Amrum to Algiers and Back: The Reintegration of a Renegade in the Eighteenth Century', *Central European History* 36 (2003): 209–33.
101. Simon Ockley, *South-West Barbary* (London, 1713), 36.
102. Ibid., 8.
103. *A Description of the Nature of Slavery Among the Moors* (London, 1721), 9.
104. William Berriman, *The Great Blessing of Redemption from Captivity* (London, 1722), 22, 23.
105. *Description of the Nature of Slavery*, 8, 9, 10, 11.
106. Eliza Haywood, *The Fair Captive* (London, 1721).

107. [Robert Chetwood], *The Voyages and Adventures of Captain Robert Boyle* (London, 1726), 34.
108. See *A True Relation of the Inhumane and Unparallel'd Actions, and Barbarous Murders of Negroes or Moors* (1672), and Gerald MacLean, *Looking East: English Writing and the Ottoman Empire before 1800* (Basingstoke, 2007), chapter 8, 'A View from the West: Young American Writing about the Maghrib'.
109. Muhammad Rabiʻ ibn Muhammad Ibrahim, *The Ship of Sulaiman*, trans. John O'Kane (London, 1972), 232.
110. Daniel Defoe, *A Plan of the English Commerce* (London, 1728), 323; and see *Captain Singleton*, ed. Shiv K. Kumar (Oxford, 1990): 'I myself [Defoe] had an adventure in a ship bound to Rotterdam, that was taken by an Algerine man of war in the mouth of the River Thames and in sight of Harwich,' 278.

CHAPTER 5

1. John Sanderson, *The Travels of John Sanderson in the Levant, 1584–1602*, ed. William Foster (London, 1931), 50.
2. George Manwaring, 'A True Discourse of Sir Anthony Sherley's Travel into Persia', in Edward Denison Ross, ed., *Sir Anthony Sherley and his Persian Adventure* (London, 1933), 192. Sandys notes that Cairo is inhabited by '*Moores, Turks, Negroes, Jewes, Copties, Greeks*, and *Armenians*', George Sandys, *A Relation of a Journey begun An. Dom: 1610* (1615), 122–3.
3. The myth of Prester John did not die completely: 'The people are naked, Moors and Mahometans of religion, yet subject to Prester John,' wrote Richard Cocks in 1612. A few months earlier, in May, an Armenian reported on 'the Prester John or the Ethiopian Emperour', who had '300,000 men armed with lances and swords', and who rules a region that includes 'a mountain called Phillassa, which is inhabited by Jews', *Letters received by the East India Company from its Servants in the East, 1602–1613*, ed. Frederick Charles Danvers (London, 1896), 217, and 191–4.
4. French writers produced 'sixty original 17th century travel narratives to the East', most of them ecclesiastical; Michael Harrigan, *Veiled Encounters: Representing the Orient in 17th-Century French Travel Literature* (Amsterdam and New York, 2008), 22, 24.
5. See Anne Wolf, *How Many Miles to Babylon? Travels and Adventures to Egypt and Beyond, from 1300–1640* (Liverpool, 2003). The earliest English consul to Aleppo, William Barrett, arrived in about 1580; Alfred C. Wood, *History, A History of the Levant Company* (1935); rpt. (London, 1964), 255.
6. W. H. and H. C. Overall, eds., *Analytical Index to the Series of Records Known as the Remembrancia* (London, 1878), 54–5.
7. Thomas Gainsford, *The Glory of England* (1618), 192.

8. Thomas Smith, *Remarks upon the Manners, Religion and Government of the Turks, Together with a Survey of the Seven Churches of Asia, as they now lye in their Ruines* (1678), 152–3.
9. Franklin Le Van Baumer, 'The Conception of Christendom in Renaissance England', *Journal of the History of Ideas* 6 (1945): 131–56, 136.
10. Samuel Chew, *The Crescent and the Rose: Islam and England During the Renaissance* (New York, 1937), 61–5; Edward Gibbon, *The Decline and Fall of the Roman Empire*, ed. J. B. Bury, 7 vols. (London, 1898), 6: 271.
11. Aaron Hill, *A Full and Just Account of the Present State of the Ottoman Empire* (London, 1709), 182; Gainsford, *Glory of England*, 288.
12. John Locke in Richard Hakluyt, *Principal Navigations, The Principal Navigations: Voyages, Traffiques and Discoveries of the English Nation* (1589); rpt. 8 vols. (London, 1910), 3: 20.
13. Marshall T. Poe, *'A People Born to Slavery': Russia in Early Modern European Ethnography, 1476–1748* (Ithaca, NY, 2000), 148.
14. Quoted in Alastair Hamilton, 'The English Interest in the Arabic-Speaking Christians,' in G. A. Russell, ed., *The 'Arabick' Interest of the Natural Philosophers in Seventeenth-Century England* (Leiden, 1994), 30–53, this passage 34.
15. R. J. Roberts, 'The Greek Press at Constantinople in 1627 and its Antecedents', *The Library* 22 (1967): 13–43.
16. Negotiations also allowed for the arrival of Greeks seeking financial assistance; see *CSPD, 1633–34*, 280–1, 423.
17. John Evelyn, *Diary*, ed. E. S. de Beer, 6 vols. (Oxford, 1955), 1: 14.
18. On Lukaris, see George A. Hadjiantoniou, *Protestant Patriarch: The Life of Cyril Lukaris (1572–1638), Patriarch of Constantinople* (Richmond, VA, 1961).
19. As Charles G. D. Littleton observes, Pocock changed Book VI because it 'contained frivolous legends and fables ... wrongly ascribed to the Muslims', 'Ancient Language and New Science: The Intellectual Life of Robert Boyle', in Alastair Hamilton, Maurits H. Van Den Boogert and Bart Westerweel, eds., *The Republic of Letters and the Levant* (Leiden, 2005), 151–73, this passage 157.
20. Edward Pococke, *Liturgiae Ecclesiae Anglicanae, Partes praecipuae ... In Linguam Arabicam traductae* (Oxford, 1674).
21. For a list of names of some of the students, see John B. Pearson, *A Biographical Sketch of the Chaplains to the Levant Company Maintained at Constantinople, Aleppo and Smyrna, 1611–1706* (Cambridge, 1883), 44.
22. Girolamo Dandini, *A Voyage to Mount Libanus* (1698), 20. The work was first published in 1656.
23. See Asad Rustum and Fu'ad Afram al-Bustani, eds., *Lubnan fi 'ahd al-Amir Fakhr al-Din al-Ma'ni al-Thani* (Beirut, 1969), and Sandys, *Relation*, 212.
24. Mazin Tadros, 'Fishers of Men, 'the Jesuits in Bilad al-Sham, 1625–1660' (PhD dissertation, SUNY-Albany, 2009), 180. Our thanks to Dr Tadros.
25. *Calendar of the Clarendon State Papers*, 5 vols. (Oxford, 1872, 1969–70), 5: 189.

26. Richard G. Hovannisian, ed., *The Armenian People from Ancient to Modern Times*, 2 vols. (Basingstoke, 1997), 1: 324.
27. Philip J. Stern, ' "A Politie of Civill & Military Power": Political Thought and the Late Seventeenth-Century Foundations of the East India Company-State', *Journal of British Studies* 47 (2008): 253–83.
28. For the attractiveness of Catholicism, see Robert M. Haddad, 'Conversion of Eastern Orthodox Christians to the Unia in the Seventeenth and Eighteenth Centuries', in Michael Gervers and Ramzi Jibran Bikhazi eds., *Conversion and Continuity: Indigenous Christian Communities in Islamic Lands, Eighth to Eighteenth Centuries* (Toronto, 1990), 449–60.
29. John Covel, *Some Account of the Present Greek Church* (Cambridge, 1720), xvii.
30. Bibliothèque Nationale, Orienteaux, Paris, Ms Arabe 312.
31. On the fear of contamination, see Raymond A. Mentzer, 'The Huguenot Minority in early modern France', in James D. Tracy and Marguerite Ragnow, eds., *Religion and the Early Modern State: Views from China, Russia, and the West* (Cambridge, 2004), 185–206.
32. Sandys, *Relation*, 150.
33. Ephraim Pagitt, *Christianography: Or, The Description Of the Multitude and sundry Sorts of Christians, in the World, Not Subject to the Pope* (1634; rpt. 1674), 25. Pagitt notes the Christians in Antioch, 'mingled with *Mahumetans*', 26, and that 'Christians inhabite mingled with Mahumetans and Pagans, a great part of the Orient', 32.
34. Paul Rycaut, The *Present State of the Greek and Armenian Churches, Anno Christi, 1678* (London, 167), 14; and see 311 where Rycaut observes that the Greeks, like the Ottomans, keep 'up their Daughters, with the same retirement and distance, from the view of men'; on intermarriage, see 314–15.
35. See Molly Greene, *A Shared World: Christians and Muslims in the Early Modern Mediterranean* (Princeton, NJ, 2000) chapter 6.
36. Hill, *Full and Just Account*, 183.
37. M. Corneille de Bruyn, *A Voyage to the Levant: or, Travels in the Principal Parts of Asia Minor, the Islands of Scio, Rhodes, Cyprus, &c.* Trans. W. J. (London, 1702), 183.
38. Hill, *Full and Just Account*, 187.
39. Smith, *Remarks*, 69
40. Rycaut, *Greek and Armenian Churches*, 4.
41. *The Estate of Christians, living under the subiection of the Turke* (1595), 6.
42. George Meriton, *A Geographical Description of the World* (1671), 133.
43. William Lithgow, *The Totall Discourse of The Rare Adventures and Painefull Peregrinations* (1632); rpt. Glasgow, 1906, 208.
44. Ibid., 236–7.
45. Fynes Moryson, *An Itinerary Containing His Ten Yeeres Travell* (1617); rpt. 4 vols. (Glasgow, 1907), 2: 30–1.
46. Ibid., 2: 20–1.

47. Ibid., 2: 14.
48. Sandys, *Relation*, 181; Heylyn, *Cosmographie in foure Bookes* (1652), bk 3: 122.
49. Sebastian Munster, *A Briefe Collection and compendious extract of straunge and memorable things* (1572), 41.
50. Giovanni Botero, *Relations of the Most Famous Kingdoms and Common-wealths*, trans. Robert Johnson (1601; rpt. 1608), 557.
51. Abdal-Rahman al-Marrakishi al-Suktani, *Kitab al-Ajwiba al-Fiqhiyya*, Rabat, National Library, Ms Jeem 1016, fols. 280–3.
52. Thomas Roe, *The Embassy of Sir Thomas Roe to India, 1615–19*, ed. William Foster (1899); rev. 1926; rpt. New Delhi, 1990, 313, 559.
53. Pietro della Valle, *The Travels of Sig. Pietro della Valle, A Noble Roman, Into East-India and Arabia Deserta* (1665), 475.
54. Rupert A. Hall and Marie Boas Hall, eds. and trans., *The Correspondence of Henry Oldenburg*, 5 vols. (Madison, WI, 1965–68), 1: 410.
55. *Four Treatises Concerning the Doctrine, Discipline and Worship of the Mahometans* (London, 1712), 170.
56. See Nabil Matar, 'The Toleration of Muslims in Renaissance England: Practice and Theory', in John C. Laursen, ed., *Religious Toleration from Cyrus to Defoe: The Variety of Rites* (New York, 1999), 127–46.
57. Moryson, *Itinerary*, 2: 34.
58. Sandys, *Relation*, 173.
59. T. B., *A Journey to Jerusalem: Or, a Relation of the Travels of Fourteen English-Men, in the Year, 1669* (1672), 13.
60. Rycaut, *Greek and Armenian Churches*, 21.
61. John Locke, *Two Tracts on Government*, ed. Philip Abrams (Cambridge, 1967), 130.
62. See also Nabil Matar, 'John Locke and the "Turbanned Nations"', *Journal of Islamic Studies* 2 (1991): 67–77.
63. BL Add Ms 22910, fo. 242.
64. Ibid, fo. 186.
65. Ibid., fo. 245.
66. Ibid., fo. 246.
67. Ibid., fo. 247.
68. Edmund Bohun, *A Geographical Dictionary* (1691), n. 'Palestina'.
69. Heylyn, *Cosmographia*, bk 3: 70.
70. Meriton, *Geographical Description*, 150.
71. Lewes Roberts, *The Marchants Map of Commerce* (1638), part 2, chapter 64.
72. Kenneth Nebenzahl, *Maps of the Holy Land* (New York, 1986), 85; Jerry Brotton, *Trading Territories: Mapping the Early Modern World* (London, 1997), 152.
73. Abraham Ortelius, *Theatrum Orbis Terrarum, The Theatre of the Whole World* (1606), 109.
74. Ibid., 110.

75. Ibid., 114.
76. See R. V. Tooley, 'Maps of Palestine in the Atlas of Ortelius', *The Map Collector* 3 (June 1978): 28–31.
77. See Marcel R. van den Broecke, *Ortelius Atlas Maps: An Illustrated Guide* ('t Goy, 1996), plates 170–3 and 180.
78. Early modern travel writing about Palestine in Arabic remains chiefly in manuscript. For an important printed account awaiting translation, see 'Abd al-Ghani al-Nabulsi, *Al-hadra al-unsiyyah fi al-safara al-qudsiyyah*, ed. Akram Hasan al-'Ulabi (Beirut, 1991).
79. See Hakluyt, *Principal Navigations*, 3: 72–82.
80. See Sandys, *Relation*, 158–201.
81. Purchas, *Hakluytus Posthumus*, 7: 464.
82. Fuller, *Pisgah-Sight*, bk. 4, 18; and see Gerald MacLean, 'Strolling in Syria with William Biddulph', *Criticism* 46: 3 (Summer 2004): 415–40.
83. See Heylyn, *Cosmographia*, bk 3: 70–98.
84. See Nabil Matar, 'Two Journeys to Seventeenth-Century Palestine', *Journal of Palestine Studies,* 29 (2000): 66–79.
85. Robert Morden, *Geography Rectified: Or, A Description of the World* (1680); rpt. 1693, 361.
86. Henry Maundrell, *A Journey from Aleppo to Jerusalem in 1697*, ed. David Howell (Beirut, 1963), 35, 118.
87. Richard Helgerson, *Forms of Nationhood: The Elizabethan Writing of England* (Chicago, 1992), 107.
88. George Abbot, *A Briefe Description of the Whole World* (1599); rpt. 1664, 133. For a seventeenth-century account about the fertility of Palestine, see al-Nabulsi, *Al-hadra al-unsiyyah*, 78–91, and see Nabil Matar, 'Orthodox, Sunni, and Anglican in Palestine, *c.*1642–1697', forthcoming in Judy Hayden and Nabil Matar, eds., *Through the Eyes of the Beholder: Images of the Holy Land in the Early Modern Period* (Leiden, 2011).
89. James Shapiro, *Shakespeare and the Jews* (New York, 1996), 147.
90. Sanderson, *Travels*, 95–121.
91. Lithgow, *Totall Discourse*, 257; Sandys, *Relation*, 148.
92. Lynn Glaser, *Indians or Jews? An Introduction to a Reprint of Manasseh ben Israel's The Hope of Israel* (Gilroy, CA, 1973), 49.
93. [George Phillips], *The Present State of Tangier* (1676), 42.
94. Heylyn, *Cosmographie*, bk 3: 106. For studies of Jews in the Ottoman Empire, see Aryeh Shmuelevitz, *The Jews of the Ottoman Empire in the Fifteenth and Sixteenth Centuries* (Leiden, 1984), esp. chapter 4, and Stanford J. Shaw, *The Jews of the Ottoman Empire and the Turkish Republic* (New York, 1991), chapter 3.
95. Bernard Lewis, *The Jews of Islam* (London, 1984).
96. George Abbot, *A Briefe Description of the Whole World* (1599; rpt. 1664), 105.
97. Sandys, *Relation*, 146.
98. Lancelot Addison, *The Present State of the Jews* (1675), 7–8.

99. Moryson, *Shakespeare's Europe*, 489.
100. Manwaring, 'True Discourse', 188.
101. Ottaviano Bon, *A Description of the Grand Signour's Seraglio, or Turkish Emperor's Court*, trans. Robert Withers (1650); rpt. 1653, 56–7; and see Gainsford, *Glory of England*, 191.
102. William Biddulph, *The Travels of certaine Englishmen into Africa, Asia, Troy, Bithnia, Thracia, and to the Blacke Sea* (1609), 73; Heylyn, *Cosmographie*, bk 3: 106.
103. 'The fatal and final Extirpation and Destruction of the Jews out of the Empire of Persia, begun in 1663' first appeared in John Evelyn, *Three Late Famous Imposters* (1669), and was later reprinted in Nathaniel Crouch, ed., *Two Journeys to Jerusalem* (1692).
104. See Cecil Roth, 'The Jews of Jerusalem in the Seventeenth Century: An English Account', *Journal of the Jewish Historical Society of England*, pt 2 (1935): 99–104.
105. Wheeler M. Thackston, trans. and ed., *The Jahangirnama, Memoirs of Jahangir, Emperor of India* (New York and Oxford, 1999), 40.
106. Sandys, *Relation*, 189.
107. Ibid., 147.
108. See David Katz, *Philo-Semitism and the Readmission of the Jews to England, 1603–1655* (Oxford, 1982), and John Toland, *Reasons for Naturalizing the Jews in Great Britain, and Ireland, on the Same Foot with All Other Nations* (London, 1714).
109. Sandys, *Relation*, 147. Sandys adds that the Jews' 'familiar speech is Spanish: yet few of them are ignorant in the *Hebrew, Turkish, Moresco*, vulgar *Greeke*, and *Italian* languages', 148.
110. Addison, *Present State*, 9.
111. See Gerald R. Cragg, *Puritanism in the Age of the Great Persecution, 1660–1688* (New York, 1971), and on the Clarendon Code, see Christopher Hill, *The Century of Revolution, 1603–1714*. 1961; rpt. (London, 1974), chapters 14, 15.
112. George Philips, *The Present State of Tangier* (1676), 43–51.
113. Leah Sumbel, *Memoirs of the Life of Mrs. Sumbel,* 3 vols. (London, 1811), 1: 190–239. Our thanks to Khalid Bekkaoui for this reference.
114. Henry Blount, *A Voyage Into the Levant* (1636), 113–15.
115. For interest in the Ten Lost Tribes, especially in the context of Native Americans, see Glaser's *Indians or Jews*.
116. Thomas Fuller, *A Pisgah-Sight of Palestine and the Confines Thereof* (1650), bk 5: 191–3.
117. Hill, *Full and Just Account*, 328.
118. See Nabil Matar, *Islam in Britain, 1558–1685* (Cambridge, 1998), chapter 5.
119. John Harrison, *The Messiah Already Come. Or Proofs of Christianitie* (Amsterdam, 1613; rpt. 1619).

120. See Mercedes García-Arenal and Gerard Wiegers, *A Man of Three Worlds: Samuel Pallache, a Moroccan Jew in Catholic and Protestant Europe* (Baltimore, MD, 2003), chapter 3.
121. *The Restauration of the Jewes: Or, A True Relation of their progress and Proceedings* (1665), 1, 3.
122. Petrus Serrurier, *The Last Letters, To the London-Merchants and Faithful Ministers* (1665); *A Brief Relation of Several Remarkable Passages of the Jewes, In their Journey out of Persia, and Tartaria toward Jerusalem* (1666); and see Michael McKeon, 'Sabbatai Sevi In England', *AJS Review* 2 (1977): 131–69.
123. Paul Rycaut, *The History of the Turkish Empire, From the Year 1623, to the year 1677* (1680), 204.
124. See Gershom Scholem, *Sabbatai Sevi, The Mystical Messiah, 1626–1676* (Princeton, NJ, 1973), especially units 5 and 6.
125. *CSPD, Addenda, 1660–85*, 104 (7 June 1664).
126. E. M. G. Routh, *Tangier: England's Lost Atlantic Outpost, 1661–1684* (London, 1912, 276.
127. TNA CO 279/30 fo. 293v. (15 Dec 1682).
128. TNA SP 71/2 fo. 64v. The account was later printed as *The Present State of Algiers*, attached to Phillips' *Present State* (1676).
129. Simon Ockley, *An Account of South-West Barbary* (London, 1713), 28, 29.
130. TNA SP 41/34 fo. 288.
131. TNA SP 71/16 fos. 403–4 (26 December 1715).
132. John Noorthouck, *A New History of London: Including Westminster and Southwark* (1773), 301.
133. TNA CO 91/1 fo. 195 (20 August 1725).
134. Lucien Wolf, 'Status of the Jews in England after the Re-Settlement', *Jewish Historical Society of England* 4 (1899–1901): 177–91; A. S. Diamond, 'The Community of the Resettlement, 1656–1684, A Social Survey', *Jewish Historical Society of England, Transactions* 24 (1970–73): 134–50; David Katz, 'The Abendana Brothers and the Christian Hebraists of Seventeenth-Century England', *Journal of Ecclesiastical History* 40 (1989): 28–52.
135. *CSP, Foreign, 1581–82*, 49.
136. So Paris O'Donnell, 'Pilgrimage or "anti-pilgrimage"? Uses of mementos and relics in English and Scottish narratives of travel to Jerusalem, 1596–1632', *Studies in Travel Writing*, 13 (2009): 125–39, this passage 136 n. 9. In 1669, T. B. reported seeing a list of all English visitors to Jerusalem between 1561 and 1669 (*Journey to Jerusalem*, 83) and the number is less than O'Donnell suggests.
137. In a letter sent to 'the one in authority' [*sahib al-amr*] he claims knowing Hebrew, Syriac, Turkish, Latin, French, and Arabic, 'which is my real language'; BL Ms Burney 367, fo. 200. See also Alastair Hamilton, 'An Egyptian Traveller in the Republic of Letters: Josephus Barbatus or Abudacnus the Copt', *Journal of the Warburg and Courtauld Institutes* 57 (1994): 123–50.

Abudacnus's *The True History of the Jacobites of Egypt* was published in 1692 to ensure that English readers could distinguish between the 'Old Jacobites of Aegypt, and New Jacobites of England'; see 'Epistle to the Reader'.
138. Richard Hakluyt, *Divers voyages touching the discoverie of America* (1582), 3.
139. See Claire S. Schen, 'Greeks and "Grecians" in London: The "Other" Strangers', in Randolph Vigne and Charles Littleton, eds., *From Strangers to Citizens* (Brighton, 2001), 268–75.
140. Purchas, *Hakluytus Posthumus*, 3: 15.
141. Robert Coverte, *A True and Almost Incredible Report of an Englishman* (1612), 40.
142. See Sandys, *Relation*, 168, 169, 178.
143. What follows is indebted to Ina Baghdiantz, 'The Armenian Merchants in New Julfa: Some Aspects of their International Trade in the Late Seventeenth Century' (PhD dissertation, Columbia University, 1993), chapter 7; and R. W. Ferrier, 'The Armenians and the East India Company in Persia in the Seventeenth and Early Eighteenth Century', *Economic History Review*, 2nd Series, 26 (1973): 38–62.
144. Cited from Ferrier, 'Armenians', 47.
145. Foster, ed., *English Factories*, 64, 9.
146. Ferrier, 'Armenians', 48 n. 7.
147. Cited ibid., 54 n. 3.
148. Foster, ed., *English Factories*, 66.
149. Manwaring, 'True Discourse', 193.
150. *CSP, Colonial, East Indies, China, and Japan, 1513–1616*, 172; and see 186 (10 June 1609).
151. Pagitt, *Christianography*, 18.
152. M. Garayzabal, *A Brief Relation of the late Martyrdome of five Persians Converted to the Catholique Faith by the reformed Carmelites* (Douai, 1623), sig. A3v.
153. Herbert, *Relation* (1634), 69, and John Chardin, *Sir John Chardin's Travels in Persia*, trans. Edmund Lloyd, 2 vols. in 1 (London, 1720), 1: 140–7.
154. See Vahe Baladouni and Margaret Makepeace, eds., *Armenian Merchants of the Seventeenth and early Eighteenth Centuries* (Philadelphia, PA, 1998).
155. Mawsuli in Matar, *In the Lands of the Christians* (New York, 2003) 102, 105.
156. Baghdiantz, 'The Armenian Merchants', 201; see also R. W. Ferrier, 'The Agreement of the East India Company with the Armenian Nation 22nd June 1688', *Revue des etudes arméniens* 7, n.s. (1970): 427–43.
157. BL Add Ms 61542 fo. 49 (4 July 1707).
158. Covel, *Some Account*, xvii. For an alternative view to Covel's, see Marie-Carmen Smyrnelis, 'Les Armeniens catholiques aux XVIIIeme et XIXeme siécles', *Revue du Monde Arménien moderne et contemporain* 2 (1995): 25–44.
159. Joseph Pitts, *A True and Faithful Account of the Religion and Manners of the Mohammetans* (Exeter, 1704), 169, in Daniel J. Vitkus, ed., *Piracy, Slavery and Redemption: English Captivity Narratives in North Africa, 1577–1704*, 331.

160. Vartan Gregorian, 'Minorities of Isfahan: The Armenian Community of Isfahan, 1587–1722', *Persian Studies* 7 (1974), 652–80, this passage 666–7. Photographs of those churches and their interiors appear in John Carswell, *New Julfa: The Armenian Churches and Other Buildings* (Oxford, 1968).
161. Baldouni and Makespeace, eds., *Armenian Merchants*, 53.
162. Daniel Defoe, *Captain Singleton*, ed. Shiv K. Kumar (Oxford, 1990), 272.
163. BL Add Ms 61493 fos. 43v, 47r.
164. Narcissus Luttrell, *A Brief Historical Relation of State Affairs from September 1679 to April 1714*, 6 vols. (Oxford, 1857), 6: 577. For the letter see TNA SP 71/15 fo. 237 (8 June 1710).
165. Ibid., fos. 277–8.
166. Ibid., fos. 237–9; and see TNA SP 71/16 fo. 238.
167. TNA SP 71/15 fo. 249.
168. *The Speech of His Excellency Don V. Zary* (London, 1710).
169. Ibid.
170. TNA SP 71/15 fo. 233.
171. Ibid., fo. 259.
172. TNA SP 44/113 fo. 408.
173. TNA SP 71/15 fo. 275.
174. TNA SP 71/16 fo. 270.
175. TNA SP 71/15 fos. 289–93.
176. Ibid., fo. 293.
177. TNA SP 71/16 fo. 256.
178. *The Post Boy* (From Tuesday March 25. To Thursday March 27 March. 1712), #2633. The reference to the *Gazette* appears in a letter by Jones of 3 January 1713, TNA SP 71/16 fo. 34.
179. Ibid., fo. 34.
180. Ibid., fo. 24.
181. Ibid., fo. 32.
182. TNA SP 71/16 fo. 76.
183. Ibid., fo. 57v.
184. The Jesuits established themselves in Istanbul in 1609 and in New Julfa thirty years later; Richard G. Hovannisian, ed. *The Armenian People from Ancient to Modern Times*. 2 vols. (Basingstoke, 1997), 1: 323.
185. Ockley, *South-West Barbary*, 41.
186. Ibid.
187. David Green, *Queen Anne* (New York, 1970), 316.
188. TNA SP 102/4 fo. 119.
189. Ibid.
190. Sir John Child, while governor of the East India Company, however, seems to have had fewer scruples. Alexander Hamilton reports that during the 'War of Bombay' in 1686, Child sent 'Mr. *George Weldon* and *Abraham Navaar* a *Jew*' to negotiate at the court of Aureng Zebe 'under the Name of *English*

Ambassadors'; *A New Account of the East-Indies: Being the Observations and Remarks of Capt. Alexander Hamilton*, 2 vols. (London, 1739), 1: 224.

191. TNA PROB 32/60 fo. 23 (28 September 1716), signed by Davidis Chiriaco.
192. Mohammad Taghi Nezam-Mafi, 'Persian Recreations: Theatricality in Anglo-Persian Diplomatic History, 1599–1827' (PhD dissertation, Boston University, 1999), 11, 26.
193. Franciscus de Billerbeg, *Most rare and straunge discourses, of Amurathe the Turkish emperor* (1584). See also the translations from the Italian, Giovanni Tommaso Minadoi, *The History of the Warres betvveene the Turks and the Persians*, trans. Abraham Hartwell (London, 1595).
194. Manwaring, 'True Discourse', 192.
195. Ibid., 209, 218.
196. Jenkinson in Hakluyt, *Principal Navigations*, 2: 21.
197. John Cartwright, *The Preachers Travels Wherein is set downe a true Journall to the confines of the East Indies* (1611), 97.
198. Abbot, *Briefe Description*, 105.
199. Gainsford, *Glory of England*, 24.
200. Knolles, *Generall Historie*, 464.
201. Roe, *Embassy*, 123.
202. Lancelot Addison, *The Life and Death of Mahumed* (1679), 57.
203. See the 1650 documents, 'Moores and Armenian merchants' and 'Armenien and Persian merchants', in Baldouni and Makepeace, eds., *Armenian Merchants*, 47.
204. Herbert, *Relation* (1634), 160, 159.
205. Ibid., 153–8.
206. Rudolph P. Matthee, 'Between Aloofness and Fascination: Safavid Views of the West', *Persian Studies* 31 (1998): 219–46, this passage 222.
207. Ibid., 229 and n. 43.
208. Chardin, *Travels*, 2: 159.
209. Pococke, *Specimen*, 24–6, 260–5.
210. BL Ms Harleian 6189, fos. 161–7. See Henry Stubbe, *The Rise and Progress of Mahometanism*, ed. Nabil Matar (New York, forthcoming).
211. David Jones, *A Compleat History of the Turks, From their Origin in the year 755, to the year 1718*, 4 vols. (1719), 3: 67, and chapter 5 generally.
212. Chardin, *Travels*, 1: 219. In May 1652, Shah 'Abbas II's secretary told a Dutch ambassador that the Dutch could expect the same immunities as the English 'when they had don such service to the Crowne of Persia as the English nacion had don', cited in Foster, ed., *English Factories . . . 1651–1654*, 124.
213. For a similar observation about French attitudes, see Harrigan, *Veiled Encounters*, 155.
214. Thomas Hyde, *Historia Religionis Veterum Persarum, eurumque Magorum* (Oxford, 1700); see Nora Kathleen Firby, *European Travellers and their Perceptions of Zoroastrians in the 17th and 18th Centuries* (Berlin, 1988).

215. Clements R. Markham, ed., *The Voyages of Sir James Lancaster, to the East Indies* (1877; rpt. New Delhi, 1998), 7.
216. Ibid., 97, 96; William Bedwell's translation of the letter appears ibid., 95–7.
217. Herbert, *Relation* (1634), 129.
218. William Parry, *A New and Large Discourse of the Travels of Sir Anthony Sherley* (1601), 23, 10; and see Chloë Houston, '"Thou glorious kingdome, thou chiefe of Empires:" Persia in early seventeenth-century travel writing', *Studies in Travel Writing* 13: 2 (June 2009): 141–52.
219. Hakluyt, *Principal Navigations*, 3: 286.
220. See Gerald MacLean, *Looking East: English Writing and the Ottoman Empire before 1800* (Basingstoke, 2007), chapter 5, 'The Sultan's Beasts: Encountering Ottoman Fauna'.
221. Purchas, *Hakluytus Posthumus*, 9: 46.
222. Ibid., 9: 38–9.
223. Roe, *Embassy*, 195.
224. Ibid., 270.
225. Ibid., 274, 275.
226. Ibid., 275–6, 345.
227. Ibid., 276.
228. Kenneth Parker, ed., *Early Modern Tales of Orient: A Critical Anthology* (London, 1999), 13.

CHAPTER 6

1. Jean Baptiste Tavernier, *The Six Voyages of John Baptista Tavernier, Baron of Aubonne*, trans. John Phillips (1677), 60.
2. On the wide use of English broadcloth known as 'çuka', see Christoph Neumann, 'How Did a Vizier Dress in the Eighteenth Century', in Faroqhi and Neumann, eds., *Ottoman Costumes*, 181–217, especially 190; and see Halil Inalcık, *Economic and Social History of the Ottoman Empire, Vol One. 1300–1600* 1994; rpt. (Cambridge, 1997), 353.
3. Verney, Frances Parthenhope and Margaret M. Verney, eds. *Memoirs of the Verney Family During the Seventeenth Century* (1892); rev. ed., 2 vols, London, 1907, 2: 263.
4. Sanjay Subrahmanyam, 'Connected Histories: Notes towards a Reconfiguration of Early Modern Eurasia', *Modern Asian Studies* 31 (1997): 735–62, lines quoted 750; and see Andre Gunder Frank, *Re-Orient: Global Economy in the Asian Age* (Berkeley and Los Angeles, 1998).
5. Donald Quataert, ed., *Consumption Studies and the History of the Ottoman Empire, 1550–1922* (Albany, NY, 2000), Introduction, 4, and see 5–7, 10–11. See also Rudi Matthee, 'Exotic Substances: The Introduction and Global Spread of Tobacco, Coffee, Cocoa, Tea and Distilled Liquor, Sixteenth to Eighteenth Centuries', in Roy Porter and Mikulas Teich, eds., *Drugs and Narcotics in History* (Cambridge,

1995), 24–51, and John E. Wills, 'European Consumption and Asian Production in the Seventeenth and Eighteenth Centuries', in John Brewer and Roy Porter, eds., *Consumption and the World of Goods* (London, 1993), 133–47.
6. Keith Thomas, *The Ends of Life: Roads to Fulfilment in Early Modern England* (Oxford, 2009), 111.
7. Leslie Peirce, 'The Material World: Ideologies and Ordinary Things', in Aksan and Goffman, eds., *The Early Modern Ottomans*, 213–32, this passage 214–15.
8. See Maxine Berg, *Luxury and Pleasure in Eighteenth-century Britain* (Oxford, 2005), 46–84, especially 49–50.
9. John Sweetman, *The Oriental Obsession: Islamic Inspiration in British and American Art and Architecture, 1500–1920* (Cambridge, 1988), 1–72.
10. Ibid., 16; and see Gerald MacLean, *Looking East: English Writing and the Ottoman Empire before 1800* (Basingstoke, 2007), 39–41; Berg, *Luxury*, 79–80.
11. William Lithgow, *The Totall Discourse of The Rare Adventures and Painefull Peregrinations* (1632); rpt. Glasgow, 1906, 58.
12. William Congreve, *Way of World*, 4: 240–1.
13. [Charles II], *By the King. A Proclamation for the Suppression of Coffee-Houses* (1675).
14. Colin Imber, *Ebu's-su'ud: The Islamic Legal Tradition* (Edinburgh, 1997), 93–4; and see James Grehan, 'Smoking and "Early Modern" Sociability: The Great Tobacco Debate in the Ottoman Middle East (Seventeenth to Eighteenth Centuries', *American Historical Review*, 111: 5 (December 2006): 1352–77, and Ralph Hattox, *Coffee and Coffeehouses: The Origins of a Social Beverage in the Medieval Near East* (Seattle, WA, 1985), 43.
15. Donna Landry, *Noble Brutes: How Eastern Horses Transformed English Culture* (Baltimore, MD, 2008).
16. Peirce, 'Material World', 230, and Selma Akyazici Özkoçak, 'Coffeehouses: Rethinking the Public and Private in Early Modern Istanbul', *Journal of Urban History* 33 (2007): 965–86; this point, 971.
17. James I, *A Counter Blaste to Tobacco* (1604), sig. Bv.
18. Samuel Rowlands, 'The Devils health-drinker', in *The Knave of Clubbes* (1609), sig. E4v.
19. C. T., *An Advice how to Plant Tobacco in England* (1615), sig. B4v.
20. [Brathwaite, Richard], *The Smoaking Age*, in *A Solemne Joviall Disputation, Theoreticke and Practicke* (1617), 197; and see 155 where Pluto advises Tobacco: 'Plant thy selfe in the eye of the Citie: set mee the picture of some sallow-faced Blackamoore, or a Virginia-man, for that will rather draw custome upon the Frontespice of thy doore.'
21. Muhammad al-Saghir ibn Muhammad al-Ifrani, *Nuzhat al-Hadi*, ed. 'Abd al-Latif al-Shadhili (Casablanca, 1998), 248.
22. *Nasihat al-Ikhwan*, National Library, Rabat, MS Kha Meem 100, fos. 301, 297.
23. Ibid., fo. 312.
24. Ibid., fo. 299.

25. See Muhammad Hajji, 'Al-Tabgh fi al-Maghrib', in *Jawlat Tarikhiyya* (Beirut, 1995), 580-6.
26. 'Abd al-Karim Lafqun, 'Muhaddid al-Sinan fi Nuhur Akhwan al-Dukhan', Royal Library of Rabat, MS 6929: 33, fos. 52–3.
27. See *Wasf al-Mamalik al-Maghribiyya*, trans. 'Abd al-Wahid Akmir (Rabat, 1997), 177–8.
28. Muhammad al-Mannuni, *Rakb al-Hajj al-Maghribi* (Tetuan, 1953), 21; and see Grehan, 'Smoking', who cites a version of this incident from Egyptian sources, 1352.
29. 'One of the first colonial goods imported by English merchants into Turkey was tobacco, around 1600. It soon became a widely consumed commodity in Turkey,' Inalcık, *Economic and Social History*, 359.
30. Grehan, 'Smoking', 1362.
31. Cited by Cemal Kafadar, 'A History of Coffee,' unpublished working paper.
32. Grehan, 'Smoking', 1362 n. 45.
33. On the Kadızadeli movement, see Madeline Zilfi, 'The Kadızadelis: Discordant Revivialism in Seventeeth-Century Istanbul', *Journal of Near Eastern Studies* 45 (1986): 251–69, and Cemal Kafadar, 'Janissaries and other Riffraff of Ottoman Istanbul: Rebels without a Cause?', in Baki Tezcan and Karl. K. Barbir, eds., *Identity and Identity Formation in the Ottoman World* (Madison, WI, 2007), 113–34.
34. Thevenot, *Travels*, 62.
35. Katib Çelebi, *The Balance of Truth*, trans. Geoffrey Lewis (London, 1957), 50–1.
36. Ibid., 51, and see Inalcık, *Economic and Social History,* 359.
37. Katib Çelebi, *Balance*, 51.
38. Ibid., 52, 58.
39. Grehan, 'Smoking', 1355.
40. Alfred C. Wood, *A History of the Levant Company* (1935); rpt. London, 1964, 76.
41. See MacLean, *Looking East*, 39.
42. Cited by Audrey W. Douglas, 'Cotton Textiles in England: The East India Company's Attempt to Exploit Developments in Fashion, 1660–1721', *Journal of British Studies* 8: 2 (1969): 28–43, at 30.
43. See William Foster, ed., *The Voyage of Nicholas Downton to the East Indies, 1614–1615* (1939; rpt. New Delhi, 1997), xxviii.
44. Michel Morineau, 'The Indian Challenge: Seventeenth to Eighteenth Centuries', in Sushil Chaudhury and Michel Morineau, eds., *Merchants, Companies and Trade: Europe and Asia in the Early Modern Era* (Cambridge, 1999), 243–75, this passage, 243.
45. Ibid., 244.
46. On Hargreaves and Arkwright, see *ODNB*; James Butterworth, *A Complete History of the Cotton Trade* (Manchester, 1823), 76–93; and R. S. Fitton, *The Arkwrights: Spinners of Fortune* (Manchester, 1989).

47. Washing, bleaching, and dyeing are all ancient arts that made their way westward from Egypt and Babylon. By 1480 the London fullers who bleached grey cloth formed their own guild, later merging with the Guild of Cloth Workers in 1527. Dyeing was a more complicated process than bleaching, involving minerals and costly dye-stuffs many of which needed to be imported. Dyers in London and Yorkshire became the Company of Dyers in 1472 and were subsequently regulated by Parliamentary Acts permitting and restricting the colours and materials they might produce. The rivers and streams of Lancashire supplied the vast quantities of fresh water needed for washing, bleaching, and rinsing by the rapidly expanding industries that grew up there during the seventeenth century specializing in the making and dyeing of fustians that blended flax yarn with imported cotton. See: Geoffrey Turnbull and John Turnbull, *A History of the Calico Printing Industry of Great Britain* (Altrincham, 1951), 1–30; Butterworth, *Complete History*, 1–75; Alfred Wadsworth and Julia de Lacy Mann, *The Cotton Trade and Industrial Lancashire, 1600–1780* (Manchester, 1931), 15.
48. Turnbull and Turnbull, *History*, 1951, 18.
49. Douglas, 'Cotton Textiles', 32.
50. *The true Case of The Silk-Throwsters, Weavers and Dyers, with Their Petition to the Parliament* (1689), broadside.
51. *Considerations Humbly offered to the Right Honourable the Lords Spiritual and Temporal in Parliament Assembled* [1689?], 2.
52. *Querical Demonstrations Writ by Prince Butler, Author of the Eleven Queries Relating to The Bill for Prohibiting East-India Silks and Printed Callicoes* [1699?], broadside.
53. *Five Queries Humbly Tender'd, Relating to the Bill for Prohibiting the Consumption of East-India Silks, Bengals and Printed Callicoes* [1696?], broadside.
54. Richard Steele, *The Female Manufacturers Complaint* (London, 1720), 10.
55. See Douglas, 'Cotton Textiles', 35–6.
56. Daniel Defoe, *A Review of the State of the British Nation*, 4: 152 (31 January 1708), 606.
57. Daniel Defoe, *A Brief State of the Question Between the Printed and Painted Callicoes and the Woollen and Silk Manufacturers... The Third Edition* (1719; rpt. London, 1720), sig. A4.
58. Turnbull and Turnbull, *History*, 21.
59. Edward Baines, *History of the County Palatine and Duchy of Lancaster*, 4 vols. (London, 1836), 2: 397; and see Turnbull and Turnbull, *History*, 23, and Wadsworth and Mann, *Cotton Trade*, 118–9.
60. Alexander Ross, *Pansebeia, or: A View of all Religions in the World* (1653; rpt. 1675), 58; Evliya [Çelebi] Efendi, *Narrative of Travels in Europe, Asia, and Africa, in the Seventeenth Century*, trans Joseph von Hammer, 2 vols. (London, 1834, 1850), 1: 3.
61. See William Seaman, *The Reign of Sultan Orchan Second King of the Turks. Translated out of Hojah Effendi* (1652), 27.

62. Ivan Kalmar, 'Jesus Did Not Wear a Turban: Orientalism, the Jews, and Christian Art', in Ivan Davidson Kalmar and Derek J. Penslar eds., *Orientalism and the Jews* (Waltham, MA, 2005), 3–31.
63. See, for example, Jan van Dornicke, 'The Adoration of the Magi' (late 1520s); Gaudenzio Ferrari, 'The Holy Family with a Donor' (late 1520s); Jacobo Bassano, 'Christ healing the Lame Man' (fl. 1510–1592); Marcello Fogolino, 'Adoration of the Kings' (fl. 1519–48); Sisto Badalocchio, 'Susannah and the Elders' (c.1610); Francesco Caior 'Judith with the Head of Holofernes' (c.1630–35); Rembrandt, 'The Descent from the Cross' (1633); Pietro Berretini, 'Hagar and the Angel' (c.1637–38); Jacob Jordaens, 'Boaz' (c.1641–42); Mattia Preti, 'Salome with the Head of John the Baptist' (c.1648).
64. See Rubens' 'Portrait of Mulay Ahmad', and the mysterious musician in Rembrandt's 'Musical Company'.
65. Edward Halle, *Hall's Chronicle: Containing the History of England during the reign of Henry the Fourth,* ed. Sir Henry Ellis (London, 1809), 513. See also Maria Hayward, 'Symbols of Majesty: Cloths of Estate at the Court of Henry VIII', *Furniture History* (2005): 1–11.
66. Sweetman, *Oriental Obsession*, 12.
67. H. B. Rosedale, *Queen Elizabeth and the Levant Company* (London, 1904), 16.
68. Susan A. Skilliter, 'Three Letters from the Ottoman "Sultana" Safiye to Queen Elizabeth I', in S. M. Stern, ed., *Documents from Islamic Chanceries* (Oxford, 1965), 148.
69. Robert Schwoebel, *The Shadow of the Crescent: The Renaissance Image of the Turk (1453–1517)* (New York, 1967), 178.
70. Lithgow, *Totall Discourse,* frontispiece.
71. Henry Blount, *A Voyage Into the Levant* (1636), 98.
72. George Gascoigne, 'Councill given to Master Bartholomew Withipoll', in *The Complete Poems of George Gascoigne,* ed. W. Carew Hazlitt, 2 vols. (London, 1869), 1: 375.
73. Amanda Wunder, 'Western Travellers, Eastern Antiquities, and the Image of the Turk in Early Modern Europe', *Journal of Early Modern History* 7 (2003): 89–119, this phrase 115.
74. The Marquesse Virgilio Malvezzi, *Il Davide Perseguitato, David Persecuted,* trans. Robert Ashley (1647; rpt., 1650), 14.
75. John Trapp, *A Commentary or Exposition upon all the Epistles* (1647), 678.
76. Cited by Abdeljelil Temimi, *Etudes d'Histoire Morisque* (Zaghouan, Tunisia, 1993), 77.
77. George Sandys, *A Relation of a Journey begun An. Dom: 1610* (1615), 63. Robert Baron quoted those words and added a long footnote on the use of the turban to his play, *Mirza: A Tragedie* (1647), 179–80.
78. Samuel Purchas, ed. *Hakluytus Posthumus, or, Purchas His Pilgrimes* (1625); rpt. 20 vols. Glasgow, 1905–7, 9: 113.
79. William Biddulph, *The Travels of certaine Englishmen into Africa, Asia, Troy, Bithnia, Thracia, and to the Blacke Sea* (1609), 72.

80. Giovanni Botero, *Relations of the Most Famous Kingdoms and Common-weales,* trans. Robert Johnson (1601; rpt., 1608), 267.
81. Sandys, *Relation,* 56.
82. Robert Daborne, *A Christian Turn'd Turke* (1612), sig. F2v. In 1892, when Frances Parthenope Verney compiled the *Memoirs of the Verney Family,* she referred to the turban still preserved at Claydon House which had belonged to Sir Francis Verney, a fellow pirate of Ward, 1: 63–8.
83. Jean Dumont, *A New Voyage to the Levant* (1696), 326.
84. Trapp, *Commentary,* 679. See also Ross, *Pansebeia* (1675): Muslim children 'are circumcised about eight years of age; the Child is carried on horse back, with a Tullipant on his head', 173.
85. Sandys, *Relation,* 63.
86. Jean Baptiste Tavernier, *Collections of Travels through Turkey into Persia, and the East Indies,* trans. John Phillips and Edmund Everard (1684), 176 [mispaginated '169' at sig. Y4v].
87. *The Arrivall and Intertainements of the Embassador, Alkaid Jaurar Ben Abdella* (1637), frontispiece portrait, 5.
88. Charles Fitz-Geffry, *Compassion towards Captives chiefly towards our brethren and country-men* (Oxford, 1637), sig. **.
89. See the illustration from Francis Knight's *Relation* reproduced on the cover of Vitkus, ed., *Piracy.*
90. Edward Kellet and Henry Byam, *A Returne from Argier. A Sermon Preached at Minhead in the County of Somerset* (1628), 31.
91. Ibid., 75.
92. Ibid., 32.
93. Ibid., 41.
94. Ibid., 75.
95. Thomas Pellow, *The History of the Long Captivity and Adventures of Thomas Pellow, in South-Barbar.* (London, 1739), 16.
96. Paul Rycaut, The *Present State of the Greek and Armenian Churches, Anno Christi, 1678* (London, 1679), 288, 289.
97. Tavernier, *Collections,* 176 [mispaginated '169' at sig Y4v].
98. John Dryden, *Don Sebastian* (1690), 102.
99. 'A Broad-Side Against Coffee: Or, The Marriage of the Turk' appears within a tract catalogued in the Wing *STC* at J147 under King James I, *Two Broad-Sides Against Tobacco* (1672); the illustration appears 63.
100. Samuel Pepys, *The Diary of Samuel Pepys,* eds. Robert Latham and William Matthews, 11 vols. (Los Angeles and Berkeley, CA, 1970–83), 7: 378 (21 November 1666).

101. John Evelyn, *Diary*, ed. E. S. de Beer. 6 vols. (Oxford: Clarendon, 1955), 3: 464–5 (18 October 1667); and see Charlotte Jirousek, 'Ottoman Influences in Western Dress', in Faroqhi and Neumann, eds., *Ottoman Costumes*, 231–51.
102. Evelyn, *Diary*, 4: 266. The painting is reproduced on the cover of Nabil Matar, *In the Lands of the Christians* (New York, 2003).
103. Wilfrid Blunt, *Black Sunrise: The Life and Times of Mulai Ismail Emperor of Morocco, 1646–1727* (London, 1951), 191 n. 4, citing a report from the memoirs of the French ambassador, Saint-Olon.
104. Janusz J. Tomiak, 'A British Poet's Account of the Raising of the Siege of Vienna in 1683', *Polish Review* 5 (1966): 66–74, this passage 70.
105. Joseph Addison, *The Tatler* 161 (20 April 1710), in Donald F. Bond, ed., *The Tatler*, 3 vols. (Oxford, 1987), 2: 401.
106. Joseph Morgan, *A Compleat History of the Piratical States of Barbary* (London, 1750), v.
107. Landry, *Noble Brutes*, 4; see also Miklos Jankovich, *They Rode into Europe: The Fruitful Exchange in the Arts of Horsemanship between East and West*, trans. Anthony Dent (London, 1971).
108. Ibid., 5.
109. Ibid., 16.
110. Ibid., 17, 20.
111. Joan Thirsk, *Horses in Early Modern England: For Service, for Pleasure, for Power* (Reading, 1978); and see Peter Edwards, *Horse and Man in Early Modern England* (London, 2007).
112. Landry, *Noble Brutes*, 82.
113. Fynes Moryson, *Shakespeare's Europe: A Survey of the Condition of Europe at the end of the Sixteenth Century, being Unpublished chapters of Fynes Moryson's Itinerary (1617)*, ed. Charles Hughes (1903); rpt. New York, 1967, 47; compare John Fryer, *A New Account of East India and Persia, Being Nine Years' Travels, 1672–1681*, ed. William Crooke (1698; rpt. 3 vols., London, 1909), 1: 251.
114. Edward Terry, *A Voyage to East-India* (1655), 139.
115. Ibid., 140.
116. Ogier Ghiselin de Busbecq, *The Four Epistles of A. G. Busbequius Concerning his Embassy into Turkey*, trans. Nahum Tate (1694), 27.
117. Ibid., 163–4.
118. John Sanderson, *The Travels of John Sanderson in the Levant, 1584–1602*, ed. William Foster. London, 1931, 15.
119. G. Dyfnallt Owen, ed., *Manuscripts of the Marquess of Bath Preserved at Longleat: Volume 5, Talbot, Dudley and Devereux Papers, 1533–1659* (London, 1980), 126.
120. Landry, *Noble Brutes*, 86.
121. *CSPD, 1657–8*, 96.
122. *CSPD, 1657–8*, 97.
123. John Ogilby, *Africa, being an Accurate Description of the Regions of Ægypt, Barbary, Lybia, and Billedulgrid* (1670), 17.

124. Evelyn, *Diary*, 4: 398–9.
125. Ibid., 4: 399.
126. Ogilby, *Africa*, 17.
127. Berg, *Luxury*, 20.

CONCLUSION

1. Lancelot Addison, *Life and Death of Mahumed* (London, 1679).
2. See Khalid Bekkaoui, 'White Women and Moorish Fancy in Eighteenth-Century Literature', in Saree Makdisi and Felicity Nussbaum, eds., '*The Arabian Nights' in Historical Context: Between East and West* (Oxford, 2008), 153–166.
3. See *CSP, Colonial Series, East Indies, China and Japan, 1617–1621*, 293.
4. *CSP, Colonial Series, East Indies, China and Japan, 1513–1616*, 465 (1 May 1616).
5. *CSP, Colonial Series, East Indies, China and Japan, 1617–1621*, 273.
6. Philip J. Stern, ' "A Politie of Civill & Military Power": Political Thought and the Late Seventeenth-Century Foundations of the East India Company-State', *Journal of British Studies* 47 (2008) 264.
7. See C. R. Boxer, *The Christian Century in Japan, 1549-1650* (Berkeley and London, 1951), chapters 7 and 8.
8. TNA SP 71/4 fo. 187.
9. TNA SP 71/17 fos. 135r–v. From 'Additional Articles of Peace' between Morocco and Britain, 10 July 1729.
10. See Gerald MacLean, *Looking East: English Writing and the Ottoman Empire before 1800* (Basingstoke, 2007), 47–55.
11. William Foster, ed., *The English Factories in India, 1651–1654* (Oxford, 1915), 282.
12. *CSP, Colonial Series, East Indies, China and Japan, 1513–1616*, 368 (10 January 1615).
13. Antony Wild, *The East India Company: Trade and Conquest from 1600* (London, 1999), 24.
14. As J. S. Bromley observed: 'there can be no real study of British Gibraltar which fails to explore its economic relations with the Maghreb', 'Letter-Book', 29.
15. Mehmet Bulut, *Ottoman-Dutch Economic Relations in the Early Modern Period, 1571–1699* (Hilversum, 2001), 131.
16. Richard Hakluyt, *The Principal Navigations: Voyages, Traffiques and Discoveries of the English Nation* (1589; rpt. 8 vols. London, 1910), 2: 66.
17. Ibid., 2: 172.

Works Cited

MANUSCRIPT SOURCES

National Library of Morocco, Rabat
Ms Dal 1878, *Ibraz al-Wahm al-Maknun min Kalam Ibn Khaldun aw al-Murshid al-Mahdi li-rad ta'an Ibn Khaldun bi Ahadith al-Mahdi*
Ms Kha Meem 100, *Nasihat al-Ikhwan*
Ms Jeem 1016, *Kitab al-Ajwiba al-Fiqhiyya*

Royal Library of Rabat
6929: 33, 'Abd al-Karim Lafqun, 'Muhaddid al-Sinan fi Nuhur Akhwan al-Dukhan'

Beyazit Devlet Library, Istanbul University
Mustafa bin Ibrahim Safi, *Zubdetu't-tevarih*

Bibliothèque Nationale, Orienteaux, Paris
Ms Arabe 312

British Library
Add Ms 6115
Add Ms 22910
Add Ms 29921
Add Ms 47028
Add Ms 61493
Add Ms 61535
Add Ms 61536
Add Ms 61542
Burney 367
Cotton Nero B.viii
Cotton Nero B.xi
East India Company Court Minutes, B/11
Harleian 6189
Sloane 2439
Sloane 2755
Sloane 3511

The National Archive (formerly Public Records Office), Kew, London
CO 77/1
CO 91/1
CO 279/30
FO 113/1
FO 113/3
FO 335/19
PROB 32/60
SP 12/240
SP 14/90
SP 16/373
SP 29/441
SP 34/31
SP 41/34
SP 44/113
SP 71/1
SP 71/2
SP 71/3
SP 71/4
SP 71/11
SP 71/12
SP 71/14
SP 71/15
SP 71/16
SP 71/17/II
SP 71/22/I
SP 71/22/III
SP 71/23/II
SP 71/27
SP 71/31
SP 71/27/III
SP 97/19
SP 102/4
SP 105/109

All Soul's College, Oxford
Owen Wynne MSS, XII: 144 and XXII: 84.

PRINTED SOURCES

Place of publication for pre-1700 imprints is London, unless otherwise indicated. Lengthy titles have been abbreviated.

Abbot, George. *A Briefe Description of the Whole World.* 1599; rpt. 1664.
Abbott, G. F. *Under the Turk in Constantinople: A Record of Sir John Finch's Embassy, 1674–1681.* London, 1920.

Abudacnus, Josephus. *The True History of the Jacobites of Ægypt.* Trans. E. Sadleir. 1692.
Abun-Nasr, Jamil M. *A History of the Maghrib In the Islamic Period.* 1971; rev. rpt. Cambridge, 1993.
An Act for continuation of the Act for redemption of Captives. 1652. [Wing, STC E1013]
An Act for continuation of the Act of redemption of Captives. 1652. [Wing, STC E1014]
An Act for the Redemption of Captives. 1650. [Wing, STC E119C]
'An Act for the Relief of the Captives, taken by Turkish, Moorish, and other Pirates, and to prevent the taking of others in time to come'. Printed with *An Act for the better Raising and Levying of Mariners, Sailers, and others.* 1641. [Wing, STC E1099A].
Addison, Joseph. *The Tatler.* Ed. Donald F. Bond. 3 vols. Oxford, 1987.
Addison, Lancelot. *The Present State of the Jews.* 1675.
—— *West Barbary or, A Short Narrative of the revolutions of the Kingdoms of Fez and Morocco.* Oxford, 1671.
—— *The Life and Death of Mahumed.* London, 1679.
'Africanus, Leo' [Hasan ibn Muhammad al-Wazzan al-Fasi]. *Della Descrittione dell'Africa.* Venice, 1550. Trans. John Pory, *A Geographical Historie of Africa, Written in Abrabicke and Italian by John Leo a More, borne in Granada, and brought up in Barbarie.* 1600.
Aksan, Virginia and Daniel Goffman, eds., *The Early Modern Ottomans: Remapping the Empire.* Cambridge, 2007.
Alam, Muzaffar and Sanjay Subrahmanyam. *Indo-Persian Travels in the Age of Discoveries, 1400–1800.* Cambridge, 2007.
The Alcoran of Mahomet, Translated out of Arabique into French . . . And newly Englished, for the satisfaction of all that desire to look into the Turkish Vanities. 1649.
The Ale-wives complaint against the coffee-houses in a dialogue between a victuallers wife and a coffee-man, being at difference about spoiling each others trade. 1675.
Alpino, Prospero. *La Médecine des Égyptiens, 1581–1584.* Trans. Raymond de Fenoyl. 2 vols. Cairo, 1980.
The Amours of the Sultana of Barbary. 1689.
Anderson, Sonia. *An English Consul in Turkey: Paul Rycaut at Smyrna, 1667–1678.* Oxford, 1989.
Andrea, Bernadette. *Women and Islam in Early Modern English Literature.* Cambridge, 2007.
Arber, Edward, ed., *Edward Webbe, Chief Master Gunner, His Travailes. 1590.* London, 1868.
—— ed., *A Transcript of the Registers of the Worshipful Company of Stationers: from 1640–1708.* 3 vols. London, 1913.
Archer, John Michael. *Old Worlds: Egypt, Southwest Asia, India, and Russia in Early Modern English Writing.* Palo Alto, CA, 2001.
Armitage, David. *The Ideological Origins of the British Empire.* Cambridge, 2000.
Ansari, Humayun. *'The Infidel Within': Muslims in Britain since 1800.* London, 2004.

The Arrivall and Intertainements of the Embassador, Alkaid Jaurar Ben Abdella, with his Associate, Mr. Robert Blake. 1637.
Articles of Peace & Commerce Between The Most Serene and Mighty Prince Charles II . . . And The Most Illustrious Lords, The Bashaw, Dey, Aga, Divan, And Governours of the Noble City and Kingdom of Tripoli in Barbary. 1677.
Auvry, Michel. *Le Miroir de la charité chrétiene*. Aix, 1663.
B., T., *A Journey to Jerusalem: Or, a Relation of the Travels of Fourteen English-Men, in the Year, 1669*. 1672.
Bacon, Francis. *The Works of Francis Bacon*. Ed. James Spedding et. al. 14 vols. London, 1857–90.
Baghdiantz, Ina. 'The Armenian Merchants in New Julfa: Some Aspects of their International Trade in the Late Seventeenth Century'. PhD dissertation, Columbia University, 1993.
Baines, Edward. *History of the County Palatine and Duchy of Lancaster*. 4 vols. London, 1836.
Baladouni, Vahe and Margaret Makepeace, eds., *Armenian Merchants of the Seventeenth and early Eighteenth Centuries*. Philadelphia, PA, 1998.
Barbour, Richmond. *Before Orientalism: London's Theatre of the East*. Cambridge, 2003.
Barendse, R. J. *The Arabian Seas*. London and New York, 2002.
Baron, Robert. *Mirza: A Tragedie, Really acted in Persia, in the Last Age*. 1647.
Bartels, Emily. *Speaking of the Moor: from Alcazar to Othello*. Philadelphia, PA, 2008.
—— *Spectacles of Strangeness: Imperialism, Alienation and Marlowe*. Philadelphia, PA, 1993.
Baxter, Richard. *The Reasons of the Christian Religion*. 1667.
Bayly, C. A. *Imperial Meridian: The British Empire and the World, 1780–1830*. London, 1989.
Beazley, C. Raymond. *Voyages and Travels mainly during the 16th and 17th Centuries*. 2 vols. 1903; rpt. New York, 1964.
Bedwell, William. *Mohammedis Imposturae: that is, A Discovery of the Manifold Forgeries, Falshoods, and horrible impieties of the blasphemous Seducer Mohammed*. 1615.
Behn. Aphra. *The Moor's Tragedy*. 1676.
Bekkaoui, Khalid. *In Moorish Thraldom: Narratives by White Women Captives inNorth Africa*. Basingstoke, forthcoming.
—— 'White Women and Moorish Fancy in Eighteenth-Century Literature'. In Saree Makdisi and Felicity Nussbaum, eds., *'The Arabian Nights' in Historical Context: Between East and West*. Oxford, 2008: 153–66.
Ben-Na'eh, Yaron. 'Hebrew Printing Houses in the Ottoman Empire'. In Gad Nassi, ed., *Jewish Journalism and Publishing Houses in the Ottoman Empire and Modern Turkey*. Istanbul, 2001: 35–82.
Berg, Maxine. *Luxury and Pleasure in Eighteenth-Century Britain*. Oxford, 2005.
Berriman, William. *The Great Blessing of Redemption from Captivity*. London, 1722.

Biddulph, William. *The Travels of certaine Englishmen into Africa, Asia, Troy, Bithnia, Thracia, and to the Blacke Sea*. 1609.

de Billerbeg, Franciscus. *Most rare and straunge discourses, of Amurathe the Turkish emperor that now is with the warres betweene him and the Persians*. 1584.

Blome, Richard. *Geographical Description of the Four Parts of the World*. 1670.

The bloody siege of Vienna: A Song. [1688].

Blount, Henry. *A Voyage Into the Levant*. 1636.

Blunt, Wilfrid. *Black Sunrise: The Life and Times of Mulai Ismail Emperor of Morocco, 1646–1727*. London, 1951.

Bohun, Edmund. *A Geographical Dictionary*. 1691.

Bon, Ottaviano. *A Description of the Grand Signour's Seraglio, or Turkish Emperor's Court*. Trans. Robert Withers. 1650; rpt. 1653.

Bond, Donald F., ed., *The Tatler*. 3 vols. Oxford, 1987.

Botero, Giovanni. *Relations of the Most Famous Kingdoms and Common-wealths*. Trans. Robert Johnson. 1601; rpt. 1608.

Bovilsky, Lara. *Barbarous Play: Race on the English Renaissance Stage*. Minneapolis, MN, 2008.

Boxer, C. R. 'Anglo-Portuguese Rivalry in the Persian Gulf, 1615–1635'. In Edgar Prestage, ed., *Chapters in Anglo-Portuguese Relations*. Watford, 1935: 46–129.

—— *The Christian Century in Japan, 1549–1650*. Berkeley and London, 1951.

[Brathwaite, Richard]. *The Smoaking Age, Or, The Man in the mist: With the Life and Death of Tobacco*. In *A Solemne Joviall Disputation, Theoreticke and Practicke: briefly Shadowing the Law of Drinking*. 1617: 82–199.

Braudel, Fernand. *The Mediterranean and the Mediterranean World in the Age of Philip II*. Trans Siân Reynolds. 2 vols. 1966; rpt. New York, 1972.

Brenner, Robert. *Merchants and Revolution: Commercial Change, Political Conflict, and London's Overseas Traders, 1550–1663*. Cambridge, 1993.

A Brief Relation of the late Martyrdome of five Persians. Douai, 1623.

A Brief Relation of Several Remarkable Passages of the Jews. 1666.

Brightman, Thomas. *A Revelation of the Apocalyps*. Amsterdam, 1611.

—— *A Most Comfortable Exposition of the Prophecie of Daniel*. Amsterdam, 1635.

Brissac, Philippe de Cossé, ed. *Les Sources Inédites de l'Histoire du Maroc: Archives et Bibliothèques de France—Dynastie Filalienne*. 6 vols. Paris, 1953.

Broadley, Alexander Meyrick. *The Last Punic War: Tunis Past and Present*. 2 vols. Edinburgh and London, 1882.

van den Broecke, Marcel R. *Ortelius Atlas Maps: An Illustrated Guide*. 't Goy, 1996.

Bromley, John Selwyn. 'A Letter-Book of Robert Cole: British Consul-General at Algiers, 1694–1712' (1974). Rpt. in J. S. Bromley, *Corsairs and Navies, 1660–1760*. London, 1987: 29–42.

Brooks, Francis. *Barbarian Cruelty, Being A True History of the Distressed Condition of the Christian Captives*. 1693.

Brotton, Jerry. 'Carthage and Tunis, *The Tempest* and Tapestries', in Peter Hulme and William H. Sherman, eds., *'The Tempest' and its Travels*. London, 2000, 132–7.

—— and Lisa Jardine. *Global Interests: Renaissance Art Between East and West.* London, 2000.

—— *Trading Territories: Mapping the Early Modern World.* London, 1997.

Brummett, Palmira. 'A Kiss is Just a Kiss: Rituals of Submission along the East-West Divide'. In Matthew Birchwood and Matthew Dimmock, eds., *Cultural Encounters Between East and West: 1453–1699.* Newcastle, 2005: 107–31.

Bruyn, M. Corneille de. *A Voyage to the Levant: or, Travels in the Principal Parts of Asia Minor, the Islands of Scio, Rhodes, Cyprus, &c.* Trans. W. J. London, 1702.

Buchanan, Harvey. 'Luther and the Turks 1519–1529', *Archiv für Reformationsgeschichte* 47 (1956): 145–60.

Bulut, Mehmet. *Ottoman-Dutch Economic Relations in the Early Modern Period, 1571–1699.* Hilversum, 2001.

Burton, Jonathan. *Traffic and Turning: Islam and English Drama, 1579–1624.* Newark, DE, 2005.

de Busbecq, Ogier Ghiselin. *The Four Epistles of A. G. Busbequius Concerning his Embassy into Turkey.* Trans. Nahum Tate. 1694.

Butterworth, James. *A Complete History of the Cotton Trade.* Manchester, 1823.

B[utton]., J[ohn]. *Algiers Voyage in a Journall.* 1621.

C., S. *The Famous and Delectable History of Clerocreton and Cloryana.* [c.1660].

Cabanelas, Dario. 'Ortas Cartas del Sultan de Marruecos Ahmad al-Mansur a Felipe II', *Miscelanea de Estudios Arabes y Hebraicos* 7 (1958): 13–14.

Caille, J. 'Le commerce anglais avec le Maroc pendant la seconde moitie du XVI siècle', *Revue Africaine* 84 (1940): 186–219.

Calendar of the Clarendon State Papers. 5 vols. Oxford, 1872, 1969–70.

Canny, Nicholas, ed., *The Oxford History of the British Empire, Volume I: The Origins of Empire.* Oxford, 1998.

The Capitulations and Articles of Peace. Constantinople, 1663.

Carr, Cecil T., ed., *Select Charters of Trading Companies, A.D. 1530–1707.* London, 1913.

Carruthers, Douglas, ed., *The Desert Route to India.* London, 1929.

Carswell, John. *New Julfa: The Armenian Churches and Other Buildings.* Oxford, 1968.

Cartwright, John. *The Preachers Travels Wherein is set downe a true Journall to the confines of the East Indies.* 1611.

Casale, Giancarlo. *The Ottoman Age of Exploration.* Oxford and New York, 2010.

Cason, Edmond. *A Relation of the whole proceedings concerning the Redemption of the Captives in Argier and Tunis.* 1647.

Castries, Henri de. *Les Sources Inédites de l'Histoire du Maroc... Archives et Bibliothèques D'Angleterre.* 3 vols. Paris, 1918–35.

—— *Les Sources Inédites de l'Histoire du Maroc de 1530 à 1845. Dynastie Saadienne, Archives et Bibliothèques de France.* 2 vols. Paris, 1905–11.

Chamberlain, John. *The Letters of John Chamberlain*. Ed. Norman Egbert McClure. 2 vols. Philadelphia, PA, 1939.

The Character of a Coffee-House. Wherein Is contained a Description of the Persons usually frequenting it, with their Discourse and Humours. 1665.

Charant, Antoine. 'A Letter, in answer to divers Curious Questions Concerning the Religion, Manners, and Customs, of the Countrys of Muley Arxid King of Tafiletta'. In Roland Frejus, *The Relation of a Voyage Made into Mauritania in Africk, By the Sieur Roland Frejus of Marseilles, by the French King's Order in the Year 1666*. 1671.

Chardin, John. *Sir John Chardin's Travels in Persia*. Trans. Edmund Lloyd. 2 vols in 1. London, 1720.

[Charles II, king of England]. *By the King. A Proclamation for the Suppression of Coffee-Houses*. 1675.

Charles-Roux, François. *Les Echelles de Syrie et de Palestine au XVIIIe siècle*. Paris, 1928.

[Chetwood, Robert]. *The Voyages and Adventures of Captain Robert Boyle*. London, 1726.

Chew, Samuel. *The Crescent and the Rose: Islam and England During the Renaissance*. New York, 1937.

Clay, William Keatinge, ed., *Liturgies and Occasional Forms of Prayer Set Forth in the Reign of Queen Elizabeth*. Cambridge, 1847.

Clouse, R. 'The Influence of John Henry Alistead on English Millenarian Though in the Seventeenth Century'. PhD dissertation, State University of Iowa, 1963.

Coles, Paul. *The Ottoman Impact on Europe*. London, 1968.

Colley, Linda. *The Ordeal of Elizabeth Marsh: A Woman in World History*. London, 2007.

Comelin, François and Philémon de la Motte. *Etat des Royaumes de Barbarie, Tripoly, Tunis et Alger*. Rouen, 1703.

—— —— and Joseph Bernard. *Voyage pour la Redemption des Captifs, Aux Royaumes D'Alger et de Tunis*. Paris, 1720. Trans. Joseph Morgan, *A Voyage to Algiers and Tunis, For the Redemption of Captives*. London, 1735.

Considerations Humbly offered to the Right Honourable the Lords Spiritual and Temporal in Parliament Assembled. [1689?].

A coranto Relating diverse particulars concerning the newes out of Italy, Spaine, Turkey, Persia, Bohemia. 1622.

Coryate, Thomas. *Coryats Crudities 1611*. Intro. William M. Schutte. London, 1978.

Cotter, Holland. 'The Splendor of Tapestries Both Opulent and Complex'. *New York Times*, 15 March 2002.

Charles Cotton, trans. *The Fair One of Tunis*. 1674.

Coulter, Laura Jane Fenella. 'The Involvement of the English Crown and its Embassy in Constantinople with Pretenders to the Throne of the principality of Moldavia between the years 1583 and 1620, with particular reference to the pretender Stefan Bogdan between 1590 and 1612'. PhD dissertation, University of London, 1993.

Covel, John. 'Dr. Covel's Diary'. In Theodore J. Bent, ed., *Early Voyages and Travels in the Levant*. London, 1893: 101–287.
—— *Some Account of the Present Greek Church*. Cambridge, 1720.
Coverte, Robert. *A True and Almost Incredible Report of an Englishman*. 1612.
Cragg, Gerald R. *Puritanism in the Age of the Great Persecution, 1660–1688*. New York, 1971.
[Crouch, Nathaniel] 'B., R.' *The English Acquisitions in Guinea and East-India*. London, 1700.
[Crouch, Nathaniel] 'D., R.' *The Strange and Prodigious Religions, Customs, and Manners of Sundry Nations*. 1683.
Crouch, Nathaniel, ed. *Two Journeys to Jerusalem*. 1692.
Crown, Thomas. *Darius, King of Persia*. 1688.
Cunningham, Allan. 'Dragomania: the Dragomans of the British Embassy of Turkey', *St. Antony's Papers* 2 (1961): 81–100.
[D., R.] *A True Relation of the Adventures of Mr. R. D.* 1672.
Daborne, Robert. *A Christian Turn'd Turke*. 1612.
Dalrymple, William. *White Mughals: Love and Betrayal in Eighteenth-Century India*. New York, 2002.
D'Amico, Jack. *The Moor in English Renaissance Drama*. Tampa, FL, 1991.
Dan, Pierre. *Histoire de Barbarie et de ses corsairs*. Paris, 1637.
Dandini, Girolamo. *A Voyage to Mount Libanus*. 1698.
Danvers, Frederick Charles, ed., *Letters received by the East India Company from its Servants in the East, 1602–1613*. London, 1896. [volume 1 of 6; later volumes edited by Foster]
D'Aranda, Emanuel. *Relation de la captivité et liberté du Sieur Emanuel d'Aranda, Jadis Esclave à Alger*. Brussels, 1662. Trans. John Davies, *The History of Algiers and It's Slavery*. 1666.
Davies, William. *A True Relation of the Travailes and most miserable Captivitie of William Davies, Barber-Surgion of London*. 1614.
Day, John, William Rowley, and George Wilkins. *The Travailes of The Three English Brothers*. 1607.
Defoe, Daniel. *A Brief State of the Question Between the Printed and Painted Callicoes and the Woollen and Silk Manufacturers . . . The Third Edition*. 1719; rpt. London, 1720.
—— *A Plan of the English Commerce*. London, 1728.
—— *A Review of the State of the British Nation*, 4: 152 (31 January 1708).
—— *Robinson Crusoe*. London, 1721.
—— *Captain Singleton*. Ed. Shiv K. Kumar. Oxford, 1990.
Denham, John. *The Sophy*. London, 1642.
A Description of the Nature of Slavery Among the Moors. London, 1721.
A Description of Tangier, The Country and People Adjoyning. 1664.
Dew, Nicholas. *Orientalism in Louis XIV's France*. Oxford, 2010.
Diamond, A. S. 'The Community of the Resettlement, 1656–1684, A Social Survey', *Jewish Historical Society of England, Transactions* 24 (1970–3): 134–50.

Dimmock, Matthew. 'Britain and the Prophet Muhammad: Precedents and Paradigms'. Unpublished paper delivered at 'Britain and the Muslim World: Historical Perspectives', University of Exeter, April 2009.
―― *Newe Turkes: Dramatizing Islam and the Ottomans in Early Modern England.* Aldershot, 2005.
―― ed. *William Percy's 'Mahomet and His Heaven'*. Aldershot, 2006.
al-Din, Hasan Taj. *The Islamic History of the Maldive Islands.* Ed. Hikoichi Yajima. 2 vols. Tokyo, 1984.
Dinar, Ibn Abi. *Kitab al-Mu'nis fi Akhbar Ifiqiyah wa Tunis.* Ed. Muhammad Shammam. Beirut, 1993.
Domínguez, Javier Lobato and Angel Martín Esteban. *Reales Alcazares de Sevilla.* Barcelona, 1998.
Douglas Audrey W. 'Cotton Textiles in England: The East India Company's Attempt to Exploit Developments in Fashion, 1660–1721', *Journal of British Studies* 8: 2 (1969): 28–43.
Doyle, Peter, ed. *Butler's Lives of the Saints: October.* Collegeville, MN, 1996.
Dryden, John. *Aureng-zebe.* 1676.
―― *Don Sebastian.* 1690.
Dumont, Jean. *A New Voyage to the Levant.* 1696.
Dunton, John. *A True Iournal of the Sally Fleet.* 1637.
Dursteler, Eric R. *Venetians in Constantinople: Nation, Identity, and Coexistence in the Early Modern Mediterranean.* Baltimore, MD, 2006.
Edwards, Peter. *Horse and Man in Early Modern England.* London, 2007.
Edwardes, Michael. *Ralph Fitch: Elizabethan in the Indies.* London, 1972.
Ekin, Des. *The Stolen Village: Baltimore and the Barbary Pirates.* Dublin, 2006.
Eldem, Edhem. 'Capitulationss and Western Trade'. In Faroqhi, ed., *History of Turkey*: Cambridge, 2006, 283–335.
―― 'Istanbul: From Imperial to Peripheralized Capital'. In Edhem Eldem, Daniel Goffman and Bruce Masters, *The Ottoman City between East and West: Aleppo, Izmir, and Istanbul.* Cambridge, 1999: 135–206.
Elizabeth I, queen of England. *Elizabeth I, Collected Works.* Ed. Leah S. Marcus, Janel Mueller, and Mary Beth Rose. Chicago, 2000.
Elliot, Adam. *A Modest Vindication of Titus Oates the Salamanca-Doctor From Perjury.* 1682.
Elmarsafy, Ziad. *The Englightenment Qur'an: The Politics of Translation and the Construction of Islam.* Oxford, 2009.
The estate of Christians, living under the subiection of the Turke. 1595.
Evelyn, John. *Diary.* Ed. E. S. de Beer. 6 vols. Oxford: Clarendon, 1955.
―― *The History of the Three Late Famous Imposters.* 1669.
Evliya [Çelebi] Efendi. *Narrative of Travels in Europe, Asia, and Africa, in the Seventeenth Century, by Evliya Efendi.* Trans Joseph von Hammer. 2 vols. London, 1834, 1850.

An Extract of several Letters Relating to the Great Charity and Usefulness of Printing the New Testament and Psalter in the Arabick Language. 1720; rpt. London, 1721.

F[arewell], C[hristopher]. *An East-India Colation, or, A Discourse of Travel.* 1633.

Faroqhi, Suraiya, ed., *The Cambridge History of Turkey, Volume 3: The Later Ottoman Empire, 1603–1839.* Cambridge, 2006.

Faroqhi, Suraiya and Christoph Neumann, eds., *Ottoman Costumes: From Textile to Identity.* Istanbul, 2004.

Farouk, Ahmed, ed., *Relation en forme du journal du voyage pour la rédemption des captifs, aux royaumes de Maroc et d'Alger.* St Denis, 2000.

Favata, Martin A. and Jose B. Fernandez, eds., *The Account: Alvar Nunez Cabeza de Vaca's Relacion.* Houston, TX, 1993.

Fawcett, Charles, ed., *The English Factories in India, 1678–1684, vol.3 (New Series) Bombay, Surat, and Malabar Coast.* Oxford, 1954.

—— *The English Factories in India, 1670–1677, vol. 4 (New Series) The Eastern Coast and Bay of Bengal.* Oxford, 1955.

Ferrier, R. W. 'The Agreement of the East India Company with the Armenian Nation 22nd June 1688', *Revue des etudes arméniens* 7, n. s.(1970): 427–43.

—— 'The Armenians and the East India Company in Persia in the Seventeenth and Early Eighteenth Century', *Economic History Review*, 2nd Series 26 (1973): 38–62.

—— 'The European Diplomacy of Shah 'Abbas I and the First Persian Embassy to England', *Iran* 11 (1973): 75–92.

—— 'The Terms and Conditions under which English Trade was Transacted with Safavid Persia', *Bulletin of the School of Oriental and African Studies* 49 (1986): 48–66.

Figueras, Tomas Garcia and Rodrituez Joulia Saint-Cyr. *Larache, Datos para su Historia en el Siglo XVII.* Madrid, 1973.

Finett, Sir John. *Finetti Philoxenis: Som Choice Observations of Sir John Finett Knight, And Master of Ceremonies to the two last Kings.* Ed. James Howell. 1656.

Finkel, Caroline. *Osman's Dream: The Story of the Ottoman Empire, 1300–1923.* London, 2005.

Firby, Nora Kathleen. *European Travellers and their Perceptions of Zoroastrians in the 17th and 18th Centuries.* Berlin, 1988.

Firth, Katharine R. *The Apocalyptic Tradition in Reformation Britain, 1530–1645.* Oxford, 1979.

Fisher, Godfrey. *Barbary Legend; War, Trade and Piracy in North Africa, 1415–1830.* Oxford, 1957.

al-Fishtali, Abu Faris 'Abd al-Aziz. *Manahil al-safa' fi ma'athir mawalina a-shurafa'.* Ed. 'Abd al-Karim Karim. Rabat, 1972.

Fitton, R. S. *The Arkwrights: Spinners of Fortune.* Manchester, 1989.

Fitz-Geffry, Charles. *Compassion towards Captives chiefly towards our brethren and country-men.* Oxford, 1637.

Five Queries Humbly Tender'd, Relating to the Bill for Prohibiting the Consumption of East-India Silks, Bengals and Printed Callicoes. [1696?].

Floor, Willem. 'The Dutch and the Persian Silk Trade'. In Charles Melville, ed., *Safavid Persia: The History and Politics of an Islamic Society.* London, 1996: 323–68.

Folke, Dahl. *A Bibliography of English Corantos and Periodical Newsbooks, 1620–1642.* London, 1952.

Forell, George W. 'Luther and the War against the Turks', *Church History* 14 (1945): 256–71.

A forme to bee used in Common praier every Wednesdaie and Fridaie, within the citie and Dioces of Norwiche: to excite all godlie people to praie unto God for the deliverie of those christians, that are now invaded by the Turke. [1565].

Foster, William, ed., *Early Travels in India: 1583–1619.* 1921; rpt. New Delhi, 1968.

—— *England's Quest of Eastern Trade.* 1933; rpt. London, 1966.

—— ed. *Letters Received by the East India Company from its Servants in the East.* 6 vols. London, 1896–1902. [volume 1 edited by Danvers]

—— ed., *The English Factories in India, 1624–1629.* Oxford, 1909.

—— ed., *The English Factories in India, 1630–1633.* Oxford, 1910.

—— ed., *The English Factories in India, 1634–1636.* Oxford, 1911.

—— ed., *The English Factories in India, 1637–1641.* Oxford, 1912.

—— ed., *The English Factories in India, 1646–1650.* Oxford, 1914.

—— ed., *The English Factories in India, 1651–1654.* Oxford, 1915.

—— ed., *The English Factories in India, 1655–1660.* Oxford, 1921.

—— ed., *The English Factories in India, 1661–1664.* Oxford, 1923.

—— ed., *The Voyage of Nicholas Downton to the East Indies, 1614–1615.* 1939; rpt. New Delhi, 1997.

—— ed., *The Voyage of Thomas Best to the East Indies, 1612–14.* 1934; rpt. Delhi, 1997.

Four Treatises Concerning the Doctrine, Discipline and Worship of the Mahometans. London, 1712.

A fourme to be used in common prayer every Sunday, Wednesday and Fryday for the preservation of those Christians and their Countreys that are now invaded by the Turke. [1566].

A fourme to be used in common prayer every Wednesdaye and Fryedaye within the cittie and diocs of London, for the delivery of those Christians that are now invaded by the Turke. 1565.

Foxe, John. *The Acts and Monuments of John Foxe.* 1563. Rpt. ed. George Townsend. 1843–49; rpt., 8 vols., New York, 1965.

Francisco, Adam S. *Martin Luther and Islam.* Leiden, 2007.

Frank, Andre Gunder. *Re-Orient: Global Economy in the Asian Age.* Berkeley and Los Angeles, 1998.

Franklin, William. *A Letter from Tangier Concerning the Death of Jonas Rowland the Renegade, and other strange Occurences since the Embassadors Arrival here.* 1682.

Friedman, Ellen G. 'Christian Captives at "Hard Labor" in Algiers, 16th–18th Centuries', *International Journal of African Historical Studies* 13 (1980): 616–32.
—— *Spanish Captives in North Africa in the Early Modern Age.* Madison, WI, 1983.
Fryer, John. *A New Account of East India and Persia Being Nine Year's Travels, 1672–1681.* Ed. William Crooke. 3 vols. London, 1909.
Fuller, Thomas. *A Pisgah-Sight of Palestine and the Confines Thereof.* 1650.
Gainsford, Thomas. *The Glory of England.* 1618.
Galland, Antoine. *Relation de l'Esclavage d'un Marchand de la Ville de Cassis, à Tunis.* Paris, 1809.
Games, Alison. *The Web of Empire: English Cosmopolitanism in an Age of Expansion, 1560–1660.* New York, 2008.
Gannun, Abdallah, ed., *Rasa'il Sa'adiyya.* Tetuan, 1954.
Garayzabal, M. *A Brief Relation of the late Martyrdome of five Persians Converted to the Catholique Faith by the reformed Carmelites.* Doway, 1623.
Garcia, Humberto. 'Turning Turk, Turning Heretic: Joseph Pitts of Exeter and the Early Enlightenment, 1670–1740'. In Gerald MacLean, ed., *Britain and the Muslim World: Historical Perspectives* Newcastle, UK, forthcoming.
Garcia-Arenal, Mercedes and Gerard Wiegers. *A Man of Three Worlds: Samuel Pallache, a Moroccan Jew in Catholic and Protestant Europe.* Baltimore, MD, 2003.
Gascoigne, George. *The Complete Poems of George Gascoigne.* Ed. W. Carew Hazlitt. 2 vols. London, 1869.
[Gee, Joshua]. *Narrative of Joshua Gee of Boston, Mass.* Hartford, CT, 1943.
Gee, Joshua. *The Trade and Navigation of Great-Britain Considered.* Glasgow, 1750.
Georgivits, Bartholomeus. *The Ofspring of the house of Ottomanno.* Trans. Hugh Goughe. 1570.
al-Gharbi, Muhammad. *Bidayat al-hukm al-Maghribi fi al-Sudan al-gharbi.* Baghdad, 1982.
Gibbon, Edward. *The Decline and Fall of the Roman Empire,* ed., J. B. Bury. 7 vols. London, 1898.
Goffman, Daniel. *Britons in the Ottoman Empire, 1642–1660.* Seattle, WA, 1998.
—— 'Izmir: From village to Colonial Port City'. In Eldem, Goffman and Masters, eds., *The Ottoman City.* Cambridge, 1999: 79–134.
—— 'Negotiating with the Renaissance State: The Ottoman Empire and the New Diplomacy'. In Aksan and Goffman, eds., *Early Modern Ottomans.* Cambridge, 2007: 61–74.
Geuffroy, Antoine. *The order of the greate Turckes courte, of hys menne of warre, and of all hys conquestes, with the summe of Mahumetes doctryne. Translated out of Frenche. 1524* [sic]. 1542.
Grehan, James. 'Smoking and "Early Modern" Sociability: The Great Tobacco Debate in the Ottoman Middle East (Seventeenth to Eighteenth Centuries', *American Historical Review* 111: 5 (December 2006): 1352–77.
Gregory, John. *Gregorii Opuscula, or Notes & Observations upon some passages of Scripture.* 1650.

Glaser, Lynn. *Indians or Jews? An Introduction to a Reprint of Manasseh ben Israel's The Hope of Israel*. Gilroy, CA, 1973.

Green, David, *Queen Anne*. New York, 1970.

Greene, Molly, *A Shared World: Christians and Muslims in the Early Modern Mediterranean* (Princeton, NJ, 2000), chapter 6.

—— 'The Ottomans in the Mediterranean'. In Aksan and Goffman, eds., *Early Modern Ottomans*. Cambridge, 2007: 104–17.

Greene, Robert. *Selimus: Emperor of the Turks*. 1594.

Gregorian, Vartan. 'Minorities of Isfahan: The Armenian Community of Isfahan, 1587–1722', *Persian Studies* 7 (1974): 652–80.

Gully, Adrian. *The Culture of Letter-Writing in Pre-Modern Islamic Society*. Edinburgh, 2008.

Habib, Imtiaz. *Black Lives in the English Archives, 1500–1677*. Aldershot, 2008.

Haddad, Robert M. 'Conversion of Eastern Orthodox Christians to the Unia in the Seventeenth and Eighteenth Centuries'. In Michael Gervers and Ramzi Jibran Bikhazi, eds., *Conversion and Continuity: Indigenous Christian Communities in Islamic Lands, Eighth to Eighteenth Centuries*. Toronto, 1990: 449–60.

Hadjiantoniou, George A. *Protestant Patriarch: The Life of Cyril Lukaris (1572–1638), Patriarch of Constantinople*. Richmond, VA, 1961.

al-Hajari, Ahmad ibn Qasim. *Kitab Nasir al-Din 'ala'l-Qawm al-Kafirin*. Eds. and trans. P. S. Van Koningsveld et al. Madrid, 1997.

Hajji, Muhammad. 'Al-Tabgh fi al-Maghrib'. In *Jawlat Tarikhiyya*. Beirut, 1995.

Hakluyt, Richard. *Divers voyages touching the discoverie of America*. 1582.

—— *The Principal Navigations: Voyages, Traffiques and Discoveries of the English Nation*. 1589; rpt. 8 vols. London, 1910.

Hall, Rupert A. and Marie Boas Hall, eds. and trans., *The Correspondence of Henry Oldenburg*. 5 vols. Madison, WI, 1965–8.

Halle, Edward. *Hall's Chronicle: Containing the History of England during the reign of Henry the Fourth, and the succeeding Monarchs, to the end of the reign of Henry the Eighth*. Ed. Sir Henry Ellis. London, 1809.

Hamilton, Alastair, 'An Egyptian Traveller in the Republic of Letters: Josephus Barbatus or Abudacnus the Copt', *Journal of the Warburg and Courtauld Institutes* 57 (1994): 123–50.

—— 'The English Interest in the Arabic-Speaking Christians'. In Russell, ed., *'Arabick' Interest*: 30–53.

—— Maurits H. Van Den Boogert and Bart Westerweel, eds., *The Republic of Letters and the Levant*. Leiden, 2005.

—— *William Bedwell The Arabist, 1563–1632*. Leiden, 1985.

Hamilton, Alexander. *A New Account of the East-Indies: Being the Observations and Remarks of Capt. Alexander Hamilton*. 2 vols. London, 1739.

Hanway, Jonas. *An Historical Account of the British Trade over the Caspian Sea: with a Journal of Travels from London through Russia into Persia*. 4 vols. London, 1753.

Harakat, Ibrahim. *Al-Siyasah wa-al-Mujtama'fi al-'Asr al-Sa'adi*. Al-Dar al-Bayda', 1987.

Harrigan, Michael. *Veiled Encounters: Representing the Orient in 17th-Century French Travel Literature*. Amsterdam and New York, 2008.

Harrison, John. *The Messiah Already Come. Or Proofs of Christianitie*. Amsterdam, 1613; rpt. 1619.

Hattox, Ralph. *Coffee and Coffeehouses: The Origins of a Social Beverage in the Medieval Near East*. Seattle, WA, 1985.

Hayward, Maria. 'Symbols of Majesty: Cloths of Estate at the Court of Henry VIII', *Furniture History* (2005): 1–11.

Haywood, Eliza. *The Fair Captive*. London, 1721.

Hebb, David Delison. *Piracy and the English Government, 1616–1642*. Aldershot, 1994.

Helgerson, Richard. *Forms of Nationhood: The Elizabethan Writing of England*. Chicago, 1992.

H[erbert], T[homas]. *A Relation of some Yeares Travaile, Begunne Anno 1626. Into Afrique and the greater Asia, especially the Territories of the Persian Monarchie: and some parts of the Orientall Indies, and Iles adjacent*. 1634. Revised edition: *Some Yeares Travels into Africa and Asia the Great, Especially describing the Famous Empires of Persia and Industant. As also Divers other Kingdoms in the Oriental Indies, and Iles Adjacent*. 1638.

Herbert, Thomas. *Thomas Herbert: Travels in Persia, 1627–1629*. Ed. William Foster. London, 1928.

Heylyn, Peter. *Cosmographie in foure Bookes*. 1652.

Heywood, Thomas. *The Fair Maid of the West, Parts I and II*. Ed. Robert K. Turner. Lincoln, NE, 1967.

Higgins, Iain Macleod. 'Shades of the East: Orientalism, Religion, and Nation in Late Medieval Scottish Literature', *Journal of Medieval and Early Modern Studies* 38: 2 (2008): 197–228.

Hill, Aaron. *A Full and Just Account of the Present State of the Ottoman Empire*. London, 1709.

Hill, Christopher. *The Century of Revolution, 1603–1714*. 1961; rpt. London, 1974.

Hillgarth, J. N. *The Mirror of Spain, 1500–1700*. Ann Arbor, MI, 2000.

Historical and Critical Reflections upon Mahometanism and Socinianism. London, 1712.

Historical Manuscripts Commission Report on the Manuscripts of Allan George Finch. 2 vols. London, 1913.

Historical Manuscripts Commission Report on the Manuscripts of the Family of Gawdy. London, 1885.

Hoblos, Farouk. 'The European as Seen by the Inhabitants of the Syrian Coast during the Ottoman Period'. In Bernard Heyberger and Carsten-Michael Walbiner, eds. *Les Européens vus par les Libanais à l'époque ottomane*. Beirut, 2002: 43–58.

Hopkins, J. F. P., trans. *Letters from Barbary, 1576–1774*. Oxford, 1982.

Houston, Chloë. ' "Thou glorious kingdome, thou chiefe of Empires": Persia in early seventeenth-century travel writing', *Studies in Travel Writing* 13: 2 (June 2009): 141–52.

Hovannisian, Richard G., ed., *The Armenian People from Ancient to Modern Times*. 2 vols. Basingstoke, 1997.

Huntington, Samuel P. *The Clash of Civilizations And the Remaking of World Order*. 1997; rpt. London, 2002.

Hurewitz, J. C., ed., *The Middle East and North Africa in World Politics*. New Haven and London, 1975.

Hyde, Thomas. *Historia Religionis Veterum Persarum, eurumque Magorum*. Oxford, 1700.

Ibrahim, Muhammad Rabi' ibn Muhammad. *The Ship of Sulaiman*. Trans. John O'Kane. London, 1972.

al-Ifrani, Muhammad al-Saghir ibn Muhammad. *Nozhet Elhadi. Historie de la dynastie saadienne au Maroc, 1511–1670*. Trans. O. Houdas. 2 vols. Paris, 1888, 1889.

—— *Nuzhat al-Hadi*. Ed. 'Abd al-Latif al-Shadhili. Casablanca, 1998.

Imber, Colin. *Ebu's-su'ud: The Islamic Legal Tradition*. Edinburgh, 1997.

Inalcik, Halil. *Economic and Social History of the Ottoman Empire, Vol One. 1300–1600*. 1994; rpt. Cambridge, 1997.

Indulgences issued to raise money to fight the Turks or to ransom captives. Westminster, 1480.

Jacob, James R. *Henry Stubbe, Radical Protestantism and the Early Enlightenment*. Cambridge, 1983.

James I, king of Great Britain. *A Counter-Blaste to Tobacco*. 1604.

[James I, king of Great Britain]. *Two Broad-Sides Against Tobacco*. 1672.

Jankovich, Miklos. *They Rode into Europe: The Fruitful Exchange in the Arts of Horsemanship between East and West*. Trans. Anthony Dent. London, 1971.

Jasanoff, Maya. 'Measured Reciprocity: English Ambassadorial Gift Exchange in the 17th and 18th Centuries', *Journal of Early Modern History* 9 (2005): 348–70.

Jardine, Lisa. 'Hooke the Man: His Diary and His Health'. In Jim Bennett, Michael Cooper, Michael Hunter, and Lisa Jardine. *London's Leonardo: The Life and Work of Robert Hooke*. Oxford, 2003.

Jirousek, Charlotte. 'Ottoman Influences in Western Dress'. In Faroqhi and Neumann, eds., *Ottoman Costumes*: 231–51.

[Jones, David]. *A Compleat History of the Turks, From their Origin in the year 755, to the year 1718*. 4 vols. London, 1719.

Jourdain, John. *The Journal of John Jourdain, 1608–1617*. Ed. William Foster. Cambridge, 1905.

Kafadar, Cemal. 'A History of Coffee', unpublished working paper.

―― 'Janissaries and other Riffraff of Ottoman Istanbul: Rebels without a Cause?' In Baki Tezcan and Karl. K. Barbir, eds., *Identity and Identity Formation in the Ottoman World*. Madison, WI, 2007: 113–34.

Kalmar, Ivan. 'Jesus Did Not Wear a Turban: Orientalism, the Jews, and Christian Art.' In Ivan Davidson Kalmar and Derek J. Penslar, eds., *Orientalism and the Jews*. Waltham, MA, 2005: 3–31.

Katib Çelebi. *The Balance of Truth*. Trans. Geoffrey Lewis. London, 1957.

Katz, David. 'The Abendana Brothers and the Christian Hebraists of Seventeenth-Century England', *Journal of Ecclesiastical History* 40 (1989): 28–52.

―― *Philo-Semitism and the Readmission of the Jews to England, 1603–1655*. Oxford, 1982.

Kellet, Edward and Henry Byam. *A Returne from Argier. A Sermon Preached at Minhead in the County of Somerset*. 1628.

[Ketton, Robert of, trans.] *Mahometis Abdallae filii theologia dialogo explicata; Hermanno Nellingaunense interprete. Alcorani epitome*. [Vienna? Nürnberg?] 1543.

al-Kharazi, Badi'a. *Tarikh al-kanisah al-nusraniyah fi-al-Maghrib al-Aqsa*. Rabat, 2007.

King Charles His Letter to the Great Turk. 1642.

Klarwill, Victor von, ed. *The Fugger News-Letters, Second Series*. Trans. L. S. R. Byrne. London, 1926.

Knight, Francis. *Relation of Seaven Yeares Slaverie under the Turks of Argeire*. 1640.

Knolles, Richard. *The Generall Historie of the Turkes . . . With a continuation* [by Thomas Nabbes]. 1603; 'The fifth edition'. 1638.

Knox, Robert. *An Historical Relation of the Island Ceylon*. 1681.

Knutson, Roslyn L. 'Elizabethan Documents, Captivity Narratives, and the Market for Foreign History Plays', *English Literary History* 26 (1996): 102–10.

Lach, Donald F. *Asia in the Making of Europe. Volume I: The Age of Discovery*. Chicago, 1965.

Landry, Donna. *Noble Brutes: How Eastern Horses Transformed English Culture*. Baltimore, MD, 2008.

Lane-Poole, Stanley. *The Barbary Corsairs*. London, 1890.

Lanquet, Thomas. *Coopers Chronicle unto the late death of Queen Marie*. 1560.

Lawrence, A. W. *Trade Castles and Forts of West Africa*. London, 1963.

Le Blanc, Vincent. *Les voyages fameux du Sieur Vincent Le Blanc*. Paris, 1648. Trans. Francis Brooke, *The World Surveyed; or the Famous Voyages and Travailes of V. Le Blanc*. 1660.

Leonard, Irving A. 'A Shipment of *comedias* to the Indies', *Hispanic Review* 2 (1934): 39–50.

Le Van Baumer, Franklin. 'The Conception of Christendom in Renaissance England', *Journal of the History of Ideas* 6 (1945): 131–56.

―― 'England, the Turk, and the Common Corps of Christendom', *American Historical Review* 50 (1944): 26–43.

Lewis, Bernard. *The Jews of Islam*. London, 1984.

Lithgow, William. *The Totall Discourse of The Rare Adventures and Painefull Peregrinations*. 1632; rpt. Glasgow, 1906.
Littleton, Charles G. D. 'Ancient Language and New Science: The Intellectual Life of Robert Boyle'. In Hamilton, Van Den Boogert and Westerweel, eds. *Republic*: 151–73.
Locke, J. Courtenay, ed., *The First Englishmen in India*. London, 1930.
Locke, John. *Two Tracts on Government*. Ed. Philip Abrams. Cambridge, 1967.
Longino, Michèle. *Orientalism in French Classical Drama*. Cambridge, 2002.
Luke, John. *Tangier at High Tide: The Journal of John Luke, 1670–1673*. Ed. Helen Andrews Kaufman. Paris, 1958.
Luttrell, Narcissus. *A Brief Historical Relation of State Affairs from September 1679 to April 1714*. 6 vols. Oxford, 1857.
Mabro, Judy. *Veiled Half-Truths: Western Travellers' Perceptions of Middle Eastern Women*. 1991; rpt. London, 1996.
McDowell, Joan Allgrove. 'Elizabethan Embroidery at Hardwick Hall'. *Hali* 10: 4 (July–August 1988): 16–25.
McJannet, Linda. *The Sultan Speaks: Dialogue in English Plays and Histories about the Ottoman Turks*. New York, 2006.
—— 'The Translator as Emissary: Continental Works about the Ottomans in England'. In Brinda Charry and Gitanjali Shahani, eds., *Emissaries in Early Modern Literature and Culture: Mediation, Transmission, Traffic, 1550–1700*. Aldershot, 2009: 147–66.
McKeon, Michael. 'Sabbatai Sevi in England'. *AJS Review* 2 (1977): 131–69.
Maclean, John, ed. *Letters from George Lord Carew to Sir Thomas Roe, 1615–1617*. London, 1860.
MacLean, Gerald. 'East by North-East: The English among the Russians, 1553–1603'. In Jyotsna Singh, ed., *A Companion to the Global Renaissance*. Oxford, 2009: 163–77.
—— *Looking East: English Writing and the Ottoman Empire before 1800*. Basingstoke, 2007.
—— 'Milton Among the Muslims'. In Andrew Hadfield and Matthew Dimmock, eds., *The Religions of the Book: Conflict and Co-Existence, 1400–1660*. Basingstoke, 2008: 180–94.
—— 'Milton, Islam and the Ottomans'. In Sharon Achinstein and Elizabeth Sauer, eds., *Milton and Toleration*. Oxford, 2007: 284–98.
—— 'Performing at the Ottoman Porte in 1599: The Case of Henry Lello'. In Ralf Hertel, ed., *Cultures at Play: Encounters with the East in the Early Modern Age*. Aldershot, forthcoming.
—— 'Re-siting the Subject'. In Amanda Gilroy and Wil Verhoeven, eds., *Epistolary Histories: Letters, Fiction, Culture*. Charlottesville, VA, 2000: 176–97.
—— 'Slavery and Sensibility: A Historical Dilemma'. In Brycchan Carey and Peter Kitson, eds., *Slavery and the Cultures of Abolition: Essays Marking the British Abolition Act of 1807*. Cambridge, 2007: 173–94.

—— 'Strolling in Syria with William Biddulph', *Criticism* 46: 3 (Summer 2004): 415–40.
—— *The Rise of Oriental Travel: English Visitors to the Ottoman Empire, 1580–1720.* Basingstoke, 2004.
al-Malibari, Zayn al-Din ibn 'Abd al-Aziz. *Tuhfat al-mujahidin fi ba'd akhbar al-burtughaliyin.* Trans. Muhammad Husayn Nainar. Madras, 1942.
Malvezzi, The Marquesse Virgilio. *Il Davide Persequitato, David Persecuted.* Trans. Robert Ashley. 1647; rpt. 1650.
Mancini, Augusto. 'Per lo Studio della leggenda di Maometto in Occidente'. *Rendiconti della R. Accademia Nazionale dei Lincei*, 6th series, X (Rome, 1934): 325–49.
Mandeville, John. *The Travels of John Mandeville.* 1900; rpt. New York, 1964.
al-Mannuni, Muhammad. *Rakb al-Hajj al-Maghribi.* Tetuan, 1953.
Manwaring, George. 'A True Discourse of Sir Anthony Sherley's Travel into Persia'. In Edward Denison Ross, ed., *Sir Anthony Sherley and his Persian Adventure.* London, 1933.
Markham, Clements R., ed., *The Voyages of Sir James Lancaster, to the East Indies.* 1877; rpt. New Delhi, 1998.
Marshall, P. J. 'The English in Asia'. In Canny, ed., *Oxford History of the British Empire*: 1: 264–85.
—— ed., *The Oxford History of the British Empire, Volume 2: The Eighteenth Century.* Oxford, 1998.
Massinger, John. *The Renegado.* 1630.
Masters, Bruce. 'Aleppo: The Ottoman Empire's Caravan City.' In Edhem, Goffman and Masters, eds., *Ottoman City*: 17–78.
—— *Christians and Jews in the Ottoman Arab World: The Roots of Sectarianism.* Cambridge, 2001.
Matar, Nabil. www.hull.ac.uk/caravane/documents/sourcesmatar.pdfbar
—— 'Ahmad al-Mansur and Queen Elizabeth I'. *Journal of Early Modern History* 12 (2008): 55–76.
—— *Britain and Barbary, 1589–1689.* Gainesville, FL, 2005.
—— *Europe Through Arab Eyes, 1578–1727.* New York, 2009.
—— 'The 1609 Expulsion of the Moriscos in Early Modern British Thought', *Explorations in Renaissance Culture* 35 (2009): 132–49.
—— *In the Lands of the Christians.* New York, 2003.
—— *Islam in Britain, 1558–1685.* Cambridge, 1998.
—— 'John Locke and the "Turbanned Nations"', *Journal of Islamic Studies* 2 (1991): 67–77.
—— 'The Last Moors: Maghariba in Britain, 1700–1750', *Journal of Islamic Studies* 14 (2003): 37–58.
—— 'The Maliki Imperialism of Ahmad al-Mansur: The Moroccan Invasion of Sudan, 1591'. In Elizabeth Sauer and Balchandra Rajan, eds., *Imperialisms: Historical and Literary Investigations, 1500–1900.* New York, 2004: 147–61.

Matar, Nabil. 'Orthdox, Sunni, and Anglican in Palestine, c. 1642-1697'. In Judy Hayden and Nabil Matar, eds., *Through the Eyes of the Beholder: Images of the Holy Land in the Early Modern Period*. Leiden, 2011.

—— 'Some Notes on George Fox and Islam', *The Journal of the Friends' Historical Society* 55 (1989): 271–6

—— 'The Toleration of Muslims in Renaissance England: Practice and Theory.' In John C. Laursen, ed., *Religious Toleration from Cyrus to Defoe: The Variety of Rites*. New York, 1999: 127–46.

—— *Turks, Moors, and Englishmen in the Age of Discovery*. New York, 1999.

—— 'Two Journeys to Seventeenth-Century Palestine', *Journal of Palestine Studies* 29 (2000): 66–79.

—— and Rudolph Stoeckel. 'Europe's Mediterranean Other: The Moor.' In Andrew Hadfield and Paul Hammond, eds., *The Arden Critical Companions*. London, 2004: 230–52.

Mather, James. *Pashas: Traders and Travellers in the Islamic World*. New Haven and London, 2009.

Matthee, Rudolph P. 'Between Aloofness and Fascination: Safavid Views of the West,' *Persian Studies* 31 (1998): 219–46.

—— 'Exotic Substances: The Introduction and Global Spread of Tobacco, Coffee, Cocoa, Tea and Distilled Liquor, Sixteenth to Eighteenth Centuries'. In Roy Porter and Mikulas Teich, eds., *Drugs and Narcotics in History*. Cambridge, 1995: 24–51.

—— *The Politics of Trade in Safavid Iran: Silk for Silver, 1600–1730*. Cambridge, 1999.

Maundrell, Henry. *A Journey from Aleppo to Jerusalem in 1697*. Ed. David Howell. Beirut, 1963.

The Mens Answer to the Womens Petition Against Coffee. 1674.

Mentzer, Raymond A. 'The Huguenot Minority in early modern France'. In James D. Tracy and Marguerite Ragnow, eds., *Religion and the Early Modern State: Views from China, Russia, and the West*. Cambridge, 2004: 185–206.

Meriton, George. *A Geographical Description of the World*. 1671.

Meshkat, Kurosh. 'The Journey of Master Anthony Jenkinson to Persia (1562)'. MA thesis, University of Oslo, 2005.

Meunier, Dominque. *Le Consulat Anglais à Tetouan sous Anthony Hatfeild [sic] (1717–1728)*. Preface by Chantal de La Véronne. Tunis, 1980.

Meyerstein, E. H. W., ed., *Adventures by Sea of Edward Coxere*. New York and London, 1946.

Milton, Giles. *Samurai William: The Adventurer who Unlocked Japan*. New York, 2002.

Mindanoi, Giovanni Tommaso. *The History of the Warres betweene the Turks and the Persians*. Trans. Abraham Hartwell. 1595.

The Moderate Intelligencer, no 215 (26 April – 2 May 1649).

Montesquieu, Charles de Secondat. *Persian Letters*. Trans. C. J. Betts. Harmondsworth, 1973.

Morden, Robert. *Geography Rectified: Or, A Description of the World*. 1680; rpt. 1693.
Morgan, E. Delmar and C. H. Coote, eds., *Early Voyages and Travels to Russia and Persia by Anthony Jenkinson and Other Englishmen*. 2 vols. London, 1886.
Morgan, Joseph. *A Complete History of Algiers*. 2 vols. London, 1728.
—— *A Compleat History of the Piratical States of Barbary*. London, 1750.
Morineau, Michel. 'The Indian Challenge: Seventeenth to Eighteenth Centuries'. In Sushil Chaudhury and Michel Morineau, eds., *Merchants, Companies and Trade: Europe and Asia in the Early Modern Era*. Cambridge, 1999: 243–75.
Moryson, Fynes. *An Itinerary Containing His Ten Yeeres Travell*. 1617; rpt. 4 vols. Glasgow, 1907.
—— *Shakespeare's Europe: A Survey of the Condition of Europe at the end of the Sixteenth Century, being Unpublished chapters of Fynes Moryson's Itinerary (1617)*. Ed. Charles Hughes. 1903; rpt. New York, 1967.
The Most Ancient and Famous History of the Renowned Prince Arthur. 1634.
Moüette, Germain. *Relation de la Captivité du Sr. Moüette dans les Royaumes de Fez et de Maroc*. Paris, 1683. Trans. 'Travels in the kingdoms of Fez and Morocco during his eleven years' captivity in those parts'. In *A New Collection of Voyages and Travels into several Parts of the World, none of them ever before Printed in English*. London, 1711: 1–115.
Munster, Sebastian. *A Briefe Collection and compendious extract of straunge and memorable things*. 1572.
al-Nabulsi, 'Abd al-Ghani. *Al-hadra al-unsiyyah fi al-safara al-qudsiyyah*. Ed. Akram Hasan al-'Ulabi. Beirut, 1991.
[Narborough, John]. *Articles of Peace & Commerce Between The Most Serene and Mighty Prince Charles II . . . And The Most Illustrious Lords, Halil Bashaw, Ibraim Dey*. 1676.
Neau, Elias. *Account of the Sufferings of the French Protestants*. 1699.
Nebenzahl, Kenneth. *Maps of the Holy Land*. New York, 1986.
Newes from divers countries as, from Spaine, Antwerpe, Collin, Venice, Rome, the Turke. 1597.
News from Sally: Of A Strange Delivery of Foure English Captives. 1642.
Nezam-Mafi, Mohammad Taghi. 'Persian Recreations: Theatricality in Anglo-Persian Diplomatic History, 1599–1827'. PhD dissertation, Boston University, 1999.
Nicholl, Charles. 'Field of Bones'. *London Review of Books* (2 September 1999), accessed online 12 July 2009.
Nicolay, Nicholas de. *The Navigations, Peregrinations and Voyages, made into Turkie*. Trans. Thomas Washington. 1585.
Nixon, Anthony. *The Three English Brothers. Sir Thomas Sherley his Travels, with his three yeares imprisonment in Turkie*. 1607.
Noorthouck, John. *A New History of London: Including Westminster and Southwark*. London, 1773.

North, Roger. *The Life of the Honourable Sir Dudley North, Knt.* Ed. Montague North. London, 1744.
Ockley, Simon. *An Account of South-West Barbary.* London, 1713.
—— *A History of the Saracens.* 2 vols. London, 1708, 1718.
O'Donnell, Paris. 'Pilgrimage or 'anti-pilgrimage'? Uses of mementos and relics in English and Scottish narratives of travel to Jerusalem, 1596–1632', *Studies in Travel Writing* 13 (2009): 125–39.
Ogborn, Miles. *Indian Ink: Script and Print in the Making of the English East India Company.* Chicago, 2007.
Ogilby, John. *Africa: Being An Accurate Description of the Regions of Ægypt, Barbary, Lybia, and the Billedulgerid.* 1670.
Okeley, William. *Eben-Ezer: Or, A Small Monument of Great Mercy appearing in the Miraculous Deliverance.* 1675.
An Ordinance for continuation of one Act of Parliament, Entituled, An Act for Redemption of Captives. 1653.
Orr, Bridget. *Empire on the English Stage, 1660–1714.* Cambridge, 2001.
Ortelius, Abraham. *Theatrum Orbis Terrarum, The Theatre of the Whole World.* 1606.
Overall, W. H. and H. C. Overall, eds., *Analytical Index to the Series of Records Known as the Remembrancia.* London, 1878.
Overbury, Thomas. *A True and Perfect Account of the Examination, Confession, Tryal, Condemnation, and Execution of Joan Perry.* 1676.
Ovington, John. *A Voyage to Surat in the Year 1689.* 1696.
Owen, G. Dyfnallt. ed. *Manuscripts of the Marquess of Bath Preserved at Longleat: Volume 5, Talbot, Dudley and Devereux Papers, 1533–1659.* London, 1980.
Oxford, University of. *Britannia Rediviva.* Oxford, 1660.
Oxford, University of. *Vota Oxoniensia pro serenissimis Guilhelmo Rege et Maria Regina.* Oxford, 1689.
Özkoçak, Selma Akyazici. 'Coffeehouses: Rethinking the Public and Private in Early Modern Istanbul', *Journal of Urban History* 33 (2007): 965–86.
P., M. *A Character of Coffee and Coffee-Houses.* 1661.
Pagitt, Ephraim. *Christianography: Or, The Description Of the Multitude and sundry Sorts of Christians, in the World, Not Subject to the Pope.* 1634; rpt. 1674.
Pailin, David. *Attitudes to Other Religions: Comparative Religion in Seventeenth- and Eighteenth-century Britain.* Manchester, 1984.
Painter, William. *The palace of pleasure beautified.* 1566; rpt. 1567.
Pandon, Charles. *Copie d'Une Lettre Envoyee de Coutron en Calabre.* Lyons, 1587.
Pannier, Jacques. 'Calvin et les Turcs' [Mélanges], *Revue Historique* 180 (1937): 268–86.
Parker, Kenneth, ed., *Early Modern Tales of Orient: A Critical Anthology.* London, 1999.
Parr, Anthony, ed., *Three Renaissance Travel Plays.* 1995; rpt. Manchester, 1999.
Parry, William. *A New and Large Discourse of the Travels of Sir Anthony Sherley.* 1601.

—— *A Particular Narrative of the Burning of the Port of Tripoli, Four Men of War, Belonging to the Corsairs, By Sir John Narbrough . . . 14 Jan 1676*. 1676.
Pascoe, C. F. *Two Hundred Years of the S.P.G.: An Historical Account of the Society for the Propagation of the Gospel in Foreign Parts, 1701–1900*. London, 1901.
Pearson, John B. *A Biographical Sketch of the Chaplains to the Levant Company Maintained at Constantinople, Aleppo and Smyrna, 1611–1706*. Cambridge, 1883.
Peirce, Leslie. *The Imperial Harem: Women and Sovereignty in the Ottoman Empire*. Ithaca, NY, 1993.
—— 'The Material World: Ideologies and Ordinary Things'. In Aksan and Goffman, eds., *Early Modern Ottomans*. Cambridge, 2007: 213–32.
Pellow, Thomas. *The History of the Long Captivity and Adventures of Thomas Pellow, in South-Barbary*. London, 1739.
Pennell, C. R., ed., *Piracy and Diplomacy in Seventeenth-Century North Africa: The Journal of Thomas Baker, English Consul in Tripoli, 1677–1685*. Rutherford, NJ, 1989.
Pepys, Samuel. *The Diary of Samuel Pepys*. Eds. Robert Latham and William Matthews. 11 vols. Los Angeles and Berkeley, CA, 1970–83.
—— *The Tangier Papers of Samuel Pepys*. Ed. Edwin Chappell. London, 1935.
Phelps, Thomas. *A True Account of the Captivity of Thomas Phelps at Machaness in Barbary*. 1685.
Philippson, John [Sleidanus]. *A briefe Chronicle of the foure principall Empyres. To witte, of Babilon, Persia, Grecia, and Rome*. Trans. Stephan Wythere. 1563.
—— *The Key of Historie*. 1627.
[Phillips, George]. *The Present State of Tangier*. 1676.
Pignon, Jean. 'Un document inédit sur la Tunisie au début du XVII siècle', *Les Cahiers de Tunisie* 33 (1961): 109–219.
Pitts, Joseph. *A True and Faithful Account of the Religion and Manners of the Mohammetans*. Exeter, 1704.
Plantet, Eugène. *Correspondance des Beys de Tunis et des consuls de France avec la Cour de France, 1577–1830*. 3 vols. Paris, 1893–99.
Pococke, Edward. *Liturgiae Ecclesiae Anglicanae, Partes praecipuae . . . In Linguam Arabicam traductae*. Oxford, 1674.
—— *Specimen Historiae Arabum*. Oxford, 1650.
Poe, Marshall T. *'A People Born to Slavery': Russia in Early Modern European Ethnography, 1476–1748*. Ithaca, NY, 2000.
Pool, John J. *Studies in Mohammedanism, Historical and Doctrinal*. Westminster, 1892.
Prasad, Ram Chandra. *Early English Travellers in India*. 1965; rpt. Delhi, 1980.
Prideaux, Humphrey. *The True Nature of Imposture Fully Display'd in the Life of Mahomet*. 1697; rpt. 1697, 1698 (twice).
Purchas, Samuel, ed., *Hakluytus Posthumus, or, Purchas His Pilgrimes*. 1625; rpt. 20 vols. Glasgow, 1905–7.
Quataert, Donald, ed., *Consumption Studies and the History of the Ottoman Empire, 1550–1922*. Albany, NY, 2000.

Querical Demonstrations Writ by Prince Butler, Author of the Eleven Queries Relating to The Bill for Prohibiting East-India Silks and Printed Callicoes. [1699?].
[Qur'an]:
—— *Machumetis Saracenorum principis, eiúsque successorum vitae, ac doctrina, ipséque Alcoran . . . quae . . . Petrus abbas Cluniacensis . . . ex Arabica lingua in Latinam transferri curavit . . . Cum Philippi Melanchtonis praemonitione . . . Haec omnia in unum volumen redacta sunt, opera & studio Theodori Bibliandri.* Basle, 1543.
—— *L'Alcorano di Macometto, nel qual si contiene la dottrina, la vita, i costumi, et le leggi sue. Tradotto nuouamente dell-Arabo in lingua Italiana.* [Venice], 1547.
—— *Alcoranus Mahometicus oder: Tuerckenglaub aus des Mahomets eygenem Buch genañt Alcoran und seinen 124 darinn begriffenen Azoaris, in ein kurtz Compendium zusammen gebracht . . . durch . . . Henricum Leuchtern.* Frankfurt am Mayn, 1604.
Rawlins, John. *The Famous and Wonderful Recovery of a Ship of Bristol.* 1622.
Rawlinson, H. G. *British Beginnings in Western India, 1579–1657.* Oxford, 1920.
Refik, Ahmed. *Onuncu Asr-i Hicride Istanbul Hayati (1495–1591).* Istanbul, 1988.
Regla, Juan. *Estudios sobre los moriscos.* 3rd edn. Barcelona, 1974.
The Restauration of the Jewes: Or, A True Relation of their Progress and Proceedings. 1665.
Rheinheimer, Martin. 'From Amrum to Algiers and Back: The Reintegration of a Renegade in the Eighteenth Century', *Central European History* 36 (2003): 209–33.
Rice, Warner G. 'The Moroccan Episode in Thomas Heywood's "*The Fair Maid of the West*"', *Philological Quarterly* 9 (1930): 131–40.
—— 'The Sources of Massinger's "*The Renegado*"', *Philological Quarterly* 11: 1 (1932): 65–75.
Riley, Stephen T. 'Abraham Browne's Captivity by the Barbary Pirates, 1655'. In *Seafaring in Colonial Massachusetts.* Boston, MA, 1980: 31–42.
Roberts, Lewes. *The Marchants Map of Commerce.* 1638.
Roberts, R. J. 'The Greek Press at Constantinople in 1627 and its Antecedents', *The Library* 22 (1967): 13–43.
Roderiquez, Dario Cabanelas. 'Ortas Cartas del Sultan de Marruecos Ahmad al-Mansur a Felipe II', *Miscelanea de Estudios Arabes y Hebraicos* 7 (1958): 13–14.
Roe, Thomas. *The Embassy of Sir Thomas Roe to India, 1615–19.* Ed. William Foster. 1899; rev. 1926; rpt. New Delhi, 1990.
—— *The Negotiations of Sir Thomas Roe in his Embassy to the Ottoman Porte from the Year 1621 to 1628 Inclusive.* London, 1740.
Rosedale, H. G. *Queen Elizabeth and the Levant Company. A Diplomatic and Literary Episode of the Establishment of our Trade with Turkey.* London, 1904.
Ross, Alexander. *Pansebeia: or, A View of all Religions in the World.* 1653; rpt. 'The Fifth edition, Enlarged and Perfected'. 1675.
Ross, Edward Denison, ed., *Sir Anthony Sherley and his Persian Adventure.* London, 1933.

Roth, Cecil. 'The Jews of Jerusalem in the Seventeenth Century: An English Account', *Journal of the Jewish Historical Society of England*, pt. 2 (1935): 99–104.
Routh, E. M. G. *Tangier: England's Lost Atlantic Outpost, 1661–1684*. London, 1912.
Rowlands, Samuel. *The Knave of Clubbes*. 1609.
Rubiés, Joan-Paul. *Travel and Ethnology in the Renaissance: South India through European Eyes, 1250–1625*. Cambridge, 2000.
Rubiés, Joan-Paul. *Travellers and Cosmographers: Studies in the History of Early Modern Ethnology*. Aldershot, 2007.
Russell, Alexander. *The Natural History of Aleppo. Containing A Description of the City, and the Principal Natural Productions in its Neighbourhood*. 1756; 2nd edition, 2 vols. London, 1794.
Russell, G. A., ed., *The 'Arabick' Interest of the Natural Philosophers in Seventeenth-Century England*. Leiden, 1994.
Rustum, Asad and Fu'ad Afram al-Bustani, eds. *Lubnan fi 'ahd al-Amir Fakhr al-Din al-Ma'ni al-Thani*. Beirut, 1969.
Rycaut, Paul. *The History of the Turkish Empire, From the Year 1623 to the year 1677*. 1680.
—— *The Present State of the Greek and Armenian Churches, Anno Christi, 1678*. London, 1679.
—— *The Present State of the Ottoman Empire*. 1667; rpt. 1670.
Ryley, J. Horton. *Ralph Fitch, England's Pioneer to India*. London, 1899.
S., T. *The Adventures of (Mr T. S.) An English Merchant, Taken Prisoner by the Turks of Argiers*. 1670.
Sabbagh, Leila. *al-Jaliyat al-urubbiya fi bilad al-sham fi al-'ahd al-uthmani fi al-qarnayn al-sadis 'ashar wal sabi' 'ashar*. 2 vols. Beirut, 1989.
Saldanha, Antonio de. *Cronica de Almançor, Sultan de Marrocos (1578–1603)*. Ed. Antonio dias Farinha, trans. Leon Bourdon. Lisbon, 1997.
Sanderson, John. *The Travels of John Sanderson in the Levant, 1584–1602*. Ed. William Foster. London, 1931.
Sandys, George. *A Relation of a Journey begun An. Dom: 1610*. 1615.
Savory, Roger M. *Iran under the Safavids*. Cambridge, 1980.
—— 'The Sherley Myth', *Iran* 5 (1967): 73–81.
Schen, Claire S. 'Greeks and "Grecians" in London: The "Other" Strangers'. In Randolph Vigne and Charles Littleton, eds., *From Strangers to Citizens: The Integration of Immigrant Communities in Britain, Ireland, and Colonial America, 1550–1750*. Brighton, 2001: 268–75.
Schmidt, Jan. 'Between Author and Library Shelf: The Intriguing History of Some Middle Eastern Manuscripts Acquired by Public Collections in the Netherlands Prior to 1800'. In Hamilton, et al., eds., *Republic of Letters*: 27–53.
Scholem, Gershom. *Sabbatai Sevi, The Mystical Messiah, 1626–1676*. Princeton, NJ, 1973.
Schwoebel, Robert. *The Shadow of the Crescent: The Renaissance Image of the Turk (1453–1517)*. New York, 1967.

Seaman, William. *The Reign of Sultan Orchan Second King of the Turks.* Translated out of Hojah Effendi, an eminent Turkish Historian. 1652.

Serrurier, Petrus. *The Last Letters, To the London-Merchants and Faithful Ministers.* 1665.

Settle, Elkanah. *The Empress of Morocco.* 1673.

Setton, Kenneth M. *Western Hostility to Islam and Prophecies of Turkish Doom.* Philadelphia, PA, 1992.

Shapiro, James. *Shakespeare and the Jews.* New York, 1996.

Shaw, Stanford J. *The Jews of the Ottoman Empire and the Turkish Republic.* New York, 1991.

Sharb, Ahmad Bu. 'Mawarid al-Maghariba al-muqimin bi-l-Burtughal khilal al-qarn al-sadis 'ashar', *Majalat Kuliyat al-Adab wa-l 'Ulum al-Insaninyah* 19 (1994): 87–103.

—— *Magharibah fi al-Burtughal.* Rabat, 1996.

Shmuelevitz, Aryeh. *The Jews of the Ottoman Empire in the Fifteenth and Sixteenth Centuries.* Leiden, 1984.

—— *A short forme of thankesgeving for the delyverie of the isle of Malta from the invasion and long siege thereof by the great armie of the Turkes.* 1565.

Skilliter, Susan A. 'Three Letters from the Ottoman "Sultana" Safiye to Queen Elizabeth I'. In S. M. Stern, ed., *Documents from Islamic Chanceries.* Oxford, 1965: 119–57.

—— *William Harborne and the Trade with Turkey, 1578–1582.* Oxford, 1977.

Smith, Henry. *Gods Arrow Against Atheists.* 1593; rpt. 1604.

Smith, Richard L. *Ahmad Al-Mansur.* New York, 2006.

Smith, Thomas. *Remarks upon the Manners, Religion and Government of the Turks, Together with a Survey of the Seven Churches of Asia, as they now lye in their Ruines.* 1678.

Smyrnelis, Marie-Carmen. 'Les Arméniens catholiques aux XVIIIeme et XIXeme siècles', *Revue du Monde Arménien moderne et contemporain* 2 (1995): 25–44.

The Speech of His Excellency Don V. Zary. London, 1710.

Speed, John. *The Theatre of the Empire of Great Britain.* 1611.

[Spragge, Edward]. *Articles of Peace & Commerce Between The Most Serene and Mighty Prince Charles II . . . And The Most Illustrious Lords, The Bashaw, Dai, Aga, and Governours of the Famous City and Kingdom of Algiers.* 1677.

Spratt, T., ed., *Autobiography of The Rev. Devereux Spratt.* London, 1886.

St. Olon, François Pidou de. *The Present State of the Empire of Morocco.* Trans. Peter Motteux. 1695.

Staden, Johann von Hans. *The True Story of His Captivity 1557.* Trans. and ed. Malcolm Letts. London, 1928.

Stanhope, Alexander. *Spain Under Charles the Second; or, Extracts from the Correspondence of the Hon. A. Stanhope . . . 1690–1699.* Ed. Philip Henry, 1840; 2nd ed., London, 1844.

Steele, Richard. *The Female Manufacturers Complaint.* London, 1720.

Steensgaard, Niels. 'Consuls and Nations in the Levant from 1570–1650', *The Scandinavian Economic History Review* 15 (1967): 13–54.
Stern, Philip J. '"A Politie of Civill & Military Power": Political Thought and the Late Seventeenth-Century Foundations of the East India Company-State', *Journal of British Studies* 47 (2008): 253–83.
Stodart, Robert. *The Journal of Robert Stodart*. Ed. E. Denison Ross. London, 1935.
Stow, John. *A Survay of London*. 1598.
Strachan, Michael. *Sir Thomas Roe, 1581–1644: A Life*. London, 1989.
Stubbe, Henry. *The Rise and Progress of Mahometanism*. Ed. Nabil Matar. New York, forthcoming.
Subrahmanyam, Sanjay. 'Connected Histories: Notes towards a Reconfiguration of Early Modern Eurasia', *Modern Asian Studies* 31 (1997): 735–62.
Sumbel, Leah. *Memoirs of the Life of Mrs. Sumbel*. 3 vols. London, 1811.
Sweetman, John. *The Oriental Obsession: Islamic Inspiration in British and American Art and Architecture, 1500–1920*. Cambridge, 1988.
T., C. *An Advice how to Plant Tobacco in England*. 1615.
Taafe, Francis. *Count Taaffe's Letters from the Imperial Camp*. 1684.
Tablit, Ali. 'Algerian-British Relations: 1585–1830'. In Abduljelil Temimi and Mohammed-Salah Omri, eds., *Actes du Ier Congrés International sur: Le Grande Bretagne et le Maghreb: Etat de Recherche et contacts culturels*. Zaghouane, Tunisia, 2001: 197–212.
Tadros, Mazin. 'Fishers of Men, the Jesuits in Bilad al-Sham, 1625–1660'. PhD dissertation, SUNY-Albany, 2009.
Tappe, E. D., ed. *Documents concerning Rumanian History (1427–1601) collected from British Archives*. Hague, 1964.
Tasso, Torquato. *Godfrey of Bulloigne*. Trans. Edward Fairfax. 1600.
Tavernier, Jean Baptiste. *The Six Voyages of John Baptista Tavernier, Baron of Aubonne*. Trans. John Phillips. 1677.
—— *Collections of Travels through Turky into Persia, and the East-Indies*. Trans. John Phillips and Edmund Everard. 1684.
Taylor, Joan. *The Englishman, the Moor and the Holy City*. Stroud, Gloucestershire, 2006.
al-Tazi, 'Abd al-Hadi. 'Muhammad ibn Haddu', *Academia* 2 (1985): 55–80.
Teltscher, Kate. *India Inscribed: European and British Writing on India 1600–1800*. Delhi, 1995.
Temimi, Abdeljelil. *Etudes d'Histoire Morisque*. Zaghouan, Tunisia, 1993.
Teonge, Henry. *The Diary of Henry Teonge*. Ed. G. E. Manwaring. London, 1927.
Terry, Edward. *A Voyage to East-India*. 1655.
de Testa, Marie and Antoine Gautier. *Drogmans et diplomates européens auprès de la Porte ottomane*. Istanbul, 2003.
Thackston, Wheeler M., trans. and ed., *The Jahangirnama, Memoirs of Jahangir, Emperor of India*. New York and Oxford, 1999.

Thévenot, Jean de. *The Travels of Monsieur de Thevenot into the Levant*. Trans. Archibald Lovell. 1687.
Thirsk, Joan. *Horses in Early Modern England: For Service, for Pleasure, for Power*. Reading, 1978.
Thomas, Keith. *The Ends of Life: Roads to Fulfilment in Early Modern England*. Oxford, 2009.
Timberlake, Henry. *A True and Strange Discourse of the Travailes of two English Pilgrimes*. 1603.
Tolan, John V. *Saracens: Islam in the Medieval European Imagination*. New York, 2002.
Toland, John. *Reasons for Naturalizing the Jews in Great Britain, and Ireland, on the Same Foot with All Other Nations*. London, 1714.
Tomiak, Janusz J. 'A British Poet's Account of the Raising of the Siege of Vienna in 1683', *Polish Review* 5 (1966): 66–74.
Tooley, R. V. 'Maps of Palestine in the Atlas of Ortelius', *The Map Collector* 3 (June 1978): 28–31.
Toomer, G. J. *Eastern Wisdome and Learning: The Study of Arabic in Seventeenth Century England*. Oxford, 1996.
Toon, Peter, ed., *Puritans, the Millennium and the Future of Israel*. Cambridge and London, 1970.
Touili, Mohammed, ed., *Correspondance des Consuls de France à Alger, 1642–1792*. Paris, 2001.
Tournefort, Joseph Pitton de. *Relation d'un voyage du Levant*. 2 vols. Paris, 1717.
Trapp, John. *A Commentary or Exposition upon all the Epistles, and the Revelation of John the Divine*. 1647.
A Transcript of the Registers of the Worshipful Company of Stationers: From 1640–1708 A. D. 3 vols. London, 1913.
The true Case of The Silk-Throwsters, Weavers and Dyers, with Their Petition to the Parliament. 1689.
A True Copy of a letter sent from Vienna, September the 2d, N. S. by an eminent English officer. 1683.
A True Declaration of the estate of the Colonie in Virginia. 1610.
A True Narrative of a Wonderful Accident, Which occur'd upon the Execution of a Christian Slave at Aleppo in Turky. 1676.
A True and Perfect Relation of the Happy Successe & Victory Obtained against the Turks of Argiers at Bugia. 1671.
A True Relation of the Inhumane and Unparallel'd Actions, and Barbarous Murders of Negroes or Moors. 1672.
Turnbull, Geoffrey and John Turnbull. *A History of the Calico Printing Industry of Great Britain*. Altrincham, 1951.
Tuwat, Al-Tahir Muhammad. *Adab al-rasa'il fi al-Maghrib al-Arabi*. Algiers, 1993.
Tyerman, Christopher. *England and the Crusades, 1095–1588*. Chicago and London, 1988.

Ungerer, Gustav. *The Mediterranean Apprenticeship of British Slavery*. Madrid, 2008.
―――― 'Portia and the Prince of Morocco', *Shakespeare Studies* 31 (2003): 89–129.
Valle, Pietro della. *The Travels of Sig. Pietro della Valle, A Noble Roman, Into East-India and Arabia Deserta*. 1665.
Verney, Frances Parthenhope and Margaret M. Verney, eds., *Memoirs of the Verney Family During the Seventeenth Century*. 1892; rev. ed., 2 vols, London, 1907.
Vickers, Brian, ed., *Shakespeare: The Critical Heritage*. 6 vols. London, 1974–81.
Vitkus, Daniel J. ed., *Piracy, Slavery and Redemption: English Captivity Narratives in North Africa, 1577-1704*. With an Introduction by Nabil Matar. New York, 2001.
―――― *Turning Turk: English Theatre and the Multicultural Mediterranean, 1570–1630*. New York, 2003.
―――― ed., *Three Turk Plays from Early Modern England*. New York, 2000.
Wadsworth, Alfred and Julia de Lacy Mann. *The Cotton Trade and Industrial Lancashire, 1600–1780*. Manchester, 1931.
Wakefield, C. 'Arabic Manuscripts in the Bodleian Library: The Seventeenth-Century Collections'. In Russell, ed., *'Arabick' Interest*: 128–46.
Walker, Julia M. *The Elizabeth Icon, 1603–2003*. Basingstoke, 2004.
Wallington, Nehemiah. *Historical Notices of Events Occurring Chiefly in the Reign of Charles I*. 2 vols. London, 1869.
Walton, Izaak. *The Lives of John Donne, Sir Henry Wotton, Richard Hooker, George Herbert, Robert Sanderson*. Ed. George Saintsbury. London, 1973.
Wasf al-Mamalik al-Maghribiyya. Trans. 'Abd al-Wahid Akmir. Rabat, 1997.
Weiss, Gillian Lee. 'From Barbary to France: processions of redemption and early modern culturally identity'. In Giulio Cipollone, ed., *La Liberazione dei 'Captivi' tra Christiantà e Islam*. Vatican, 2000: 789–805.
―――― 'Back from Barbary: Captivity, Redemption and French Identity in the Seventeenth- and Eighteenth-Century Mediterranean'. PhD dissertation, Stanford University, 2002.
Wernham, Richard Bruce ed. *List and Analysis of State Papers, Foreign Series, Elizabeth I, July 1590 – May 1591*. 7 vols. London, 1969.
―――― *The Return of the Armadas*. Oxford, 1994.
Wheeler, J. Talboys, ed., *Early Travels in India: Being Reprints of Rare and Curious Narratives of Old Travellers in India in the Sixteenth and Seventeenth Centuries: First Series, comprising Purchas's Pilgrimage and Travels of Van Linschoten*. Calcutta, 1864.
Wild, Antony. *The East India Company: Trade and Conquest from 1600*. London, 1999.
[Wilkins, George]. *Three Miseries of Barbary: Plague, Famine, Civill Warre. With a relation of the death of Mahamet the late Emperour*. [1607].
Willan, T. S. 'Some Aspects of English Trade with the Levant in the Sixteenth Century', *English Historical Review* 70 (1955): 399–410.
―――― *Studies in Elizabethan Foreign Trade*. 1959; rpt. Manchester, 1968.
―――― *The Early History of the Russia Company, 1553–1603*. 1956; rpt. Manchester, 1968.

Willard, A. M. 'The Import Trade of London, 1600–1640'. PhD dissertation, University of London, 1956.

Wills, John E. 'European Consumption and Asian Production in the Seventeenth and Eighteenth Centuries'. In John Brewer and Roy Porter, eds., *Consumption and the World of Goods*. London, 1993: 133–47.

Wilson, C. H. 'Cloth Production and International Competition in the Seventeenth Century', *EHR*, 2nd series, 13 (1960): 209–21.

Windler, Christian. 'Diplomatic history as a field for cultural analysis: Muslim-Christian relations in Tunis, 1700–1840', *The Historical Journal* 44 (2001): 79–106.

Windus, John. *A Journey to Mequinez, The Residence of the Present Emperor of Fez and Morocco*. London, 1725.

Wolf, Anne. *How Many Miles to Babylon? Travels and Adventures to Egypt and Beyond, from 1300–1640*. Liverpool, 2003.

Wolf, Lucien. 'Status of the Jews in England after the Re-Settlement', *Jewish Historical Society of England* 4 (1899–1901): 177–91.

The Women's Petition Against Coffee. Representing to Publick Consideration the Grand Inconveniences accruing to their Sex from the Excessive Use of that Drying, Enfeebling Liquor. 1674.

Wood, Alfred C. *A History of the Levant Company*. 1935; rpt. London, 1964.

Woodcroft, Bennet, ed., *Appendix to Reference Index of Patentees of Inventions*. London, 1855.

Woodward, David. *Maps as Prints in the Italian Renaissance*. London, 1996.

Wright, Denis. 'Great Britain'. In Ehsan Yarshater, ed., *Encyclopaedia Iranica*, Volume XI, Fascicle 2. New York, 2002: 200–24.

Wunder, Amanda. 'Western travellers, eastern antiquities, and the image of the Turk in early modern Europe', *Journal of Early Modern History* 7 (2003): 89–119.

Yerasimos, Stephan. *Les Voyageurs dans l'Empire Ottoman (XIVe–XVIe siècles): Bibliographie, Itinéraires et Inventaire des Lieux Habités*. Ankara, 1991.

Yermolenko, Galina, ed., *Roxolana in History and Literature*. Aldershot, 2010.

Yurdusev, A. Nuri, ed., *Ottoman Diplomacy: Conventional or Unconventional?* Basingstoke, 2004.

Yurtbaşi, Metin. *A Dictionary of Turkish Proverbs*. Ankara, 1993.

Zilfi, Madeline. 'The Kadizadelis: Discordant Revivalism in Seventeeth-Century Istanbul', *Journal of Near Eastern Studies* 45 (1986): 251–69.

Index

'Abbas, Shah 64, 69, 71, 109, 181
Abbot, George 173, 174, 189, 195
Abdella, Alkaid Jaurar Ben 19, 219
Abi Dinar, Ibn Abi 137–8
Abraham, Marcus 180
Addison, Joseph 222
Addison, Lancelot 175, 176, 189, 231
Africanus, Leo 17, 148
agents, and writings on Islamic world 4, 89–90
Aghia Sophia mosque 18
Ahmed I, Sultan 207
Ajmer 92
Akbar, Shah 40, 67, 71, 166
Aldersey, Laurence 17, 171
Aldworth, Thomas 91, 100
Aleppo 7
   and Christian churches 95
   and first Arabic-script press 16
   and living conditions of Britons 91
Algiers 22
   and Christian worship in 95
   and consuls to 83
   and factors in 84–5
   and Jewish community 178
   and living conditions in 93–4
ambassadors:
   and Moroccan embassy to London 182–8
   and Ottoman Empire 82, 122
      Finch's embassy 114–21
      political interventions 81–2
   and role of 62, 63, 81
   see also living conditions; working conditions
Andaluz, Muhammad 184
Anglo-Dutch wars 2
Anne, Queen 182, 183–4, 187

archaeology, and Britons in Islamic world 101–2
Argenter, Lucas 158–9
Arkwright, Richard 211
Armenians 156, 180–2
   and Anglo-Armenian relations 180–1
   and geographic spread of 181–2
   and integration of 182
   and trade 180–1
   see also Zary, Bentura de
art:
   and Islamic admiration of European 84
   and representations of Muslims 29–30
   and turbans 215–16
Arundel, Sir Matthew 225–6
Ashby, John 120
Ashley, Robert 217
assimilation, and dangers of 110
Audellay, John 83
Aureng-zebe 2, 9

Baines, Sir Thomas 112, 114, 119, 121
Baker, Francis 106
Baker, Thomas 102, 109–10, 111
balance of power, and British view of Islamic world 9
Balfour Declaration 197
Barbary Company 2, 51, 79, 84, 85
Barbary pirates 7, 82, 86, 230
   see also piracy
Barbatus, Josephus 180
Bard, Henry 83
Barendse, R J 7
Barker, Edmund 193
Baron, Robert 191
Barrington, Francis 106
Barton, Edward 47, 82, 94, 98, 174, 216

Baxter, Richard 37
Becudo, Matias 51
Bedwell, William 33, 160
Beg, Muhammad 'Ali 71
Beg, Muhammad Hussain 104–5
Behn, Aphra 4
bell-ringing 87
Bendish, Sir Thomas 226
Berriman, William 152
Best, Thomas 74, 91
Bibliander, Theodor 32
Biddulph, William 38, 96–7, 98, 100, 175, 217
Blackman, Captain Jeremy 98
Blake, Robert 18
Blome, Richard 144
Blount, Henry 3, 176, 216
Bogdan, Stefan 62–3, 78
Bohun, Edward 169
Bon, Ottaviano 38
books, and Britons in Islamic world 100–1
Bradshaw, Edmund 18
Brathwaite, Richard 204–6
Braudel, Fernand 126, 130–1
Brèves, François Savary de 97
bribery, and gift-giving 109
Brightman, Thomas 4, 27
British Empire:
    and commercial imperative 236–8
    and origins of 23
Broach 91–2
Brooks, Francis 19, 149
Brotton, Jerry 170
Broughton, Hugh 27
Browne, Abraham 149
Bruyn, Corneille de 102, 163
Brydges, John 120
Burghley, Lord 51, 67
Busbecq, Ogier Ghiselin de 224–5, 227
Byam, Henry 219, 220

Cadiz 56, 57
calico 14, 202, 209–14
    and attempts to ban trade in 211, 212, 213
    1721 Act 214
    abuses of 213–14
    and debates over 211–12
    and domestic production 214
    and growth in demand for 210
    and impact on class boundaries 213
    and imports of 210
    and lobbies against 210–11
    and objections to 210
    and satirical writings 212
Calvin, John 26, 60
Cambridge University 4
Camroni, Caspar 159
Capitulations, Grant of (1629) 17
captives 7
    and consuls' responsibilities 112
    and *fakkakin* 124
    and fear of conversion 139, 140
    and hiring of 100
    and lack of royal/church interest in 129, 139
    and liberation from Salé 139–40
    and North Africa 86, 87, 126
    and Parliamentary action on behalf of 142
    and persistence of Islamic habits on return 151
    and petitions on behalf of 139
    and ransoming of 152
        raising money for 142, 143
    and religious orders to negotiate ransoms 125–6
    and suspicion of returning 128–9, 139
    and women 129–30
captivity, literature of 25, 124, 126, 154–5
    and demonisation of Islam 126–7
    and features of 127
        post-1640 accounts 131–2
        pre-1640 accounts 130–1
    and Hakluyt's *Principal Navigations* 128
    and image of Muslims 7, 25, 126–7, 142, 154–5, 232
    and influence of 127–8
    and post-1640 accounts 140–54
        advocacy of conquest 140, 141, 151–2
        attitudes towards Islam and Muslims 141, 146, 149, 150–1
        Brooks (Francis) 149
        D'Aranda (Emanuel) 143–4
        Elliot (Adam) 147–8
        features of 131–2

French accounts 144
heroic and plucky Englishmen
    145–6, 147–9
informative nature of 141, 144,
    148–9, 150
Knight (Francis) 140–1
Knox (Captain Robert) 147
limited nature of 149–50
Ockley (Simon) 151–2
Okeley (William) 146
Phelps (Thomas) 148–9
Pitts (Joseph) 150–1
public interest in 144–5
ransomer's account 152
romance 153–4
Spratt (Devereux) 141–2
and pre-1640 accounts 132–40
    advocacy of conquest 137
    attitudes towards Islam 138
    commercial factors 138
    Davies (William) 136–7
    Elliott (Robert) 137
    features of 130–1
    first English account 133–4
    first European accounts 133
    Foxe (John) 133–4
    Haselton (Richard) 134–6
    hostility to Catholicism 134, 135–6
    intelligence functions of 136–7
    Middleton (Sir Henry) 138
    New World captivity 132–3
    official discouragement of 138, 140
    Red Sea 138
    relatives' view 135, 136
    religious meaning 133–4
    Webbe (Edward) 134
Capuchins 95
Carew, Lord 137
Cartwright, John 189
Cartwright, Ralph 108, 172–3
Carvajal, Antonio Fernandez 179
Casale, Giancarlo 86
Cason, Edmond 142
Cecil, Sir Robert 57
Cervantes, Miguel de 133
Chardin, Sir John 3, 164, 191–2, 192–3
Charles I 11, 70, 139
Charles II 20, 77, 79, 118, 143, 202, 226
chartered companies 2, 235–6
    and establishment of 14, 81
    and political interventions 81
    and reports on Islamic world 4,
        89–90
    see also Barbary Company; East India
        Company; Levant Company
Chetwood, Robert 153
Child, Sir Joshua 5
Chios, and consuls to 83
Christendom, and definition through
    religious 'others' 39
Christianity:
    and Britons in Islamic world 103–4
    and churches in Islamic world 94–5
    and image of Muslims as enemies
        of 26–8
    and Islamic preservation of holy
        sites 165
    and materialism 200
    and Muslim converts to 20–1
        absence of missionary projects 123,
            232
    see also eastern Christians; Greek
        Orthodox Christians
Church Mission Society 197
Civil War, English, and impact on
    Britons abroad 103–4
clothes, and significance of 216–17
coffee:
    and closure of coffee houses 202
    and controversies surrounding 203–4
    and historical similarity to tobacco 203
    and introduction to England 160
    and moral and juridical anxieties
        over 200
    and stigma attached to 202, 203
Cole, Robert 98, 108, 110, 111
Coles, Paul 199
collectors, and Britons in Islamic
    world 101–2
colonialism 10, 155
    and India 233
    and North Africa 233
    and Persian Gulf 233
communications, and Britons in Islamic
    world 106–7
Companie des Indes 236
Connock, Edward 99, 109
Conopios, Nathaniel 160

consuls:
    and captives 112
    and characteristics of 83
    and disciplining of 83
    and dissuading converts 110
    and exchanges of royal portraits 84
    and expenses incurred by 110–11
    and length of service 110
    and network of resident 79–80
    and North Africa 84, 85, 122
    and Ottoman Empire 122
    and piracy 112
    and questionable behaviour of 111–12
    and role of 81, 82
    and social background 96
    and supervision of 84
    and tariffs 112
    and writings on Islamic world 4, 89–90
    see also living conditions; working conditions
consumerism, and Christian and Muslim approaches to 200–1
converts, religious:
    Christian to Islam 21, 103
        attempts to dissuade 110
        captives 139, 140
        fear of forced conversion 87
        first English 239n1
        marriage to Muslim women 97–8
        reconversion to Christianity 219–21
        white turbans 217–18
    Islam to Christian 20–1
        absence of missionary projects 123, 232
Coptic Christians 180
Coryate, Thomas 15, 20, 71, 76
Costa, Mendez de 179
Cotterel, Sir Clement 183
Cotton, Sir Dodmore 70, 71
Covel, John 92, 112, 113–14, 116, 117, 119, 162, 168, 182
Coventry mystery plays 28
Coverte, Captain Robert 180
Crete 161, 163, 231
Cromwell, Oliver 142, 166, 226
Crowther, John 68
Crusades, and impact on British attitudes 10
currants 201

Daborne, Robert 43, 218
Dallam, Thomas 101
Dandini, Girolamo 161
D'Aranda, Emanuel 143–4
Dartmouth, 1st Earl of (William Legge) 183, 184, 185
Davenant, William 20
Davies, John 143
Davies, William 136–7
De Azevedo, Jeronimo 75
De Vaca, Alvar Nunez Cabeza 132
Defoe, Daniel 147, 155, 182, 210, 213–14
Denham, John 191
Dimmock, Matthew 29
diplomatic relations, Anglo-Islamic 42, 77–8
    and Anglo-Moroccan relations:
        Bentura de Zary's embassy 182–8
        Elizabeth I's diplomacy 43–5, 49–61
    and Anglo-Ottoman relations 115
        Finch's embassy to Istanbul 114–21
    and British Islamic diplomats 63–4
    and Elizabeth I's personal diplomacy 42, 43–5, 62
        impact of death of 62
        legacy of 78
        Morocco 49–61
        Ottoman Empire 45–9, 54
    and James I 62–3, 136, 137
    and Mughal Empire 71–7
        East India Company 72–7
        Fitch-Newberry expedition 71
        Mildenhall's mission 71–2
        trade 72–7
        use of naval power 74
    and role of ambassadors 62, 63
    and Safavid Empire:
        commercial motives 66
        East India Company 68–9
        first Persian ambassador to London 69–71
        Fitch-Newberry expedition 67
        Jenkinson's embassy 64–6
        Levant Company 67–8
        silk trade 68–9
    and Stuart monarchs 43, 62–3
disease, and Britons in Islamic world 105
Dormido, David Abrabanell 179
Downton, Nicholas 75

drink, and Britons in Islamic world 104–5
Dryden, John 4, 221
Du Ryer, André 36
Ducket, Geffrey 189
Dumont, John 218
Durson, Captain John 19

East India Act (1813) 86, 233
East India Company 2, 236
  and area of operation 7–8
  and calico trade 210, 211
  and centralized administration 87–8, 107, 235–6
  and colonialism 233
  and commercial imperative 236–7
  and disciplining of consuls 83
  and factors 87–8
    local languages and measures 88, 89
  and government functions of 86
  as imperial masters 123
  and Mughal Empire 72–7
  and naval actions 85, 86
  and reports on Islamic world 4, 8, 89–90
  and Safavid Empire 68–9
  and use of force 9, 122
eastern Christians 25–6, 158–69
  and Anglican view of 159–60
    conversion hopes 160–1, 168–9, 197
    Protestant-Catholic rivalry 160
  and attempts to militarize 161, 162
  and British encounters with 156
    challenge posed by 157
  and Catholic missionaries 162
  and economic value of 161
  and European Protestant view of 159–60
  and Greek Christian visitors to England 158–9
  and heterogeneity of 162
  and interest in 158
  and Islamic preservation of holy sites 165
  and Islamic toleration 165–7
  and manipulation of 161
  and plans to transport to New World 161–2
  and portrayal as victims 157, 163–5, 169
  and relations with Muslims 162–3, 168
  and resentment at western conversion attempts 162
Edirne, and Mehmed IV's festival in 115–16
Edwards, William 86, 92
Elizabeth I 1, 2
  and commercial imperative 236–7
  and excommunication of 78
  and Ottoman Empire 14
    present of clothes from 216
  and personal diplomacy of 42, 43–5
    legacy of 78
    Morocco 49–61
    Ottoman Empire 45–9, 54
  and piracy 43
Elliot, Adam 147–8
Elliott, Robert 137
Elmarsafy, Ziad 37
English thought, and Islamic world in:
  and first contacts between 13–18
  and images of:
    in art 29–30
    enemies of Christianity 26–8
    theatre 4, 28–9, 58, 61
    visual imagery 29–30
  and India 14
  and Islam 31–9
    admiration of 37
    association with Ottomans 32, 41, 163–4
    contrasted with Christianity 32–3
    first translation of Qur'an 34–7
    harem 38
    iconoclasm 37
    misrepresentations of 31–2
    oriental studies 34
    in Persian-Indian region 40–1
    Pitts' account of 38–9
    use of Arabic sources 33–4
  and Ottoman Empire 14–15
  and Persia 14
  and personal contacts 18–26
    consuls and merchants 23–4
    friendships 18, 19
    migrants 21–3
    Muslim visitors to England 19–21
    piracy 24–5
  see also captivity, literature of; images of Muslims and Islam

INDEX

Evelyn, John 160, 177, 221, 222, 227–8
Evliya Çelebi 90, 215

factors:
   and characteristics of 81, 83
   and East India Company 87–8
      local languages and measures 88, 89
   as first settlers in Islamic world 81
   and network of resident 79–80, 81
   and North Africa 84, 85, 87, 88, 122
   and Ottoman Empire 122
   and role of 81
   and writings on Islamic world 4, 89–90
   see also living conditions; working conditions
Fairfax, Edward 29
fakkakin 124
Farewell, Christopher 91, 92, 105
Faroqhi, Suraiya 15
Fenell, Lawrence 101
Finch, Sir John 18, 82, 95
   as ambassador to Istanbul 112
   anti-Greek pro-Latin policy 118
   attends Mehmed IV's festival at Edirne 116–17
   Christian disputes in Jerusalem 117–18, 120
   deterioration in relations 120
   negotiation of capitulations 118–19
   received by Mehmed IV 119
   secures approval for naval action 119–20
   seizure of the *Mediterranean* 114–15
   and death of 121
   and friendship with Baines 114
Finett, Sir John 69
Fishtali, 'Abd al-Aziz al- 49, 50, 51, 52, 53, 56–7, 60
Fitch, Ralph 67, 71, 194
Fitz-Geffrey, Charles 219
Fitzgerald, Colonel John 177
Fletcher, John 166
food, and Britons in Islamic world 104–5
Fox, George 4, 37
Foxe, John (English captive) 133–4
Foxe, John (English puritan preacher) 26–7
Friedman, Ellen G 127
Frizell, James 22

Fuller, Thomas 176
funerals 94

Gainsford, Thomas 159, 189
Galata 90
   and Christian churches 94–5
Gardiner, Captain Thomas 143
Gee, Joshua 149
geography of Islamic world 5–6
   and Anatolia and eastern Mediterranean 6
   and North African Ottoman regencies 6–7
   and Persian-Indian region 7–8
George I 19, 187
Georgievits, Bartolomeus 133
Gibbon, Edward 159
Gibraltar 178, 234, 236
Gibson, William 181
gift-giving 109–10
Glover, Lady Anne 94
Glover, Sir Thomas 62–3, 82, 97, 98
Goddard, John 106, 110
Goffman, Daniel 81
Gombroon (Bandar Abbas) 69
Goodwin, John 111
Goodwin, Thomas 27
Goughe, Hugh 133
Grafton, Richard 31
graveyards 94
Greaves, Richard 10
Greek Orthodox Christians:
   and Anglican view of 159–60
      conversion hopes 160–1
      Protestant-Catholic rivalry 160
   and attempts to militarize 161, 162
   and disputes in Jerusalem 117–18
   and economic value of 161
   and European Protestant view of 159–60
   and Greek Christian visitors to England 158–9
   and plans to transport to New World 161–2
Greene, Robert 28
Greene, Thomas 4
Gregory, John 34
Grelot, Guillaume Joseph 3
Grotius, Hugo 160
Guinea Company 2

Habib, Imtiaz 20–1
Haddu, Mohammad ibn 19, 147, 222
Hakluyt, Richard 11, 17, 45, 67, 128, 180, 236, 237
Hamet, Lucas (James) 19
Harborne, William 5, 81
harem, and English perceptions of 38
Hargreaves, James 211
Harrison, John 18, 83–4, 177
Harvey, Sir Daniel 94, 115, 118
Haselton, Richard 134–6
Hawkins, William 11, 16, 23, 61, 72–4, 180
Haywood, Elizabeth 153
health, and Britons in Islamic world 105
Helgerson, Richard 172
Henin, Jorge de 207
Henry VIII 216, 223
Herbert, Admiral Arthur 83
Herbert, George 132
Herbert, Sir Thomas 38, 70–1, 191, 194
Heylyn, Peter 165, 172, 174, 175
Heywood, Thomas 4, 22, 61
  and *The Fair Maid of the West* 58
Hill, Aaron 32, 163, 176
Hill, Christopher 27
Hindus 194
Hoby, Sir Edward 56
Holy Land:
  and English anger at Muslim control of 169
  and Islamic preservation of holy sites 165
  and mapped as religious space 170–1
  and viewed through biblical past 171–3
Hooke, Robert 147
Hormuz 66–7, 69
horses, imports from Islamic world 202, 222–8
  and admiration of 224, 227–8
  and first evidence of 223–4
  and hunting 228
  and improving native stock 225–6
  and interest in eastern methods of horse management 224–5
    contrasted with European methods 225
  and interest in origins of eastern horses 226–7
  and military motives 228
  and transformation of English equestrian culture 222–3
Hortop, Job 132–3
Howard, Sir Philip 221
Hyde, Edward 100
Hyde, Sir Thomas 3, 10, 89, 193

iconoclasm 37
Ifrani, Muhammad al-Saghir al- 206
illness, and Britons in Islamic world 105
images of Muslims and Islam:
  in art 29–30
  and captivity literature 7, 25, 126–7, 142, 154–5, 232
  in Christian thought 26–8
  as military and expansionist threat 231–2
  and North Africa 230
  and Ottoman Empire 231
  and Persian-Indian region 231
  in theatre 4, 28–9, 58, 61
  and visual imagery 29–30
India:
  and British military presence 5
  and colonialism 233
  and East India Company reports on 4, 89–90
  and English perceptions of Islam in 194–6
  in English thought 14
  and first English accounts of 11
  and fortified settlements in 5, 79, 80, 86
Isfahan 22
Islam:
  and Christian converts to 21, 103
    attempts to dissuade 110
    fear of forced conversion 87
    marriage to Muslim women 97–8
  and English perceptions of 31–9
    admiration 37
    association with Ottomans 32, 41, 163–4
    contrasted with Christianity 32–3
    first translation of Qur'an 34–7
    harem 38
    iconoclasm 37
    misrepresentations of 31–2
    Mughals 194–6

Islam: (cont.)
 oriental studies 34
 in Persian-Indian region 40–1
 Pitts' account 38–9
 use of Arabic sources 33–4
 in English writings on Islamic
  world 8–9, 10–11
 and materialism 200
 and religious toleration 165–7
Islamic world:
 and engagement with Britain 4–5
 and factors affecting English attitudes
  towards:
  balance of power 9
  Crusades 10
  extent of English publications on
   9–10
 and first-hand accounts of 3–4
 and heterogeneity of 156
 as multi-religious society 163
 and non-Muslim population 6
 and openness of 15–16, 167, 233–4
 and regions of 5–6
  Anatolia and eastern
   Mediterranean 6
  North Africa 6–7
  Persian-Indian 7–8
 and religious toleration 165–7
 and social harmony amongst religious
  communities 163
 see also diplomatic relations,
  Anglo-Islamic; English thought,
  and Islamic world in; images of
  Muslims and Islam; peoples of the
  Islamic world
Ismail, Mulay 19, 182, 187
isolation, and Britons in Islamic
 world 106–7
Israel, Manasseh ben 174
Istanbul 22, 79
 and British ambassadors in 82
 and Christian churches 94
 and Christian funerals and
  graveyards 94
Izmir 79, 90–1

Jahangir, Shah 16, 71, 72, 74, 75, 76,
 101, 195
 and religious toleration 166, 196

James I:
 and *Counter-Blaste to Tobacco* 204
 and foreign policy 62–3, 78, 136, 137
 and piracy 43
janissaries 99
Jansz, Cornelius 59
Jenkinson, Anthony 10, 17, 23, 64–6,
 189, 193
Jerusalem:
 and Christian disputes under Ottoman
  rule 117–18, 120
 and Islamic preservation of holy
  sites 165
Jessey, Henry 175
Jesuits 95, 180
Jews:
 and attempts to convert to
  Christianity 176–7, 197
 and attitudes towards 174–5
 and banished from Tangier by
  English 177–8
 and British encounters with 25, 156,
  174
 challenge posed by 157
 and coexistence with Muslims 175–6
 and envy of 175
 and Islamic tolerance of 175, 176
 and opposition to readmission to
  England 176
 and portrayal as victims 157, 175
 and presence in Islamic world 174
 and Sabbatai Sevi 177
 and trade 178
 and viewed through biblical
  history 176
Jones, David 192
Jones, Sir Harford 71
Jones, Jezreel 100, 108
Jourdain, John 138

Kalantar, Khoja Phanoos 182
Kalmar, Ivan Davidson 215
Kara Mustafa Pasha, Merzifonlu 99, 115,
 120, 121
Karlowitz, Peace of (1699) 15
Katib Çelebi 208–9
Kellet, Edward 219, 220
Kerridge, Thomas 10, 89, 97
Khurram, Prince 76

INDEX 329

Kirke, Colonel Percy 178
Knight, Francis 140–1, 152
Knights of the Order of St Stephen
    125–6
Knolles, Richard 6, 164, 189, 231
Knox, John 60
Knox, Captain Robert 147
Köprülü Mehmed Pasha 115, 117, 119,
    120

Lach, Donald F 2
Lafqun, 'Abd al-Karim 207
Laicksteen, Peter 171
Landry, Donna 202, 223, 226
language 88, 89
    and translators 100
Laqani, Ibrahim al- 207
Laud, Archbishop William 102, 140, 160
Laxton, Thomas 102
Leachland, John 97
Lee, Hugh 181
Leigh, John 234
Lello, Henry 62
Lepanto, battle of (1571) 30
Leslie, Walter 63
Levant Company (originally Turkey
    Company) 2, 122
    and area of operation 6
    and reports on Islamic world 4
    and Safavid Empire 67–8
Lewis, Bernard 174
Lewis, Erasmus 185
Lewis, Gabriel 97–8
Lisdam, Henry du 232
Lithgow, William 15, 43, 103, 164, 174,
    201, 216
Liverpool Moslem Institute 1
living conditions (Britons in Islamic
    world) 87, 90
    and Christian churches 94–5
    and communications with home 106–7
    and funerals and graveyards 94
    and hiring local help 99–100
    and housing and residential areas:
        India 91–2
        North Africa 93–4
        Ottoman Levant 90–1
    and illness 105
    and isolation 106–7

and leisure pursuits 100, 102–3
    archaeology 101–2
    books and reading 100–1
    food and drink 104–5
    hunting 102
    music 101
    natural history 101
    sport 102
and local hostility 105–6
and marriage:
    to local Christians 96–7
    to Muslim women 97–8, 99
and religion 103–4
and wives and children 98
Locke, John 167–8
Loddington, Benjamin 107, 111
London, and Muslim visitors to 19–21
Lukaris, Cyril 160
Luke, John 100
Luther, Martin 26, 60

Mabro, Judy 38
Macaulay, Thomas Babington 113
McJannet, Linda 133
Madras, and fortification of 5, 79, 86
Mahilli, Ahmad Ibn Abi 207
Mainwaring, Sir Henry 137
Malik, 'Abd al- 45
Mandeville, Sir John 31–2
Mangy, Anthony 140
Mansel, Sir Robert 9
Mansur, Ahmad al- 42, 45, 85
    and conquest of Sudan 55
    and Elizabeth I 49–56, 57–61
Manwaring, George 3, 156, 188–9
maps 88–9
    and Palestine 170–2
Mariani, Paulo 48
Marlowe, Christopher 4
Maronites 161, 169, 180
Marrakesh 22
marriage:
    to local Christians 96–7
    to Muslim women 97–8, 99
    and use in trade policy 122–3
Marsh, Elizabeth 129
Martin, James 103–4
Martin, Samuel 106, 110
Martin, William 91

Massinger, John 4
material goods, and trade with Islamic
    world 2, 199
  Christian and Muslim views of
      materialism 200–1
  domestic imitations 201
  domestication of commodities 201
  impact of 199–200, 229
  mutual benefits from 201
  'Oriental Obsession' 201
  see also calico; coffee; horses; tobacco;
      turbans
Mattee, Rudolph 191
Maundrell, Henry 91, 102–3, 172
Mawsuli, Hanna al- 182
Mayflower 61
Meade, Joseph 27
medicine, and Islamic influences 3
Mehmed III 45, 49, 101
Mehmed IV 95, 115–16
Meknes, and ransoming of captives 152
Mercedarians (Order of Our Lady of
    Mercy) 125
merchants:
  and characteristics of 81
  as first settlers in Islamic world 81
  and local languages and measures 88,
      89
  and network of resident 79
  see also living conditions; working
      conditions
Meriton, George 164
Methwold, William 101, 104
Middleton, Sir Henry 72, 74, 126, 138
Mielich, Hans 29
Mildenhall, John 71–2
military force, and British use of 5, 9, 122
Milton, John 27, 176
Minorca 236
minorities, and heterogeneity of Islamic
    world 156
miracle plays 28
Moldavia 62, 82
Montagu, Lady Mary Wortley 6
Montesquieu, Charles-Louis de Secondat
    Baron de 2
Morden, Robert 17, 172
More, Henry 27
More, Sir Thomas 26

Morea 161
Morgan, Joseph 34, 100, 110–11
Moriscos 10, 41, 85, 136, 137
Morocco:
  and Anglo-Moroccan relations:
    Bentura de Zary's embassy 182–8
    Elizabeth I's diplomacy 43–5,
        49–61
  and Christian churches 95
  and engagement with Britain 4–5
  and living conditions in 93–4
  and naval power 85
  and tobacco 206–7
Moryson, Fynes 18, 99, 105, 165, 167,
    175, 224
mosques, and first British 1
Moüette, Germain 144
Mughal Empire:
  and Anglo-Mughal relations 71–7
    East India Company 72–7
    Fitch-Newberry expedition 71
    Mildenhall's mission 71–2
    trade 72–7
    use of naval power 74
  and engagement with Britain 4–5
  and English perceptions of Islam
      in 193–6
  and fragmentation of 2
  and naval weakness 86
Mughals 156
  and English perceptions of religion
      of 193–6
Mukarrab Khan 72, 74, 75
Munn, Thomas 68
Munster, Sebastian 133, 165–6
Murad III, Sultan 17, 45, 48, 49, 81
Murad IV 202, 208
Muscovy Company 64
music, and Britons in Islamic world 101
mystery plays 28

Nantes, Edict of 164
Naqd 'Ali Beg 69–71
Narborough, Sir John 119–20
national identity:
  and costume 216–17
  and representations of Muslims 30
natural history, and Britons in Islamic
    world 101

naval power:
  and British use of 9, 74, 85, 86
  and East India Company 85–6
  and Mughal Empire 86
  and North African Ottoman regencies 85, 136
Nebenzahl, Kenneth 170
Newberry, John 66–7, 71
newsbooks, and reports on Islamic world 3–4
Nezam-Mafi, Mohammad Taghi 188
Nicolay, Nicholas de 3
Nicusi, Panayoti 117
Nointel, Charles-François de 117
North Africa:
  and British engagement with 6–7
  and British migrants 21–2
  and characteristics of 85
  and Christian worship in 95
  and colonialism 233
  and consuls in 84, 85, 122
  and engagement with Britain 4–5
  and European colonialism 10
  and factors in 84, 85, 87, 88, 122
  and image of Muslims 7, 230
  and naval power 85, 136
  and reports on Islamic world 4
  and small size of English population 95–6
  and strategic importance of 236
  see also Morocco
North, Dudley 112, 113, 117, 119

Ockley, Simon 21, 34, 151–2
Ogilby, John 144, 226–7, 228
Okeley, William 131–2, 146
Oldenburg, Henry 166
Olufs, Hans 151
O'Neill, Hugh 57
oriental studies 34
Ortelius, Abraham 170–1
Osborne, John 110
Ottoman Empire:
  and ambassadors to 82
    Finch's embassy 114–21
    political interventions 81–2
  and Anglo-Ottoman relations 115
    Elizabeth I's diplomacy 45–9, 54
    Finch's embassy 114–21
    James I 62–3
  and change in English attitude towards 6
  and Christian churches 94–5
  and engagement with Britain 4–5
  and English association with Islam 32, 41, 163–4
  in English thought 14–15
  and English trade with 17
  and image of Muslims 231
  as multi-religious society 163
  and Pact of Umar 94
  and portrayal in Christian theology 26–7
  and tobacco 207–9
    attitudes towards 208–9
    domestic production 209
Ovington, John 98, 104
Oxford University 4
  and Greek College 160–1
Oxwick, John 91–2

Paddon, Captain George 178, 187
Pagitt, Ephraim 162, 181
Painter, William 28–9
Palestine:
  and English anger at Muslim control of 169
  and few English travellers to 180
  and mapped as religious space 170–1
  and viewed through biblical past 171–3
Pallache, Samuel 177
Pandon, Charles 129
Pariente, Solomon 177
Parker, Kenneth 196
Parry, William 194
Peele, George 61
Peirce, Leslie 200
Pellow, Thomas 98, 129, 151, 220
peoples of the Islamic world:
  and British encounters with 197
  and heterogeneity of Islamic world 156
  see also eastern Christians; Jews; Mughals; Shi'ites
Pepys, Samuel 4, 93, 104, 142–3, 221
Percy, William 33

Persia:
  and East India Company reports on 4
  and English confusion over Shi'ite beliefs 188–92
  in English thought 14
  and English writings on 192
  and silk 14
Persian-Indian Islamic region:
  and British experience of Islam in 40–1
  and colonialism 233
  and English trade with 7, 14
  and image of Muslims 231
  see also India; Mughal Empire; Persia; Safavid Empire
personal contacts, British-Muslim 18–26
  and consuls and merchants 23–4
  and friendships 18, 19
  and literature of captivity 25
  and migrants to Islamic world 21–3
  and Muslim visitors to England 19–21
  and piracy 24–5
  and working in Muslim countries 108
Phelps, Thomas 148–9
Philip II 50, 51, 52, 54
Philippson, Joannes 14
Philips, Miles 132–3, 134
pictures, and images of Muslims 29
Pindar, Sir Paul 63
piracy 21–2, 24–5
  and consuls' responsibilities 112
  and Elizabeth I 43
  and North Africa 85
  and seizure of the *Mediterranean* 114–15
  see also Barbary pirates; captives
Pitts, Joseph 38–9, 150–1, 182
Pitts, William 19
Pius V, Pope 78
plague 105, 113–14, 119
Pocock, Edward 3, 10, 18, 34, 102, 160, 192
Pool, John J 1
Pope, Alexander 184, 222
Portugal, and Mughal Empire 74, 75
Pory, John 148
Prester John 156–7
Preston, Ralph 103
Prideaux, Humphrey 4, 34, 39
'Prince Butler' 212

printing, in Islamic world 16
Purchas, Samuel 17, 77, 138, 172, 217, 237

Qa'id, Mahmud al- 53
Quilliam, William Henry 239n1
Qur'an, and translations of 31
  first English 34–7

Ralapolus, Anastatius 159
Raleigh, Sir Walter 204
Raye, William 102
Riley, Henry 226
Robert of Ketton 31, 32
Roberts, Lewes 169
Roe, Sir Thomas 3, 16, 24, 60, 72, 75–7, 78, 166, 189, 233
  as ambassador in Istanbul 82
  as ambassador to Mughal court 92
  as collector 102
  and Islam in India 194–6
romance, and literature of captivity 153–4
Ross, Alexander 4, 36–7, 215
Ross, Thomas 36
Rowlands, Samuel 204
Royal Society 101
Rycaut, Sir Paul 3, 16, 18, 24, 38, 92, 112, 167, 182, 191, 231
  and Anglo-Ottoman relations 115
  and mixing of Muslims and Christians 162
  and Royal Society 101
  and Sabbatai Sevi 177
  and turbans 220–1
Rymer, Thomas 19

Safavid Empire:
  and Anglo-Safavid relations:
    commercial motives 66
    East India Company 68–9
    first Persian ambassador to London 69–71
    Fitch-Newberry expedition 67
    Jenkinson's embassy 64–6
    Levant Company 67–8
    silk trade 68–9
  and engagement with Britain 4–5
  and English trade with 17

Safi, Mustapha ibn Ibrahim 47
Safi, Shah 17, 96
Safiye, Sultana 45, 47–9
St Olon, Pidou de 150
Saldanha, Antonio de 55
Salé, and liberation of captives 139–40
Sanderson, John 15, 48, 98, 156, 174, 225
Sandys, George 3, 16, 97, 165, 167, 174–5, 217, 218
Saris, Captain John 103
Scaligar, Joseph 216
Schrot, Christian 171
Settle, Elkanah 4
Sevi, Sabbatai 177
sexual relations, and Christian-Muslim liaisons 98–9
Sgrothen, Christian 171
Shakespeare, William 67
Sharpe, Samuell 3
Sherley, Lady Teresa Sampsonia 61
Shi'ites 156, 188–93
    and English confusion over beliefs of 188–92
    and English writings on 192
ships' captains:
    and maps 88–9
    and writings on Islamic world 4, 89–90
Shirley, Sir Anthony 3, 5, 63–4, 175
Shirley, Sir Robert 3, 5, 15, 61, 64, 68, 69–70, 71, 110, 175
silk trade 209, 210
    and Persia 14, 68–9
Skilliter, Susan 45, 47
Skinner, Daniel 111
slave trade 79, 255n2
Sloane, Hans 149
Smith, Henry 33
Smith, Thomas 3, 18, 24, 159, 163, 164, 168
Society of the Propagation of the Gospel 104
Spain:
    and Anglo-Spanish rivalry 13, 45, 50, 51, 53, 56, 77
    and decline of 2
    and Morocco 50, 52, 57, 59
    and Shirley's mission to 64, 69
Spanish Succession, War of the 2

Speed, John 172
sport, and Britons in Islamic world 102
Spratt, Devereux 95, 141–2, 146
Staden, Hans 132, 150
Staper, James 91
Steel, Richard 68
Steele, Benjamin 106
Steele, Richard 201, 212
Stella, Tileman 171
Sterry, Peter 27
Stevenson, John 34–6
Stow, John 172
Stubbe, Henry 4, 37, 192
Stubbs, George 202
Stuckley, Thomas 50
Süleyman 'the Magnificent', Sultan 14, 15
Surat 72, 74, 75, 123
    and living conditions of Britons 91, 92
    and resident factors 80
Sutton, Sir Robert 108

Tahmasp, Shah 10, 17, 66, 193
Tangier 22–3, 144, 233
    and Jews banished from 177–8
tapestries, and images of Muslims 29
tariffs 112
Tasso, Torquato 29
Tate, Nahum 227
Tavernier, Jean Baptiste 3, 105, 164, 198, 218
tea 104
Teonge, Henry 15–16, 102
Terry, Edward 77, 92, 194, 224
textiles:
    export of English cloth 198
    imports from Islamic world 198, 199, 202
    and Islamic influence on 209
    see also calico
theatre:
    and captivity 133, 153
    and Islamic world in 197
    and representations of Muslims 4, 28–9, 58, 61
theology, Christian, and portrayal of Muslims 26–8
Thévenot, Jean de 3, 208
Thirty Years War 13
Thomas, Keith 200

Thomason, George 36
Thomson, Thomas 108
Timberlake, Henry 18, 43
Tipton, John 83
tobacco 203–9
    and association with Africa 204–6
    and controversies surrounding 203–4
    and English export to Islamic world:
        Morocco 206–7
        Ottoman Empire 207–9
    and historical similarity to coffee 203
    and Islamic associations of 202
    and Islamic jurists:
        championed by 207
        denounced by 206, 207
    and James I's *Counter-Blaste to Tobacco* 204
    and moral and juridical anxieties over 200
    and Morocco 206–7
    and Ottoman Empire:
        attempts to ban 207–8
        attitudes towards 208–9
        domestic production 209
        introduction into 207
    and smoking as alien practice 204
    and stigma attached to 203
Toland, John 176
toleration, religious, and Islamic world 165–7
Tomson, Jasper 16
Towerton, Captain 103
trade, England and Islamic world 79, 121–3
    and centralized administration of 235–6
    and economic integration 199
    and Elizabeth I's diplomacy 43–5
    and impact of 199
    and Mughal Empire 72–7
    and network of residents 80
    and openness of 233–4
    and Ottoman Empire 17
    and Persian-Indian region 7, 14
    and primacy of in dealings with 236–8
    and regulation of 79–80
    and Safavid Empire 17, 66–8
        silk trade 68–9
    see also material goods, and trade with Islamic world

translators 100
Trapp, John 217, 218
Trinitarians (Order of the Most Holy Trinity) 125
Trinity House 139
turbans 202
    and anxiety over 218, 219
    and artistic representations of 215–16
        significance of 215
    and Christian denunciation of 219–20
    and coffee house keepers 221
    and converts to Islam 217–18, 219
        reconversion to Christianity 219–21
    as gauge of English attitude toward Islam 214–15
    and significance of clothes 216–17
    as symbol of Islam 215
        declining power of 222
    and white turbans 217–19
        converts to Islam 217–18
        as distinguishing sign 218–19
        sign of Islamic identity 217
    and worn by Englishmen 221
        returning travellers 216
        Tudor court 216
Turkey Company 2, 67
    see also Levant Company
Tyler, Alexander 222

Umar, Pact of 94
universities, and study of Islamic world 4, 6
Utrecht, Peace of (1713) 2, 186, 187

Valle, Pietro della 166
Verney, Edmund 198, 221
Verney, John 101, 105, 107, 198
Virginia Company 22
visual imagery, and representations of Muslims 29

Walton, Isaac 101
Ward, John 15, 22, 43, 103, 218
Watson, Richard 110
wealth, and Christian and Muslim approaches to 200–1
Webbe, Edward 116, 134
Wells, Leah 176
Whitehead, John 149

Wilson, Thomas 181
Wilton, Richard 3
Winchilsea, Second Earl of (Heneage Finch) 118
Windus, John 150, 152
women, as captives 129–30
Wood, George 211
Worde, Wynkyn de 32
working conditions (Britons in Islamic world):
  and expenses incurred by consuls 110–11
  and gift-giving 109–10
  and length of service 110
  and local customs and protocols 108–9
  and personal contacts 108
Wrag, Richard 47
Wunder, Amanda 216

York mystery plays 28
Young, Gilbert 145

Zary, Bentura de 181–2, 187–8
  as Moroccan ambassador to England 182–8
  acquiring animals 184
  audience with the Queen 187
  death of 187
  under house arrest 185–6
  official reception 183–4
  prepares to return home 184–5